Trapped in the Abyss

TRAPPED IN THE ABYSS
No Way Out

R.T. Page

Copyright © [2022] by [R.T. Page]

All rights reserved. No part of this book may be reproduced or used in any manner without written permission of the copyright owner except for the use of quotations in a book review.
For more information, address: rtpage2022@outlook.com

FIRST PAPERBACK EDITION 2022

Book design by PublishingPush

978-1-80227-395-3 (paperback)
978-1-80227-396-0 (ebook)

Contents

Acknowledgements xi

Preface xiii

Introduction 1

Part 1
Chapter 1: The Pain 5

Chapter 2: Who am I? 79

Chapter 3: Darker Days 93

Chapter 4: The Suffering Continues 119

Part 2
Chapter 5: Understanding the Different Types of Mental Health Disorders 179
    Bipolar Disorder 180
    Depression 180
    Mania 181
    Living with bipolar disorder 182
    What causes bipolar disorder? 183
    Psychosis 184

Schizophrenia 185
Schizophrenia syndrome 185
Schizoid Personality Disorder (SPD) 188
Schizoaffective disorder 189
Body dysmorphic disorder (BDD) 192
Anxiety disorder 194
Panic attacks 196
Borderline Personality disorder (BPD) 199
Depression 202
Anger 208
Stress 215
Eating problems 220
Hoarding 227
Obsessive-compulsive disorder (OCD) 231
Paranoia 238
Tardive dyskinesia 245
Seasonal affective disorder (SAD) 248
Suicidal feelings 251
Post-traumatic stress disorder (PTSD) 256
Trauma 259
Dissociation and Dissociative disorders 263
Postnatal depression and perinatal mental health 269

Chapter 6: The truth about some mental health afflictions 277

Chapter 7: Money, Money, Money 285

Chapter 8: The other side of pain 301

Chapter 9: How to overcome and cope with mental health afflictions 311

Regular exercise 313
Veganism 316
Cognitive behavioural therapy (CBT) 321
Figure 1: Cognitive Behaviour 323
The mind 326
Reading... 326
Meditation 330
Medication 333
The Gray's Line method 337
Figure 2: Gray's Line 338
Colour... 340
Present moment focus 342
The best case scenario rule 346
The mental grinder 348
Figure 3: The Mental Grinder 349
Audio record 351
Taking regular time outs and going on vacation 352
Sleeping and resting well 357
Alcohol, caffeine and nicotine 361
Nicotine 366
Caffeine 370
Deep breathing 372
Figure 4: Breathing 375
Figure 5: The Theory A and Theory B approach 380
Laughter 381
Learn what triggers your mental health problems 384
Be okay with not having control over everything 385
Anxiety Blueprint.. 386

Challenge your negative thoughts 387
Figure 6: Situation, Reaction and Learning point record 388
Acupuncture 389
Embrace moments of stillness and quietness 392
New habits that help to improve yourself 394
Having a positive attitude and setting goals 397
Keep reminding yourself that these moments (anxiety and panic attacks) will pass 398
Remind yourself that you are normal 400
Consider playing different frequencies 401
Join self-help groups 406
Family and friend intervention 407

Epilogue 410
List of useful contacts in the UK for mental health conditions 411
   Anger Problems 411
   Body Dysmorphic Disorder (BDD) 415
   Borderline personality disorder (BPD) 417
   Depression 419
   Dissociation and dissociative disorders 422
   Eating problems 425
   Hoarding 428
   Obsessive-compulsive disorder (OCD) 430
   Anxiety and panic attacks 432
   Paranoia 434
   Post-traumatic stress disorder (PTSD) 436
   Postnatal depression and perinatal mental health 440
   Psychosis 446

Schizophrenia 447
Schizoaffective disorder 449
Seasonal affective disorder (SAD) 451
Stress 453
Suicidal feelings 455
Tardive dyskinesia (TD) 459
Trauma 461

Bibliography 467

Acknowledgements

I would like to thank my wonderful girlfriend, for all the help and support that she gave me during the difficult time I had going through this. She is very patient with me and always gives me advice and comes up with ways I could, and still can, improve my affliction.

I'd like to thank my mom, dad and sister who have also helped guide me through the difficult times that I faced with my condition. They showed nothing but patience, understanding and support. It was my mom who encouraged me to seek professional help, so without her, I don't know where I would be today. My therapist, Matthew, was also a great help. He helped me to further understand my condition and gave me ways that I could use to manage it. One must understand that in a lot of cases you may not be able to completely rid yourself of your mental health problem, but you can find the tools to help you manage it and live the happy and healthy life that you once had.

I would also like to thank all my friends that knew about my condition and were helpful and supportive throughout. Without them, I would also be completely lost. I'm lucky to have had all the support that I received. It has helped me a great deal. I'm not completely out of the dark yet but I now have the tools necessary to manage and cope with my problem. It's important that you confide in people you can trust as they can be very supportive, especially when you feel alone. I don't know where I would be without all the help I received along the way through this journey so I'm extremely grateful for it.

Preface

I would like you to try and imagine you are the person described in this story. By the time you get to the end, it's likely you won't see the world and your life in quite the same way. I used my own experience, books I've read, and programmes I've watched, as well as anecdotes and wisdom from some of the wonderful, and not so wonderful, people I have met in my life to bring this book to fruition and deliver the message to you, the readers, the way I know how.

I realised that one man's story is every man's story, as I once read. I want to share this story with you, I want people to realise that no matter what you are going through you are not alone, that someone out there understands your pain, that if you lose yourself, you can find yourself again, and that sometimes you have to lose yourself to then find out who you truly are. For me, in sharing my personal story, which I've kept private for so many years, I came to the realisation that surrendering to it and letting it go was the best way to liberate myself – hence why I'm sharing it with you. I hope this will inspire at least one person; if it does, then I will know I was right in sharing it with everyone. I realise some will judge and some will empathise, but as long as people feel something, that's all I could ask for. The truth is that most of us are scared to be ourselves for the fear of being rejected and not accepted, but also because we are scared to be great. A lot of us are also afraid of failure. But as Walt Disney said, "the difference between winning and losing is most often not quitting". Don't give up; be impeccable with your word. Don't give up on your dreams. We don't plan to fail; we fail to plan. Don't be afraid of failure: not to have tried at all is true failure. You have to keep trying and eventually, you will succeed. Thomas Edison failed over ten thousand times while trying to get a lamp to work, but he didn't give up and eventually he got it to work. What that says is that every experiment that failed is one step closer to success Also, remember that your best teacher is your last mistake. To get something you never had, you have to do something you never did. We spend most of our lives running away from who we are, denying who we are, living externally, trying to find solutions to our problems by creating other problems to distract ourselves. But we lie to ourselves and hope these new problems are the solution. The great Henry David Thoreau said: "the masses of men live in quiet desperation. What we know as resignation is actually confirmed desperation". Most of us don't chase our dreams, we imagine, but never follow through. We limit ourselves and thus spend our entire lives living in desperation. During my experience, I caught the indubitable revelation that our thoughts cause our feelings, and I became obsessed with feeling neurotic and thinking there was a constant threat around me. This obsession had initially appeared as a distorted sound, then it became a habit and in its final devastating stage, an obsession, one that seized my entire existence. Scientists say it takes 66 days on average to form a new habit; I say it takes a minute to create your life, to make a decision... to shift your paradigm and rebuild the world in your own image. This was something I discovered once I learned the secret.

Everything we choose to do, and even not do, is born in the mind. If at some point in your life you choose to ignore who you are to fit in or conform, eventually this will cause some form of anxiety disorder, as the things you begin doing and saying stop resonating with your core frequency. This is what happened to me; this was the scariest but most rewarding experience I have ever had in my life. Many times, I felt like giving up, wondering if this was punishment for some transgressions I'd committed, wondering if it was my fault. I think the worst part wasn't the experience itself but the feeling of despair, and that there didn't seem to be a way to break free of this overwhelming monster I had very carefully created!!

I once heard the saying, "if you change the way you look at things, the things you look at change" and so here I am today.

Introduction

I have written this book to outline the struggles I have encountered with my mental health, specifically with social anxiety disorder and psychosis which was mainly through unabating auditory hallucinations that came from other people. I hope this book can raise awareness for sufferers of all mental health disorders and provide some helpful tips in dealing with and coping with this rather arcane subject. The book gives an account of my everyday struggle, and brings to light the most salient aspects of my affliction. Everything I have covered is germane and will hopefully raise awareness in this subject.

The way I have structured this book is that I have started by giving my everyday experiences with social anxiety disorder and my psychosis so you, the reader, can get a comprehensive understanding of the specific affliction I have suffered from. All mental health disorders, although similar, are entirely different. The first part of the book covers my mental health issues. Later in the book, I have then gone into the hidden science and studies surrounding this topic. I have also included a sort of guide and useful tips to help overcome mental health issues. This covers topics such as meditation, acupuncture, present moment focus, psychopharmacology and the different medications that can be taken and how they affect you. I have also covered different breathing techniques and exercises that can be employed to cope with an episode you may have, and also the effects of alcohol, tobacco and caffeine on mental health. I have found a lot of the methods I have researched extremely useful and they have helped me in my journey. Mental health disorders are rife and many people, anyone, can be affected by them. Whether you suffer from it yourself or you know someone who suffers from it, this book will apprise you and give you a greater knowledge of this topic. This will give you the tools you need, not only to alleviate your mental health issues but also to help others do the same. Life these days can be very challenging and demanding and it's not uncommon for one to be subjected to mental health issues. I never knew I would be affected by it, but at the same time, I have learned a great deal about it, and how to help others overcome it. It can be the worst feeling. You can feel isolated and alone. No one understands your plight. Sometimes it can even feel like the 'flat affect.' I have even had some suicidal thoughts which again is something I could have never imagined as a young boy growing up, but the reality of life is a lot more menacing at times. Things can get dark and it's easy for one to lose oneself. It's important to note that our minds are constantly in use. Sometimes overuse is essentially one of the effects of a mental health issue. You find that you spend most of your time thinking about it even when you are not in a stressful situation. It's torture. I have gone through this and can attest to this fact.

My only hope is that you read the book through and take something away from it. I wouldn't have been able to write this book without the help of all of the amazing people I have met in my life. I'm using my experience to represent myself in whatever light

INTRODUCTION

it puts me in; as long as it can help at least one person, then I have achieved my goal. I hope you enjoy the book and can share it with people you know.

Part 1

Chapter 1: The Pain

Have you ever been in a place so dark, so lonely that you begin to wonder if it's even real? Sequestered, constantly asking yourself when the nightmare will end? Asking yourself how you got there and why? Being seized by fear, uncertainty and anxiety at the prospect of being around people and out in public, vulnerable, exposed, little. I have. The thing we have to realise is that our bodies are like a twenty-four-hour live broadcast of our feelings that everyone can see, and even feel. Our body is our subconscious mind, we may not always realise it but it's always giving off an energy that resonates with how we feel at every moment. I used to, and to an extent still, feel as if everyone I come into contact with looked at me with contempt, that they can feel every single nerve that courses through my body, that everyone can see how lost and afraid I am. This so-called place became my new home. A place where darkness gets trapped and can't escape, a hole, space, 'a nowhere,' a place where only I exist, a place where only I suffer.

This is my story, it's about me losing myself and then starting to become myself all over again.

I remember waking up at 4 am one early winter morning, a forlorn figure laying in my cold bed, so timid, so meek, my limp body lay there and emptiness filled my soul, it seemed that feeling alone had become the only feeling I could discern anymore. On the verge of depression, head filled with macabre thoughts, in a state of lassitude, feeling hopeless, suffering, and no one hearing my screams or understanding my pain. Having sleepless nights spent perpetually thinking, longing for something different. I had become obsessed with what I hated and feared the most. What I realised, later on, was that I had to lose my mind and come to my senses.

My head hurt, I could feel my breathing was slow and precise, my neck was tight, my mouth was dry, my eyes heavy, I was shaking, I had lost all my strength and self-belief, my body felt so heavy.

I wondered what time it was? I remember thinking, "I'm here again I've woken up in a complete daze," unaware of how I got here; my head was thumping just as fast and furiously as my heart was beating. "What time is it?" I didn't even want to look because reality lies to no one. "What time did I fall asleep?" The last thing I remembered was being awake watching an episode of "Friends". That is what my life had become – a perfect imperfectness, a life of routine, hopelessness and solitude, a perpetual brown study but also a life of longing, isolation and confusion. A change that I could never comprehend. A hole that had no bottom, but the feeling of falling couldn't escape the pit of my stomach; my heart had been permanently moved to my stomach. It felt like a vortex, I was in a place in between who I was and who I had become. I felt like this every second of every day. I was sick and tired of feeling sick and tired. I got up and walked sluggishly towards the wall as the moonlight illuminated through my bedroom window, I saw my shadow and thought, "I wish I was it and it was me; actually, I wish

I could be invisible. I turned the lights on and I then walked back towards the mirror. I tiptoed as I knew my floor always squeaked near where the light switch was and the last thing, I wanted was to hear my flatmates suddenly moving or talking, because I knew to me that would be a censure by them to express their anger at my noisiness. No matter what anyone said, whether I could hear it or not, but especially when I couldn't hear what was said, I'd always find a negative interpretation for it in my mind. "They all hate me. Why was I born?"

I toddled over to the mirror, careful and precise with my steps. I planted my feet and looked in the mirror unsure of what I was supposed to think of myself, unsure of who I was but just knowing my soul had gone to a place where no soul should go. A sort of abyss, or an endless road to perdition. I guess I was hoping the mirror would change my reflection, but how would that happen? The pain I felt was indescribable; it completely consumed my existence. I was a wretched inscrutable entity, full of despair and fear. I remember wanting to just disappear at that moment. I hadn't yet mustered up the courage to end everything. So, like the coward I was, I gently walked back towards the light switch, turned the light off and walked over to my bed and went back to sleep, hoping that I would never wake up again.

It's amazing how I could even face people at work and friends and even have a conversation without feeling sorry for myself. They would ramble on about their wonderful blissful lives full of joy and purpose, while I stood there pretending to share the same sentiments, feigning happiness. If only they knew how broken I was inside, how many times I had contemplated suicide, how sad I always felt, how lonely I was.

But I couldn't show this to anyone. it was my biggest secret. In a way, the prison I had built for myself was my freedom. People live in one of two places, fear or freedom. I convinced myself that I was free and the only way that was possible was to never feel sorry for myself.

I seemed to ask myself more and more questions every day... more than I could ever answer. Why did I feel this way all the time? Why did I feel like I couldn't be my true self, that everyone was judging me, that everyone was scrutinizing me? Even if it was a simple 'hello' I muttered to someone it felt as if the way I said it was different to everyone else. I felt as if the way I smiled at someone during a conversation was seen as something other than what it was – a 'smile'.

The next morning at around 5 am I was ruffled and woken up by the sound of my alarm and I thought to myself, "Here goes another day that I have to endure". I remembered that it was going to be extremely busy at work because we had a big group checking into our hotel, so I already knew my anxiety was going to have a field day with me. It always got its way with me; I couldn't suppress it. It ruled me. I remember thinking that I wished I knew the exact time they would come so I could plan accordingly and take my lunch break at that exact time, to avoid feeling exposed and vulnerable, alone! And to avoid having to deal with the concourse of them in the hotel lobby, looking for a fitting distraction while patiently waiting to be assigned their rooms. After all, that's what anxiety is – it's the desire to escape the present moment.

CHAPTER 1: THE PAIN

After very reluctantly reaching over to hit the snooze button on my alarm, I then moved over back to my bed and just closed my eyes and I disappeared. I felt like I was squeezing something very tightly but then realised I wasn't. What seemed like 10 seconds later I heard my alarm sounding again. This time I woke myself up meekly and then sat up on my bed thinking of the pure dread I faced ahead, I knew from that point onwards I was going to be a nervous wreck, a wretched man. I vacillated between going to work or not going in at all. I had to do an early shift on the front desk as a receptionist which was meant to start at 8 am and finish at 5 pm. I was contracted to do night shifts but due to a colleague calling in sick, I had decided to cover that shift – besides it wasn't for free.

I sat on my bed for about 15 minutes and was just drifting in and out of reality. I looked at the clock and saw it was about 5:15 am at that point and didn't know why time never protected me; it always seemed to want to expose me. I always preferred night shifts as it was considered 'unsociable hours' or the 'graveyard shift,' which appealed to me as I generally saw fewer people and I worked alone. This is very common with anxiety – you do things at times when people generally aren't around to avoid social interactions.

I finally got up and already felt my legs trembling, I started imagining every conceivable situation I'd be faced with at work, not only that but on the way there, too. From walking out of my front door down the stairs and to my car, I didn't want to see anyone, but that was as realistic as me winning the lottery twice! I remember a time that I couldn't even leave my flat for three weeks on end, which I refer to as the "the dark days".

I staggered downstairs, to the bathroom. I lived in a three-bedroom flat. My room was upstairs and was huge, reminding me more and more of how alone I was. Then there were two bedrooms downstairs, one of which had an en-suite bathroom and the other was a cubbyhole-like room. I knew my flatmates quite well. One room was occupied by Jasmine and the other by a more senior citizen who was a kind and hearty man who I'd known for some time. It was by sheer coincidence that when I was looking for a flat to rent when my parents had moved out of the United Kingdom, that a family friend was looking for a tenant to rent a room. Godsent, so I thought.

It was early November, I remember vividly, and the bathroom was so cold. I put the heating on; luckily for me, it was a fan heater and had an immediate effect. It seemed like the cold only exacerbated my anxiety. I turned on the water, hopped in the shower and focused on that and not what was coming next. I quickly learned that anxiety disorder makes you realise how many things in your life you take for granted before you are afflicted by it. I finished showering. It felt like it took hours to do so but that was because my mind was clouded by my thoughts; all I ever did was think. Thinking is the biggest cause of unhappiness and the biggest misuse of your imagination. I knew that once I stepped foot outside my front door, my protective shell would have been destroyed and I was going to be attacked, not physically, but emotionally and psychologically.

I got dressed upstairs in my bedroom; it took me like two minutes to put on each shoe and about 10 minutes to iron my shirt. Whew! "Here we go", I thought. I was dressed and ready to leave my sanctuary… well the safest place for me during this experience – my room. My anxiety disorder had started a few months prior whilst still living at home with my parents; this part I will get to a bit later as it is very germane to my story.

I said a quick prayer and just asked God to clear my path at least for the day ahead, although I didn't truly believe that would happen. I locked my door and headed downstairs for the front door. I was already sweating, my heart was palpitating, my stomach churning, I had pins and needles, felt dizzy, needed the loo, my eyes were wide. I was scared but still alive. Once I got out of my front door, it was a three-story complex, I immediately heard another person's front door open so I stopped dead in my tracks, my heart felt like it did the same. I didn't want to see anyone; of this I was certain!! I could hear it was a man, probably a blue-collar worker, a typical lad, confident, gregarious and without a care in the world. Just by the sheer heaviness, speed and sureness of his steps I could tell he was a threat to me, he would see this timid man and would then display some kind of impudent attitude towards me, I was beginning to realise that my fear was seeing people, especially men, as I perceived them to be more of a threat than women. But my worst fear was of them murmuring or hurling insults at me, scorning me or ridiculing me. Why? I guess because I believed I was all of these negative things. I didn't know who I was anymore. I allowed a figment of my imagination to condition my outlook on reality; it was an obsession, not a sickness. Looking back now, I think maybe they saw me as a threat rather than me seeing them that way.

I waited until the sound of his footsteps had faded and finally heard the downstairs main entrance door open and shut so I knew whoever it was had gone – gone to continue leading their perfect life.

I realised I had to be stealthy and get to my car quickly. Perception. Was I a solipsist? Solipsism is the philosophical idea that only one's mind is sure to exist. So, the knowledge of anything outside of one's own mind is unsure; therefore, the external world and other minds cannot be known and might not exist outside the mind.

I got to the door downstairs, took a deep breath and headed outside. Birds were singing, so free, so peaceful, I always marvelled at nature's beauty. It was very misty outside. I walked rapidly and briskly but quietly, careful not to tread on any rubble or foliage that would make a loud noise and attract attention to myself. The walk to my car typically took about a minute. As you get downstairs you are immediately walking parallel to a massive field, but it's gated and above you, all the balconies of other residents sit, a potential threat: up there they seem so big, down here I feel so small. They are at a vantage point, safe, ominous. I always used to dread that someone would be standing on their balcony and would spit on my head or throw something at me, laugh at me while talking to his beautiful wife, laugh at my pain, know how I feel and see how nervous I was!! And then bang! "Oh God!!" someone had coughed but it was dark I couldn't see where the person was; it was a man, you could hear by the sound of it, probably in his forties. I immediately felt vulnerable, looking around to see where he was, but I couldn't see. I looked to my left and then above me at the balconies and then to the left again and finally right and there he was, in the field. Sure enough, he was staring at me as he walked through the opaque mist. His eyes fixed on me, I felt as if he was watching my every step, almost like a cheetah does before it attacks its prey, I quickly looked away and pretended I was indifferent to his presence. I heard nothing. I had never known this sort of feeling before, that a look could make me feel so vulnerable and unsure of myself. It felt like every person I came into contact with was simply an extension of my thoughts. I didn't know what was real anymore and what wasn't. The walk to my car seemed to take an eternity but I finally got there.

I drove a black Vauxhall Astra; it was a 2007 registered car, a good motor, reliable, with the markings of a car that had survived the test of time and it had tinted windows throughout. Having tinted windows was, as you can imagine, perfect for me as it was harder to be seen by pedestrians and other road users in general, I bought the car with tints on the front windows and back windows. It was a black car so it allowed me to get away with having tints on the front as well. Apparently, you need at least 70% light to show through the front windows and 75% through the windscreen, but anyway I would only care about this if the police ever wanted to know my name.

I started my car and headed off to work. It was a Tuesday morning at dawn, and I was aware traffic would be relatively smooth at that hour, at least before I got near Shepherd's Bush. One of the triggers for my anxiety was being stuck in traffic or being in busy places with large queues. When I was in traffic, I couldn't help but pay attention to every person, car and event that was going on in the fear that someone would hoot their horn at me for some reason, or that someone would yell obscenities at me as I drove past for whatever reason. I was always tense and unable to relax. I was always worrying and always believed something bad would happen. They say the word 'fear' is an acronym for 'false evidence appearing real.' I was in a constant state of fear and it controlled my life. I would ruminate constantly; at some point, I felt like I was losing touch with reality. I hardly ever drove with my windows down even during the summer, or if I did, I'd play my music very loudly just to ensure I wouldn't be able to hear anything clearly if anything contumelious was said by someone. I remember always feeling like someone would throw something at my car from another car as I sat in traffic, or as traffic was moving slowly, that some delinquent teenage group led by a youngster eager to act tough and craving the acceptance from his peers, would throw something at my car or hurl insults at me as I drove past. Any sound I heard that I didn't recognise I'd immediately associate to these things. It was a constant thought; it was torture. Why did I deserve this? I was drowning in my own imagination. I later found out that I didn't only have a social anxiety disorder but a new onset of psychosis, which explained a lot. So, I experienced auditory hallucinations most of the time. I heard, and sometimes saw things others didn't. I would experience delusions, too. The problem is they felt very real when they happened but I learned that they are beliefs that no one else shares and that other experiences or perceptions show they can't actually be true. I only understood what this meant later on but at its worst, I believed everything to be real that I was hearing.

Luckily, though, I had enough petrol in my car as I'd filled it up the previous week. I did this deliberately as it meant fewer trips to the petrol station, at least until it ran low. I realise now that I organised my life in such a way that I'd only need to do things as and when necessary, to minimise the "exposure" to people. I had a fear of being around people. We all have an unconscious cloak that tells us we are safe in seemingly innocuous social situations; it's what makes us put down our guard. But is it a mirage? Is it only a generally accepted thing because it simply exists? I realised I was stuck when I suddenly became conscious of this unconscious cloak and so began this road of self-micro management and I became exceedingly efficient at it. If survival becomes everything, does the existence of happiness dissipate? Surely the two cannot co-exist. I once heard this saying – "the human mind is designed for survival; your mind isn't designed to be happy, that's your job" – these words are very true.

Strange because my nature is to be very sociable. Who am I? I always went to two specific petrol stations as they were typically not busy. I was now on the dual carriageway at this point and traffic was looking okay, I was beginning to feel somewhat relaxed, which was extremely rare for me when I was out in public. I reclined a bit in my seat and let the drive come to me; I lit a cigarette, rolled down my window as I was on the dual carriageway and it just felt magical. Moments aren't necessarily magical; I believe getting lost in the moment is what's magical. I recall that I kept wishing there wouldn't be any delays along the way. Later on, I realised how powerful our thoughts can be and how the seven hermetic principles played a role in my life. These include the principle of mentalism which states that "the all is mind; the universe is mental." The principle of correspondence, also known as the law of attraction which states "As above, so below, as below, so above. As within, so without, as without, so within." The principle of vibration which says "nothing rests; everything moves; everything vibrates." The principle of polarity states that "Everything is dual, everything has poles and everything has its pair of opposites; Like and unlike are actually the same; Opposites are identical in nature, but different in degree;

Extremes meet; All truths, are but half-truths; All paradoxes may be reconciled." The principle of rhythm states that "Everything flows out and in; Everything has its tides; All things rise and fall." The principle of cause-and-effect states "Every cause has its effect; Every effect has its cause." Finally, we have the principle of gender. It states that "Gender is in everything; Everything has its masculine and feminine principles. These principles are powerful and very relevant to our lives as human beings.

My workplace was a two-hour drive away from where I lived; it was based in South Kensington near the Royal Albert Hall, a bustling, affluent area in London, 'haute societe' as they call it... I worked in a small forty-bedroom private hotel, owned by a wealthy Arab family.

Just like that the rug got pulled from under my feet; the connection between man and machine suddenly became mechanical, meaningless, just flipping a switch or unplugging a charger, I finished enjoying my cigarette even though I had only smoked half of it, but it didn't matter because I was approaching a traffic light. I could feel the blood rushing around my body and almost colliding into my organs; the feeling was here; I was a passenger sitting in the driver's seat. I lost control and again survival was all I could think of. I realised later on that when I had an anxiety attack nothing else mattered at that moment; it was my centre, and everything I conceived or saw or heard was altered in what I now know as the mental grinder to match my core thoughts at that moment. I took as long as I could before coming to a complete halt. I remember checking the rear-view mirror about eight times as well, and that wasn't because you are taught to during your driving lessons. I could feel my left leg shaking uncontrollably, I had to take my hands off the gear knob to control it from losing functionality. The sort of nerves I was feeling at that point I'd imagine was the type of nerves one would feel after discovering that their dearest love was cheating on them. This feeling was all because I feared people's attention in the traffic would suddenly be drawn to me in my car, and they would insult me even though I had tinted windows. It wasn't like my car was bright yellow either. I just felt like my energy would attract their attention somehow. It had to; of this, I was convinced. I felt that they would sense my uneasiness as I impatiently looked in anticipation at all my rear view and side mirrors. I remember then getting angry because the traffic lights were taking so long to change. I let out a scream of frustration, more I think because of how I always felt, as opposed to the traffic light taking forever to change. I felt so uncomfortable even though it was a completely normal innocuous situation. What was wrong with me? I didn't choose this!!! It wasn't people's attention that unsettled me, it was rather what they did with the attention I gave back to them that unsettled me, I learned later on.

Green. Go. "Yes, finally, thank God that's over" I remember thinking to myself.

As I continued with my journey there was an Audi driver behind me, typical as they say, tailgating me and had been doing so for a while. I got more and more agitated the longer he was behind me. It almost felt as if he could see me, but I knew he couldn't. But I was convinced he could, so I thought as far back into my journey as I could to see if I could remember cutting in front of someone or driving unreasonably slow in front of someone, perhaps, to find an answer as to why he was tailgating me. Yes, I took it personally; I took most things personally back then. See the pain I caused myself, but I couldn't seem to help myself. I knew he had an issue with me, I wanted to sort of "disarm" him so I became docile, and quickly decided to move out of the right-hand lane to let him pass. I know the right lane is for overtaking but I was driving fast enough and overtaking other cars. What happened to my placid, imperturbable nature? This wasn't me. I was living like I was being chased all the time or stalked. Every normal situation, became threatening to me in the sense that I felt someone would have a problem with me, whatever I did: the way I walked, the way I looked, the way I spoke, the gentility which I once possessed had perished. Everyone loves the confidence they see in others. It's a way of that person saying: "It feels so good to be me" and this makes them attract other people's attention and interest, but yet so many people lack gentility when it comes to being themselves. I learnt these things once I had begun to take my life back. I now envied confident people, mainly men – people that walked tall, stood as if they were hanging by their teeth, had good eye contact with others, who said things that made others listen attentively, that men respected and that women longed for. The sort of people who would be extolled even when they were not in the room. People that were able to express themselves exactly how they wanted to without hesitation. People who were so sure of themselves and trusted themselves. I had this once upon a time, but it was gone and I feared, gone for good.

I realise that there are probably many people in the world who suffer from something similar but at the time I felt I was the only person on earth who did; I felt so alone. The truth is how can a weeping man expect to be helped when most of the people around him are weeping, too? How can a strong, proud man ask for help when he believes he is the shepherd? How can I show my weakness? Doesn't this discredit me as a man? I kept asking myself this over the years. But I didn't realise that I wasn't weak; I was brave and I was strong. Bravery is where vulnerability meets a momentary lack in fear.

I was only a few minutes from Shepherd's Bush at this point. It's funny. I wanted the journey to end but I didn't want to get to work and be around so many people. I wished I could just keep driving and driving and never stop. The hordes of people were increasing which made me realise I was nearing the city. I began seeing tourists being washed away by all the corporate people. It was like watching an unabating tsunami washing away everything in its path. All these white-collar people on their merry way to an important job, programmed, automated, lost. It was like they were in a trance. The worst part of my journey was fast approaching – it was just after the Shepherd's Bush roundabout. I always liked roundabouts, not sure why but I just liked them. I found it interesting that the first one ever built was in Letchworth Garden City in 1909. Shepherd's Bush – it was built up, where the rat race began so to speak, so fast, so noticeable, just never stopped. I turned left and exited the roundabout as I entered Holland Park Avenue. I could feel my senses spiking. All of a sudden, I noticed everything, every sound, every person, even the man in blue jeans and a black bomber jacket who dropped his wallet as he walked – there was no way I could stop and inform him, surely someone else would have? I didn't want to attract attention to myself. Luckily traffic wasn't as bad as I'd anticipated. As I drove further along Holland Park Avenue, I could see those early morning delivery drivers from Tesco's, and then from Sainsbury's. As they carefully and meticulously ticked off items on the ever-present inventory on a clipboard. I always used to think, "why can't I own a huge business?" How proud and fulfilled the founders must have felt. Sam Walton of Walmart, Jeff Bezos of Amazon, Peter Thiel of PayPal, Mark Cuban – the list is endless and I'm not on it. But as Albert Einstein said: "Only those who attempt the absurd can achieve the impossible." Knowing how to think empowers you far beyond those who know what to think. Most of us are taught to limit ourselves in terms of what we can achieve.

I remember driving as quickly as possible. I just didn't want to be stuck in traffic. I didn't want people to have a chance to see me and judge me. The traffic was moving quite swiftly I remember the wind was turbulent and howling with such vigour and a light drizzle had started.

I passed the last morning delivery truck within sight and came up towards a roundabout which was five minutes from my workplace. My heart started to beat so rapidly again I could feel my fingers curling up, making steering seem more difficult. I could feel my toes curl, I could feel my head pound – I knew I was about to enter a world of complete uncomfortableness, a world that had become my existence, a world full of confusion of pain and suffering. I was stuck behind the eight ball. As I said, I'd never done a lot of day shifts previously. I worked there for about two years and my worst fear was the upcoming London 2012 Olympic Games because we had to host a big group of guests. The fear of the situation was worse than the situation itself. I think in most cases I got so caught up in preparing and worrying about what was going to happen that by the time it happened I was in such a state. I began wishing I was back in my room.

I had just turned on to Merton Avenue at this point, which was one minute away from my workplace I sensed the terror; the fear crawled up my spine and throughout my body. I drove slowly taking as much time as possible. It was approximately 7:50 am at this point and I had 10 minutes to get into work. I just didn't want to face reality, just the feeling of being exposed once again, feeling vulnerable. There it was – my final turn before I turned into the road where my workplace was located. To make matters worse, just as I turned onto Cecil Road, there it was! My worst nightmare – a couple. I spotted a woman and a man standing there. For some reason, I always felt more anxious when I saw couples. I felt like the man would be threatened by me – not necessarily a physical threat, just my presence would make him feel demasculinized, and as a consequence of this, he would have to prove that he wasn't feeling threatened and that he would stand his ground, so to speak. You see, I'm very tall and quite muscular. Anyone who didn't know me would perceive me as a masculine, virile man. So, a lot of the time I would pay more heed to the man and everything and any little thing that he did – what he looked like, if he gave a glance in my direction. I would always assume it was with contempt, with hatred, with anger. I could never imagine something positive was going through his head. I also wonder if this had something to do with the "ladder inference"? Maybe I kept relating any situation involving a couple as threatening and hostile due to a previous experience of being scrutinised and challenged. Also, say for instance if I ever heard him and his partner having a conversation, perhaps, and I heard something inscrutable, I would assume it was something about me – something negative. I have always felt this way whenever I spotted a couple, whether they were in a shop with me, walking past me or towards me on the street, far away, the feeling would be the same in my stomach. It was a similar feeling when I was with a female and a man or couple were in our vicinity… It was absolute torture and I was doing it all to myself. When did this all begin? When will it end? Is this how my life story goes?

That couple stopped just in the front of a building. Luckily, they weren't paying attention to me. I then needed to find a place to park my car. There were no parking spaces available. I once heard a story told by David Schirmer, an investment trainer – he said he was somehow always able to get parking spaces wherever he went. He would imagine it and visualise the parking space that he wanted, and exactly where he wanted it, and he would always get it or near enough. This part of the story I will get to later is related to the law of attraction or law of correspondence, one of the 7 hermetic principles in the emerald tablet. When I started to realise the power I had and how to apply certain principles to my life things changed drastically. It was like I changed my reality with just my thoughts and feelings. As I mentioned, if you change the way you look at things, the things you look at change. Bob Proctor said, "if you can think it in your head, you can hold it in your hand." We are all so powerful and it just takes knowing the power that we possess to get what we want.

I DON'T need this. I had to circle a few times before a space became available so I parked, sat in my car for a minute and prepared myself. One thing I was always taught, even before this affliction, was deep breathing does calm and centre the mind, taking it from a state of panic to tranquillity relatively well. I got out of the car, locked the door and crossed the road just as I spotted a group headed in my direction. I tried my best to avoid eye contact and hoped I wouldn't hear any chatter between them as I know I would interpret it as insults towards me. I walked very nervously towards the front door. These were old Victorian buildings converted into a hotel. I knew it was going to be very, very upbeat, very busy and yet I knew I'd still feel all alone and hide my sorrow with a painful smile. I got to the door and got even more nervous as that group was striding towards me, well past me actually – I remember getting more frustrated and anxious the more steps they took. I abruptly pressed the buzzer on the door and hoped whoever was on shift would open the door quickly. "Hurry up!" I thought. They did. I pushed open the door, walked in, saw Patrick and greeted him. He was about 37 years old, 15 years older than me, a French man, he had a very GQ look, very suave and well-groomed, extremely confident and sure of himself. I was once just like this, but no more. I remember always wishing I could be more like Patrick once I became such an anxious wreck. Behind him was Marie, a very sweet woman in her early fifties, she was always a very congenial character. She greeted me. She said, "Hello Steven, how are you today?" I said, "I'm fine thanks!" but I didn't look at her, I looked at the floor. But what I was doing was listening to see if Patrick would open my wounds. He didn't. What a basket case I was. There was an elephant in the room for a minute, but the tension was soon cut when the phone rang and Patrick promptly answered it. I was relieved. I wish more people like Marie existed, people that don't necessarily solve your problems but make you feel positive and give positive energy, or at least don't project their negative energy onto you. Patrick was a very stern sort of character, very stoic, so as you can imagine he could make you feel very uncomfortable, especially because he was a deputy manager at my hotel. Every time he saw me, he probably thought, "Oh bless his little cotton socks".

I walked straight downstairs without paying any notice to any of the patrons in the breakfast room which was located just to the left of the reception office. I was so glad it was a small hotel. I once worked in a prodigious hotel that had no less than 340 bedrooms, several conference and banqueting suites, a gym, a fully-fledged restaurant and a spa – "Wow!". I often imagined how it would have been if I'd still been working there with my mental health issues. I couldn't have managed it, I don't think. Too frenetic, too many people, no time for yourself, people borrowing your thoughts. No thanks.

Once I got downstairs, I used the lavatory, dipped my face in water and tried my best to cool down and calm down, I hadn't even started my long 10-hour shift, and I had already broken into a profuse sweat. I was used to sweating due to my anxiety, so I always made sure to use plenty of deodorant, especially in warmer climates.

I then stepped very timorously out of the lavatory, just as one of the housekeepers walked by, who was always in her own world but never failed to throw a mirthful smile my way with a slight head nod; she exuded warmth and friendliness. I always felt at ease around her but only when no men were present. A few feet away from the downstairs lavatory, which was designated for the staff, there was a kind of staffroom, which had an old table inside it, a few chairs and a microwave. A lot of the staff members would frequent it on their breaks but it comforted no one so not many people stayed in there for very long. Behind it was also a cloakroom which somehow housed a few staff lockers, which were popular amongst the catering staff members as several of them kept their work apparel, ties and shoes there and just past that, further along the corridor, the maintenance office where Martin usually was. The door was shut, thank God! I could hear him inside there rummaging through some stuff. He was an elderly fellow, one resigned to do this work until he could work no more, a very genuine, likeable fellow. nonetheless, but not nice enough for me to believe he wouldn't insult me covertly, or even overtly, where it mattered. He always had one of those stories, you know, that you had to listen to and pretend to find funny. Particularly the one about his son having once played semi-pro rugby, and being so disorientated after being tackled ferociously, that he ran with the ball to the wrong try line thinking it was the right one. Poor Martin, he seemed to be lost in time. That particular story was only funny the first time – by the twentieth time, it became exasperating. I felt for the new receptionist, Rachel, a petite blonde of about 34 years of age. She was the new receptionist when Martin cornered her and delighted her with one of his famous stories, but she took it well and didn't let the smile on her face wither away. I was privileged enough to witness this, that was one of my happier days before this prison my brain dwelled in. She was a single mother I'd heard, just working to make ends meet and take care of herself and her kids, I heard she was once an architect for about 10 years but that was another story. I've always had the utmost respect for young single mothers – they stand in front of a great example. As I say, Martin was harmless; a slim lone figure, his attire always a bit dishevelled, he had a slight hunch and crooked teeth. A heavy smoker. I remember once, I came to work and greeted him in the hallway and smoke was coming out of his mouth as he spoke. But anyway, that's Martin, just stuck in his ways; stuck in an endless routine which he called his life.

I needed a cigarette, probably two, I thought to myself. So went outside at the back to the staff designated area, parked my backside on the bench, reached over and grabbed the ashtray took a cigarette out of the box and lit it. "Why do I smoke?" I thought and remembered how cigarettes came about in the first place and how they were initially brought on after the wars as a stress reliever for soldiers, or a test, and even with the news of cancer rates rising, how especially in America, there was a petition to make it acceptable for women to smoke, too. More money, more evil. But anyway, I'm no better. The nicotine mocked me every day.

Two housekeepers came to the smoking area, Sarah and Ana. It was funny, whenever you saw them, it was like they were joined at the hip, speaking in their own language. I guess they found solace being from the same country and all. Fair enough they were very demure and quiet, almost made me feel like I was still a confident person but who was I kidding. They just gave a little acknowledgement of my presence, finished their cigarettes and headed back inside. I carried on sitting down alone, with my thoughts and lit my third cigarette. I wanted coffee but knew that would have affected my nerves adversely. I never used to realise that our thoughts are what create our feelings – this became very stark to me once I understood it properly, later on. It's like I was sitting on a goldmine the whole time unbeknownst to me, hidden in plain sight. A comfortable seat one could say. I just sat there and let myself disappear for a moment.

CHAPTER 1: THE PAIN

I used to watch countless videos on methods and ways to overcome anxiety and depression, ways to become happy and motivated. I realised that anxiety eventually leads to depression if untreated. What's worse is when being stuck in this impregnable crazy 8 cycle, one minute you are depressed, the next frustrated and angry. Sick and tired of being sick and tired.

This is how *Sunshine and Showers Positive Mental Health* breaks it down:

When we feel like we don't have control, we fall into one half of the Crazy 8 cycle. (Picture a sideways 8 or an infinity sign.) If we prefer variety and love more than certainty and significance, we jump into the sadness and depression side of the 8 first. We feel upset with life, we aren't happy with ourselves or others around us; and overall things just look blue. We look to others for support (we get love), and we get people to behave in ways toward us that they wouldn't usually (we get variety).

But because, as human beings, we can't always stay in the same state, after some time we tip over into the other half of the Crazy 8 and become angry and frustrated. We yell, or demand things from others, or blame others loudly for things going on in our lives. And so, from this, we get certainty (for sure we get their undivided attention), and significance (they listen to us and do what we say).[1]

---

1 SAS, 'Are You Stuck in a Crazy Eight?', *Sunshine and Showers Positive Mental Health*, 2013 <http://www.sunshineandshowers.co.uk/1/post/2013/04/are-you-stuck-in-a-crazy-eight.html> [accessed 30 August 2021].

I began to understand how some people become depressed. One of the causes, I think, is doing something you don't truly have any passion for over a long period of time. I felt alone, every second of every day. It's funny I felt more alone when I was around people than when I was alone on my own. One of my favourite inspirational videos, which in the beginning did not affect me because, you see, I didn't have faith in it. I couldn't possibly see how these few words and ways to shift my paradigm would manifest into the happiness I yearned for. It took me so long to realise the secret. The words in the video went something like this:

When you choose to feel in a constant state of worry, you subjugate yourself with the conflict in your life and it can limit what you can do in your life. The world is turning around you and you can't do anything, you can't concentrate; no one wants to be around someone like that. Sometimes in life when you fall and don't feel like you have the strength to get back up you put on a mask, you come to school, pretend everything's ok when it's not.

Depression happens in one of two ways: intrinsically or extrinsically. Depression, frustration, anxiety, pain disillusion, it's all part of the process of becoming a better version of yourself. It happens spiritually and physically in the world. We have to choose whether to give up or keep on going. You have to ask yourself, 'are you going to believe in yourself but also be there for yourself?' You'll never believe people when they say you're a failure or that no one likes you, cares about you; people ask how you are and you say fine, but you're not fine.

Life's a journey. With depression you have to realise you're not alone, you're not the first to go through it and won't be the last, but you can overcome it and make a difference to someone else suffering with it. It can seem like what you are going through makes life seem hopeless, but the pain is temporary – it lasts a minute, a day, a month, years but eventually it will subside and something else will take its place. But if you quit it will last forever.

Imagine in your life you're going through something now with someone 10 years older than you, or 10 years ahead who has gone through the same thing as well, and they came to you and said: "You know what? I know how it feels. I've been there. I've gone through what you're going through now, but I'm still here." All we can do is either give up or keep going, give up, or get up. When you fail, try again and again and again.

As the Chinese say there are three ways to gain wisdom: first, by reflection, which is the most noble, second by imitation, which is the easiest way, and third, by experience, which is the hardest way. Life is an experience. Happiness is the journey, not the destination. We all have to get back up when we fall and once, we master that we must help others. Each one, teach one. There are three ways to live your life: make things happen, watch things happen or wonder what happened.

These were some of the words that I'd constantly repeat to myself to keep me on a positive frequency. This only became meaningful once I started to realise there was something else on the other side of pain. This relates to one of the hermetic principles, polarity.

I opened my eyes and was ready to go and commence my shift. The day would have gone quickly considering the amount of administrative work that needed doing. I put out my cigarette and headed to the door, taking one last deep breath as I mounted the narrow staircase.

"Hey, guys!"

There was an awkward moment of silence. It felt as if everyone could hear my heart beating loudly and echoing across the reception lobby. Marie and Patrick both just stared at me. I remember swallowing a big gulp of saliva, just wondering when the group was going to be arriving. I asked Marie in a very timorous tone and she replied, "around noon". The thing is, she said it so casually just like another normal day at the office, but to me, this news almost gave me a heart attack. As soon as I heard it I remember experiencing an overwhelming feeling of dread. Imagining all the voices I'd hear insulting me brought back that all too familiar feeling: my stomach was churning, my fingers were numb, I was breathing faster, started sweating and so on. But then I thought to myself, it'll be okay, "I Will Survive".

The reception area was very, very small, comprising of a front desk and immediately to the left of that was a little breakfast lounge, and behind that was a bar that had seen better days. Nevertheless, I did like the cosy feeling the reception and breakfast area gave me. It felt secure and compact. Safe to some degree in comparison to much larger franchise hotels. As for my affliction, I don't understand when it started, I don't understand why it started, I just know that whenever I was in social situations, I always felt some form of ridicule or some form of judgement, or a murmured insult or gesture would be thrown my way. It got to a point where the idea of nothing happening seemed weird to me. It became my norm to constantly live in fear of being insulted in one way or another, especially by other men. My worst fear was being in the presence of groups of teenagers, with young virile boys wanting to maybe impress their friends or female counterparts at my expense. The same went for the young adult crowd, the twenty-somethings. It's funny because ordinarily, I would be part of one of those groups, yet seeing them now terrified me more than anything. It was torture; I was constantly in that state of wondering where the next "attack" would come from and consequently, how badly I would tense up, be seized by overwhelming dread, thinking someone, particularly a male, would spot me in a crowd or smaller setting, and be overcome by the need to insult me in some way. It's just the way my brain worked and it got to the point where I couldn't discern between reality and a figment of my imagination. At its worst, I was unable to leave my home for about three weeks on end. I felt extremely isolated. When I did finally muster up the courage to be "normal" it would involve doing groceries at around 3 am. Or only doing home delivery grocery shopping. I remember once I came out from hiding and had to jump on the bus, as I wasn't driving at the time; it felt so alien to me. I felt like I was sticking out like a sore thumb, but not only that, everything felt strange, like the air hitting my face as I waited at the bus stop. The moment when a stranger laid eyes on me, I felt as if I was naked or wasn't human.

I asked Marie how many people we were expecting from the group, how many rooms we had to block for them and how long they were staying. I remember asking all these questions as if nothing else in my life mattered. For me, I guess it was a form of managing the problem, but I wonder if it perpetuated it. I once heard that to be free you must surrender to everything. Where my anxiety and psychosis were concerned I did everything but that.

The group was to occupy 30 rooms. So we certainly had our hands full. The whole saga was to last three weeks and none of the staff would have a day off. All for a lousy little bonus at the end of it. So negotiable. I couldn't wait for Patrick to leave; his presence made me very uncomfortable and in a perpetual state of consternation. Sure enough, he was soon to leave as I could see him sifting through some documents. I knew this was a sign he was about to make off. "Thank God," I thought.

"OK, guys I'll leave you to it," Patrick remarked, as he skedaddled from the reception desk. Surely, he had more important things to do. I breathed a sigh of relief, and sat down, taking my position at the reception desk. As I said, it was a small area – compact, small but efficient.

I logged in to the in-house system and checked the arrivals list. And there it was – 30 rooms, most of which were for double occupancy and some even triple. We offered single rooms, standard double rooms, deluxe double rooms, suites and finally the apartment room. I sat there and just tried to gather my thoughts and compose myself. "It will pass very soon," I said to myself. One thing I later learned was a way to cope or manage anxiety attacks is to repeat this sentence – "there's nothing I can do about this right now" – over and over again. Drum it into your brain. One way or another your brain will eventually believe in something if you repeat it to yourself enough times and condition yourself to believe in it. Talking therapy, like cognitive behavioural therapy (CBT), medication or self-help books can also help. Visiting early intervention teams which usually consist of psychiatrists, psychologists, social workers, support workers, etc., is very helpful, too, as they can identify the specific mental health problem you have and tailor the treatment for it. I found it very important to learn my triggers, which was being in busy places around a lot of people. I found ways to relax like deep breathing exercises which I will cover later, and also present moment focus.

    I felt my stomach doing cartwheels and my left leg then began to tremble profusely as I sat there helpless, a shrinking violet, awaiting my impending doom. I'd rather have been anywhere else in the world right then than there. It felt a bit weird being in on the day shift. Even though there were no arrivals as yet, just the early morning sun shining through the breakfast room window, and the sound of hooting horns and London's exasperating traffic gave me a feeling that serenity could never exist without chaos in this city. A perfect way to describe London. At this point, it was about 8:15 am and I couldn't shake this feeling. I felt this way daily over the slightest things and I hated, absolutely hated, changes to daily patterns. It's like everything most people complain about or want to escape from, like the stultifying tedium of a monotonous job, or a not so challenging walk in the park or that phone call from your friend telling you about the new girl he fancies, just became my comfort zone and I refused to leap into the unknown for fear of having no control and being vulnerable. The truth, I later realised, was that control is an illusion. It was a Sunday and breakfast was generally served later on

Sundays – around 8 am. No patrons had come down to indulge yet. The sweet breakfast lady, Ana, was so hardworking, shy and modest. She just came to work, did her job, smiled and went home. She never got involved with all the drivel and claptrap that tends to engulf the typical office environment. We served continental breakfast which was made up of freshly made and delivered croissants with other delicious pastries, ham, salami, cheese, bread and rolls, bagels, yoghurt, a vast array of oats and cereals, tea, coffee, fruit bowls, boiled eggs. I must admit it was yummy and quick to prep. Preparing breakfast was one of my duties towards the end of my night shift. I finished at 7 am and would begin preparing breakfast around 5 in the morning. That's around the time the fresh bread and pastries would be delivered. Strangely, the delivery guy was one person from who I didn't seem to hear anything insulting. Well, it did happen once, but I believe it because it's the only time that I recall that he seemed to be in a bit of a huff – other than that he was a very friendly lad. I think he said he was of Polish descent. The night before would have been Jason's shift. There were three other night duty managers. So, it was me, Jason who was a young Irish guy and a fairly new recruit, Dan who was very quiet and kept to himself a lot, and finally Enrique, a very loud, flamboyant Spanish lad, who was just so excited at the prospect of being in London – it was a holy grail to him. He would often wax lyrical about the capital at any opportunity he could get, talking about how fantastic the eateries are, the nightclubs, the people, but not the weather. I pitied him. But I guess perspectives define each individual's reality. To me, Spain, where he was from, seemed a much nicer prospect even though I hadn't been there. I heard a lot of positive things about it, namely the beaches, the weather and the general atmosphere. But who am I kidding – I'm terrified of being around people. I can't even enjoy those things anymore. I have been damned.

At this point, Marie had also left for her sanctuary in the downstairs "managers' offices", lucky them. I heard footsteps coming down the stairs getting louder and louder as my heart beat faster and faster. We had a lift, but as the hotel was only four floors and there was only space for one lift many customers opted to use the staircase. An elderly gentleman emerged in my peripheral view on the top right. The reception desk faced the stairs so you were on display as soon as a customer came down them. I greeted him with a bashful "good morning" to which he replied "good morning" with a look of certainty, but I quickly broke eye contact, started randomly clicking the mouse and fixed my eyes on the screen to pretend I was engrossed in the workload I had for the day. I'm sure he understood and didn't wonder why I broke eye contact in the middle of our gaze; did he think I was rude? Did my smile seem sincere? "Oh my God!" "I hope he won't insult me now." These were very often my thoughts with the interpersonal moments I shared with people. I remember even thinking as I took my gaze off him that I would listen out to see if he did say something offensive to me, "he must, I know he will". I heard nothing, "but the day has just begun", I thought.

I saw him disappear around the corner into the breakfast room and cheerfully greet Ana, I heard the sound of him picking up his plate and helping himself to the continental buffet breakfast. Soon I thankfully forgot he was even there. I needed to find something else to worry about. Some time passed with many guests of the few rooms we didn't have allocated to the Olympic group, coming down to the breakfast area. Most just gave me a brief passing greeting, except this one older woman who was a regular at my hotel. I felt comfortable around her and she always put her hands on the table, so to speak. We indulged in some conversation, me mainly doing the listening, of course, such was her loquacious nature. I would almost freeze up as people walked by, noticing us in conversation, and I would hope no Mr Eddy, who was another regular guest, would come and become the centre of our conversation. I couldn't relax even when I felt comfortable. She soon left and went on her usual morning run. "See you soon," I remarked. By this point, the breakfast room was in full flow, plates clanging, chatter and laughs filling the atmosphere. Then came a man – he emerged from the lift as I heard the doors open. He had a very grumpy countenance. I'd seen him once, months before, but he stared at me, I looked at him and tried to greet him but he had already looked away at that point. I was sure I heard him utter something offensive to me, or was he murmuring to himself – I couldn't tell. Perhaps he was just talking to himself, expressing his censure at the recent project he was assigned to by his boss? He was the corporate type; tailored suit, cufflinks, and he had a walk that embodied certainty like he was on a mission. The thing was, what was I to do – go and confront him? Ask him if he had said something? That seemed so awkward to me at that moment. I didn't know what to do. Was I to just sit there and be a punching bag?

They say anxiety can be caused by bad childhood experiences like neglect, a lack of affection or a traumatic event, your current life situation or even drugs and medication. Psychosis is caused by trauma, physical illness or injury, alcohol and smoking or even prescribed medication, lack of sleep, bereavement or genetic inheritance. No one in my family or extended family has a history of mental health problems. I did indulge in smoking weed at university and I stopped maybe a year before these problems started. My psychologist suggested that may be why. He also told me that it may be attributed to childhood experiences, possibly being bullied or being neglected. I was never neglected but at times I did feel left out at school, or at least I always felt like I was different, and I still do.

I remember when I used to work in Victoria, in another hotel near Buckingham Palace. It was a 10-minute walk to my hotel from Victoria station, one of the busiest in London. I was walking and a group of twenty-something-year-old boys were walking in front of me; they were all of mixed origin. Black, white, Asian and I think, bi-racial. The sight of them immediately made my heart freeze for a moment, I then gathered my thoughts, awaiting my impending doom. I knew they were going to take exception to my presence or notice something about me. I wasn't doing anything but walking to work but somehow, I knew they would pay heed to my presence, and at last one of them would have something insolent to say to me. I slowed my walking down and began pacing my steps as I quickly thought of a way I could re-route and take another road to work, but I wasn't aware of an alternate route. I just had to face my fears. I remember stopping dead in my tracks covertly undid my shoelace as I bent down only to then re-do it as slowly as was humanly possible to buy some time so that they could get further ahead. But as I stopped about 30 metres behind them so did they. One of the members of the group was making jokes with a few fellow members of the entourage and suspending their walking every few seconds. I just kept thinking in my head "hurry up" and "for God's sake walk", and the more I did that the more they seemed to slow their pace. It was almost like my thoughts and feelings were manipulating the universe to put things into place to reflect just that. Was this power? Surely not. How can it be powerful if I'm attracting exactly what I don't want? I just wanted the ground to swallow me up at that moment. I worked night shifts there as well, I think it's very obvious why – so it wasn't particularly busy on the street. I just had the train journey to put up with, and now this. Why do I feel something bad is going to happen? Someone is going to insult me or hurl derisive comments to entertain the group at my expense. Is there something wrong with me? I never used to feel this way this consistently, and I don't know what to do. Sure enough, the boys halted and then they turned around and my cover was blown. I had nowhere to hide I just had to keep walking, feigning confidence as I did so. I made every attempt to not make eye contact with any of them. As they turned, I felt they could immediately sense my discomfort. Like predators, they preyed on it. Eyeing the target, looking for a moment of weakness in which to strike. Fake it till you make it? I guess so, if that even made sense to me. Buddha said, "all that we are is a result of what we have thought." This became abundantly clear to me later on. One of them on the end said something – it arrived at my ears, a sort of cacophony, it was indecipherable. But as always, my brain insisted on interpreting it as an insult hurled in my direction. What I usually would do when I didn't fully comprehend what was said is I would then use my secondary senses, my eyes. If I noticed the supposed culprit gazing at me ominously, or with a sort of guilty look – one which asked the question, "what are you going to do about it?", I'd also then look at their companions to see if they are giving me the "Oh my God I hope he didn't hear that, will he do anything about it?" look. My brain was constantly at work, constantly working, never at rest and peace. Can you imagine going through that? Especially where human beings are concerned. The ability to have a very innocuous and friendly conversation even with your best, most trusted friend, or your family members and you are certain they are in some way insulting you or have a problem with you. It's torture. I remember on many occasions contemplating suicide. I couldn't live that way.

The white boy on the end had the look of "yeah, what? What are you going to do about it!!!" And then at that moment, I knew he said something insulting towards me for no reason, just because I was born. How can I address such a thing? I knew I wanted to. To be honest, at that moment I wasn't intimidated by the fact that I was grossly outnumbered; I just really almost wanted clarity and certainty that what was said was for a reason. I couldn't think of one, so what I did was then create one. It must have been the way I looked at him. Which was completely innocent, but not to him. What else could it be? I TOOK IT ALL IN MY STRIDE. If someone were aware of my affliction and witnessed this moment, they would have been able to say I had all this going on in my head because I was good at hiding it, living with this pain and pretending I was okay. But it was destroying me inside. Eating my soul.

As they turned and the boy on the end gave me that look, my interpretation of this look was that it was ominous (but I guess this was because I used emotion to rationalise it, as my psychologist once told me). My first instinct was to give a look back which exclaimed, "stop looking at me," because I was sure it would attract others' attention to me. I mean what else was there to look at in that moment. I knew if the group collectively looked at me at the same time they would have had a problem with me. Luckily most of them were so engrossed in their conversation that they paid me no mind, but the one boy did and it affected me. If only he knew what it made me feel like. Don't get me wrong… people look at people. I'm talking specifically about the look when it FEELS like someone is looking into your soul, seeing your most vulnerable and sensitive feelings, and you believing they can so easily sense it. I later realised I was more afraid of that than the actual "offending" itself.

Once they looked at me, and then looked back towards each other and ahead, I made haste and quickened my step, taking the opportunity to pass them, making sure to give them a wide berth as I did, and marched on to work making sure to ignore any further misinterpretations of words they were saying to each other. One stone's throw was enough.

I came up with this analogy that when in the presence of a crowd or a small group it's like being surrounded by mirrors which give a three-hundred-and-sixty-degree view or reflection of you standing in the middle. At least one of the reflections will not be flattering. One of the people won't like what they see. It's like I once heard about the rule of 10. It states that in an average taken of 10 people, three will like you, three won't like you and 4 will be indifferent. My interpretation of that is more like 1 or 2 won't mind you, 1 will actually like you and 6 or 7 won't like you. It won't take much for the indifferent people to dislike you. Another way to say it is, it would take much less for them to not like you than it would for them to like you. It's just human nature, it seems, these days. People are

CHAPTER 1: THE PAIN

trying so hard to live outside of time. No one stops and looks and sees – I mean really looks. They just judge, categorise and move on. Easy as pie. I later learned that when we judge others, we actually judge ourselves. That's why people nowadays are unable to love thy neighbour because true love when you think about it is just a glorified form of acceptance. How can most accept when most judge first. The only reason this can be so is because of experiences, how we feel and just a lack of acceptance.

The breakfast room was now quietening down. With most guests heading out for the day as they were staying for more than a night. Some, I was informed, were in the country for the London twenty twelve Olympics, while others were probably on business or just for leisure. I checked the departures list for the day and saw that we only had two departures scheduled. I was relieved. The last thing I wanted was a queue of people waiting to check out in a small area. That in itself is normal in a large hotel, but in a small compact hotel, large queues are less common. I checked the customer accounts, for the departures. They were names I didn't recognise. This was my second year here. By that point, I knew all the regulars. There was what I presumed was a married couple (one of my worst nightmares), a Mr and Mrs Keith Wilson, and then the second check-out was for a single guest in a single room who went by the name Mr Jonathan Levy. Most hotels' departure time is around 11 am or 12 noon and arrival time, meaning times whereby patrons could check-in, is usually around 2 or 3 pm. In our hotel check-in time was 3 pm and check-out time was 11 am. This gave the housekeepers enough time to clean the rooms and spruce them up for the next guests. The breakfast room was almost silent now. I quickly got up and looked and saw a single patron, deeply preoccupied with whatever she was reading in the newspaper. I always wondered how true the things that are portrayed in media are. Nevertheless, it certainly didn't matter to the average train commuter and white-collar worker. It was better than people watching you at such close proximity, or counting how many times the person sitting opposite you picks their nose. At this point, Ana came back upstairs. I think she must have gone for a smoke. She gave me a hearty smile and proceeded to restock the breakfast table with more food. It was unlikely many more patrons would come for breakfast seeing as there was hardly anyone in the hotel. We were at full capacity for that night onwards due to the arrival of the group but had they not stayed we would have been at, like, 30% occupancy. I suppose in a normal year without Olympics around that time of the year it would make sense. I tried to gather my thoughts as I heard Ana in the background moving things around, refilling empty drink jars, removing dirty plates, as they clanged. It was a cacophony of sounds only heightening my senses. At this point, I needed a "sedative" not a "stimulant" so to speak. I was busy on the system just looking around at some metrics when I heard "doors opening" and I knew someone was about to emerge from the lift. I could hear chatter and laughter, in slightly croaky voices. I could tell they were both smokers. They approached the desk and gave me a friendly smile. "Here we go". They asked to check out and as I'd seen, they had paid on arrival which was great. It meant a very fleeting exchange. Mr Wilson handed me the key card. I started getting uncomfortable at this point as his partner had nothing else to do but stare at me. I felt like it was a pyrotechnics display and that I was on stage. What could possibly be so interesting

CHAPTER 1: THE PAIN

about staring at me as I carried out a very monotonous check-out process? I saw they had been in room 27, one of our better rooms. I clicked on the checkout button as the balance owed was zero, and quickly put the key card in the "checkout" box, ready to be reset and reused. Mr Wilson asked if all was settled and if anything else needed doing, and I advised him that it didn't but still, there was almost a hesitance by him to accept it. Like he wanted something else from me. I gave a wry smile and wished them well. At this moment he said something I didn't quite comprehend. I thought I heard the word "idiot" so I said, "Sorry?" to which he replied with a laugh saying, "Oh sorry, I said is that it". I smiled again and the awkward tension was finally broken. They left and wished me a nice day. Even though he repeated what he had said I asked myself if he was telling the truth. He must have wanted to offend me and needed to. I was too used to thinking this way, you see. What's worse is sometimes I would only pick up insulting words once a conversation was over and the person had left my presence or vice versa. It's like a playback in my brain and a word would pop up. Was it real? I don't know, but I felt and believed it must have been. I felt that I couldn't do this anymore. It was like any encounter I had with people, especially with men, made me anxious about the next interaction I'd have. This couldn't have been normal, but it had become normal to me. I'd even run through scenarios before the conversations would happen. Carefully thinking through how I would avoid offending people or disarm them, so they wouldn't have a reason for taking an immediate dislike to me. It was torture.

About an hour and a half passed and the front desk was rather quiet. There wasn't much to do. I then heard the doorbell ring and looked at the CCTV monitor; we had this, I guess, to distinguish between who was a prospective customer or a staying customer or a serial killer. We would on occasion leave the door wide open too but this was rare. I was delighted to see that it was a guy wearing a baby blue shirt and navy trousers and carrying a red sort of rucksack. He seemed impatient and was fiddling with some letters – it was the postman! I was rather happy, as with all the experience I had with them they weren't always concerned with balderdash. They had targets to meet and every second counted. I buzzed him in, and drew in one big breath of air. He walked briskly towards the front desk whistling to himself as he did so. "Good morning," I said, to which he replied with half a smile and a slight nod of the head. He probably wouldn't remember me if he came the next day, I thought. Just how I like it. Sometimes I wish I was invisible anyway. He handed me the letters and headed back to the door hastily and headed off to carry out the rest of his days' work. I stood up and told Ana I'd be back and that I had to quickly place the letters in their respective pigeon holes. This was downstairs near Patrick's office. I scurried back upstairs, quickly enough to make sure that any customer waiting wouldn't have needed to wait for too long. As I opened the door that separated the staircase from the lobby area I immediately turned right and saw a tall gentleman standing there, frustratedly tapping his key card on the table. He gave me a blank look, one of censure and impatience. I quickly apologised and remember thinking at that moment that explaining why I had left the desk unattended would only give him more reason to unleash his fury on me, so I remained quiet. I walked past him, sat down at the desk and asked if he was checking out. His response, very aloof and unfriendly was a simple glance towards his key card and then directing me to take it from him, so I did. He just took off before I could get another word in. The good thing is the machine that cuts the keys could also be scanned for room recognition purposes. So, I figured out that it was Mr Levy. I clicked on his account, moved the cursor of the mouse to the room balance button, and saw that it was zero. I then moved the cursor to the check-out button and clicked it, and checked him out of the system. So now I felt a bit more relaxed as one part of the day's job was done for good. Early check-outs before the end of a customers' stay were rare in our small hotel. We did offer a pro-rata refund. This was easy to process on the user-friendly system. So, it wouldn't throw me off if it did happen. It didn't happen.

It was about 11 am at this point. All departures had left and the breakfast room was empty. Ana, the breakfast lady and part-time housekeeper, had already tidied it up. There was a quiet atmosphere now in the reception and I was comforted by the ambient sound of the fridge that was behind me in the bar area. It only then dawned on me that I was alone in the front lobby/reception area and I found it peaceful to not have to deal with any other energies and consciousnesses but my own. It was so placid and calming. But then I thought that it wouldn't last. When did it ever? My phone vibrated; we were always told to keep them away from the desk but there was no camera at reception so like most other front desk agents I had my phone on me, on vibrate. It was a message from my friend Joe, just catching up with me. We went to university together in Greenwich and he was what I considered to be a very close friend. But once this affliction progressed that changed as I couldn't even enjoy the simple little talks we used to have, or the outings we embarked on.

As I was putting my phone away the reception phone rang. It had a very loud tone and for some reason, no one thought to reduce the volume. I didn't want to tamper with it so I left it.

"Hello, you are through to King's Hotel. You are speaking to Steven. How can I help you?"

"Oh, good morning, hi, thanks. Erm, I wanted to enquire about your availability for myself and my partner over the Olympic period from the 25th July until the 13th August. Do you have any availability?" It was a lady with a slightly northern English accent calling.

I then responded by saying, "thank you for your call, but unfortunately, we don't have any available rooms at the moment. Should there be any cancellations you are more than welcome to try and book in the next few days, either on our website, booking.com, lastminute.com, Agoda, GTR or call us directly." I knew that was unlikely but I said it to potentially placate a disappointed customer.

"Oh no!" she said, "that's alright. Thanks for your help".

Normally I would have checked the room map and availability to see how we were looking for the next few days to check if anything was available, but I just wanted to get off the phone. Despite it being a woman, I sensed I was on a loudspeaker as I heard a lot of background noises and immediately felt uncomfortable, and assumed someone else was listening in. Maybe her partner would hurl insults at me. I was a complete passenger. Not just that, but a scared one. I realised later on that when we feel anxious, we must find a reason why. If there isn't one, we will create one. The brain sends a message to the rest of the body to go into survival mode. Fight or flight, as they call it. Once that chain of events has happened you are forced to acknowledge the signal sent by the brain, and then find a cause for it. Sometimes there's no threat at all. This is what I later learned that I had. Kind of like the burnt toast effect which is just a false alarm. When it seems as if there's a threat of danger of the toast causing a fire it turns out that it isn't anything harmful. It's just a bit of burnt toast. With me, I had an oversensitive mind that would often make me overreact to things that weren't threatening.

I hung up the phone and then released the tension in my body. I remembered there was a direct debit going out that day for two apps I had self-developed and published on Google play store. I sneakily opened up a new tab, checked my bank account and saw the eight pounds had been debited. I then checked the app development platform and smiled to myself. That's pretty cool. "You have your own app," I thought. Albeit, a simplistic one but it was still an achievement. I remember hearing the saying, "if your first attempt at anything was exceptional, you should have been doing it way before then." One of the apps was a social platform where I'd raise topics regularly around the world for people to discuss and also to interact with one another, give access to news feeds, etc., and the other was a basic hub in which customers could access all UK leading supermarkets websites and offers.

I closed the windows down and erased the browsing history and went back onto Opera. I saw the financials for this group's upcoming stay and saw the hotel generated circa £80,000 for this Olympic season. If only I had that much money in my account, the things I would do! I wondered if I would still care if I constantly heard insults from people. Then I thought, if money can't buy you time, how can it buy you peace? Over the next hour, a couple of the housekeepers and senior management walked past the reception desk, occasionally acknowledging me with the odd smile or dry witty comment. I guess somehow this helps time pass by. It was nigh on 2 pm and I knew the group was soon to arrive. Would they come in droves or would they come in batches? I wasn't to know, but one thing was for sure and that was that I certainly didn't hesitate to think of all the worst possible scenarios: The key machine becoming faulty, or one of the members of the group insulting me, laughing at my expense, being grumpy and unhappy with the room allocations, needing me to meet their needs in other ways which we don't typically offer as receptionists, them thinking our 4-star hotel was sub-par and overpriced, them not enjoying the amenities we offered or the breakfast – the thoughts were endless. It was like I was throwing them into a pit and once it was full with my thoughts, I could stop filling it. The problem was the pit was bottomless. I guess it's true what they say – overthinking is the biggest cause of unhappiness. I once heard the saying that people are just an extension of your thoughts. I now understand what that means today.

For this period there was a consensus to install ice cream machines specifically for the group – vending machines and their own Dutch beverages. Of course, as staff members, we could also indulge in these things. The hotel was located on a very busy road in Kensington. I wondered where they would park their bus. And I wondered what I'd say to them to get them excited and looking forward to their stay. Then I thought, simplicity is the highest form of sophistication. I don't need to sell anything – it's already been sold. Just smile, be nice, calm and welcoming. Advise them on some of the local eateries, bars and sights to see, like the natural history museum, Royal Albert Hall, Hyde Park, the local Chinese delightful restaurant that everyone loves called 'Wong's Buffet', or the lovely Italian restaurant called 'De Rossi's'. That's it. Talk about what I know and not try and compete with their expectations of me. I was rationalising my thoughts. But they have guides who would have done their research already or have been informed by our corporate members and senior members of this, surely. I had no idea what time the group was arriving. I assumed it wouldn't be too long after 3 pm, although technically they could have come even earlier as the rooms were prepared for them as a matter of priority, but they didn't. I also remembered that Marie said that she thought they would arrive at around noon. I was constantly looking at the clock.

What happened next really startled me. I received a call from management downstairs asking if the group had arrived yet as they were due. My heart skipped a beat. It all felt very real.

Sigmund Freud listed three things that cause us discomfort on earth. 1. Is the pain and dissolution of our bodies, i.e., time and ageing. 2. Outside forces, things out of our control which I think at this period in time was my biggest cause of pain. 3. The last thing is pain caused by other people, for example, being betrayed and let down.

I was always anxious: before a situation, during a situation and after the situation in preparation for the next situation. It was a perfect cycle of perdition. I just wish I did something about it earlier when I first spotted the signs. Once I became a victim of it I was living outside of my body and in my mind. If I only knew that we live in every cell in our body, not just in our mind as we think. Our body is our subconscious mind. I never knew that it was always imperative to check your body language, stand tall as if hanging from your teeth. Give good eye contact, smile a lot. All this puts your body back in a steady flow of energy. If your mind is healthy but you are not physically fit, this will lead to disharmony in the body (the system) over time. Everything must be in balance for you to be truly happy. I never even knew what chakras were and that we have seven points on our spinal column which are connected to the various organs and glands through the body. These chakras are responsible for disturbing the life energy which is also called Qi or Prana. When I later learned these things, it was a breakthrough for me, and I will share this with you.

I didn't even go for lunch. I couldn't bear the exposure in a bustling place such as Kensington. I just kept a yoghurt and mini cereal box from breakfast for myself as well as a croissant. I kept it in the bar fridge and got up to eat it. I was starting to get the shakes. Every spoonful of yoghurt I scooped fought with my hand to go into my mouth. The food prevailed. I also felt very dehydrated. It's like all the water in my body was absorbed. I wouldn't dare consume any diuretics. The urge to urinate was overwhelming. I headed to the lavatory which was just a few steps from reception on the same floor. So, leaving the front desk unmanned for a moment was okay, I thought. Besides, it was very quiet and not much was going on. In previous years I would always be excited about the Olympics but in 2012 I dreaded it, not only because I had to work non-stop during that time, but because everywhere would be busy. I hoped I was wrong. The maintenance guy, Peter came through the reception lobby door from his downstairs office. He was a contractor who we only saw about twice a week but he was reliable and kept himself to himself. Wasn't much of a small talker. My kind of people. He walked past me and greeted me and headed upstairs via the staircase with a toolbox that looked like it could fix an aeroplane. And then it happened. I saw a crowd of people congregating at the front door. I was just staring at the CCTV screen feeling beside myself. As much as I knew they were coming it still shocked me when they just appeared. It was first one group of them, consisting of about seven people, then shortly after that another consisting of about nine people until eventually there were at least forty individuals. They weren't ringing the doorbell as yet, just engaged in chatter amongst themselves and then I guess the guide, it must have been, walked up to the door and pressed the bell. My heart started beating out of my chest. I wanted to call Patrick downstairs and summon him to come and deal with them. I wanted no part of it. I sunk into my seat but after three rings I finally opened the door and the herd came crashing in. The key cards were already pre-cut, and the different guests were already assigned to their rooms. It consisted of members of the company, Heineken, Unilever and some others I didn't even know of. All of a sudden, the reception area looked something like a queue at immigration in the airport. "This is my worst nightmare. I have to be perfect or I will be mocked and insulted." The group leader was the first to emerge into my view. He was a tall, well-spoken man, with a slight Dutch accent and carried himself very well. He greeted me. I acknowledged him as best as I could, careful to not seem perturbed and uncomfortable. I just kept thinking, I hope the group stays out of sight and doesn't also circle around him with their hands and eyes unoccupied with something else but me. But that's exactly what happened. Before

I knew it there were about 10 others in my line of sight staring at me, anxiously awaiting something I couldn't offer them, but the majority of the group, forming something like a procession, were out of sight. It almost felt like I had to frisk each one or interact with each one before the moment would pass. I advised them that their rooms were ready and the keys were cut and that we just needed to cross-reference his checklist with our systems to know who would be assigned to what room. The awkward moment of silence was broken and it gave me solace; at least some of them didn't find me that interesting and continued with their chatter. I heard a cackle and I immediately felt anxious. I looked up only to still see the 10 people from the group staring into my soul not even blinking or moving. I kept a smile on my face, careful to not give myself away. The group leader was called Dennis. He and I agreed that I would read the names on our system as well as their room numbers and hand the keys to him to give to them. So we did. Each one formally acknowledged me as they stepped forward to get their key card. It was going fairly smoothly. I knew it was only because there was something else to fill the moment other than just me, and them with nothing to do. I guided most of them to their respective rooms and at this point, there were only about 15 members left to be given their keys. This group was a lot quieter and reserved, probably the more senior members of the respective companies. One of the names made me want to laugh, his name was Wesley Von Toon. But of course, I had to remain professional. He certainly fit the name in my eyes. He stepped forward gave me a warm smile and thanked me, and headed to the room. The next woman approached the desk as her name was read out, carrying the joke she had heard from the other members of the group with her and communicating it directly to my eyes. I knew they had made a derisive remark about me. Surprise, surprise! To impress the woman? I don't know if she realised that making fun of me to make her react was an insult to her. I just ignored it. I was too relieved and focused on the fact that this moment was almost over and I could breathe again. I never knew I could hold my breath longer than a navy seal diver. "I could do with being submerged underwater after the way I feel if I don't drown in my sweat before that," I remember thinking.

The lady left and took the inappropriate energy with her. There were now just two guests left. They both received their room keys at the same time and headed off. The guide had stated that the guests were going to get some desperately needed rest and then later would probably come down, in droves I assumed, to get some light refreshments and perhaps go for dinner. "I won't be here," I thought but I hid that thought in the smile I gave him in acknowledgement of his comment. He grabbed his keys and asked me if it was okay to sit in the bar and he helped himself from the fridge provided for them for their stay. I could only hear it open and close as I assume he grabbed a cold Heineken. He disappeared into the back of my consciousness, a bit more than a whisper away. I literally couldn't believe I had done it. Even if I was to see them again it surely wouldn't be as bad as the first time, would it? I was reviewing that moment for at least 20 minutes, carefully going through each fleeting interaction I had with each guest. Shockingly, there was no playback evidence of an insult, just that awkward moment when two or three of the last of the group received their keys, and I sensed they were giggling at me and sent their messenger to make sure that I knew it. Well, at least that's how it felt. It was fast approaching 5 'o clock and I certainly had a shadow. I couldn't wait to leave but then began focusing on the traffic that lay ahead. "Wonderful," I thought. Jason would be in tonight for the night shift. "My turn is coming soon." I wondered what they would have been like if they'd been inebriated, loud and obnoxious. The joys of the night shift. I went on to the employee portal website to have a look at the rota as I was curious as to who was going to take over from me, seeing as I was to finish at an unusual time. It was Dana, a part-timer, she had kids as well and did two shifts per week. Today was her shift. She was okay, amenable, a bit quirky and in her own world.

Dennis emerged from the bar and lounge area, thanked me and headed to his room. The entire time before that I could hear the sound of movement reverberating throughout the entire building. It was an interesting sensation I felt when I was paying attention to it. A mix between if and when someone would call reception, or just come down to ask for something or if they were in their rooms, confused as to how to operate certain amenities and if they were pleased with the quality of the hotel. The thoughts hurried around my head, without time for me to validate each one. They would then rush to my body and I would become them. It was nearing the end of my shift and all I kept thinking was that the day was nearly done and, "I will soon be out of here." No one passed reception. I assumed they all had a briefing on the time they'd all need to congregate in the reception area. Dana appeared on the CCTV monitor. If you had seen me at that moment, you would have thought I had won the lottery. That little moment was everything to me. It sounds pathetic but you would have to walk in my shoes to understand.

CHAPTER 1: THE PAIN

This anxiety, this entity itself, refuses to let you live your life without its presence. If it could form as a thing it would undoubtedly be large and offensive in its form. It commanded attention and refused to be left out of my daily proceedings. It pushed me out the way and then pulled me along. It's true, as the saying goes, the battle is always between how you feel and what you know? I feel in a constant state of panic and dread but I knew I should have been calm and that nothing was going on. Calm is who I am and anxious is who I thought I was supposed to be. I let Dana in; she was as ebullient as ever and full of positive energy. "Hey gorgeous," she said. to which I replied with a sheepish, "Hello Dana," while wrapping my response in a bashful smile. "I'll be back in a minute," she said. I wondered if she was going to quickly indulge in some sort of ten-minute yoga session before commencing her shift; she had bags of energy and a lot to share, it seemed. I sat there waiting, constantly looking at the clock hoping she would come back and that I would be able to hand over to her before anyone appeared to delay my departure. I heard some noise upstairs and my heart reacted before my mind did, but my mind quickly joined the party. It was short-lived as Dana appeared, almost skipping as she came. I wish I was as positive and carefree as she was. She was of a mixed ethnic background, white English mixed with Iranian and Caribbean. She had curly black hair, hazel eyes, tanned skin and a beautiful smile. She was about five foot five, and had a slim build but the lower half of her body was very curvaceous. She was a dahlia, a nubile, energetic, charming, smart 23-year-old woman. "So how are we looking?" she said. I almost thought she was referring to how she looked and I nearly said "beautiful" before realising what she meant. Before I tripped over my words, I explained that the group had arrived so there was no need to pull her hair out. She sighed and seemed disappointed to not have been present to welcome them to the hotel. She was definitely the most suitable person for that, an ambassador for the hotel. I told her that there were no arrivals due in general, and that we were at a hundred percent occupancy, so we couldn't take any more bookings. She asked me if I was excited about the Olympics and I told her I was – lying of course. "I can't wait to feel the electricity and buzz in the air," I exclaimed, feigning a smile. She shared the same sentiment. Small talk? I guess so. I gathered my stuff, disposed of my rubbish and wished her a pleasant shift, then headed to the lavatory to wash my face and prepare myself for the journey home.

I had only recently realised that driving to work in "the city" was feasible because they compressed the congestion zone and Kensington, at least the part I was in, the south, wasn't part of it. I scolded myself for not realising this sooner. It reminded me of all the horrible experiences I had had travelling to work via train. Three, in particular, I can never forget. I had to catch the train from Cheshunt to Seven Sisters and then from there, catch the Piccadilly line to Gloucester Road and my work place was a 5-minute walk from there. One time, a long time before my mental health problems started, I was heading for work. I used to dress in urban clothing, heavily influenced by the music I listened to and the culture that I followed. I mainly listened to UK grime and American rap music. I would have a rucksack stuffed with my work apparel. So, when I got to work, I'd change and commence my shift. On this occasion, I was anxiety-free. I can't begin to explain how much I miss being there; how do I get back? Seems impossible. The train arrived and I got in a carriage with a group of about eight millennials, sitting in typical inconsiderate fashion, spreading themselves across multiple seats and throwing a football to each other, back and forth. Not forgetting to make fun of each other as they did so. For whatever reason when I noticed them, I felt two things: one was annoyance, the other was uncertainty. But I left those thoughts where they were, careful to not fertilise and water them to grow. Anyway, I decided that the best thing to do was to move through the carriage door to the next carriage to ensure I didn't have to even face them and be perturbed by them. I was still in control of my feelings back then; I know this because I wasn't dreading such a situation before it actually happened but only reacting to it once it did. The other section of the carriage was full of commuters. The seats were not attractive. I generally would opt for a seat with no one next to it. That was just a preference thing. It meant everything, it meant nothing. I walked towards the group who were stealing the attention of all the commuters. After all, everyone generally looks forward, you can't look to the side or down for too long before it makes you stand out. I walked towards them growing increasingly tense as I did. I can't explain it; it wasn't fear, just adrenaline. It was like I was a triumphant gladiator walking toward my adversaries in war and everyone was looking to me as the bravest, strongest warrior to face the opposition. Remember what I said about the different angles of the mirror's reflection. One of the boys had his long legs spread across from his seat to the two on the other side, acting as a roadblock for passing passengers. In theory, if I just asked him to move, he would have probably obliged. I didn't. Again, it wasn't fear, it was more just to not be conspicuous and have to engage with them. They had no right to force anyone to have to engage with them just because they had safety in numbers. My theory on when people are in a big group is that they automatically feel more secure and that whatever they do is always safer because the group will invariably back them up, not necessarily violently. I wonder if these people, most of them, would behave this way when alone. Interesting. As I got to the roadblock, I assumed the boy would notice me and move his leg; for a moment it felt as if time stood still and an intense standoff was to ensue. But no, he was so engrossed with his comrades that he probably didn't even heed my presence. For some reason, I didn't ask him to move. I realised it was possible to simply step over his leg, so to speak. I clearly made a poor decision. As I was doing so, he then realised he was obstructing me and at the same as I was stepping over his leg, he was also moving his leg out of the way. Our legs made contact and I stumbled. It was a gentle stumble, hardly enough to make me lose my footing. It felt worse than it looked. I swear when I say, I felt like my clothes fell off and the whole train was just frozen staring at this incident unfold. The intensity from the onset of that feeling was making this whole thing bigger than it was. I'm talking with the benefit of hindsight, but at that moment I wasn't so aware. I locked eyes with him without uttering a word, sure in my gaze of what I thought of his disregard for others. He gave me the same stare back as if to show no weakness or fear. One thing I now know is staring at someone is a way to get them to react, change their decision or just feel uncomfortable. He then said, "I would have moved my leg if you just asked, my bad". I said nothing.

No one from his entourage uttered a word in his defence either and that was it. Someone hit the play button and then everyone carried on like it never happened. The awkward tension was cut in half. I reviewed what had transpired as soon as I sat down in the next carriage. I began dissecting the chain of events that had taken place. I concluded that I wasn't satisfied with the outcome; why I was subjected to that negligent behaviour. Why I was forced on stage against my will; don't get me wrong in the world we live in there is always going to be a nuisance in a crowd. Of the 16 personality types out of every 100, this was a certainty. But why me? Also, why didn't I just say "excuse me" and leave that moment in the past instead? It was the beginning I believe of me becoming aware of the feeling that people would provoke, test, and insult me. Moreover, with an audience witnessing. This became my biggest fear, it became my undying obsession. This lack of acceptance that I couldn't go back and change how I reacted and what people thought of my response to the "test" proved to be what led to this problem becoming exacerbated. It was eating me up inside. If I was happy with my response, then I assume they would be too, and vice versa. It was a quandary and I needed a silver bullet.

The next example I vividly remember was once again on the train, well the underground this time, on the Piccadilly line. It was during a quieter period at about nine o'clock in the evening. Again, I was heading to work. The first part of the journey on the overground train was fairly relaxed; alas the second part had to make up for that. I was sitting in solitude in the section nearest the next carriage. I hate sitting in the middle section, with relatively few people getting on and off at the various stops. When I got to Green Park this changed.

As the tube's brakes screeched bringing it to a halt, I was relishing the fact that I had so much space to myself, not squashed in like a sardine in a tin. I wish I lived in America. They have so much space there and it is more natural to give people space, whereas in places like Asia and the middle east their culture is more known for people standing very close together. London is overpopulated. Being of foreign heritage even I can admit that.

The doors opened and at this point I was in such a relaxed state I had shut my eyes, satisfied that the stops before encompassed a peaceful journey. Up to this point, I was so grateful. Before my affliction I wouldn't take notice of this, rather I'd be frustrated and angry when tranquil, calm environments were suddenly inhabited by unruly, money and impression-driven people. Going nowhere quickly. I was abruptly sobered by a concourse of people rushing onto the train, some in groups some on their own. It was like in an instant beauty had turned into a beast. I was now a passenger on many levels of consciousness. It felt like I had lost the ability to choose my thoughts. I was unsettled, the palpitations started, I started shifting in my seat, looking around for the threat and all I was getting was half looks from disinterested commuters. I only had three stops to go. After one stop two men suddenly stood up, I assume waiting to get off the train. The two people sitting next to me were relatively calm and in their own world. One I believe was an elderly English man. The other was a young oriental woman, timid in her movements. Across from me was a couple probably of European descent who would occasionally glance at me and then return to their bubble. It annoyed me but it wasn't threatening as far as I was concerned. Wait! Everything was. So, I ignored it, my attention was preoccupied with the two men by the doors waiting to exit the train. Like in the movie "Focus" the mind cannot focus on more than one thing at the same exact time coherently, and I'm not a woman. As the tube approached the next stop the two men got ready to disembark the tube. One of them barged into my leg as he was heading to the door. I was worried someone saw it like it happened to everyone at the same time, and immediately I felt the responsibility to react to it for everyone. It was a weird thought; I didn't only think about whether it was really a big deal or not and how it affected just me. I jumped up in a hurry and aggressively accosted him. At that moment I forgot who I was. It was like the real me was still sitting down and my alter ego was acting on my behalf. "What's your problem? Can't you even say sorry? Didn't you see my leg?" His friend quickly stepped in; he had a calming voice and it seemed to cool me down somewhat, but in case people were expecting more I carried on. I extended both my arms to the side and said, "Come?" I was losing this battle; I was giving the devil what he wanted. The perpetrator wasn't apologetic as such with his words or movements, but the cat had his tongue. His companion continued to gently intervene and for a moment my attention was diverted to him, listening to his words. In the moment my adversary seized the opportunity to gesticulate something that I didn't see. Another commuter stepped in and admonished him. As I looked back towards the threat, I saw nothing. I then wondered what I had missed? What did he do? I had no answers. I didn't ask as it seemed out of time. I was grateful that whatever he did do, another good person with integrity stepped in on my behalf. The two men soon walked off and I pushed the guy in the back to send another message.

When I sat back down so did everyone else it seemed. And then again it was like it had never happened. Just like that. A moment. And then nothing. I gently nodded my head at the commuter who stepped in, still wondering if I should have asked what the other guy gestured at me. But I didn't. My stop was next. I got up and left the train and the moment was gone forever. I hoped none of them remembered my face. Again, upon reflection, I wasn't satisfied with what I did. I felt I should have assailed him. Taught him a lesson but it wasn't me. I was doing what I believed people expected a big guy like myself to do. I guess there's a reason why a viral video of a big strong looking guy beating up another guy will get more views than one of a big strong man being provoked but walking away with a smile on his face. As I stepped off at Gloucester Road Station and headed for the stairs, I let out a huge scream to release the tension. It startled the mother and little boy walking past me as well as the people I saw at the top of the stairs. Their sudden silence summarised everything. I headed to work.

There were many other incidents I had on the tube. I even remember once during a rush, a man barged into me trying to make his way onto the train forgetting his patience and vision on the platform. As I was getting off the tube, I ignored it but five seconds later I ran back onto the train in front of an audience and confronted him. He had no time to process what had happened and apologised and I left. I was stuck in a perpetual state of needing to prove something according to other people's expectations of me. I always thought I was so sure of myself, but maybe this was proof that I wasn't. They say the minute you allow someone to give you value or validation you lose confidence. Looking back this is very profound and true. These incidents were so shocking to my body that I swore to avoid taking the tube and train for as long as I could. My mind was trying to protect me from the world. Or was it trying to protect me from my body?

The other time I vividly remember was again when I was on the tube, the Piccadilly line no less, on my way to work, again on the night shift. The journey was usually relatively uneventful and placid. On this occasion, I boarded the tube and sat literally behind the drivers' deck, in the last seat. Nothing in front of me and everything and everyone behind me. I was five stops away from Gloucester Road. On this day I toyed with the idea of getting off at South Kensington station. It was about a similar walking distance from my workplace as Gloucester Road. But I dared not; I tried it once before and that station was far more crowded and busier. Who was I kidding? Where isn't busy in the city? I think it was more due to not wanting to change my routine and my comfort zone. It was sacrosanct. 4 STOPS TO GO. The doors opened and a handful of commuters hopped on. There was a discarded Kleenex tissue two seats to my right. Of the people getting on an elderly gentleman sat in the second seat where the tissue was but moved it to the seat right next to me. I immediately accosted him "what the f**k are you doing?" I exclaimed. Furious at his lack of regard for me. "I didn't put it on your seat" he replied, giving me a tacit look of disdain. "You could have put it on the f**king floor. Stupid idiot!" I said. At this point, I stole everyone's breath in the carriage and there was no 'snackman' eating, who was present to help diffuse the situation. Once again, all eyes were on me. I was back here again. Did I do this to myself? Is it a self-fulfilling prophecy? The elderly man just reclined in his seat and stopped engaging. "I will stab you in your neck!" I spouted. He didn't respond. I was satisfied. To be honest I wouldn't do that unless it was life and death but again, I was entertaining peoples' perception of me. I was being me for them I wasn't being me for me. I carried on hurling insults and obscenities at this man. Never taking my eye off him fully. It was a diatribe. The man just ignored me; maybe he realised I wasn't mentally stable and might act on my empty threats. Why take a chance? My stop came up and as I was walking off, I never took my eye off my enemy, to ensure there was no sneak attack. My worst fear. I walked off and even as I got off, I looked back, still giving him the death stare. The train was silent. I don't feel people were judging, but their preconception due to the media portrayal of a man of colour, a big man at that, is a threat to their safety. When all I was doing was crying out for someone to understand me and feel my pain. Instead, I justified the media's brainwashing. I was a stereotype. I felt damned if I did, damned if I didn't. But for a moment it did feel satisfactory when he stopped responding. I was thinking for a minute that this is London and people are NOT afraid of confrontation, in fact, a lot even relish it. A lot of people are stressed up to their eyeballs with work, relationships, money issues, environment. An ideal situation to take it out on me. I didn't care; I knew no one cared or would even take a moment to wonder why I was acting out. Not because I'm aggressive and a violent person, but because if I wasn't people wouldn't even care. People don't care. It's why most people, when witnessing something bad happening to a stranger, will just sit back and watch or film it on their phone. Do it to someone they care about and they react.

CHAPTER 1: THE PAIN

I later learned that for every minute you are angry, you lose 60 seconds of happiness. My affliction was getting worse and I still didn't feel I needed some professional intervention. Regret not taking action sooner – this I did. I didn't know what to do. I was slipping further and further away from myself. These moments would eat me up and haunt me. I just hated feeling like I was being forced to react when I didn't ask for a situation in the first place. I began to sympathise with people who were diagnosed with mental health problems, when previously I had taken this for granted. It can happen to anyone and no one knows how or when. I used to wish I was five foot two and a different race so people wouldn't immediately associate my colour with strength and a heap of expectation. To be aggressive and not be tolerant. My dad once taught me that being tolerant is one of the most powerful things you can be when it comes to your fellow man. I miss being young – just happy all the time, excited about life and taking each day as it came. Life was so simple back then. I was always a cynosure amongst the people around me. I was gregarious and the 'fun' of the group. The dichotomy between who I am today and who I used to be is clear to see. I'm more sheltered and bashful, a shadow of my former self. Even during my time at university, I was very sociable, amiable and would be the life of the party. I spoke to everyone and was extroverted. How much I miss myself. It saddens me. Perhaps it's because I moved to the U.K. from South Africa, during a very crucial time in my life – my teens – perhaps that changed me somehow and I became lost and have since been trying to find myself. I had to adjust to a whole new country, new culture, new accent, and new people. I've always felt like I never truly fitted in.

I had to go through this alone; no one asked me how I felt about having to leave my home, what it meant and if I would be okay. Maybe, just maybe, this contributed to me eventually experiencing mental health problems many years later. I believe there is a link between the two. My therapist made me realise this, too, during one of our many sessions together. Finding your way home isn't always easy. Sometimes we go to places and we never find our way back home. Instead, we have to settle there, just move along with the flow of the current and adapt to the new demands of life.

But back to the day, I was telling you about when I had finished work, I got out of the lavatory, determined to get home as quickly as I could. I exited out the back door which basically was just next to the front door when you came out of it. I guess it was a subconscious thing that I'd always done in many of my jobs. My car was parked just across the road. It was a contraflow system so if I didn't manage to double back and park on the correct side facing the correct direction, I would have to make the U-turn when leaving work. I unlocked my car and couldn't have been more relieved to sit in it. I looked up and saw a man and woman engaged in conversation. They just appeared and suddenly stopped and stared at me. They were standing just in front of me to my left. I saw his hand twitch and I just thought "Please don't do any ambiguous hand gestures. please". He didn't seem particularly interested in me; I was more interested in him. I started my car made the U-turn and headed home.

There were two routes I could potentially take to get back to my area from South Kensington. Seeing as it is London there were probably about ten ways from Sunday to get home, but I had become accustomed to two. I did try a third way once but it took me through King's Cross and it was so crowded that it gave me an anxiety attack.

Where is the beauty in a rat infestation? I couldn't handle the pressure of travelling via King's Cross. I even recall on one occasion I was so tense and worked up with anxiety. I came to a stop at a set of traffic lights waiting for a group of millennials to also cross but they decided to hesitate and abort that. For whatever reason, I got so frustrated with them that when the light turned green, I jolted off and avoided making eye contact. I wasn't allowed to get off that easily. As I was driving past, I was certain one of the men of the group had spotted me, his pupils dilated and I was certain he spat on my car. Tactile hallucination? I didn't even know what that was back then. I needed a release to my tension so this was a perfect way to do so in my body and my brain. I forgot what fear and danger meant. Bear in mind this group consisted of about five men and three women, all in their twenties to my best estimate. As I raced off, I believed I spotted the tallest, biggest lad of the group give me the eye and spit at my car. It was impossible for them to just let me drive off without expressing some censure towards me. Anyone else would be let off. I believed that. I stopped my car on the side of the road, and aggressively engaged my hazard lights and handbrake, it seemed all in one swooping motion. I jumped out, leaving my keys in the ignition and the car unlocked. It was King's Cross. I RAN ACROSS THE ROAD, beating my brain as I did, not my chest. I walked up to the group from a kind of side angle, adrenaline fuelling me on, nothing else but authority over my actions. I looked for the perpetrator, spotted him, kept charging, growing more and more threatening as I did. I shoved him, and he stumbled backwards completely in shock as to what was going on. "You spat on my car!" I shouted. Time froze. I had seized the moment. Correction the moment had seized me. "YOU SPAT ON MY F**KING CAR!" He wore a half bemused looking smile and a frown on his face, unsure of what to do or say. Bear in mind it was night-time. "I'm sorry?" he said. I repeated myself. After a tense standoff and him processing all that stood before him, I think he then decided that I wasn't intending on assailing him. "Did you check to see if there was spit on your car?" he uttered. He was right but I couldn't let him know that. Besides, it was dark. I thought carefully about what my next move would be. Remember there are five men and three women as your audience. And you demanded their attention. Imagine being in that situation. Nothing was giving. He didn't assure me he hadn't spat and I didn't feel I needed to do more. Now, this part still surprises me to this day. I have no idea when I think back as to why I did it. It's totally out of character for me. I walked up to the prettiest girl in the group and grabbed her arm as a dominant alpha would. "Are you okay?" I said. She couldn't summon the will to respond so gave me a fleeting, slightly uncomfortable smile. It rippled across her lips from one corner to the other. I let her arm go as I was distracted, proving I wasn't a pushover or intimidated I now noticed one of the members of the group, probably the boyfriend of the innocent, beautiful girl, murmur something. It sounded like the name, "Nick". At least I didn't think anything else of it. I walked off and strangely didn't hear any sound from them. I had stolen their consciousness for a moment and they couldn't do anything about it. I still wasn't satisfied. This is my point. I was still in the same place. Nothing mollified me. I carried on to work, and when I got there, I took a moment to gather my composure. Did he say "Nick?" maybe one of his friends was called Nick. Nick? Nik? Knick? Nig? N**ga? Oh!!! How come I'd never heard that abbreviation before. If he meant it so strongly why abbreviate? Why not say it loud and clear like a lion's roar. Coward, I thought. Or was I the coward? In the same way that the definition of respect lost meaning to me, so did the word coward.

    The traffic was pretty awful. I was just happy that my car was heavily tinted. "That takes care of that." The front windscreen wasn't however, and every time someone would look at me just long enough for me to feel I needed to respond emotionally I would try and calm myself down again. I took my preferred way home. It was the most straightforward and had the least turns. As far as I was concerned traffic and pedestrians would plague the streets no matter what the route was that I took; it was the Olympic period and near central London. I carried on driving, and I soon approached a traffic light in an area that I knew was usually very densely populated. Most of the people were just lingering, looking around, marching along, tourists. Some were crossing the road, flagging down black cabs. Rubbernecking, I'm joking! It was chaotic and rather disorderly; something you would expect on the road in Mumbai. I squinted my eyes just as the light turned red, so as not to show emotion and attract attention with my eyes and countenance. It felt like at least a thousand people passed near or around my car in those twenty seconds that I was stationary at the light. London is overwhelming. The light turned green not a moment too soon. I sped off; I felt as narrow as a sheet of paper. I was so aware of every little feeling

I was experiencing all at the same time. It was all so intense and overwhelming, I encountered traffic at sporadic intervals. With the odd plight no less, along the way. Nothing I didn't already expect.

I was almost home and remembered that I needed some basic groceries. Living independently certainly has its ups and downs. After the day I had, I was too nervous to go to the Asda or Lidl. So, what did I do? I settled for the superette Cost-Cutter near the petrol station closest to my flat. How pathetic, right? I couldn't even afford myself the courtesy of eating decent food? On top of everything else! "My anxiety disorder caused this; my anxiety disorder caused that." What I am now starting to understand is that it begins to exacerbate other areas of your life. You feel alone and isolated. I guess in some way everything that happens in life matters. I turned onto the high road and accelerated rather quickly toward Herald's Road where the Cost-Cutter was located. I found a parking space on the road and got out and headed towards the shop. As soon as my door was open it felt as though something got out of the car with me. or something got in my car anxiously awaiting my return. I walked rather hunched over towards the shop. I crossed over the road and as I reached the other side a black golf sports car, thumping some very loud grime music, drove past me. Windows tinted front and back. The front driver's window was open halfway and smoke was pouring out of it. My heart immediately responded. It was a life and death sensation that it had induced. I know that feeling so well. It's like a shock to the system, a spike in the heart rhythm. A mild arrhythmia. That sensation immediately triggers a thought of danger or a threat that sends signals to the rest of my body, which then tenses up. I'd need to urinate, my mouth would dry up, my pupils would dilate. It's designed to protect us but surely an extended overuse of it would deplete its efficiency and end up making it go haywire. I think this was the case in my situation. At that time, seven years earlier, I had no idea of any of this, nor what it meant.

I was just hoping that the group of people in the car didn't intend on coming to the shop as well. Every step I took was filled with the dread of them entering the shop. My body became my thoughts. I opened the door, was careful with my step as I went in and decided that if anyone came in, I'd immediately rush to the counter to pay for my items and leave. Or I would stay in the shop as long as I had to until the other customers left. I was near the frozen section. I had no idea what I wanted to buy anymore. My brain was too focused on everything else. I was turned inside out. I grabbed some frozen potatoes, fish fingers, a medium-sized pizza, a loaf of bread, eggs and some concentrated fruit juice and was about ready to leave. I headed to the till still with no one present in the shop besides the clerk and myself. And then I heard distant laughter, chatter and aggression. A group of three men entered. One was black African/Caribbean, another might be middle-eastern and the third and the final one was white. I knew at once they were the occupants of the Volkswagen Golf. As I promised myself, I would leave as soon as anyone arrived to avoid feeling anxious about hearing an insult or being mocked or scrutinized or stared at, I was luckily already at the till as this happened. They were lingering behind me talking as loudly as one can imagine. All sorts of drivel and balderdash came out of their mouths. Not a care or regard for who may be listening to their coarse and sordid tone. The man at the tills' eyes was my mirror to the rear-view. Anytime I saw him look up at them I looked at his eyes for confirmation as to whether they were insulting me or making fun of me. In my mind, I would always believe I heard an insult at some point in this kind of situation, not necessarily from each member of the group but at least one of them. Without fail. I can't remember the last time I was in that sort of situation where nothing happened. I can't remember a time. This was caused by the hallucinations due to my psychosis. With every second that passed while I was still in there, I grew more frustrated by the clerk focusing on the guys and not on scanning my items and taking my payment quicker. I took my attention off the guys for a second as the clerk was ringing up the final price and then when my consciousness went back to them, I hit the playback button for the recording of five seconds that I had missed live and heard the word "c**t" forgetting that I wasn't the only person in the shop. There was the clerk, his friends. Why did I assume it was directed at me? My back was turned to these people but I was sure that still, I would annoy them. Something about me just annoyed people. How could I have gotten to such a point? I didn't accost the guys, but not out of fear – more out of exasperation. I was tired of always being the object of obscurity in the room and peoples' psychological punching bag. It was like there were countless situations where I'd walk in and people would hit me metaphorically and I couldn't do anything about it. It was stripping away my happiness and the thing I once called comfort. For a moment I was so engrossed in the sadness of not being able to escape this hell I was in that I didn't even hear the clerk alert me twice to the total price. I did the third time. Luckily, he was calm about it. I didn't want to upset anyone. My subconscious was still working, as ever. I inserted my debit card into the machine and made the payment and just wished I could disappear. By then I'd almost forgotten those three guys were even there. The damage was done. What was I to do – accost them? Who said it? Why? Did anyone say it? How do you do this without being socially awkward? Once upon a time, I did just that. I was happy to investigate and confront. But I was quickly getting sick of it. How long could I keep it up? I remember in the early days of my psychosis a close family friend who I'd confided in said these words to me – "You just need to be insulted more times, so that after that if it happens again, you won't care as much" – such veracious and profound words. I walked out of the shop, defeated mentally and spiritually. Winning one battle within a war of a thousand battles no longer placated me. I was giving up on everything. Things I once knew. Things I could discover. I got back in my car and just sat there for an hour, staring into the distance. Looking at nothing but feeling everything. I didn't care who walked past. I just wanted everything to end in that small perfect moment of desperation. I started my car and headed home I was a mere 2 minutes away and looking forward to being alone, parked away out of sight. I got into my flat and heard a noise coming from the living room. I know it must have been my flatmates, either the elderly gentleman, called Frank, or it was Jasmine, both of whom were very well known to me. We are all from the same country and very familiar with the landlady. That's another story which I will explain. I was just grateful to be home and had no space in my brain to also deal with the issues I was dealing with at home on a sporadic basis. I didn't kick this gift horse in the mouth. I sat in my room holding my head firmly in my hands and just asked "why?" How could my life be such a mess? I've always been a good, kind, amenable person. Would never hurt a fly. I didn't deserve it. I switched on my television and there was a pre-Olympic show on BBC 1. I put my food in the oven in my room as I had a microwave that had that convection and grill function. I bought this deliberately to avoid having to spend more time in the kitchen than was necessary, just to avoid interacting with my housemates and feeling like they would insult me. You have to understand the offenders were beginning to become interchangeable. What I mean is that initially I began hearing the insults from strangers and then this insidious virus became so powerful it began to affect my close relationships. Again, I will explain how this came to be. Imagine, sitting with your closest friends or family in a nice fun setting, with only laughter on your mind. But then every few moments you are sure one of them is either verbally insulting you or offensively gesticulating towards you. Close your eyes and feel what I'm saying. Your closest people are now strangers. They don't like you. You know deep down that they can't be insulting you but you feel like they are. It gets to a point where you even avoid spending time with them due to that fear. It's complete hell. It's completely dark. Imagine you are me. Then just begin to appreciate these little things you have right now. I once heard the saying, "if people were to only wake up tomorrow with what they are grateful for today, what would they have?" I read this recently and it immediately made me halt in the moment. It is so profound.

I sat down in my single-seater, a black leather sofa that my mom got for me a while back during one of her visits back to the UK. My mom is so kind and caring always making sure that I'm okay. Sometimes she coddles me but I appreciate her, nevertheless. My three-star Michelin entrée made up of potatoes and fish fingers was

CHAPTER 1: THE PAIN

now ready and the ravenous creature that I was, I attacked the food without taking a moment to enjoy it. I was due to do another day shift the following day but I knew I didn't have the willpower to motivate myself to go. It was more because of the unknown if I'm completely honest. As I sat there I made the impetuous decision to call in sick. The procedure was we had to call a sick line at least 1 hour before the commencement time of the shift in question. So, my plan was set and I must admit it gave me a joyous feeling that filled my room. I sat quietly staring through the television. Aloof. Lost in my misery and thoughts. The joy was short-lived. Time was passing by so quickly and night fell even quicker. The noise downstairs carried on steadily but I was without a care. I knew I had no reason to go downstairs except to shower. It got so bad at one point that I bought a kind of urinal container (chamber pot) that I would use in my room and empty and clean regularly as to not have to come downstairs more than I needed to. To avoid facing anyone. It sounds horrible but it worked for me seeing as I needed to urinate on a very regular basis. At some point, I believed I had an issue with my kidneys but when I had the doctor look into my blood results, they found nothing amiss. I needed to distract myself so ended up switching my Xbox 360 on. I was obsessed with Street Fighter and FIFA. On this occasion, I put Street Fighter on and played until the early hours of the morning. I set my alarm for 6 am to wake up and call the sick line. I was due to come back to my normal night shift two days after that. We usually worked on a rotation basis five or six days a week. I was looking forward to lying in for the next day and the day after; Saturday and Sunday. I was due back on my normal shift on Monday from 11 pm until 7 am, after and before the London rush. Bank holidays and weekends were always such a joy as there was hardly anyone around during those hours, at least as far as traffic was concerned.

I was beginning to get tired and had been engrossed in my video games. Needless to say, I didn't frequent the kitchen at all. I lived in total isolation. The noise had quietened down before I realised. I think my flatmates had called it a day. How sad that I always felt vulnerable and alien. It's like I had lost my basic social skills: from facial expressions to behavioural traits to general social etiquette. I stuck out like a sore thumb and I felt people's eyes reminding me of this constantly. The silence became a sort of white noise and had a calming effect. I remember back then a friend taught me about Solfeggio frequencies. It's musical frequencies that calm us, connect to our chakras and our soul and ensure our mind and body are in a cadent flow. It centres you. At these times I wasn't really listening to it, it was just on. Later, these frequencies would prove to be therapeutic and tranquilising. I got up and lay down on my bed for the first time. I just immersed myself in the moment and all I could feel was my Posturepedic bed absorbing my body, welcoming me, hugging me. I was looking forward to being off for the next two days. It was a well-deserved rest. I could switch off from the world, secure in my bubble, living on my own time. Appreciating myself.

I slowly drifted out of consciousness and into the dream world. I heard a loud bang with the receding scampers of birds in the background, the sound wave eluding me the more I was aware of it. It was daylight. I had fallen into a deep sleep. I'd woken up as if sleeping wasn't the best way to make it into tomorrow.

The Olympics came and went just like that. I stayed in that job for another year or so after that and my condition just got worse and worse. The job was okay and paid a decent salary but I knew I deserved better. Despite my affliction I know I could have landed a better job. The enemy of the great is the good, as they say. I just settled for that job knowing I could have gotten something better. Maybe it was my condition that limited me in the way that I thought. I kept on hearing insults from various people. With no help or cure in sight, I just had to live with it as if it was my broken leg. No one is perfect and we all have afflictions. I always felt like this was mine. But I never truly believed that all this suffering was for nothing. I never believed or knew when it would go away but I felt like there was more to come after it. Neither good nor bad, just more. Something. Anything.

Chapter 2: Who am I?

My alarm chimed, I looked at my phone and it was 6 am. I quickly rang the sick line, spoke to Jason who was approaching the end of his shift and told him I wasn't coming in. I was unwell. I was as succinct as possible. He wished me well and just as he tried to carry the conversation on, I said, "see you later."

It was a lovely sunny Saturday morning. I stood up and walked over to my window. I was on the 3rd floor so my room overlooked a large park that was frequented by many itinerant adolescent teens either playing football or parading around just looking for a motive, father playing football with his son, people walking their dogs, sporadic semi-professional rugby matches and even a semi-professional football practising ground. On that particular day I stood at my window, the side the field was on and just stared at the sky, marvelling at the celestial beauty. I felt free for a minute. Like anything was possible. Like I wasn't me. In the distance, I spotted a most beautiful sight. There she was. I had never seen her before. This was a very large park so all sorts of new people would catch my occasional gaze. She was wearing a white spaghetti string tube top, light blue high waisted jeans, grey and blue coloured trainers that had a glow and she had beautiful full, curly, black hair. I know what you're thinking – how could I see her from that far away? But you know, sometimes beauty commands your attention; it summons you before you even notice something is beautiful; it's like something preceding your attention already told you it was. It's a feeling; something innate. Folding myself more into myself, it seemed. As Charles Bukowski, the writer, once said, "when a hot woman meets a hermit one of them will change." Maybe I needed that. It was like she was moving in slow motion. I just stared at her and felt her. She disappeared from my viewpoint and then I got my breath back. Was she just a window to my potential? At that moment I knew there were things in the world that could remind me that things could improve. It momentarily quietened the editors in my brain that were distorting reality into a limited negative narrative.

I was brought back to reality when my phone rang. I hated speaking on the phone just as much as meeting people in person. The "curse" followed me in the waves of the sound, too. I checked my phone and saw it was my friend, Eron, calling. We went way back to school days when I first moved to the UK from South Africa as a teenager. He could talk the hind legs off a donkey. He certainly didn't run out of words to say such is his garrulous nature. He was in the year above me in a school I attended in Cockfosters, near Barnet. Fun times, Sort of.

He wanted to check up on me as we hadn't spoken for a few weeks. He also mentioned that he was heading to a shindig at a friend of his, and urged me to come along. Before he finished asking me, I already knew I wouldn't go. Just the idea of it, playing out in my head, the social awkwardness, the insults I would hear, unsure where to look and where to turn, having to avoid accosting someone due to believing they were insulting me in some manner, all these strangers. NO! NO! I couldn't. it filled me with a deep antipathy for the actual do itself. In previous years I was the one to have parties and invite people. Who am I? I've become so afraid to be myself again, but I can't, my auditory hallucinations, if that's all they are, that cause my social anxiety disorder, won't let me be me again. I like the reference in the movie "Get Out" – the real me is in the sunken place falling deeper and deeper into the abyss. Trapped. I'm throwing a rope down hoping the real me will tether to it and come back up. I can't win this on my own. I got off the phone after a 10-minute conversation with Eron and for whatever reason, in that moment I did my usual conversation review or playback to see if any insults were heard. The word 'prick' kept surfacing. My close friend. This was normal for me to believe I was hearing insults under their breath or while I was preoccupied in a verbose conversation. At this stage, I hadn't a clue what I could do to resolve this problem I had. I was none the wiser. I had no idea what was happening to me or why? I sat there filled with a combination of rage and feeling crestfallen. I believed so much that he had insulted me. Every reason I could think of as to why he wouldn't have spouted an insult at me was quickly thrown into the bin. It gradually progressed. There was a point later where I would ask people if they said something but it's not as simple as them denying it. I didn't necessarily believe them; started thinking I could hear their thoughts, it was a way for them to project their issues on me, knowing how much this affected me. Plus, constantly asking people if they had said something gets exhausting for both parties. What could I do? I just had to accept it and deal with always believing I was being insulted and ridiculed. My therapist later told me that the action of asking people was leading to a self-fulfilling prophecy. Eventually, people would run out of patience and begin to feel offended by my thinking that they did or said something so that eventually I might drive them to do just that. Eron was one of the friends I had who knew about my condition and supported me. But I trusted no one's word anymore, nor their intentions or agenda. A friend or close family member insulting me, as absurd as it sounds, and a complete stranger insulting me became interchangeable. It was all the same. The virus was at its most deadly stage. This came after years and years of suffering.

What I started to think as the years went by with this problem I had was that there were several different arguments for and against it. I had to give credence to the argument that people were indeed insulting me, mocking me, testing me as often as I saw them. Psychologists or doctors will tell us that our anxiety disorder/psychosis/schizophrenia amongst other mental health problems are caused by exposure to a traumatic or uncomfortable or embarrassing public social situation that is so horrible and unsettling that it has a lasting impact on our brains. The shock to the system and what the brain has to do to protect us completely sends our mind into a haywire overactive oversensitive state. Anxiety is natural and not negative in itself. There's a spectrum and if you have a disorder, you are on the higher end of it. This event, or series of incidents, are too overwhelming for the brain to just brush them off as a one-off. What then happens is the brain is in almost a perpetual state of panic and worry and hyperactive looking and scanning for threats around you.[2] *Where it becomes interesting is when there is no threat at all but the brain is interpreting normally innocuous situations as threatening, such is the shock and effect from a previously misinterpreted situation. Sounds, looks, words, people, environments all become threatening. That's what I believe happened to me. It's either that or people are truly saying things to me as often as I believe they are. Which is unrealistic to an average, anxiety-free person, but not to me.*

Anxiety is a physiological state characterised by cognitive, somatic, emotional and behavioural components. So, what happens somatically is that the body prepares the organism to deal with the threat. Blood pressure and heart rate increase, sweating increases, blood flow to the major muscle groups increases, and immune and digestive system functions are inhibited as a result. Externally speaking, somatic signs of anxiety usually include sweating, nausea, chest pain, trembling and pupillary dilation. Emotionally, anxiety causes a sense of dread or panic and physically you sometimes get the chills or feel nervous. Behaviourally, most of us will try and escape or avoid the source of anxiety. One must note that anxiety isn't always pathological or maladaptive. It's a common emotion along with fear, anger, sadness and happiness, and it's a vital function in relation to survival. Neural circuitry involving the amygdala and hippocampus is thought to underlie anxiety. Unpleasant and potentially harmful stimuli, such as being around people in my case, shows increased blood flow in the

---

2 Osmosis, *Generalized Anxiety Disorder (GAD) – Causes, Symptoms & Treatment*, 2016 <https://www.youtube.com/watch?v=9mPwQTiMSj8> [accessed 31 August 2021].

amygdala. All of this suggests that anxiety is a protective mechanism designed to stop the organism from engaging in harmful behaviours.

The other thing I began thinking, later on, was that contrary to popular belief, a particular event, usually social, where something very strange, eerie or frightening happens can then spark the dark chain of events. I suggest that maybe it's not so much an event in a social situation that triggers the disorder, rather being exposed to situations regularly that we take for granted, but that we don't realise we don't want to be in at all. For example, work – a lot of us don't like what we do. In social functions, we sometimes force ourselves to go to appease a friend or family, or ourselves. Shopping, standing in queues, driving especially in highly populated areas, the list goes on. The constant exposure to what we don't like and would rather avoid causes the disorder, eventually leading to an episode so to speak. Ask yourself how often do we do or go where we truly want. A walk in the park or being exposed to nature, indulging in things we are passionate about, doing things that edify us, hang around people who celebrate us. I put forward the argument that we spend too much time doing and chasing things the world tells us we should be doing. That if we don't, we will suffer. Or feel left out. I urge you to consider employing anomie and let go of the social and ethical standards that have been set for you to follow. Don't let what happened to me happen to you. That alone is the biggest lie ever. It's societal norms. Created by society, not each individual. Think if you go to the cinema alone, which some do, it's seen as an aberration. Why? Or if you sit in your car in the middle of the day for hours upon end because you enjoy it in a busy area, with wayfarers swarming the streets around you, it's seen as weird or different. Or if you wear summer clothing in winter; yes, it's cold but the looks you would get, if you catch my drift. Here's the thing. Eventually 'different' becomes a threat. God forbid there comes a day where someone challenges the status quo. It's one of the main reasons we don't accept each other as individuals; it's because we are conforming. If you think about it, Jesus, Buddha, Moses all stood alone in a belief that most ridiculed them for, because they stood for what they believed in. So, I don't think it's a question of peoples' idiosyncrasies or strange behaviour, it's more that it's always measured against. What the sheep would do and if it deviates from that, it becomes an issue. Inertia must prevail. Seriously? Living a life being who you aren't is a huge insult to living a life not being who you are. We all want to be accepted to a degree, but think to yourself would you rather be hated for being who you are or loved for being someone you are not.

One of the other things I later realised, being introspective and critical of myself but more importantly honest with myself is that I know I naturally have a problem with my attention span. Now granted the average goldfish has an attention span of five seconds and the average human is less than that; I have known for some years that I had this issue but didn't see it leading to anything else. It's conjecture, yes, but based on that fact I think there is some correlation with that to my condition. In school, even when I tried to be attentive, I would often get distracted by something, a thought, a person, a sound. It wasn't like it is now, but generally, I find it hard to fully comprehend every word someone says without getting distracted. I don't mean to. What I theorised is that when people talk to me, they sense that I'm not listening, or that whatever they have to say I don't find important or care for it, and thus they insult me. Maybe it's to check that I'm listening, maybe my brain created this measure as a way to harm itself from my frustration with not being able to fully pay attention even when I'm really trying to. Maybe because I have this problem for whatever reason, maybe with a combination of events that may have transpired in my life, being in a society like London, stress from life, not being where I want to be as yet, all my bad choices combined with my lack of attention, led to me unconsciously filling those gaps with peoples insults in their own voices and actions. I noticed myself always saying to myself that I heard it when I wasn't fully attentive. Yes, I hear and see things that are ambiguous, too. But if I was a hundred percent attentive, surely, I'd know for sure, not surmise and assume and believe it was true.

What anxiety disorder also makes you do is focus more on yourself. You become hyper self-aware, from how you walk, talk, move, dress, to every minute detail; things that in the past you'd not even register. Again, the brain being overly active trying to ensure the 'perceived danger' doesn't harm you. It's like an alarm bell. It chimes when there's a threat or problem. But with anxiety disorder, it sounds and never stops, so you are perpetually in that state. Every moment of every day and as with me it can even spread to when you are alone. The brain feeds off that energy and it will create things to trigger it. Remember, where focus goes energy flows. I started believing that perhaps it was the countenance I had, my dilated pupils the minute someone spoke to me, especially people I wasn't familiar with, or the tightness in my lips, the sunken cheeks – the passive communication that we all unconsciously exhibit. Maybe it shows as aggression or disinterest in what others have to say, and that then pushes them to retort by insulting me, even with people close to me. Where family is concerned and them knowing my true affliction, I know it can't be, but it even spread that far. I even remember at a stage when the episodes were sparser, I said to myself that I hope it doesn't spread to family and friends, but it did. Before that, I said it's only with men, and hope it doesn't spread to women, too, but it did. Law of attraction? Scary.

I sat on my single black leather sofa, planted my feet on the footrest, switched my television on and browsed through the options; no one even watches television anymore. I looked forward to the remainder of the day enjoying my own company. Not having to deal with that immediate surge of adrenaline my body gushed to my vital organs and throughout my body the minute I spotted another person, especially someone who had negative energy. You can always sense when someone's energy is amiss. It felt like everything I did, like going to a shop, answering a phone call or going for a drive, was an achievement. These everyday things became challenges and difficult obstacles. I selected an Olympic highlights programme on BBC1. It was just a review of the opening day's events and results. The USA was already way ahead. Big surprise. Although I found it interesting that although they are the greatest and most powerful country in the world the flagship of their true sovereignty comes in the form of being liberal, having diversity and offering opportunities. China, Belgium, France, UK also possess these features. 180 sovereign states out of 270 also have freedom. The USA is seventh in literacy, 27th in math, 22nd in science, 49th in life expectancy, 3rd in median household income, 4th in the labour force and 4th in exports. But what they lead the world in is their incarceration rate – 25% of the world's prison population is locked up in the USA. In the land of the free. Have we forgotten what Nixon and Reagan did to the USA with the so-called mass incarceration, war on drugs, and then Clinton's 'three strikes and you're out' mandatory minimums? Them abolishing slavery but then introducing the 13th amendment. America is a powerhouse, but they have not been magnanimous. They have subjugated the minorities for centuries. Don't get me wrong. The USA has a huge influence on the rest of the world. The USA has advanced modern science, built and developed many things, helped poor people around the world, cured disease, they cultivated the world's biggest economy and most salient to this example they, Russia, and probably China, have developed the best athletes overall.

The Olympics' opening ceremony was the day before. 27th July 2012. I remember this period like it happened yesterday. I only looked forward to specific events: mainly track and field, 100m, 200m 4x100m relays, basketball and tennis. I was so excited to see Usain Bolt shock and amaze. The highlights show was about to end. It was a beautiful sunny day, but I had now learned how to not enjoy it. I was trapped within myself. I decided I would just have a movie marathon on that day and watch some of my favourite movies. I got up, grabbed my laptop, projected it onto my TV with an HDMI cable and went to one of the movie sites I usually used. My first choice was "Inside Man". I started watching the movie, relaxed on my sofa. Just feeling free in isolation. I repudiated the idea of getting dressed and heading out just to be in the sun. It felt nice, but it also made no sense to me to do so. What I missed was the ability to do just that, without thinking and worrying about what dangers I faced out there. About halfway through the film around the scene where Denzel Washington first comes to the bank to speak with Clive Owen in person, I heard a loud bang. I instinctively hit the pause button. The walls within that building are unbelievably thin. You can almost hear someone scratch their head two floors down. To top it off they were so cheaply built they couldn't afford to put elevators in. This pesky inconvenience didn't make living there any more enjoyable. I'm not an unfit person; I do l exercise at least three days a week, but sometimes I'm so tired that the last thing I want to do is climb three flights of stairs to get to my flat and then another once I'm inside the flat itself. I had become so attuned to the different sounds; I knew it was the front door. Even though I was so aware of the sounds I heard from my room it still triggered my danger alert sensors, in other words, my overactive anxiety mechanism.

I instantly recognised that sound. It was the sound of the front door closing. It was distinctly different from the bedroom door shutting. The first thing I did was start wondering who had just arrived. Jasmine, who was about my age, was very close to Frank. It was a kind of father, daughter relationship. Her brother would also often come and visit the property. Again, I also knew him. When my parents were moving to the Emirates in late 2011, I was offered this room. Initially, I was totally against the idea of moving to Essex as I'd heard some things about the area that were not very welcoming at all. I was seeking a self-contained flat at the time. I had several viewings, mainly for self-contained flats, but the asking prices were exorbitant and I simply couldn't afford it. I was living on the poverty line, barely making ends meet, living from paycheque to paycheque. Thank God for the recent scrapping of security deposits for renting flats. It's ridiculous and unaffordable for many. I remember living in halls of residence in university and loving the experience and the independence. I hated the idea of sharing a property; this was most certainly amplified by my anxiety and psychosis disorder.

I faintly heard Jasmine's loud cackle. I heard the timber in her brother's voice. I knew it was him. His name is Jeffrey. She was very exuberant and full of energy. This was a good thing but sometimes it felt superfluous. I don't quite know why, but I immediately felt my heart drop into my stomach and adrenaline pumping profusely through my veins. Nothing had even happened yet. But I just suddenly remembered that flat sharing is flat sharing. No one knows, nor do they care about how anxious you feel when they are present. In the beginning, for the most part, I and the other tenants had a general consensus, which was that we would be considerate of each other's space, we would all clean regularly and we wouldn't be loud and disruptive. We all stuck to this agreement initially, but things would take a turn for the worse later during my tenure there. Remember the water bottle? I knew I would use it that day. I didn't plan on even stepping foot outside of my room. I just wanted to not exist, or to exist in another dimension. In the beginning, Jeffrey and I would hang out a lot, play PlayStation – endless hours of FIFA into the wee hours of the morning. But then it all changed. Of course, it did. I wasn't the same person, was I?

I hit the play button and carried on watching my film. Although I was in my room and away from any social interaction, I still felt vulnerable and uncomfortable. I didn't feel settled, nor did I feel at home. A few minutes passed and there was a steady distracting noise coming from downstairs from them. They all seemed so happy and in their own bubble. I wish I could feel that feeling again, so secure in the presence of others, especially people close to me. Now, I felt exposed no matter who I was around. This did feel less so around my sister, my nieces and my parents. Every sound I heard seemed loud and pesky in the sense that it made my heart beat faster. I was trying everything I could to stay immersed in the movie. Once again, I heard a loud bang. This time it was Frank's bedroom door.

This is something I have to give you a background on. Within the first few months of my tenure, there was a list of things that particularly bothered me. One was the cleanliness issue; some of the time dishes and other stuff were left in the kitchen area. Various stains were left in the communal bathroom. I don't need to mention where but you can use your imagination. There was an issue with respecting the communal areas as far as being considerate of others using the same space. Luggage or other personal effects being left in communal areas. Finally, there was this issue of the walls being extremely thin. This was no one's fault, just cheap material and cardboard walls. But at least when it rained no one got wet. So, when any door shut or was negligently slammed it reverberated through the flat, especially upstairs in my room. Before all the doors to the rooms and the one separating the landing from the open living room/kitchen had a Perko system installed. Basically, what it does is automatically shuts the door when it has been opened. With the walls being so thin, every time a door slammed, I would feel like a victim. There was a point where I literally felt like I was going to lose it. The doors would slam so frequently that I became so frustrated by it. It was exacerbated by the anxiety disorder that I already had. I would become anxious about when the next "slam" would come. I was always on edge at home. Eventually, I had to speak to my flatmates about it.

Chapter 3: Darker Days

I hardly had any money left, hard times. I later learned that if you work hard on your job, you can earn a living if you work hard on yourself, you can earn a fortune. I definitely needed to work on myself more. I wanted to get a few items from my local pound shop. The funny thing is that not all the things cost a pound or less. Such a gimmick. To be fair some things were a pound. It was a difficult time. I was still on sick leave from my new job. I had no other option but to take some time off work. My psychosis and social anxiety relapsed and I couldn't handle it. It started when the company hired a new member of staff who went by the name, Mohammed, a very garrulous, loud and outspoken person. He seemed harmless at first glance but after speaking to him a few times, he certainly didn't seem that way to me, anyway.

I got in my car and saw that the petrol gauge was almost empty. I had no money to fill up the petrol tank and was certainly not in the mood to take a twenty-minute walk to the shop. I just ignored it and I carried on. It was around 2 pm so traffic was rather calm, and it was a nice sunny spring day. I arrived at the store and nervously got out of the car. I noticed the car park was almost empty and this gave me a sense of relief. I walked into the shop and just as I entered, I got a call from my good friend, Angela. We used to work together a few months back but still kept in contact regularly. I was just wandering around the store. I already knew what I needed to get with my restricted budget – just a few bags of noodles, some canned beans and some bottled water and that was it. I ended up walking down every aisle at least three times. I had my hands-free kit in as I was already listening to music. This is something I usually wouldn't do as I felt it would make me even begin lip-reading, and my imagination about what people were saying would be even bigger than it already was. So again, it was a fear thing or restriction thing as I wasn't used to doing that. But either way, I just walked into the shop, tried to feign comfort and a sense of belonging there and so I spoke even louder and laughed as much as I thought was needed to prove to the rest of the world that I was comfortable when I clearly wasn't. It felt strange to me but I didn't stop. I remember at some point I was walking past the kitchen section as what appeared to be a couple were just entering that aisle from a different side with the woman in the lead and the man following rather helplessly. She didn't seem to take much notice of me but the man did. I know he was talking to her, but in my mind in a cowardly way, hiding behind her and seeing that I wasn't fully attentive as I looked away, plus I had earphones in. For whatever reason, he hurled an insult at me to impress his girlfriend. So tough. I was sure I heard the word "prick". I always felt my presence intimidated other men. Women always noticed me even though I was humble and a rather shy person. My presence hid that immediately. I found it fascinating to see peoples' behaviour change because of my presence. I wonder why I didn't use that knowledge to my advantage more, but I didn't. This was something I often would think and fear when in the presence of heterosexual couples, or mixed-gender groups, that I would be an object of ridicule but not directly to my face. In a covert manner. So, after walking on I then started thinking to myself, "I bet he wouldn't say that to my face. He isn't the type. He can only do it covertly and with a lot of factors that may render it 'unlikely' to the intended recipient, me, or that would make the average person not even need to address the insult as it was said in that manner." I was toying with the idea of confronting him or even hurling an insult at him but in a much louder more direct manner. Or maybe making a pass at his girlfriend because physically this man didn't intimidate me. What made me angry was the idea that he thought he could get away with being sly with his attempt to disrespect me. There was no conviction in his aura, he had a laboured and ponderous walk, one without purpose and vigour; he was a feeble scrawny looking guy. I created a whole war in my brain, all in an attempt to pacify myself, it seemed. I carried on walking around the store from aisle to aisle with no real purpose. I already had what I wanted in my basket. I was just toying with the idea of making a B-line for him somehow, and thinking of different reasons as to why this guy would insult me. If he did so I was thinking of ways I could also try to embarrass him in front of his female partner to pacify myself. I circled several times almost looking for him, hunting, looking to start a war over nothing.

I spotted them carefully sifting through a selection of different broomsticks as if each one had a different purpose. She was taking the lead; we men are clueless about these things. As I approached them to walk past them, I loudly exclaimed the word "idiot" while maintaining eye contact. They both looked at me, seemingly perturbed, but no one retaliated or responded. Was I a bully, or was I defending myself and proving a point? What I then did was deliberately turn and smile at the woman. I thought to myself if he was a real man, if he really had a problem with me, he would say something about my actions. Of course, he didn't. Coward!! I wasn't done yet. I went to the drink section just to pass some time, waiting to strike again.

I once heard that the way people try and take control of a situation is usually with anger. It gives a false sense that you are in control as I felt I was in this case. I was still on the phone and explained to Angela that some idiot annoyed me and she was just stupefied and asked repeatedly if I was okay as I started breathing heavily through the phone. I briefly explained what happened and she calmed me down, she knew a little bit about my condition, although I hesitated to tell her too much so as to not be so vulnerable. I eventually just got bored of walking around aimlessly. I still wasn't satisfied though. I felt like I needed to do more to make him feel stupid and to ruin his day as he had tried to ruin mine. I headed to the checkout and there they were and the best thing is I was behind him in the queue. I could sense straight away when he turned around and saw me that he felt very uncomfortable, very uneasy. I felt satisfied. This is what you deserve I thought. He twiddled his fingers, feigned a smile to his partner but he was very uncomfortable and wanted to leave. At some point, his partner even called him and he was so aloof he took a moment before answering her, such was his discomfort. You deserve it I thought, as I smirked to myself. I was listening to Angela yap on about some girl issues she had with her best friend but at the same time, I had my prey cornered. Another gentleman came from the exit doors asking the cashier if he could quickly use a basket and that he would return it and in that brief exchange, my prey sensed I was distracted. I looked back at him but he just looked away from me and at that moment the other guy asking to use the basket had also looked at me. NEVER TAKE YOUR EYE OFF YOUR ENEMY. Did he say something again? Why was this other guy also looking at me at that moment? What did I miss? He insulted me again. I'm sure he did. But how could I ask him in the middle of all that was going on? It felt so awkward. I'd look like I'm not mentally stable. But am I? I then thought, that's typical, only when he knew I was distracted and not fully aware of him, then he struck again. Coward. I still wasn't satisfied. Eventually, they finished paying and left, his partner looked at me again as they headed out, he made sure not to. I just winked at her. I walked up to the till and had my few items scanned. "That's £3.50 please sir," the cashier said. I reached into my pocket for my debit card, making sure to look through the exit door at my enemy, but they were long gone. "I can relax now," I thought. I paid, bagged my items and headed out. On the way out I told Angela I'd call her back. I saw a group of teenagers loitering around the bottom of the car park. Onto the next situation. I immediately felt nervous as I expected something to be said about me and worse from that distance. I listened out carefully but heard nothing, thankfully. It was only a short walk from the store to where I was parked. I headed off home. On the way, as I approached a pedestrian crossing, I halted and was distracted as I was sifting through my glove box, looking for a lighter so I could light my cigarette. As I looked up this middle-aged man was crossing. He had a fixed stare on me but as I kept looking back, he looked away. What did I miss while I was distracted? Did he insult me? Gesticulate towards me? Did everyone see? How could I roll my window down and ask him? That would be just too strange. I'd just have to live with not knowing.

I was starving. I hadn't done any food shopping for a couple of days and the day before I'd given in to the temptation of ordering via uber eats. It was a kind of punishment to myself by way of spending more than I needed to due to poor planning and laziness. On this particular day, I was off from work and woke up with a huge craving for fried chicken. KFC was just a 5-minute drive from where I lived. My anxiety had bad days and worse days. Today was one of those worse days. Perhaps I was being hard on myself on reflection, for indulging in fast food the day before. This is London after all. So fast-paced. Who has time to shop regularly? I headed down to my car with relative ease and comfort, with no incidents to speak of or ponder over. It was about two o'clock on a Monday during the holiday season. I didn't anticipate much traffic and as my wheels swept across foliage beneath them, I gracefully headed off to satisfy my hedonistic urge. I got there and there were no cars in the queue; of course, I preferred the drive-thru for obvious reasons. The day was being good to me, the sun was shining, my music lifted my spirits even higher. I got to the intercom system and placed my order – I went for the three-piece colonel's meal. After some confusion with the lady on the intercom, she finally heard my order. I advised her that I wanted the three piecemeal without a drink. My understanding was it came to £4.19. I got to the window, excitedly inserted my card and pin into the PDQ machine, waited about thirty seconds and got my food. I didn't even check the contents of the bag; I went to that KFC a lot and never really had any issues. I found that doing that in the face of the customer service representative would spark some disdain toward me. I drove off eager to indulge in the fresh chicken; it smelled delightful. At a set of traffic lights, I thought to myself let me just have a quick look, and so I did. Devastated! All I saw was three pieces of chicken in the bag, with some condiments and that was it. No fries. Suddenly rage filled my body and mind. Previously that particular lady always gave me a death stare. Then my mind entered that dark place. I thought, "Did she do this on purpose?" "Did she want a reaction?" "Her life must be so pathetic so she takes it out on selected patrons." I circled round and headed back; I was there within two minutes. A queue. "Here we go," I thought. From peace to war in a moment. I was behind two other cars, anxiously awaiting my interaction with this lady. When I spoke on the intercom this time I spoke in a very stern, stoic manner so as not to show weakness. I meant business. She advised me to just come to the window as she claimed she didn't understand what I was saying over the intercom, so I obliged. Of the two cars ahead, the one at the window was stuck there for ages. The tension was building up in my body, I kept thinking how dare this puerile woman do such a thing. For what? The more I thought about it the more it seemed like that moment would never end; blood was crashing into the different parts of my body and rage emerged. I couldn't mollify myself. It was 'fight' all the way. I waited 10 more seconds and when I saw the car was still there, I let out a huge clamorous scream of frustration. Luckily my window was closed and no one heard as I wasn't there for them. Moments after that car left and the man in front of me "too cool for school" casually put his car into gear and moved forward to get his order. He was moving in slow motion and it then felt like he had spotted me in his rear-view mirror and he, too, was also enjoying provoking me and watching me have a meltdown. I realise a lot of the time when unhappy people know what ticks you off, they will most likely exacerbate it. Well, if you let them. When you are thinking with your feelings you most likely will let them. I spotted him get his order and take about 15 seconds doing nothing before deciding to drive off; he was really pushing my buttons; it's like KFC had hired him to give me another slap. As he finally drove off, I gave him the middle finger, held it in position long enough that if he was deliberately trying to get a rise out of me, which I thought he was, his pompous self wouldn't be able to help but look in the rear-view and smile to himself – 'self-fulfilling prophecy'. Nothing came of it; he just drove off and disappeared into the traffic. It was the showdown. All of a sudden, this time there was another customer rep who looked like a trainee, taking orders. Just my luck, an audience! She immediately emerged into view as I got to the window and she saw the look of censure on my face. Calmly she asked what had happened. I explained and she advised that the £4.19 was only for chicken but the fries included was an extra £1.09, she said it in such a convincing, placid way that I couldn't even argue. At that moment my rage and anxiety dissipated. It released the tension that I was holding on to. I relented and agreed to pay the extra for the fries but as I reached for my card she said I didn't have to worry; she went and got the fries and said just to be aware for the next time. This time I looked in the bag of fries, I didn't trust her, I was momentarily distracted by that. I drove off without as much as a thank you. I still didn't feel satisfied. About two minutes into the journey, I reviewed the interaction the second time. "f** k y**" I heard it play in my mind over and over again. I was convinced she said it to me at that moment when I looked in the bag as she handed me the fries. What gives her the right, even on duty to insult me, covertly, when I'm not fully attentive? Why? I didn't deserve this? See, stressful situations exacerbate psychosis. I paid for a service and I get insulted for it. She was a woman. I ignored it but somehow had a grudge for the next time I would see her. I couldn't reason with myself to believe she didn't say that to me. With the trainee observing I was certain she did, to almost show off, display a false sense of arrogance and that "untouchable" vibe. Was I wrong? I don't know. But what I do know was some time back I was very confrontational. I will let you in on some of the exchanges I had with people. I had made progress one way or another. At least I could now avoid accosting people. But I relapsed sometimes. Once, I met someone who was also in an aggressive and confrontational mood and things didn't really go well. What I didn't realise was that I was also potentially putting myself in danger. What I'd like you to feel mainly is that this was a constant thing where interpersonal matters were concerned. I'm only giving some examples. But it was incessant, unabating. It was torture.

Another time I had my friend Victoria coming to visit me as she often did. She was a very nice person, very altruistic, generous to a fault. She also suffered from anxiety so to some degree she understood my plight. We had met at a recent job I had. The two of us hit it off like two peas in a pod. We were inseparable, she was like my best friend at the time. I had to quickly go and get some snacks to humour my guest. I was somewhat in a hurry as always, but nevertheless, I headed out to my local Iceland store to get a few things. It was a Saturday and around 4 pm so I had a feeling it might not be busy in the supermarket and I was right. I arrived outside, parked my car and headed inside. I didn't quite know what to get so ended up circling the supermarket a few times. I eventually picked up some kit-kat chocolate, some marshmallows, pringles, peanuts, some frozen pizzas and drinks. There was a guy in there, who worked there, who never really greeted me but always heeded my presence. It felt weird. But I never heard anything insulting from him. He was somewhat of an enigma to me, or maybe looking back that was simply because I always noticed him when he was working, regularly giving me glances and appearing next to me under the guise of stocking shelves. I always made sure to keep circling the checkout area as the tills were always grossly undermanned, with more people having cigarette breaks than they were working. It was typical. I saw my opportunity so headed to the till. There was one elderly lady ahead of me. Thankfully I timed it perfectly as out of the corner of my eye I saw a horde of people entering, but I knew I'd probably be finished by the time they queued up. I hated people standing around me, especially impatiently waiting behind me in a queue. It made me feel exposed and uncomfortable, I guess not knowing what they were thinking when looking at my back, so to speak. I looked to my right and saw an African man walking around glancing at every item. He was talking on the phone and I could hear he had a strong accent. I deliberately looked away so as not to give him that familiarity look for him to notice me and want to give me his attention. I couldn't quite discern what he was saying but at some point, I thought I heard him say something insulting. I wasn't sure but his energy didn't seem hostile although he moved as if he did notice me in some way. I heard "beat you," I was a regular in this store and I thought how weird and socially awkward it would be if I accosted him about this. I gave him the benefit of the doubt. He was engrossed in his phone call and it probably wasn't what I even heard. Why would he say that? I didn't even look at him. I didn't have a look of anger or aggression on my face. It couldn't be. I still had a niggling feeling that he may have gotten away with insulting me. Why can't I just let go and accept if I'm not sure? Why did I always insist on thinking the worst? I later applied one of the techniques proposed to me by my therapist which was the "likelihood someone said something insulting" and "think of a best-case scenario", basically why would someone just insult me and if I didn't clearly hear an insult or word, just assume it was at least neutral, not aimed at me. or it was something positive. I paid and left the store still feeling like I had left something behind as always. I headed home and spent a lovely day with my friend.

I remember one day vividly. It was one of my better days. I had just had a good gym session in my room. I was fortunate to have a very large room filled with numerous pieces of gym equipment, both for cardiovascular and weightlifting. Needless to say, I didn't attend a gym due to my anxiety. I remember one experience when there was a guy who seemed to be fixated on me. Every time I looked his way, he was staring at me. I wonder about this saying – if you think someone is looking at you it probably means you are looking at them. But I could immediately sense the attention he gave to me. I always found it funny when the men would stand looking in the mirror completely narcissistic and secretly comparing themselves to the biggest guy in the gym. I am naturally a mesomorph and sensed this guy was interested in what I was doing: what weight

I was lifting, what exercise I was doing. Was it a compliment? I heard once that respect comes from admiration or fear. He didn't admire me, surely? And he didn't know me to respect me, so I could only conclude that he loathed me, or envied me. When I'm in the gym I deliberately zone out and become aloof to my surroundings. Why would someone have a problem with me for existing? Why was I letting him win? The worst part was when I went over to the weights section and a very nubile woman was there, engrossed in her workout, I remember thinking that I wished she had earphones in case he insulted me and she was the audience. To impress her? Maybe this was a self-fulfilling prophecy. I wanted so badly for it to not happen that I eventually did things to make it happen, so to speak. Maybe he sensed my discomfort and preyed on it. I heard him say the word p***y, or so I thought, and the first thing I thought to do was look over to the woman to see if she looked at me and at that moment and she did. I froze. My flight and fight sensations kicked in. Or was it my psychosis, the delusion, the hallucinations? I never knew these things back then; I only knew how to think emotionally, never rationally. I felt embarrassed, insulted, small, and didn't want to make a fool of myself or embarrass myself by accosting him or retorting. I wasn't intimidated by this individual but somehow, I decided to not think for the woman. Ever since then I have never returned to that gym.

As I mentioned, I then began working out in the comfort of my room and got used to it. On this particular day, I had to quickly head out to get basic groceries at Asda. I liked that Asda, although it was large, and at times confusing, I was usually able to cope in there. I've had one or two anxious moments but I always do. So, I headed to

Asda and was feeling good about myself, confident there was a gusto in my walk, in my talk as I spoke to the clerk at the till. I finished up and was heading out. I was amazed that there was no incident, even in my post-mortem phase I didn't recall any insults. I was heading home and then it happened. I caught a glimpse of a couple walking out of Asda towards the car park. There is a small area that all customers must pass which runs across the exit of the car park. I kept thinking "please don't cross just as I get there, please don't". I kept thinking this over and over. I even tried to drive slower and nothing was helping avoid the seemingly inevitable. I got near them and there was a moment, it's like time froze because both the man and his partner stopped dead in their tracks, I was more focused on the threat – the man – they hesitated and I lost it. I screamed in frustration, "just cross, just f**king cross". My window was shut luckily so it didn't escalate and they couldn't see me because of my tinted windows. I carried on and the moment was about to end and just at that moment I saw his hand raised, and I wondered if he was gesticulating towards me. It's like I needed something to happen to prove I was meant to feel like this about this meaningless everyday encounter. I ignored it. I just kept going. The main reason is that he didn't see me properly so it couldn't have been personal or insulting for no reason. They even waved me to carry on driving. I became a perfectionist. Any error I made or any uncertain moments caused me a great deal of anxiety because the other side of that in my mind was an insult. I was living in a hell on earth.

People are just an extension of your thoughts. As I said, it's not always men that give me undue attention – women do, too. Granted I know sometimes when you have an anxiety disorder you tend to want to think for people. Essentially scanning for a threat. It's emotional thinking. I have been told numerous times that I have a commanding presence. I am very intuitive and self-aware, maybe too self-aware for my own good. I am also very aware of other people and behavioural tendencies. We are not as unique as we think we are. At no point are we intrinsically a singular entity. Think about it – we come from our mothers, who come from their mothers and so on; we come from creation and evolution, but you get my drift. I remember once I had an appointment at the GP for a consultation as I'd been having a chronic need to urinate frequently throughout the day. I should have done something about it years back but as we men so often do, we take our health for granted. Taking things for granted has always been the one true reason things end up going wrong in peoples' lives. If I had done something about my mental health earlier you probably wouldn't be reading this right now. Or maybe I needed to lose myself to go through this journey to really understand myself and know myself. I once heard the saying, "knowing others is intelligence, knowing yourself is true wisdom; mastering others is strength, but mastering yourself is true power" – a famous quote by Lao Tzu. Amazing, so profound and true. I was going through this to become my best version.

But as I was saying I had another example to add to the many I experienced regularly. I was trapped in the abyss. I had an appointment with my GP. This service had two centres. One was based much closer to my residence and the other a bit further away in London. My appointment was at nine in the morning, of course. I was already anxious about attending as for some reason, at some point, I decided that this other centre wasn't as peaceful as the one I usually attended. But this time I had no choice as this was the only one that had available appointments. So, I headed out anyway. One thing I realised is that when you are in a hurry or don't get enough sleep this can exacerbate your anxiety. Because you are off-kilter and in a hurried unsettled state, your brain relays this message to the rest of your body, which is your subconscious mind, to also embody that feeling. You tense up, you doubt your positive thoughts, you feel on edge and this nine times out of ten will make your anxiety worse. As soon as my alarm went off, I snoozed it, my subconscious mind woke me up and I had just 30 minutes to shower and head to my appointment. I am the kind of person that always has to shower before I leave my home. Creature of habit. Anyway, I left with ten minutes to spare. I was in a frantic out-of-balance state. But I knew it was important to go there and have this assessed by a doctor. I was aggressively tailgating slow drivers trying to make it on time. Luckily there were no incidents. I knew I'd most likely need a blood test to find out my glucose levels and kidney and liver function. What I find interesting is the misconception about diabetes that people have. At some point I was convinced I had it; it's in my family. My dad has it, his sister had it and passed away at the tender age of 45, and her daughter has it, too. I felt I was therefore genetically predisposed to it. My ignorance was a statement, not a question. I then did my research and discovered, according to doctors, the definition of diabetes does have something to do with a deficiency or lack of insulin production which converts carbohydrates into glucose to give the body energy to function. The average person is taught to solely think it's consuming too much sugar which can cause it over time. Too much sugar isn't good because the body will eventually convert it to fat if it's not all metabolised and used up, but the real silent killer is fatty foods, especially foods with mucus and cholesterol i.e., fish, red meat, eggs and cheese. What happens is that over time these fat cells begin to form plaque and layers in the bloodstream which block the vital paths that feed the body the energy it needs. Essentially these blockages don't allow insulin to efficiently enter the bloodstream to mix with the carbohydrates and produce insulin. Eating red meat every day is equivalent to smoking five cigarettes a day and there are links to heart disease, diabetes and cancer due to the carcinogens as well. Eating organic and plant-based food is what's likely to reverse any plaque build-up over time. Basically, carbon-based food for a carbon-based body. The body rejects chemicals that aren't made of itself, it's a term called chemical affinity. Hippocrates himself was a strong believer in herbs over chemicals to heal the body. Genetics only has about 20% influence on whether you contract such diseases. This discovery was fascinating to me. It gives credence to the saying "people perish due to lack of knowledge"

    I arrived at the centre and managed to find parking in the ridiculously scant car park. I caught my breath and composed myself. As the car park was so quiet, I assumed it was rather empty inside. I still had five minutes to spare. "Yes! I made it." The emptiness of the car park gave me solace and false confidence. I got out of my car and locked the door. I walked towards the electric doors, they opened and I walked in. It suddenly hit me; there they were, it was full of people. For a moment I felt like I was frozen but got myself together. To make matters worse there were only two available seats out of about twenty-five in the waiting area. Rambunctious kids running around, poor mothers trying desperately to control them, elderly people waiting to get told they may have a terminal illness, the couple in the back looking like they thought it was a community centre. The worst part was the new GP system. You had to sign in on this monitor right in front of the lobby and it truly felt like everyone was watching you being shoved onto centre stage and having to perform. I needed to do it perfectly, I didn't want to look stupid or seem like I didn't know how to operate it. It was simple to use, just basic questions about your date of birth, etc. My hands were shaking as I timidly went through the process but got there in the end. I turned around trying my best to not make eye contact with anyone. Someone's name was announced and shown on the screen. He left a seat right in front of the lobby, again centre stage. I sat down and immediately felt peoples' eyes burning through my skin. I was so uncomfortable. I kept repeating to myself, "it will be over soon". I was dreading my name coming up and again everyone heeding it. I'm present in the moment but it doesn't mean I'm the reason for the moment. Your feeling tells you that you are, I later learned. A feeling is just a feeling and a thought is just a thought.

 A few people left the door to the left where you entered to see the doctor as others entered and more names popped up on the screen. Mr Steven Honu. My heart stopped. I never liked my name. I heard nothing. Room 14. I stood up, tried to walk as perfectly as I could to the door, opened it and walked in… phew. I did it. The hard part was over. I saw the doctor and he immediately put me at ease. He was very understanding and amiable. It was a quick visit and he booked a blood test for me. I thanked him and left, and as I headed to the door leading back to the "glaring eyes" section I braced myself. I kept on hoping that no one would enter as I was leaving, and it happened. An elderly lady accompanied by her daughter who wore a permanent smile approached. I let them through and didn't even receive a thank you. It annoyed me but I was too focused on surviving the next 10 seconds. I had no time to express my censure. "Why is he looking at me?" I tensed up, and walked as briskly as I could to the exit. There were two doors at the entrance/exit one wasn't an automatic door but in my state of panic and chaos, I forgot. I was frustrated as I thought this moment of stupidity didn't go unnoticed. "I know they care." They must. I pushed the button and as I did, I heard faintly, "who's that man?" from a lady with a strong, distinct, hoarse voice. I didn't want to include this but I spent five minutes in the lavatory after seeing the doctor in that area of the building, just in the hopes that the lobby area would become less populated. It didn't help.

I didn't know but I felt she had said "who's that man?" about me and not only that but in a negative sense somehow, not in a positive way. I couldn't even look back to find out. Too much pain walking through the fire to stop and look back. Why was I the centre of everyone's life in the moments I was present? Was my ego too big? Why did I feel like the centre of the universe? Or was I finding a way to prove my feelings right. I heard that if you ask your brain a question it must give you an answer at all costs and that's what I got. I got into my car headed home and didn't leave the house for the rest of that day. I don't know what I'd have done without my car. Back then, I wouldn't dare take public transport again, that's for sure.

I just want you as the reader to put yourself in my shoes, live these moments vicariously through me. Feel my pain. In the early summer of 2014, again as we all have to, I had to go do some shopping. Bachelor life. I headed to my local discount store. I just needed some water, some canned beans and spaghetti. Frugal with my spending, as money was rather scant at this point, but isn't it always. "It's easier for a camel to pass through the eye of a needle than it is for a rich man to enter the Kingdom of heaven" – I guess this quote speaks for itself, but my interpretation is that no matter how much wealth a man has amassed that alone can't grant him free access to heaven. So being broke or financially restricted doesn't mean you are a bad person. It's also not how much you have, it's what you do with it because the last shirt you wear won't have any pockets on it. I got to the store and was relieved to find that the car park was rather empty. I headed inside with certainty in my step as I knew exactly what I needed and where it was stocked. I wouldn't be in there for long. When I entered, I was filled with excitement to see that the number of shoppers was sparse. I grabbed the stuff I needed and headed to the till. I thought, "how smooth, how perfect." There was a lady in front of me with her ebullient son running all over the checkout area which cleverly stocked toys and other treats around; he was fully engrossed in touching every item they had and his mom had to repeatedly call him. He gave her the puppy dog eyes as he spotted a water gun, he so deeply desired. At first, she resisted and finally, he twisted her arm. Result. I found it humorous, not aggravating, and as I was distracted by the young boy it filled me with happiness. I walk down memory lane remembering how everything was joyous and fun when young. All kids want to do is play and have fun. It hit me then, what if someone or a couple suddenly popped up behind me and reminded me that I have to run from myself. All of a sudden, the moment I made myself aware of myself, it was survival mode again. That little moment had gone and now I had a hurried feeling and was filled with fear and dread. It was happening again. It's like the minute I stopped being anxious it found a way back to me and slapped me in the face. 'How dare you think you can live without me,' it said to me. It's like in a second, I became hyper-vigilant, hyper-aware. When you become hyper-aware you can't be relaxed and calm at the same time. Luckily no one came up behind me and the lady left. Just as she did, I thought I heard her say "little prick" but at that moment I had taken my full attention off of her, another auditory hallucination I guess, but it was just conceivable that she said it. Because she was a woman and with her child, I just changed my thought and didn't judge my thought either. That easy. I wish! I kept dwelling on it even after she left the scene. I hardly comprehended the small talk of the cashier, I just kept wondering why she would have said it, what I did to upset her. My mind fell into that bottomless pit again. I was helpless and stuck within myself, lost unable to get out. The likeliness that I'd see her again was slim to none. So why did I care even if she had insulted me? The sweet cashier, a young lady, bagged my stuff and wished me a good day. I headed off to my car, got in and headed off home.

My day wasn't done yet. Later that evening I was meant to be heading to the flat of a nice lady I was speaking to via an online dating site, one of the most popular ones – Plenty of Fish. She was intelligent and easy to talk to. I'm sapiosexual so I'm attracted to the mind and intelligence. We had been speaking for about two weeks and would spend hours on the phone laughing and getting to know one another. She had invited me round to her flat in Docklands, East London. I was excited to see her but nervous to travel to an area my mind wasn't familiar with. It immediately made me anxious when I had to go somewhere, meet someone or do something new. This of course wasn't the first time I had been invited to a "stranger's residence". I deliberately planned for our meeting to be later on in the day for two reasons. One, it meant it was dark and I would be less noticeable driving than in the day, and two, she would be less likely inclined to want to go out into a social public place to enjoy the day. I headed downstairs to my car, my heart was already racing and I almost couldn't feel my feet touching the ground with every stride, but I eventually got near my car and then I heard a loud deafening sound, definitely made by a young male, inscrutable but unavoidable. At the moment all I could think was "please don't be sitting in any of the cars around and watching me break into pieces". I looked around my peripheral and saw nothing. I was about 10 strides from my car and had already lifted my hand to quickly unlock the central locking system. I knew I was going to open the door and sit down in one motion. I just needed to be out of sight, but they wouldn't be out of my mind. I sat down and closed my door. I gathered myself and had a quick scan around for the threat. I saw nothing but heard a car door open and there they were – a group of millennials in the next but one car bay, smoking I imagined, socialising, being rebellious. I started my car, instantly reversed and left for her apartment. I was so glad that was over. I imagined what I would have done if they were all out of their car in the middle of the car park just talking, being kids, etc. In that moment I believed I wouldn't have been able to handle that level of anxiety. I knew they would have somehow insulted me or tried to antagonise me. I was about 10 minutes into the journey. She didn't live far which was a relief. I knew this area;

I sometimes passed it on my way to work. At some point, I had no idea where I was and then the anxiety really kicked in and I was just its debilitated passenger. Every time I approached a traffic light, I prayed it stayed green or if it was red that it would quickly change to green. It was like someone was chasing me. Or was it like I was afraid of being left behind? I don't know. My leg started shaking profusely, uncontrollably, as I furthered into the unknown. I was driving on what seemed like a high road, littered with superettes and people hanging around loitering and looking ominous. Young teens cackling and being very animated as they interacted with each other. You are probably wondering how I noticed all this whilst driving. I kept my eyes on the other cars and pedestrians more than the road itself. I had programmed my mind to always scan for a threat of being insulted by someone or being ridiculed or provoked, tested. I saw everything, not always clearly, but I certainly tried to. There was a road I was approaching that the sat-nav instructed me to take. I could see from a distance that a car had very inconsiderately parked in the middle of it with its hazard lights on and people moving to and from the car. I didn't dare take the turn. I avoided it, imagining waiting behind the car, them getting annoyed at me if I had to honk my horn to alert them of my presence, them insulting me and me not clearly discerning it but assuming it. No thanks, I wanted no part of that mess. I took the next turn and the navigator recalibrated. I finally arrived at her block of flats. It was fairly modern and seemed quite secure. I called her and she advised me where to park. I caught my breath, calmed down as much as I could. I got out and walked towards the entrance. It was around the corner as she had told me. I thought to myself, "I'm nearly indoors, safe, not exposed." As I walked toward the entrance, I heard some chatter but I made sure to not look around to attract more attention to myself than I already thought I had. A sore thumb, as I walked around the corner, I saw two eastern European men having a discussion at the entrance. I almost swallowed my heart, it felt like. I just did everything I could to avoid any forced, small talk or interaction with them. They luckily acknowledged me with a look but quickly carried on confabulating as they could see I wasn't interested in them in any way. Normally when I try blatantly to ignore certain people, they go out of their way to get noticed. These ones didn't. I buzzed her flat and she let me in. It ended up being a very enjoyable evening. She didn't even know the night had two parts to it. It was my secret, my stigma, my shame.

I used to regularly travel to the United Arab Emirates, specifically Dubai and Abu Dhabi. My parents lived out there as my dad got a job there around 2012. It's a beautiful country and has a lot of sights to see. Fair enough it's rather decadent and doesn't have much culture, but it's definitely an experience. I always had fun when I visited the UAE. Although overwrought about being in another country, I still enjoyed the moments I'd spend with my mom and dad as I didn't get to see them that often anymore. I visited several sights and had a whale of a time. I just felt my safety net was there again when I was around my parents. It kind of felt like being a kid again. Just being me, ebullient and happy and looking forward to the day ahead, worrying less about my affliction and the chains that bound me. Don't get me wrong, I still heard insults whenever I was out there but it was cloaked by the fact that I was on an adventure, in a different place, away from my home. Going on holiday is a must if you want to alleviate the symptoms of your mental health condition.

I discovered this based on my personal journey. It helped me a lot. You just feel different, immersed in different environments and cultures. Sometimes I look back and wonder how I was even able to travel alone with my condition. Sitting in the airport with thousands of eyes passing, gazing at me and judging me. I felt exposed. I think just the excitement of knowing I was going to see family and going to a new place that I liked helped lessen my anxiety somewhat. It was a distraction from the real world. I remember one particular event where I was in a restaurant with my parents. It was a Chinese restaurant called Chang's. The food was world-class and the service exceptional. I was sitting there fully engrossed in conversation with my parents and I had heard someone say the word 'idiot'. As I always did, I looked around to scan for the threat. I mean why was that word necessarily directed towards me and/or my parents. Why couldn't it have been about someone else? But I just knew it was about me, I was the centre of the universe, wasn't I? I knew something would burst my bubble. I could feel the walls closing in on me, my vision became blurry, my heart started racing. I saw a group of young virile men sitting to the right of me and immediately convinced myself that it was one of them who had insulted me. It completely ruined my day. For the rest of the day, I was dissecting the event and tried to understand what I had done to offend them. I had no answer. There were many occurrences like this while I was out there, but as I said it was cloaked by my general excitement at being out there. Anxiety and psychosis follow you wherever you go, it haunts you and never leaves you alone. If I could go back in time I would. But everyone probably would. Life is just about memories and moments. Most of us live in the past, some of us live in the future but very few of us live in the moment. The present moment is where all your power lies because you can shape it into whatever you want it to be, it's a choice. Fifty per cent of who you are today is determined by your past, but you can still change that going forward if you choose to. Some events are so traumatic that they completely derail you and shape your life but it's usually just a moment – it passes, the scars heal and you can re-shape it to suit you. It's all in the mind. If you can think it in your head, you can hold it in your hand.

Chapter 4: The Suffering Continues

It was now 2019 and seven years on from the first onset of my mental health disorder. I can't describe how hopeless I would sometimes feel. Like I say when your basic ability to interact with another person, man or woman, is no longer normal it can feel like you are the only person alive that can discern your situation. Without complaining too much I just feigned happiness and put on a painful smile. I wish I could explain this to every stranger I came across and interacted with, but they wouldn't care. I would look weird and they would have my leash in their hand at all times. I'd rather have cancer than be held captive, tortured and abused for the rest of my life. Neither is preferential but one only has one threat. Granted some fight cancer and overcome it with their will and other variables. But I don't understand what I'm fighting against, and if I win where that leaves me when I look in my wake. It was a Sunday evening, I remember vividly. I started a new job working as a night concierge for a private apartment rental management company on the border of Islington Angel and Hackney, the more affluent part of both respective towns. As if that mattered to my brain. My car had finally packed it in after serving me well without much resistance. My 8th car, nonetheless, in the UK. It was my favourite car, the Vauxhall Astra; it and I had an understanding. On Friday, two days prior, I had a day off from work. I went to start my car. But the car wouldn't crank over. Instead, the immobiliser light would flash repeatedly. I did a quick check to see if this was something I could fix myself but it wasn't so to cut a long story short, I contacted my breakdown company and sent a technician out to me. After 30 minutes of assessing the issue, he found no valid solution; instead, he could only tow me to my local garage. The way my car would eventually be restored to its former glory is the funny part, and I will talk about that later. On Sunday, the day I was due back at work, I had no option but to make the commute to work via public transport. It would consist of walking to the train station, hopping on a train to Liverpool Street and then jumping on a bus for approximately 30 minutes. Journey time 55 minutes on average – not bad right? Terrible. Anyone reading this who suffers from anxiety disorder knows that public transport, especially in a city like London where most rely on the public transport system to commute to work and so forth, knows the dread that can precede a daunting journey into the city. Not a corner where someone isn't hiding. I always used to liken it to a rat infestation, which is funny considering the rat race the masses are all in. Anyway, the day before, Saturday, I must have spent no less than three hours carefully studying the route I'd take, preparing for any vicissitudes I might encounter, any diversions, delays, street views. From where the bus stop was, where I'd stand, every detail. I didn't know I had that much energy to put towards anything, even my own safety. Nevertheless, I did just that. I woke up super early. Because of all the anxiety I felt, I'd tossed and turned for about six hours before eventually falling asleep at 7 am.

CHAPTER 4: THE SUFFERING CONTINUES

Who cares? No one. They walk past you like you are a part of the building infrastructure. Just an inanimate thing that exists. But when you cough too loudly you annoy them. I remember when I woke up my legs felt like jelly and my heart was beating out of my chest. How was I going to manage this journey? exposed in the big world, a commuter in the crowd, I felt so out of my comfort zone. I had become over-reliant on my car, as it allowed me to avoid and hide from social situations as far as travelling goes. I got ready and left with plenty of time to spare. It was a hot day in June, early summer in the UK. One thing I probably hated more than the public transport commute itself was sweating whilst doing it; don't ask me why, it just angered me, I can't explain it, it just did. I walked out of my flat, locking the door behind me. My whole body was pulsating with fear, feeling as neurotic as ever. I decided I wouldn't wear headphones. I didn't want a situation where I misheard something, saw an audience look at me and having even less chance of discerning what insult was thrown this time. I wanted to be alert and aware of everything, sounds, touch, smells. I wanted to be in control, but the truth is I was under control, always was. I headed out of the complex and onto the road and immediately felt like a sore thumb. All the noises of cars, chatter or other pedestrians seemed so different from when I drove past in my car with my windows open. "This can't be the same place!" I remember thinking. But it was and I had to ask its permission to go through it. It was a Sunday so it wasn't extremely busy, but then I started to think about what Monday would be like, especially as I came into Liverpool Street during rush hour. "Oh my God!" the thought alone couldn't be processed. It was surreal in my reality. I walked hastily to the station, had no noticeable encounters and didn't hear any insults. Only one English man paid undue attention to me as he passed. It made me feel uncomfortable in my own skin for a moment, but it passed. My mom used to always say a lot of moments in life, no matter how uncomfortable, they will usually only last a moment and then pass forever. When I got to the train station, I quickly purchased a ticket at the machine. I felt so exposed, like I wasn't normal. Please, I want you to imagine that feeling for a moment. A lot of you probably don't even think about such things. I do, I have to. I thought to myself that I needed an oyster card, which would be much easier, especially with the knowledge that they could be topped up online.

My train was due in three minutes, I climbed the stairs, got to my platform. It was relatively quiet, there was a concourse of people two platforms away but I was out of harm's way, I heard nothing although I was tuned in to the "insults frequency". The train came and I found a nice quiet seat. It was a new TfL train, spacious and a hybrid between underground and overground in regards to the seating plan. It was almost empty in my carriage. A group of three teenage girls noticed me, which I believed was due to my social awkwardness – it had to be apparent. The way I felt, I couldn't see how it could remain hidden. The train journey was about 25 minutes. Each time we approached a station my heart would get very heavy and my breathing airways clogged. Some people got on, some got off, and once we arrived in Stratford the majority of people, I could see within my carriage dismounted. Then I breathed a sigh of relief. But the main event was still to come. Liverpool Street. I took a deep, deep breath and braced myself. The tranquil journey to this point offered no consolation

CHAPTER 4: THE SUFFERING CONTINUES

to my mind. Anxiety doesn't work that way, unfortunately. I approached the barriers and saw herds of people moving around ten ways from Sunday. At some point, it almost felt like some of them were itinerants just wandering around, but heeding my presence, giving me a deep stare. I broke eye contact and distracted myself by imagining arriving at work with plenty of time to spare, sitting near the canal, relaxing and smoking before starting my shift. I mounted the escalators and when I got to the top it was like a switch was flipped in everyone's brains within my vicinity to look at me; why did I think I was the centre of the world? The bust stop I needed sat just in front of the escalators. Next to it was a busy pub with wondering eyes and giggles not going unheard. I overheard the word. "prick". Who knows who said it, I know it was directed at me but I didn't investigate with my eyes. Several other buses came and then drove off, I made sure to look away as they did. My bus finally came, I hopped on, showed my ticket and found an empty seat downstairs and just let the seat hug me. A few minutes later the name of the stop I needed was announced and I got off, more relieved than ever to get to work in one piece. "I did it!" – something most think of as nothing was everything to me, an achievement. I walked in 45 minutes early, greeted the manager and my colleague and told them I'd sit in the staff room until it was time to start which they acknowledged. I came down about 30 minutes later still with about 15 minutes to go before I commenced my shift. I went outside, sat in a nice quiet spot near the canal, lit a cigarette and just enjoyed the cool summer breeze; as it hit my skin it had a calming effect on me. Always being anxious meant I would often feel hot even when there wasn't a need to. It has something to do with adrenaline I believe. I started my shift. As I said I was still very new in this role. It was a prodigious private residential complex. This particular site was made up of around 450 individual apartments and comprised of 4 separate buildings. In the main building, there was a sauna, a gymnasium, steam room, massage spa, a small underground car park and a penthouse on the top floor. My company provided a concierge service as well as cleaning, maintenance and general upkeep of the building, mainly communal areas. Landlords, of course, owned individual flats and the building itself was erected by another organisation. The company was founded by a very ambitious man about 13 years prior, who had a vision. It reminded me of something I once read by Dharmesh Shah who wrote, "don't focus on trying to get £10,000, focus on trying to get 10,000 people" – find a product or service that everyone needs and harness it and develop it. Case and point with our company. We managed over 12,000 individual flats all over London and the UK, a lucrative business model. What I found particularly interesting was with the new law implemented by the government; private residential buildings of a certain size were required under the statute of the law to apportion at least 20% of their apartments to social housing. I tell you when doing the security walks at night, the difference between the private renting tenants was a far cry from the social renting tenants in the sense that you could see the difference in behaviour, how unkempt the communal areas were, the wealth division and ethnicity. The private tenants tended to be what I presume were rich kids from Asian countries and the Middle East predominantly, whose parents could afford them the luxury flat, some costing over £4000 per month. Some of them, of course, were working, skilled professionals, some business owners and entrepreneurs. The majority of them were tenants but in one of the buildings, most of the occupants were the apartment owners themselves. What difference did it make to our company? None. we got paid by both for the service we provided.

With my vast hotel and front desk hospitality experience I was quite obviously a viable candidate, and when I was called for an interview, I relished the opportunity. It turned out to be a two-stage interview, which needless to say I wasn't a fan of. But I was selected. I once learned to imagine the interviewer as a future friend during the interview, and that it was their first interview. This helped calm me down. It was a big step up from my previous abysmal job which had been full of sub-par, vituperative people with negative mindsets and an underwhelming lack of ambition. Needless to say, I was happy when I left that job. It was so bad I ended up sinking back to a very dark place in my depression due to my mental health affliction, and was signed off sick for four months before eventually leaving when I realised, I was only entitled to statutory sick pay, and not sick pay to the full amount of my salary. These were very bad financial times, to say the least, on top of all my other daily battles. How I found the will to live is beyond me, perhaps only the fear of death alone helped me. Otherwise, I would have committed suicide.

Like I said this particular job was better paying, but didn't necessarily offer room for progression. I was however enrolled to undertake a level 7 postgraduate course in tourism and hospitality management, so upon completion of that, I suspected many doors would open. I had to complete it first, though. At this point, I had already procrastinated and nine months after full payment was made, I'd still only read a few notes for my first assignment. As it was an online course; submission dates were flexible and extensions could be granted under the right circumstances.

This new role gave me a comforting feeling from the vibration I got from all staff alike, at both of the interviews. The operations director, Victor, and the site manager, Laszlo, both seemed incredibly professional, motivational and were leaders. This was something that was lacking in my previous place of employment. How wrong a first impression I got! I began working there around April 2019. Seeing as it is London and near the centre, parking is a problem. Most roads surrounding my workplace stipulated that parking was strictly for residents or one could pay and display and remain parked for no more than 4 hours without returning to their vehicle. The operational time was between the hours of 08:30 and 18:30 and until 13:30 on Saturdays. Outside of these hours was free. I was informed that my night shift started from 7 pm until 7 am. It was situated just outside the infamous ULEZ, which my car was exempt from anyway, and the congestion zone. So, it was perfect. The problem was that I was required to do two days of training on the day shift with Laszlo, just to get an overview of the basic responsibilities of the role. I dreaded this; in fact, when I received the call from him offering me the role, once he mentioned it my heart sank. It was hard enough commuting there during the day for my interviews. Both times I paid for parking. "Anxiety is expensive." I had about a week to rest before my first 12-hour training shift commenced. This was a few days before the issue I encountered with my car. The car issues happened about four days after hearing that I got the job, and about three days before I was due to start. Perfect timing. It couldn't be.

When I arrived for this particular shift Laszlo was in and so was Dela. He had other work he carried out as security and doorman, etc. He was middle-aged, somewhat confident but walked like a man who felt indignant about the way his life was treating him, if you know what I mean. He had a certain air of a lack of interest in his job and an unshakable disdain for some of the patrons, although he didn't show it to them. Then there was Laszlo. A debonair man, stern, had a sonorous voice, well-groomed, tall but somewhat hollow inside. He had a grandiloquent nature about him. I noticed his sharp tone and how he would almost berate or lambaste us, which was meant to be constructive, but he believed that in the outside world where he wasn't directly responsible for any of us, neither our work nor performance, that he could behave that way. I don't think so. This 'job' in my opinion was the biggest house he would ever own. He acted more like an inmate in prison on death row, who knew everything and was bright but at the end of the day was still in prison for a crime he was guilty of. Who cares? I felt sorry for him. He was overcompensating for something. What shocked me was that I sensed arrogance during my interview but not a trace of bitterness. I only noticed that on my first shift on training. I can't tell you how many insults I heard throughout the day, both from him and one of my other colleagues, who worked on the day shift – Dela. I met Dela in the reception lobby whilst attending my second and final interview. He was imperceptible, hard to read, smiled at me, but it had no emotion in it. So, I couldn't be surprised by his efforts to derail me on my two training days. Like I say, my affliction causes auditory delusions and hallucinations. Constantly, every time I interact with someone, male or female, I will at some point hear an insult, in their tone of voice, with the same inflection and conviction. There was no tricking myself out of disbelieving it. I have tried. I eventually began believing it was something in my facial expression that provoked people, or it offended them and they would retaliate in this way. I found it strange that when I did pay attention to the way people reacted to me they would appear to pay particular attention to my lips, or should I say the outer part of my lips near where people with dimples would have them. I won't lie. Whenever I did speak to people either in length or briefly, that area would tighten up and feel strained. I was never aware of that previously, but in recent times in my effort to either vindicate my thoughts or understand why people constantly wanted to insult me, I realised that perhaps this physiological reaction my body induced around my 'dimple' area may have been perceived as hostile in gesticulation, disinterested or an upturn of the nose. Behaviour that you would expect someone who thought they were better than others would exhibit. Or am I overthinking? I need an answer. Also, why are people so predictable in their thinking. Most people are reactive if this is, indeed, causing the problem, or at least exacerbating it. Why aren't there some people who see my facial expression and think 'oh it's not personal' or against me? Why must they react and not understand first? We are all brainwashed, I guess, and conditioned. If you see a tear on someone's face, especially someone who looks more vulnerable or meek, you assume they are sad and poignant, not that there are three different types of tears, of which one is emotional, and the other two are basal and reactive. While many are aware of the different types, they tend to associate a weaker person with emotional tears before understanding or breaking past that initial barrier. That's brainwashed. Media, etc. Need I say more?

I just noticed that once Dela and Laszlo interacted more with me during the two days I started noticing the trend, which I've seen before in several others, that they would pay particular attention to that region of my face when I spoke or listened, and their facial expression would instantly become almost dubious of me. Throughout the two days, I heard a torrent of insults. Racial, derogatory, contumelious, sarcastic in a negative way. I heard the word 'bitch' 'stupid' 'p**sy' 'black s**t' and some other racial epithets the most. On one or two occasions I would ask them to repeat what they said only to find they would say another innocuous thing or would simply not respond. I'm on probation, in a job paying better than I've ever had before. How can I offend someone by asking them if they insulted me? I'd be kicked out of the company sooner than I could fill out any paperwork. It was a catch 22 type of predicament. It seemed unthinkable to let a stranger know my problem. In the world we live in, people celebrate and rejoice amid chaos and rapaciousness. What hope did I have that people would afford me the care that I deserved? Nobody cares about me, nor do they want to. It's that simple. It's hopeless.

I remember during my second day, I was sitting at the front desk next to the supervisor, Laszlo, with his arrogance filling the room, suffocating me and Dela, too. I know it wasn't personal, but you know certain personalities are toxic for me to deal with given my circumstances, as you can imagine. Anyway, he was explaining something to me on the incipient property management improvised system that I didn't quite comprehend. I asked again and didn't get it a second time, but then he treated the patience that he had to give me as if it was an unaffordable loan he was forced to take against his will. It was at that moment I heard the word 'bitch,' not loud, not quietly, just in a normal tone, it happened in a moment when I was carefully trying to understand what he had just explained. I was deep in my brain's calculator, thinking it through, my eyes were locked on the screen and then he struck. Well, that's when I heard it. In that vulnerable moment. Do you get what I mean? Imagine that. When you are trying to think it through, for example, because you don't get it on your first day of training you get insulted, not once, and not only for that, and not only one insult. Do you see it now? My pain? My first day of training was a lot worse because when you combine the commute to work with the vortex I had to deal with there in the form of Dela and Laszlo it made for a calamitous day. For whatever reason, day two was probably not as bad as day one… It was quickly approaching 6 pm. I remember being so happy, all I wanted to do was crawl into a hole, just leave that day behind, never to be attacked by it again. Just another day in my world, unfortunately. On the first day, there were only three occasions where there was an 'unsure' moment between me and a customer. One was a customer who had come to the concierge desk asking for a parcel. Once I retrieved it from the delivery room behind us, with Laszlo paying close attention, I saw what I believed was a private joke between Laszlo and a well-known resident. It was clear that he and the guest were more than professional acquaintances. It was too awkward for me to question it but I endured it and believed wholeheartedly that it was something to do with 'see the new black guy,' as if that alone was so hilarious. I'm not playing the race card. You must be me to understand. No one can tell me how I feel. If you work in a white-collar industry with the majority of your colleagues being of a race other than yours you will feel very ostracised, especially when they are unfriendly towards you. They go to extreme lengths to make you aware of it as if I was so stupid to not realise it from the get-go.

The second incident, my worst nightmare was when a young English couple came in; they came back from what I can only assume was a busy day in the workplace, probably met up after work for a quick bite, who cares? The point is, as soon as they saw a new face – but not just any face… mine… it was almost like an immediate dissatisfaction; not with the fact that I was there, but me doing my job, for example, and being amicable and servile wasn't enough. They needed me to entertain them to validate themselves or satisfy themselves. Granted this may be in my head. But why is it a repetitive thing? Verbatim too, the things these people say to me, and the way they say them is different to my other colleagues, not only in the place of employment. The man constantly asked me pointless, meaningless, fake things about how long had I worked there, if I enjoyed it – as if he cared. Oh please!! Every time I gave him a genuine answer, he wouldn't seem satisfied, and thus an awkward few seconds would ensue. Every time I spoke like the whole world would want to hear me speak, and then be dissatisfied with me for speaking. "It infuriates me". "I just wanted to be invisible, I swear". "Get over it". "Who am I"? "You probably earn five times what I do". "Why can't you feel sorry for me, be magnanimous, why act as though you hate me? Are threatened by me"? When all I've done is smile and be professional. This world we live in is doomed.

The third incident was when a pair of cleaners came, both of Caribbean descent, I think. Very quiet and seemingly disinterested in my presence, which was rare. Laszlo directed them to the lifts and issued them with a key to the apartment that they were instructed to clean. It was a woman and a man. About 30 minutes later the man came back to reception. At that moment a customer was in the reception lobby on her phone, very attractive, one would say. Could easily steal a moment with her appearance. As he turned the corner, he glanced at her; I witnessed this and then suddenly that demure, placid nature sounded and looked more aggressive. He asked where the bins were. I misunderstood. I thought he meant a bin, any bin any size. I said we have one here, and he then said he had meant a big bin to clear out the stuff they removed from the flat. At that moment I felt stupid. I hesitated, my eyes squinted, I had to think. Then I heard it. He said 'idiot' as I was looking away. I didn't react. I could have as I was enraged, but you wouldn't know it. How dare he? Why? I was helping him!! I was even smiling. I was so angry. I bet he was trying to impress her at my expense. Why didn't he say the word directly while my attention was on him? I didn't get it at all. I dealt with this kind of thing daily but could never get used to it. The ego deals with things on a case-by-case basis, that's why. Did the lady see? Did she care? I didn't look over at her. I hoped she didn't think I was weak and a punching bag. He left; he dismissed himself.

The best part was yet to come. It was nigh on 6:30 pm and now I started feeling another anxiety for my journey home. It was probably slightly after rush hour, which helped, I thought to myself. I began winding down for the day. Reviewing all I'd learned and eager, but also not eager, to return the next day. Laszlo then said, "So tell me, what have you learned today" – so pompous. He wouldn't dare behave this way towards me in the outside world, at least not directly. I know the type of person he is. 'Big boy in a small place,' I call him. J.K Rowling said, "if you want to know what a man is like take a good look at how he treats his inferiors not his equals." This saying has stuck with me. I feigned excitement when he asked me what I'd learned and then I told him what I had taken in. He seemed fairly satisfied but had to add his signature to every moment at the end of it, so I let him. Who cares? I laughed in my head while I pretended to laugh at his silly joke. I kept thinking, 'You are the reason I will one day become rich and successful'. I gathered my belongings stored in the back and headed out. All seemed okay; the bus came quickly. I hopped on and it wasn't nearly as full as my anxiety expected it to be. I was three stops away from Liverpool Street. Almost relaxed, almost. Then it happened. A huge black man got on the bus. There were seats further back but not so many upstairs where I was sitting; in the front half, the one next to mine was the only available seat. I noticed him on the stairs ascending; the anxiety started kicking in and then the chain reaction as I knew he would sit next to me. Perfect timing! Just before I was about to dismount from the bus. My heart started racing; I felt the usual pulsating nerve in my chest, my pupils dilated, I felt faint, I started sweating, I felt hot, I was struggling to breathe and my limbs were shaking. I deliberately looked away from him to not make eye contact and make the situation more intense for I knew what was coming. I had my noise-cancelling earphones on with my music cranked up very high. However, with all that being said, all the anxious feelings, basically being deaf to the outside world at that moment, I still believe I heard 'f**k y**' and I only believed it could have been directed at me despite the bus being full. Why, why and why? Then I started THINKING 'who heard it, who saw it?' I was still looking away at this point. Every sense in my body wanted to ask him what he said, if anything. Trust me I wasn't afraid. My years of 'abuse' as I call it had almost taken the fear away. I was ready to die. I wanted to get stabbed and beaten up, I didn't care. When I finally turned my head to look, he was staring at me, eyes wide, it almost looked like hatred in them. "I don't even know you". I stared right back, no fear no tolerance to spare. I didn't look away. He sat down next to me and I had to get off a few moments later. He got up and gave me way, and I had to live with the uncertainty of if he swore at me or not for the rest of my life, whilst his life continued blissfully on, no less. If he knew my problem, he would feel sorry for me. I would. I wasn't about to attract attention by asking if he said something. Already feeling like everyone sitting behind me was burning the back of my head with their eyes and thoughts and judgments. That was enough attention. I hopped off, crossed the road, still carrying rage with me; it was heavy to carry. But I had no choice. "No one cares." "No one knows." At this point, I felt relieved but also annoyed. The tension was released, yes, but also, I wasn't allowed to give a fair reaction in a fair circumstance. Injustice. All-day, every day – that's what I call abuse. My train was about to leave at platform 17. I walked over there through the concourse of people. Many of whom stared at me as if I was from Mars. Whatever! I'm a poor, hated celebrity I guess, it's how I felt. I'm telling you it's hell. Hell!!!!

I boarded the train; there weren't many people getting on so that was good. I calmed myself down on the train journey. I arrived

CHAPTER 4: THE SUFFERING CONTINUES

at my stop, and as I was getting off and a twenty-something white guy boarded the train, his whole energy was off and aggressive, I felt. I ignored it but despite my best efforts I still heard a murmur as I walked past him, not loud enough for observers to hear, but loud enough for me to think I knew what he said. I heard 'mug' as I walked past, I let out a huge scream, I couldn't bottle it in forever. I then did it again, screaming the word 'f**k' loudly, full of pain and anguish. I found a seat on the platform and just sat there, the train pulled away and I just didn't care I know people across the platform were staring, probably insulting me. I just didn't care, I didn't care. I just don't care. Then the thoughts insidiously entered my brain, 'what if I jump in front of a train?' It would take all my pain away on this earth. I was literally contemplating suicide due to an uncertain belief. Sometimes being uncertain is worse than being certain. In my case, it was like torture. What stopped me was the love I have for my mom, dad and sister. It's worth it, staying alive to suffer, just to be able to see them again. This is what I remember thinking. I got up, probably looked like a forlorn figure. I didn't care I was in pain. I needed someone to come over and just hug me. My immediate family were all on different continents. I was alone and I was falling apart. The walk home usually takes twenty minutes to do but that night it felt more like an hour because of my complete disorientation and being jaded about my affliction. When I got home, I didn't do much, just lay in bed. I fell asleep around 9 pm and was woken up the next morning by my alarm for day two. This day was better but still not eventless. I needed my car back so badly. I relied on it so much. Gives credence to that saying that you only realise something's true value in your life once you have lost it. I had to overcome this problem. Adapt. Not outsmart or outmuscle it, but adapt to it. Sort of like the natural selection process in a way.

On Day 2 Laszlo seemed even keener on trying to make me look like I knew less about the job and role than I did the first day. I let him compete against himself. He won of course but he also lost. Dela seemed aloof and disconnected, still giving me the odd look of disdain and being unhappy with the fact that I spoke. The second day went much quicker. Again, I headed home as I did the previous day, once again by bus and train. All was okay until I got to Liverpool Street. I attempted to purchase a weekly season ticket on the TfL machine. I was charged, but the ticket wasn't added to my Oyster card. I was later refunded but, on that day, I was directed to the National Rail ticket office where I was told they could provide some help. The lady on the desk was indignant, angry at the world and every human she ever came across, unfittingly arrogant and very supercilious. She was in the wrong seat and the wrong location. Either way, she eventually charged me again but this time processed the purchase correctly. Something the automated machine failed to accomplish. I'm sure you can imagine how frustrated I was at that moment. Her demeanour wasn't helpful, nor professional. To be fair she was probably mirroring me; I was understandably annoyed, not with her, with the situation, but according to her I wasn't allowed to be, and she proved that by becoming annoyed with me. Fair. Of course, some of her other colleagues who had nothing else to do were very fixated on the exchange and paying careful attention, not because they wanted to help – if they did, they would have chimed in – they just wanted to stare and judge. One of the older men in the background saw my anger, warranted, but still took exception and,

CHAPTER 4: THE SUFFERING CONTINUES

well, you know what happened next. Whilst 80% of my conscious attention was on the lady processing the ticket, he said something. When I played the tape back in my brain, I heard the word 'p**sy' and I bet the whole world heard it and thought I was weak for not reacting. I don't care, well maybe I do care. I don't know. I headed home and to my amazement, I checked my other phone and a voice message was left for me by the mechanic to say my car was ready for collection. I was now off for a few days so it was perfect. I would be starting my night shifts by then so could drive up to work. I got a reward whilst in hell.

The next day I got up nice and early to pick up my vehicle. The mechanic there at the front desk was quite chummy with me. He seemed non-judgmental, amiable and full of energy, yet still, I heard insults. I didn't accost him, I didn't bother, I couldn't be bothered. What's the point? Around the corner, it would happen again. I just decided to focus on his seemingly positive vibe. To be fair I don't trust mechanics as far as I can throw them. I guess it was all part of his con. But at least I had some days off to enjoy myself. I just planned to stay indoors and switch off everything, including my brain. My car was in perfect condition and working even better than before. This little moment was golden to me. I headed home after two more minutes of small talk with the receptionist at the garage.

My alarm sounded and it was time to get ready for work. I was looking forward to commencing my contracted night shifts. I couldn't work on days with Dela, Laszlo and Cristina, who was the only female in the front desk concierge team. She was heavily pregnant when I first started and it was my understanding that she would soon be off on maternity leave. She had a very stoic personality, it seemed.

I never trusted women who hid their emotions and still don't. Just doesn't seem natural to me. She had a slight abrupt, condescending tone towards me but would occasionally mask it with a mirthful smile. Of course, on one occasion she muttered the words 'f**k y**' to me; she was explaining something to me on the system that I didn't understand, and again when my face tightened up, I assume that's when she decided to strike. I said nothing. How could I? How naïve did she think I was? I could never work on the day shifts; the team would make me lose my cool, I could just tell.

I arrived nice and early and had done my research on the parking restrictions in that area. Basically, it was free from 6:30 pm until 8:30 am so I was fine to park. There was always ample parking between those hours. I walked in and saw Cristian, another Romanian. Intelligent and very interested in history. He had a lot of knowledge of history, wars and so on. I'd seen him on my two days training when he and the other night staff member, Mihai, came in to take over the shift. We hadn't spoken yet so of course, I was anxious to meet and work with them both. After all, they were my shift mates. I couldn't tell much from a smile. My brain had forgotten how to interpret that. Cristian greeted me with a warm smile. I acknowledged it and smiled back and said, "I'm looking forward to the shift" to which he replied with a smile, "Yeah, hopefully, it goes fast". The shift was going fairly fast and I was taking a lot of notes and absorbing a lot of information about the role. Cristian had a quiet nature about him. I like quiet laid-back people. It kept my anxiety under check. Loud characters brought out the worst in me. They are overbearing and loquacious and that in turn can mean I'm more likely to hear them insult me regularly. Cristian had an interesting sense of humour.

CHAPTER 4: THE SUFFERING CONTINUES

He was from the part of Romania that Hungary defeated during the war. So, he spoke both languages fluently. About halfway through the shift, we were entering a much quieter period where we could engage in casual chat and recline our seats. I got more of a sense of who he was. I was sure he didn't hate me, but couldn't ignore the fact that I wasn't white. To me the two are interchangeable. However, I didn't feel like he would be a big problem to work with, due to his quiet nature. He would sporadically have moments where he would become over-talkative over trivial subjects, probably to pass time. It was in spurts. This did occasionally annoy me but it was bearable. There were many times during our first shift and other shifts when I was certain he would insult me. When explaining something to me either about the role, or history or whatever. While I didn't carefully and attentively listen to him and show interest in what he was saying I was sure he was just looking for an opportunity to insult me. I was used to this way of thinking. It happened with everyone as I said, everyone, I had a conversation with at least. Every colleague, every customer, every shop clerk, every friend, every family member, everyone. I heard Cristian say 'black sh*t' mostly, and then he would occasionally say 'black b**ch'. I don't know why. Perhaps I associated a moderate command of the English language with that use and combination of words in an attempt to insult me. In my head that was the most likely thing I'd hear from a person who didn't have a very good command of the English language as far as it is their mother tongue. Each time I would hear the insults I would ignore them. Even if I reacted it would undoubtedly happen again, I didn't see the point. I did see the point, however, in ignoring it and focusing on working and saving my money. That was the goal at all costs. But is that fair? Taking those jabs and not being able to react? Think for a minute, in comparison to how I used to accost people frequently to where I'd now gotten to. How could I keep that aggression up? I was defeated by my weakness. On the odd occasion, I would react to people but I got tired and bored of doing it every single time.

It got to around two in the morning and I could see the finish line. Two patrons stumbled in, staggering in their steps, grinning ear to ear to each other; they were inebriated. Instantly recognising me as the new guy. I started feeling anxious about the interaction that was about to come. I remembered something – that if you eat something when feeling anxious it can trick your mind into feeling at ease as no one eats when in danger. I took a bite of the biscuit I had. Not professional, but necessary. It didn't help on this occasion. They stood at the front desk and engaged me and Cristian in some claptrap. Me mainly, every time I was asked something, everyone would just stand in awkward silence paying very close attention to my responses. Was I that aberrant? Was I that commanding? I doubt it. "Leave me alone," I thought. At some point, I felt like the guy was just staring at me, forgetting Cristian was even there. I felt his energy, Then I heard him say the word 'monkey' – it was a playback while the live-action was carrying on. I felt my blood boil, my hands tense up and my back stiffen. I immediately wanted to accost him. I did nothing. The moment passed and they disappeared. My ladder inference was overused. I carried every interaction onto the next. I couldn't escape. I needed some air so I told Cristian I would head to the petrol station to buy a drink and a snack. He said it was fine so I headed out. I had been to this station before. On one occasion, I was met with a lot of hostility by the shop clerk. On this occasion,

CHAPTER 4: THE SUFFERING CONTINUES

there was a different, younger guy there, who seemed very talkative and positive. I bought two energy drinks and a bar of chocolate. Whilst I was paying a tall European woman came in. I immediately became anxious; my main fear was that he would suddenly become unfriendly and unprofessional because she was there. I turned my head as she began asking him if they sold Jack Daniels. While I was distracted by her, I knew he would strike. I was looking away and not paying attention to him at that moment as he processed the payment and waited for my receipt to print. As I turned away and back to him, I pressed play. I was sure I heard 'f**k y**' in his voice, I did nothing. Her reaction remained the same so if he had said something surely, she would have reacted. She didn't. I couldn't prove, nor disprove this. I ate it and turned around after taking my receipt like a defeated dog with its tail between its legs. I walked back to work. Just sick and tired. "Why does everyone hate me?" "Why does everyone want to insult me?" But all I said was "hello" with a smile on my face. When I got back in, I took my one-hour break in the lounge. For the first 20 minutes, I sat motionless in the dark just feeling sorry for myself. I wanted to do nothing but cry because of my pain and suffering. All the techniques I'd learned the year before in therapy did nothing to help alleviate my affliction. I stared at nothing. When I finally came back to, I just watched some funny prank videos on YouTube. I felt numb. I returned to the desk. The shift ended quickly after that and I left and drove home. Traffic at that time was very calm. The drive was enjoyable. I got in and went straight to sleep. The thing with anxiety is that you tend to sleep more than usual. I started thinking it was a sign of depression but this was never diagnosed by my doctor.

Some weeks passed, and I continued going to work. The drive on this particular day was horrible. From the moment I got onto the main road, where I lived, there were traffic jams caused by what I can only assume was temporary traffic lights. My road was so long that there were two on either end of it and I couldn't avoid either of them. I just sat there and tried to focus on finally arriving at work with plenty of time to spare. I wasn't running late as such. I just got noticeably uncomfortable when halted in traffic and was gazed upon by passing, curious eyes. It did something to me internally. At this point I was about halfway to work, feeling like I'd already been driving for an hour. I got towards Hackney, on Mare Street, a very popular, busy road in North London. There is a section or fork in the road where I needed to make a slight left to continue on my route. I was positioned correctly luckily enough, but from the corner of my eye, I could see numerous cars weren't. A lot of them needed to jump into my lane to fork left as well. I immediately started feeling anxious. It's not because I didn't want to let anyone in – it's that I wanted to do it correctly so as not to anger drivers behind me, nor the drivers I was letting in. One thing I hate was when other people hesitate and that's exactly what happened. I let one car in front of me seamlessly. It's amazing how many drivers nowadays don't even show gratitude for a kind gesture. The driver didn't blink his/her hazards to thank me. I think this frustrated me. I took that experience into the next scenario where another impatient driver wanted to merge into my lane. I was determined to not let him in because I wasn't about to be taken for granted again. It was a hot and humid day the hottest day of the year thus far, apparently. The car to my right would accelerate harshly and angle his car towards my lane bit by bit as we impatiently waited to turn and clear the traffic ahead. I didn't let him in and finally turned left. But what did I do to escalate the situation? I looked in my rear-view mirrors. I knew he would be angry and would gesticulate in his car at me. And so, he did. It was ambiguous but based on what had just transpired I know it was an offensive gesture. I could have just left it alone. After all, if he was trying to insult me there's a good chance any witnesses in his car or pedestrians witnessing this, may realise I wasn't paying attention hence why I didn't react. But as I was still reeling from the previous incident, I couldn't let it go. I immediately pulled over, let him pass and re-joined the traffic right behind him, accelerating aggressively and mouthing off and gesticulating in my car, just to exact revenge in the same way. It did make me feel better because I beat him at his own game, but lost to him at my own. This carried on for a few minutes until he finally veered off and disappeared never to be seen or heard from again. The moment passed. I was now about 10 minutes from work, in a very busy part of my journey as far as pedestrians crossing and appearing everywhere and the roads becoming narrower and more congested. My heart was racing and my pupils were dilated. My window was open and my music was fairly loud. I did this as a mechanism to drown out any outside noises, specifically insults from people. I was about four turns away from my workplace and was at a very narrow junction with a pelican crossing and hordes of people walking, and some sitting at a bustling pub/restaurant. I knew everyone was watching me. As I turned, I saw a group of what I assume were students or tourists, teens, about seven of them I think – six girls and one boy. I was sure they would pay attention to me but I was even more certain the boy would insult me as I passed. I did everything I could to not make eye contact and then I heard it – "ni**a" I pretended not to notice but as I sneakily glanced at my side mirror, I saw the entire group look at my car. I knew and was sure the boy insulted me for just being born. I didn't react. But I know it affected me. People 1000 – me Nil. I got to work still exasperated and dumbfounded by why he would insult me. I did nothing to him at all. In fact, at that moment I was fairly calm. Was it a self-fulfilling prophecy, an auditory illusion, hallucination? I don't know but it felt real. I parked my car and tried to gather myself before heading to work. I was walking down a narrow road where I had parked towards the main road where my workplace sat. Further down the road, I spotted a bald middle-aged white man engrossed in a conversation with a much younger bi-racial girl with her son next to them playing on his tricycle. Other people were passing by them but I perceived him as threatening. I was staring at him and he hadn't spotted me. The moment I looked away from him I heard that word again – "ni**a" I immediately looked back at him and her, no one was looking. I was sure he spouted the racial insult but wondered why neither he nor she looked my way. I passed them by. Then started thinking why would he say that considering she was half black at the very least. It didn't make sense but felt so real. It always did. I lost again; I did nothing. I had no energy to ask him about it, just felt awkward and I didn't want any more attention on myself than I already felt I had.

Work was just as bad on that particular day. I was working with Mihai. I was thankful it wasn't another random cover staff member with who I wasn't acquainted yet. However, on this day at numerous points, I repeatedly heard Mihai say the words "a**hole" and "b***h" to me as well as ambiguously flashing the middle finger and ball his hand into a fist to almost psyche me out. I didn't react. I was so fed up that twice I insulted him in the same way that I believed he had insulted me. I called him "b***h" and "c**t". When I said it to him, he didn't seem to react. Maybe he didn't notice, but I said it quite clearly. I just didn't care anymore about what my therapist taught me about self-fulfilling prophecies; for all I knew he was insulting me, too, during my sessions, I was sure everyone hated me anyway. A couple came in around midnight. We had music playing in the lobby and the fan turned on. Plenty of noises to muffle people's words. As they flashed passed, I was sure I heard the man say "prick" for no reason but I know I heard it while I was distracted and sifting through some paperwork. Whenever customers or delivery drivers walked in and there were two concierges on the desk, like I said before, I still noticed they would always want to acknowledge me. Why? I don't know. "Leave me alone," I thought. The minute I speak you look at me offensively or insult me, so what's the point. I was beginning to hate talking to people. I couldn't. It was dead.

Another hour passed and an Asian customer walked past us and greeted both myself and Mihai. He returned 10 minutes later with what I believe was a courtesan. Nothing less than £250 per hour. While my colleague and I were ogling at her I was certain he whispered something to her and once he stopped, I heard that word again – "ni**a". Not once did she even make eye contact with me. "What is going on I thought," I told Mihai I had to get some fresh air; I couldn't take it, I wanted to explode and physically harm anyone I saw. I needed to defuse my tension. I returned 20 minutes later; he asked if I was okay and nodded and talked no further.

What you need to understand is that this was a daily norm for me. I lived in this hell incessantly, without a clear way out. I didn't deserve it. I didn't. No one does. It got to 3 am and all I could think about was my bed. I had had enough of this day and shift. It was one of the worst ever. I had heard enough. At that moment a delivery driver came in; he had a thick accent and struggled to express himself. He did the customary look at me even though he was in a conversation with my colleague. I hid my frustration. I was sure when I hit the playback button that I heard the word "nego" which in Brazil is the same as "ni**a," I'd once read. When he came back to the desk, I asked him if he was Brazilian, he said he was. He asked why. I feigned a smile and said he looked and sounded like it. I did nothing; how could I? I couldn't win. It would happen again and again; fighting back was no longer a solution. People had an issue with me for existing. I couldn't fight that.

Psychosis can be divided into specific categories. Hearing voices, so speaking when there is no-one there, or seeing, tasting, smelling or feeling things that others do not. These experiences are called hallucinations. Holding strong beliefs that others do not share; for example, the belief that there is a conspiracy against you by MI6, or that you can hear hidden messages on television and radio being directed at you, or that someone is controlling your thoughts.[3] These beliefs are typically referred to as delusions. If it's about someone inflicting harm on you these are called paranoid delusions. If they are about being special, then these beliefs are called grandiose delusions.

---

[3] British Psychological Society, Division of Clinical Psychology, and Anne Cooke, *Understanding Psychosis and Schizophrenia*, 2017. Part 1: What is Psychosis page 10-11

Some can also experience difficulties with thinking and concentrating in such a way that it makes it hard to concentrate on other things at the same time. People can appear distracted and preoccupied. Some even talk back to the voices they are hearing. Some may talk in a way that others find hard to follow, mentioning many unrelated topics in quick succession. This is sometimes referred to as thought disorder. Of course, when you are emotionally distressed you are likely to say confusing things. Another thing that may happen is that an individual suffering from psychosis may appear inexpressive, apathetic or unmotivated, finding it hard to even prepare a small meal and look after themselves. These are known as negative symptoms: part of an illness. They can however be a result of feeling overwhelmed by experiences and trying to cope with feelings of helplessness and depression. Some people hear voices that reinforce positive messages, too. It isn't only negative voices like in my case. Cultural differences can also lead to one experiencing psychosis. It's an us and them sort of situation. Feeling and being made to feel that you are inadequate because of where you are can cause problems in the long run. I know I have experienced this, too. With racism I became paranoid. So, it contributed to me thinking I was hearing racist remarks in certain situations. I lived in South Africa and apartheid is something that greatly affected and divided the nation over there. Granted I wasn't around when it happened but you could still feel it in the air over the years when I was growing up. The separation.

Up to 10 per cent of people will at some point in their life hear a voice talking to them when there is no one there. About one person in every hundred receives a diagnosis of schizophrenia. So, in the UK alone there are about 600,000 people who have received the diagnosis.

That's from the people who have sought help about hearing voices and deem them to be distressing. A similar number of people have received a diagnosis of bipolar disorder which is also commonly known as manic depression. From time to time all of us have experienced a paranoid thought or belief. Where it becomes a problem is when it's unabating and begins to control your life and what you do. This is when professional help needs to be sought. A lot of people who have these experiences think of them as being significant in their lives. Some believe that they have religious or spiritual significance. Some explain them in terms of supernatural or religious forces or see them as giving them a deeper understanding of the meaning of the world. Like some sort of enlightenment. Parapsychology, metaphysics, the collective unconscious and higher consciousness are some examples of this here. A chemical imbalance in the brain which some attribute to hearing voices is a rudimentary way of concluding that someone has mental health problems. We all have different experiences in life that can lead us to start misinterpreting or hearing things. Each individual is different in the way they deal with these experiences. You can't just say that because one person hears voices all of a sudden that they are suffering from schizophrenia or psychosis, for example. Reasons as to why this may be happening are subject to a big debate. It could be because of current life circumstances, experiences as a child, cultural differences and many more reasons.

Many neurological and biochemical pathways in the brain are likely to be involved in experiences such as hearing voices. This is the case for all other human experiences, though. Genetics may also play a role in determining why someone will experience mental health problems in their life or not. Research compares identical and non-identical twins or biological and adoptive relatives of people that have been diagnosed with schizophrenia. GWAS (genome-wide association study) is a technique that looks at the physical health and genetic differences between people with or without a specific disease.[4] *The genetic similarities that the studies identify are associated with more than one disorder, rather a wide range of characteristics. For example, the tendency to be emotional, or problems with concentration. For some people, this can play an important role, but only as a small part, perhaps 6% according to a recent study of the complex web of interacting factors that contribute to a particular experience. An interesting finding is that someone who has a sensitive temperament may be more likely to experience psychosis if they experience hardship, abuse or trauma. Epigenetics is a new area of research. It shows how parts of our genetic mechanisms are 'switched on', 'turned on' or 'turned down' by the things that happen in our lives. So, for example, a protein that's responsible for producing a certain protein may become more or less active, so produce more or less of that protein depending on the different environment it's in.*

Psychosis is suggested to be a result of an imbalance or difference in the brain chemicals (neurotransmitters). Some evidence of this cogent comes from the effect of drugs.[5] *People who use a lot of cannabis appear to be more at risk of developing psychosis. As I said previously, I used to smoke cannabis and it was no more than*

---

[4] British Psychological Society, Division of Clinical Psychology, and Cooke. 5.1 Genetics page 38

[5] British Psychological Society, Division of Clinical Psychology, and Cooke. 5.2 Neurochemical Theories 5.3 Brain Structure and Function page 39-40

a year after I stopped that I started experiencing psychosis and anxiety. It was insidious but at its later stages, it was devastating. Neuroleptic medication, which alleviates experiences such as hearing voices, also affects neurotransmitters. There are over 100 neurotransmitters in the brain, researchers have focused on three: dopamine, serotonin and glutamate. Many neuroleptic drugs are thought to affect dopamine. They sometimes induce Parkinsonism which are abnormal movements similar to those in Parkinson's disease. Drugs like amphetamines, which increase dopamine production, can also produce psychotic-like experiences. Some newer neuroleptics are said to affect serotonin. So far, research into this has been inconclusive. It's crucial to remember that the function of all neurotransmitters is to convey information. An example is dopamine which is used as a pathway that communicates social threat or fear, hence why it's only fair to surmise that it is involved in the experience of paranoid anxiety. Interestingly, it's been discovered that most people who have a history of psychosis have also taken powerful medication for many years. Recent evidence suggests that this can cause changes to the brain, for example, a reduction of its overall size which invariably can lead to problems. Another recent study, the social defeat theory of schizophrenia has suggested that repeated experiences of being disadvantaged and socially excluded can lead to an increase in sensitivity in the dopamine pathways in the brain, which can cause an onset of psychosis. We can therefore conclude that for at least some of us our biological makeup contributes to the likelihood that we will have an experience such as hearing voices. However, despite years of research, no specific biological mechanism has been identified as being the main cause of psychotic experiences. We might all have psychotic experiences if subjected to certain types of stress but that doesn't mean our biological makeup is responsible for that. There could be many causes, our biological makeup constantly interacts with both our personal characteristics and our environment. The complex reason for one person's experiences may have little or no significance to the causes of someone else's. The problem with the idea that it's an 'issue with the brain' is that it is a sort of lazy way to assess the problem and thus people are just handed drugs to treat it which can make it even worse over time. So, a lot of money and resources have been pumped into the pharmaceutical industry and this has meant that a lot of other treatments such as talking therapies have taken second place. Also, that means a lot less money has been available to go into extensive research into mental health disorders. Corners have been cut.

The **next** day on shift I was sitting alone at the desk engrossed in my work, aware of my every facial expression, feigning relaxation. I heard the automatic doors open, and thought it was my colleague, Cristian, returning from his security walk. But it was a customer and his partner who I'd started seeing regularly. They, however always made me feel like it was the first time I saw them each time. Like I wasn't normal, neither was the exchange we would have. I quickly looked away after greeting them with a smile and heard quite clearly the word "monkey". It was happening again. I didn't show that I heard it through my countenance and general body language but I was burning inside. I guess he was trying to impress her. Showing her that he could insult me and that I wouldn't do anything about it. I was thinking for her of course. "Too much analysis will lead to paralysis." I had just had enough; I had had enough. I told myself I would kill myself as soon as I got home. I had some prescription medication in the form of aripiprazole and a few sertraline pills left. I planned to take 30 at once and just end my suffering. I couldn't do it anymore. I had given up and it was only getting worse. I recently heard the expression "reasons to live give reasons to die". I couldn't find a good reason for either at that stage in my life I must admit to you. Somehow, I got home, although I don't even remember the drive. I just knew what I had to do. When I got home, I sat in my car in the car park for a good 30 minutes, feeling hollow and empty, but comforted. I was oblivious to all the traffic around me. The happy couple about to leave home together for work with huge smiles on their faces, walking hand in hand. The single mom with the sweet little daughter so excited to just be walking and skipping, the contractor van man who I saw regularly around that time of the morning. I just kept asking myself "why?" Why was this happening to me? I truly didn't know how to escape this labyrinth and be free. I almost didn't see the point in getting out of my car and walking to my flat. But I forced myself anyway; wallowing in self-pity was a lot more appropriate in the confines of my own solitude. Not out here exposed in the world for all to not even notice, and me feel even more insignificant and alone.

I don't know how I made it to the next day; the night before I was certain that was it. I didn't know how it would end but I knew it had to end, my life. I guess I was just as scared to face and conquer my fears as I was to kill myself. Probably the fear of the unknown, but also a fear of the unthinkable. I was my own conundrum. I felt very groggy and very weary that afternoon. I woke up feeling like

CHAPTER 4: THE SUFFERING CONTINUES

I had just fallen asleep. I had to do it all over again, and for what? To pay my rent but exacerbate my mental health. Yes, exactly for that. To survive means to live for nothing but to stay alive, or to suffer but to risk death in pursuit of finding true happiness, or just suffer for nothing. I couldn't find meaning in anything anymore; everything was commingled and confusing, I couldn't tell this from that. Everything was under the rain, everything was wet.

A few hours passed and I decided to force myself to get ready. I did that relatively quickly then headed to work. I think if a mind reader was present that evening at work, they would have given me everything they possibly could to save my life. No such luck? You can only see unicorns in the distance or in your mind. In a way, "space" is also a unicorn. I wonder if that means it's all a mirage. Everything is rigged? I would often deep dive and question everything.

I was greeted by Laszlo and Prince, who both quickly scurried off and left when I arrived. It always made me laugh; as the shifts were so long and tedious by the time the people coming to takeover would arrive, the guys on the desk would almost already be walking past you as you enter the building, such was their desire to get out. Laszlo had a five o'clock shadow. It was funny. I checked the rota as I thought I was working with Cristian, but turned out I got the days mixed up and his holiday was to begin that day, not the week after as I had originally thought. Like I said, everything got wet. It was a shift with a cover. I'd heard shifts with cover staff weren't always great. Some would undermine, underperform. I heard so many stories about this. So invariably I was very anxious. Why wouldn't I be? Who will it be? Will he be kind? Will he be understanding? Will he be patient? I'd hoped it would be a quiet woman, eager to follow my lead and be a recipient of my instructions. In a word docile. Let me roll the dice against myself, surely, I will win this bet.

In he walked. He was so tall, taller than me, had a swagger in his step, a fresh army haircut and a smirk on his face, one that suggested he knew something about me and I knew nothing about him. This guy was far too confident to be cover staff; it was like he was the new supervisor on his first shift just returning from a life-changing holiday in Thailand. It was quite a sight. As he was walking, he gave me a little head nod, one of certainty and gravitas. He knew what he was about and I knew he was going to be anything but docile. He walked past me and I could smell his strong aftershave, very fitting. He wanted to know where to put his coat so I directed him to the back office, just behind the front desk where the concierges sat during the shift. He did so swiftly, positioning his coat behind a plethora of other uniforms left by other staff members on the coat rail. At this point, my heart started racing. I didn't know what to expect. I felt adrenaline coursing throughout my body. I knew that feeling; I felt it all the time. He walked up behind me ready to take his seat next to me. I turned my head towards him and saw him roll up his sleeves. He was ready. I wasn't used to leading a shift even though I was the senior member on this particular day. I hated the limelight, I hated being the focal point of anything. I was no longer sure of myself as I was once upon a time but it had to be done and no one was coming to help me nor eradicate my anxious thoughts. I introduced myself and he told me his name was Tom. He looked Eastern European and had an accent but I could tell he had lived in London for quite some time. He sat down and gazed at me with a certain intensity. I briefed him on all the duties that we needed to complete within the 12 hours. He seemed sceptical about what I can only describe as my ability to lead the shift. It was in the way he acknowledged what I was saying. There was almost a wry smile and strong gaze every time I mentioned something. It felt uncomfortable to say the least. I was worried that something would happen that would ruin the synergy between us for the shift. At this point, I was sure that I hadn't heard him say or do anything untoward. He didn't seem insolent, rather the type of person that wanted to constantly challenge me and my so-called authority as the shift leader. The duties were simple but tedious. I remember my first shift there, I wanted to quit after two days such was the arid nature of the job. It was a Sunday evening which was usually quiet and calm. It was rare to see many patrons on Sundays. A man that I didn't recognise walked in through the revolving doors; he had a brisk walk and seemed on edge and scatty. There was about a three-second walk from the doors to the desk, just enough time to analyse someone. His energy made me feel even more unsettled and I wanted to appear to Tom as if I wasn't anxious and uncomfortable. I didn't want him to see weakness and thus use that against me. I greeted the man and asked him how I could help him. He said he was there to visit someone, a lady called Sarah. I knew who she was – she was gregarious, friendly and always had people coming to visit her, both male and female. I followed our strict visitation rules and had to do a security check to ensure he was genuine. It was company policy to carry out a strict screening process before giving anyone access to the building. I explained to him that I would need to call her room to make sure that she was expecting him. He seemed upset by this and rather irritated. I began to feel even more self-conscious and then it happened. As I dialled the room, I began thinking to myself, wondering if this man had insulted me and the word 'idiot' came to my head I was convinced I had heard him say that to me in the brief exchange we had. It felt so real, I knew he called me an idiot. Tom didn't make me feel otherwise. Surely, he wouldn't have done anything or said anything to defend me. Why would he? He didn't owe me anything. Sarah finally answered the phone, she confirmed she was expecting a visitor and confirmed his name. All I kept thinking to myself was why did he insult me when all I did was do my job. I felt naked, exposed, but it was all too familiar to me; this is where I lived. The man left in a huff. Tom took out his phone and began scrolling through it like he was in pursuit of something elusive. The shift was going quite well but I was still frustrated about thinking I'd been called an idiot for no reason; always feeling like people didn't like me or that I gave off bad energy when all I was trying to do was be nice and placid. My therapist once described my behaviour as trying to be overly nice to disarm people before I'd even gotten to know how my interaction with them would be. He said I did this because I didn't want to be insulted or offended. I couldn't agree more. I wasn't myself anymore. A few hours passed, Tom had gracefully accepted his role as co-pilot and seemed to be at ease with me by then. He had done the second patrol of five. He seemed relaxed and comfortable around me which invariably made me put my guard down. This shift was going better than I thought it would, "maybe it's not everyone who hates me". We began having a chat about balderdash and trivia and he expressed to me that he was into conspiracy theories, which to some degree I was, too. I found this subject matter interesting. He began giving me a cogent argument as to why the earth was flat and why space didn't exist. I listened attentively, happy to let him have the mic. One thing about me is that I love hearing about the things people think that goes against the status quo. I had no problem indulging in that.

Just as things were seemingly going smoothly, I suddenly felt an energy from Tom that I hadn't felt earlier. He seemed more impatient and abrupt in his responses. I couldn't understand what had led him to suddenly change. It was playing on my mind and I began to feel alone again. By this time, we only had two hours to go to complete the shift. I felt like we had genuinely bonded and that he was rather fond of me. Then it happened, I heard the word 'fool'. It happened mid-conversation whilst we were winding down, coming toward the end of the shift.

You see the way it happened wasn't always in the moment, sometimes it would happen a few seconds later. It was like I had a recorder that I'd begin playing mid-conversation. Something in my brain would activate this recording and I would always hear an insult, feel someone spitting on me or offensively gesticulating at me. I couldn't escape from it. This very thing shaped my existence and has done ever since it started around the year 2011. I don't know why, I don't know how, but I know I was alone.

In the early days of this affliction, I would accost people and have outbursts. Ask them what they said or if they had done something to me physically. I remember once I was on the London underground going down an escalator to get my tube and I remember a man standing behind me with a lady, who I presume was his partner. He expectorated and I immediately assumed he had spat on me. I confronted him to his complete surprise. He asked me if I was okay and said that he would never do such a thing. We exchanged a momentary stare and then it was over. I achieved nothing. This became the theme. The more pointless accosting people became the less I was inclined to do it. Today I say nothing. I just walk around feeling like I'm getting punched all day and I do nothing. This takes its toll after a while. No one likes to be insulted, do they? Imagine that. Especially the closest people to you are constantly insulting you and deprecating you. You can't meet up with your closest friends and loved ones. It's hell. I was lost and alone. I heard things from my own therapist, the local corner shop lady, the pastor, everyone and I believed it, that's what mattered. I believed it was all real. The difficulty is realising that it is a possibility this could happen. I couldn't discern between reality and fiction. What most saw as impossible and highly unlikely, or what people wouldn't even think about, had become my reality. Imagine that.

Ten minutes were left I couldn't wait to get home.

In just a few moments Dela and Laszlo would come storming through the doors. I just sat there in silence trying to avoid any small talk with Tom that would lead to him saying something else to me. Two minutes passed and I saw Laszlo appear out of the corner of my eye – we had a wide view of the main road so you could see people from quite a distance away. Besides, I knew the way he walked; it was very distinctive. In he came with his signature nod in acknowledgement of his staff. He was the supervisor and he made sure everyone knew about it. You could tell it meant so much to him to be a supervisor; it made his shoes grow but not his feet. He walked past us, closed the back-office door behind him and got changed. Out he came adjusting his tie and belt, so proud and ready to take charge. I am someone who likes to know a little about a lot, not a lot about a little, Laszlo was the opposite.

The first thing he said to Tom was, "so did he show you the fire evacuation procedure?" With that question, I knew he wanted to try and make me look inept and undermine me. I said nothing I just gave him a mirthful smile. I handed over and just as I was leaving Dela appeared, he acknowledged me and I gave him a warm smile and headed home. Luckily at this point, I was driving and didn't have to take public transport, which was one of my worst nightmares with my psychosis and anxiety. Being out in public made me feel very vulnerable. If you have anxiety, you know that one of the worst things you can do is jump on a bus or a train. I used to get cabs or drive everywhere, even pay the congestion charge and ULEZ, just to avoid mixing with strangers on public transport. As I said anxiety is expensive.

The drive home was smooth. I loved the fact that I finished at six in the morning and managed to avoid the busy London traffic. The drive was always smooth. I worked in Islington, right near the centre of London, a very busy area.

I got home and was met by Frank. Just as I opened the door he was walking past, going towards the kitchen/living room and he greeted me. I don't know how it happened as I always tried to avoid interacting with my flatmates for obvious reasons, but somehow, we got into a lengthy conversation. I avoided talking to them as much as I could as I didn't want to hear any insults. Like I said it was interchangeable; it happened with everyone. While I was talking to him, I heard the word "stupid" – surely this wasn't true but I believed it. Even the closest people to me felt like strangers. I quickly left the living room and retreated to the safety of my room. I'd had enough of it. I didn't deserve this. I was a pariah and, in my mind, no one liked me.

By this time, it was early in the morning; when I slept most people were actively at work. I liked the idea of that. I'm not even sure why. Less interaction with people, I guess, anti-social hours to an extent even where work was concerned. I had work again later so I needed as much sleep as possible. I would normally do a HIIT (High-Intensity Interval Training) workout straight after work and then sleep, but I was beaten up by the day and I just needed some shut-eye!

I woke up feeling more anxious than usual; I don't know why. Wait – yes, I do! – I had to live another day. Another day of being insulted and spurned. It's true what they say, that you never know how strong you are until being strong is the only option you have. I got ready and luckily, I didn't see Jasmine or Jeffrey, and I think Frank had gone out. I just knew because I was familiar with all of the sounds in my flat and voices, too of course. I ran up the stairs as quickly as I could after my shower to avoid any human interaction; I was ready to leave at this point.

I left and headed to my car and once I got inside it, I breathed a deep sigh of relief and stress at the same time. Another day of not knowing who I was. The drive to work wasn't bad considering I travelled during rush hour when most people were going home, albeit in the opposite direction. There was a point, however, when I got to a specific set of traffic lights that was always teeming with people and I always felt stared at like I stood out like a sore thumb, it was my anxiety. The fear something was going to happen before it did. There was a group of builders standing nearby who seemed fascinated by my presence as I sat there uncomfortably waiting for the lights to change; it seemed to take an age. I was shaking and nervous. The light finally changed to green and I sped off; it was like I had completed a challenge. My days were full of those. That's the difference between anxiety and an anxiety disorder. We all have anxiety but it's designed to protect us when dangerous or uncomfortable situations arise – the difference is that I wake up feeling like I'm supposed to feel anxious constantly even when there's no perceived threat, and that's taxing on the mind and body.

I got to work and was parking my car but just as I was ready to get out, I saw a group of about eight millennials, boys and girls, walking as if they didn't have a care in the world. They were walking towards me and I dreaded the idea of passing them so I sat in my car and waited for them to pass, trying to pretend I was busy doing something. This is the kind of thing I would do regularly to avoid people.

I wanted to go to the co-op to get some lunch for my shift but I decided against it as I didn't want to see the hordes of people there. It was a very busy Co-op. I remember once I thought the clerk had called me a moron and before I left the shop, I let out a huge scream; it felt like time stood still when this happened, everyone just stopped. I'm six foot three so it doesn't go unnoticed when someone my size gets aggressive. I had no control over this.

I walked into work and Mihai was already there ready to start the shift. Laszlo and Dela had already left so I was happy I didn't have to speak to them, nor see them, I greeted him and sat down. I remember wondering what I would have to eat that day as I hadn't gone to the Co-op as I should have. Anxiety is expensive.

He smiled at me and greeted me. I got myself together and sat down in what I call the passenger seat in front of the CCTV control system. There were two seats, on the left you had the main computer which had access to the customer's details, room numbers, etc., (the inhouse system) and the right workstation had the CCTV screen. I sat there and got myself into work mode. Mihai and I had had some chats in the past about various subjects, some interesting, some not. The shift was dragging on. I was already done with it. I was tired and it was my last day before I was off for four days – it was four days on and four days off. It was about midnight by this point and I was starving. I guess it would be a takeaway on uber eats or Deliveroo. But I was a bit short on money and we hadn't been paid yet. So, I was going to have to bear the uncomfortable, and walk to the local petrol station to get a meal deal. It was a two-minute walk and I believed it would be less busy because of the time. I told Mihai I was about to take my break and he acknowledged that. I headed out the front doors; I couldn't wait to eat; my stomach was rumbling and I was ravenous. I walked and at first didn't see a single person but then I suddenly heard loud music fast approaching. My heart started beating fast, I started sweating and could feel my legs get weaker. Just as I arrived at the petrol station a car pulled up, seemingly full of people. I couldn't avoid this interaction. I just hoped only one of the car's occupants would come into the shop. Everyone got out. It was three men and two females all in their twenties. They all looked at me as I walked past feeling so exposed. I heard nothing – it was like as soon as they saw me, they all stopped what they were doing to look at me, it was a weird feeling. I just remember thinking "I need to do this as quickly as possible". Then it dawned on me. It was Friday.

CHAPTER 4: THE SUFFERING CONTINUES

My least favourite day of the week. Simply because more people are usually out and usually inebriated, loud and energetic. I was now an introvert, you see. I was the only person in the shop. I wasn't even looking at what I wanted to eat properly, all my focus was on the car outside wondering when they would enter the shop. I picked up a sandwich and cheese and onion Walker's crisps. I dropped the sandwich as I was so nervous. I quickly picked it up and got myself a Red Bull as well. I can't even remember what sandwich I got. Just as I was walking to the counter to pay a tall, European woman entered the shop with the aid of a tall man, she was clearly drunk. She was stumbling around the shop and the clerk was taking his sweet time. I just wanted to get out of there. As I was paying the drunk woman leaned in front of me and asked the shop clerk where the wine was; her scent was like a mixture of perfume and cigarettes. At this point, I was overwhelmed and didn't know how to calm myself down and tell myself that everything was okay. She stumbled over to the snacks section and I had a moment of relief. The shopkeeper was scanning my items as if he was paid to move slowly. I wanted to scream at him to hurry up. I said nothing.

THEN I HEARD THE DOOR OPEN.

Three of the occupants of the white 1 series BMW walked in loud and jovial, volume turned all the way up. I never understood why an entire group of people needed to enter a little shop together when only one person is going to pay. Maybe to carry the stuff? I mean they obviously weren't there to do their Sunday groceries. At this point, I couldn't help but focus on everything but myself. The drunk woman shouted across the shop "excwuse me, dya have Skittles?" As I was momentarily distracted by this I remember thinking that

I heard the clerk say, f**k you. I knew it!! He was waiting for an audience to embarrass me. No wonder he was taking so long to process my items. That's the problem with anxiety – time moves slower. It feels like it. Anxiety is the desire to escape the present moment and that's exactly how I felt. I didn't like the fact that when I was distracted that's when he decided to insult me, in my mind.

I grabbed my stuff and scurried out of the shop. Luckily the three people were in another aisle. I didn't see them. As I walked out the drunk girl smiled at me; her partner just looked through me. Here I was walking back to work wondering what was wrong with me. I was fed up and tired of being tired. I remember that night I sat in the staff room staring at everything and staring at nothing, feeling run down and empty and contemplating suicide once again. I was tired of suffering in silence. Would anyone miss me? Even notice I was gone. I doubt that. When mental health problems become severe, we tend to eventually think about suicide. I was at that stage. I had discussed this with my therapist and that's when he prescribed anti-depressants for me.

I got back to the building feeling slightly breathless from my brisk walk. I also felt an immense sense of sadness. I know Mihai could see it, he knew what I was going through, I know he did, and he was happy about that. I know he hated me. Why wouldn't he? Everyone else did. I walked straight past him and retreated to the staff common room where we would usually spend our 1-hour lunch breaks. The light was off and I just left it that way. It fitted my saturnine mood. I felt depressed and just sat down on the sofa and stared at nothingness, in the dark, alone. When I finally snapped out of it I just started crying. I hate to admit it but a grown man can shed a tear for reasons other than a mind-blowing orgasm. We are all human, full of emotions and unsure what to do with them. I started eating my sandwich, it tasted like nothing. I just lay down on the sofa and closed my eyes, trying my best to escape somewhere, anywhere, just away from my existence, but it didn't work. I remember thinking of ways in which I could kill myself. None came to mind at first but the more I thought about it the more ways began to appeal to me. I would go to the 33rd floor, access the roof, only the staff had the key for the door, I would jump off and finally be free. Somewhere else. My alarm chimed and it was time for me to go back to hell, downstairs. I reluctantly stood up as blood rushed to my brain. I psyched myself up to go and continue my shift. Who was I fooling? It was torture. There was no way around it. I headed downstairs and saw a gentleman at the desk, I think he was a resident as he was asking Mihai for his parcel. He received his parcel and luckily didn't even notice me. I sat down at the desk and just stared into the abyss, I was trapped there and couldn't escape.

A few hours passed and the shift was survivable, despite the horrible moments I experienced around my break time. THEN SOMETHING HAPPENED.

The fire alarm started sounding. My heart started racing, was everyone going to come out of their rooms and I would be in a situation where I would have to do a roll call on my own as the desk had to always be manned by at least one occupant. I checked the fire alarm panel and saw that the trouble zone was in the basement where the car park, gym and spa were. I took the initiative and told Mihai I would go and investigate. I didn't want to be the one answering the plethora of phone calls that would pour in and people coming to the desk or evacuating. I would take my sweet time down there deliberately to avoid seeing anyone or feeling anything. I went to the problem area which in this case was the boiler room, one of the areas we would have to cover when doing our security walk. We would take turns. There were other ad hoc duties around the job that you would only find out about on the actual shift. I didn't see any sign of smoke or anything amiss or out of place. Everything seemed normal but I wasn't going back just yet. Emergency fans were turned on automatically and it sounded like sitting near the engines on a Boeing 747. I loitered a little bit in the boiler room walking around acting as if I was doing something. I just wanted time to pass and this to be done with. After about 10 minutes I started thinking it was time to go back and report to Mihai and let him know my findings in the boiler room. When I arrived, there was quite a crowd with several people standing around, about seven different residents, all looking bemused, perplexed and slightly nervous. I can only assume everyone was waiting on me, my worst nightmare. Just at that moment where you are being judged and scrutinized. I was a leader deep down but I had lost the lead. I didn't make eye contact with any of them I just focused on Mihai. I briefed him on my supposed findings and tried to feign confidence and assurance that everything was under control and that I had taken care of it. I hadn't done anything. I just hoped no one would know. But the more they were staring at me the less confident I felt. A lady approached the desk and asked what was happening and if it was safe for her to return to her flat. I began speaking and Mihai interjected and advised her that, yes, it was safe and there was no fire. At this point, we had already silenced the alarm after about two minutes of

CHAPTER 4: THE SUFFERING CONTINUES

it ringing. It was around 3 am and most residents would have been asleep. They were too important in their fields of work or studies to be awake at such hours. It was a shame Robert wasn't there; he was a neurosurgeon, one of very few in the world. He always had good energy and was lovely to me. I went to the back office and sat down. I couldn't sit out there in front of all of these people, thinking I'm the centre of attention and that they were there to judge me, not there because they were worried about the fire alarm. That's the thing with anxiety – it makes you feel like you are the centre of the universe and everything is about you and how you feel in the moment.

I heard my name. I held my breath, clenched my fist, scratched my nose, starting profusely shaking my leg and wiped the sweat off my forehead before I heeded to the summoning – it was Mihai's voice. I kept thinking of a million scenarios of what was waiting out there for me. Mainly who would be watching and listening to our conversation. "Do you want some Haribo's?" I breathed a deep sigh of relief. No one was there. Thank God.

All the customers had gone back to their rooms. I was so shocked that I didn't hear anyone insult me. I actually started to feel a bit relaxed for a moment but it didn't last long because the minute I became conscious that I felt relaxed was the minute the anxiety woke me up and took over. We only had a few hours to go to finish the shift. I was sitting at the desk but felt I had been there for too long so decided to take a walk and get some fresh air. I explained to Mihai that I was going to check the boiler room again, even though on CCTV he would see I wasn't. I didn't care. I went outside and lit a cigarette whilst I circled the complex. It was four separate buildings all connected via the basement level. It was a hotspot for thieves and muggings, so I was told. Once, I saw a man being held at knifepoint. I did nothing; it was far away but I just wanted to avoid human interaction and not get involved. It had nothing to do with being afraid physically. I just didn't want anyone to insult me. It was the strangest thing. How could life be that difficult? I had lost touch with the normal things in life that we all take for granted. The basic ability to interact with another person without believing I was being insulted. The most difficult thing was that I would hear things come from the people closest to me. I know that I should have realised the chances of that happening were very slim but I still believed it nevertheless. No one can understand the pain I was in, feeling so lost and alone.

 I got back to the front desk and just sat down and remained silent. In typical fashion, Mihai tried to engage me in a trivial conversation and I just didn't warm to it. I just sat there, cold in the cold and just spaced out. I wanted to be alone but I had to finish the shift with him. It was like he was enjoying the fact that he could tell that I wasn't okay. Well, at least that's what I believed. A few more hours passed and it was now six in the morning. We would often have contractors coming in to perform tasks in the flats between six and eight in the morning. Sometimes it was the maintenance of the building, checking the sauna and gym and the pool amongst other things. A man walked in dressed in a navy jumpsuit. He was fairly tall and had a fresh comb-over, English, and seemed like a typical bloke. He came to the desk and approached me. There were usually two of us and I always found it strange that people would tend to approach me. In any event, he just informed me that he was there to perform some maintenance and checks on the boiler room. I

CHAPTER 4: THE SUFFERING CONTINUES

acknowledged him and reached into the drawer to my right to get the contractor's login sheets. I handed him the pen and he scribbled down a peculiar signature. I got up and handed him one of the keys at the back for the boiler room and as I did so he muttered something – something I later could only discern as the word c**t. I felt that feeling again. Why does everyone hate me? All I was doing was my job or was it a self-fulfilling prophecy. I immediately looked over at Mihai hoping he would somehow save me, I guess and reprimand the man for what he had said. Mihai said nothing. I was still convinced I had been insulted.

The man returned and told Mihai this time that he had finished his checks. He returned the keys and signed the contractor sheet. Just before he headed off, I asked him if he said something to me when I gave him the keys. All he said was that he couldn't remember and headed off. I was so glad to see the back of him. The entire time that he was in the basement all I wanted to do was confront him. I became obsessed with this feeling and a lot of the time it infuriated me. The idea that someone felt like they had the right to offend me as they pleased, I wasn't a victim. I was going to fight this battle. They say the best way to take control of a situation is through anger. Who was I fooling I had no control at all. The shift ended. The last two hours raced through. I was so happy to leave and get inside of my bed. I didn't see anyone in my flat either which was great as well. I set my alarm I fell asleep.

Another time I had no fuel in my car and I was running late for my shift. It was a shift with a cover again. I had no idea who it was going to be and how it would go. I would be working with cover staff over the next few weeks as Christian was off on holiday. Apparently, he was off to Spain. Lucky him. I hated the fact that I had no petrol and because I was in a hurry, I had no time to go to my local petrol station where I felt comfortable, as I knew everyone and was used to it. What they don't tell you about anxiety is that we are reluctant to change. We like patterns and routines. Comfort zones. I felt safe in mine and hardly ventured out of it, not by choice anyway. I had to pick a random petrol station which I had never been to before and the thought terrified me. Who was going to be there? Would they insult me? Would it be busy? I had no choice. I pride myself on my punctuality so I couldn't afford to lose time by going to my local petrol station and risk being late.

    I got to the petrol station and it was extremely busy, it was a large one and had about 20 pumps. I found an empty one and braced myself before I got out to fill my car. Petrol prices there were exorbitant but I had no choice. Anxiety is expensive. As soon as I stepped out of the car, I felt that familiar feeling again, my eyes became heavy, my heart started racing, my palms felt sweaty, I needed to urinate, my breathing became very short and shallow. I was afraid. I started filling up my tank, nervous and hands shaking just pretended I couldn't see anyone and just at the corner of my eye a car pulled up behind me. All I could make out was that it was a man and a woman, Greek looking. I ignored them. As soon as the door opened, I heard something inscrutable and I knew I was being addressed but I didn't look back. I could feel his eyes on me, seeing my weakness and knowing I was fearful. I felt like people would prey on that if they knew the truth about my affliction. A minute passed and I was done. I scurried into the shop and realised I needed food for my shift so I bought a meal deal. I headed to the till and queued

CHAPTER 4: THE SUFFERING CONTINUES

up behind two other customers. I just wished they wouldn't look back at me and that they would hurry up. It was two men; one Asian and the other was on the phone so he was distracted. The first man finished paying and headed out of the shop. As he walked past me, I could feel his eyes penetrating my skin and opening me up inside. I breathed deeply and then the moment passed. The guy in front of me was engrossed in a conversation with what sounded like a client. He was discussing something about a mortgage. He paid and then left without even acknowledging me. Thank God. It was finally my turn to pay. As soon as the clerk saw me his energy changed, he became more rigid and more unfriendly. I wasn't paranoid I could see it clearly. I finally paid and turned to leave the shop. I headed to my car jumped in and sped off. I realised that being late and rushing had exacerbated my anxiety and psychosis. I got to work with five minutes to spare. I rushed inside and was greeted by Laszlo. He engaged in his usual balderdash and I didn't entertain it. Less is more with him. No curtailment was needed. He handed over to me and advised me that I was going to work with an agency cover staff member. I nodded and he left soon after. The new guy arrived, slightly scatty looking and very bedraggled. He was of average height, in his early twenties, slim and looked North African. He had an Irish accent and was very intriguing. His name was Alex. I couldn't figure him out but we seemed to have a lot in common, I later learned. He was into a lot of self-help stuff. Like books, ted talkers and more. We got on very well and it turned out to be the best shift I had ever had with anyone. He wasn't insubordinate, nor did he try to undermine me. He just got on with it and didn't complain about the job once. After a seemingly perfect shift and with just an hour to go he suddenly changed towards me. Was it something I did or said? I asked myself and I couldn't find an answer. The inevitable happened. He insulted me. Just during our conversation, he seemed off with me, distant, non-responsive. I couldn't understand what I had done wrong. I tried everything I even started brown-nosing him at some point which didn't seem to work. I liked his personality and character as he didn't seem like a typical 21-year-old, he was smart, had substance and didn't have the FOMO syndrome that most millennials did, I found. He called me a prick; I know I heard this correctly. It just came out of nowhere. What was it about me that seemed to get peoples' backs up? After I heard him say this to me. I just felt sad. Then it happened again – he called me stupid mid-conversation. I didn't know what to do. It was too frequent. That was the thing, depending on the length of interactions and interpersonal encounters I had with people, especially men, that determined how many insults I would hear. I remember having an interview before this job and I had heard about six insults from the man interviewing me.

It was a perpetual hell. A fire that never stopped burning my soul.

I just sat there quietly for the remainder of the shift. I disengaged and was left feeling rather crestfallen. There was no hope for me. Everyone hated me, I was a pariah. I didn't confront him on the subject. I just took the blows and felt helpless and hopeless. It was a sign of things to come.

I remember when I was young, I was so gregarious and amenable. People loved me and I loved them. I was popular and loved being around people. This was a far cry from what I had become. I had a fear of people, if there was ever such a thing. I wouldn't wish this on any enemy of mine. It was horrible. Just horrible.

Laszlo came marching in, in typical fashion, hardly graceful he was, ready to take charge and save the world. I left in a hurry, tail between my legs and feeling sorry for myself. To think I couldn't turn to any close relative or friend of mine for help as I heard insults from them, too, was the worst and most painful part of this problem. Alex didn't even say goodbye to me – he just left. I headed to my car and suddenly had the urge to cry. It was pathetic how low I felt and how lonely I felt.

The drive home was tedious as there was a large build-up of traffic on the way, it was usually the case if I left 10 minutes late. I got home and just sat in my car, closed my eyes. I nodded off and was woken up by the sounds of a little boy laughing. He looked so innocent and happy. blissful. I missed being young; I wish I could do it all over again and undo everything.

They say anger by definition is a self-inflicted punishment we put on ourselves as a result of other people's mistakes. I never understood this years back. It's a choice; our minds tell us to react and we do so with anger at times because it helps us take control. Yes, I was always angry but then I just started feeling sad. I dealt with this for years upon years. Nothing but me could turn the situation around. When you feel like you are in the right, or aren't in the wrong, and yet people still tell you otherwise it is likely to lead to feelings of anger and frustration, but eventually, sadness and loneliness, feeling misunderstood and unloved. After all, love is simply acceptance. If you can fully accept someone for who they are and not judge them or criticise them, that's love. Everything else is an attempt to control them for your benefit or for the sake of your mind. The mind has difficulty not knowing when asked a question. It's designed for survival, not comfort – that part is down to you. This sums up how I constantly felt. I felt like people were not accepting me for who I was. People were prejudging me, violating me, insulting me, looking at me with disdain. This was all new to me, this experience, but it got old very quickly and I tried and tried to replace it with something new on many occasions. Nothing seemed to work. Just an incessant torture. It's why I contemplated suicide so many times. I couldn't keep waking up if this is all life had become. I didn't see the point. It became hopeless when I started punishing myself and marginalising myself to appease other people and disarm them. It was pathetic I couldn't go for a walk in the park without other people dictating to me how I should feel. I was out in the open but in a prison serving a life sentence for a crime I didn't commit.

I woke up feeling sad and excluded. I just missed being me, I was lost but had to live another day. Go through the motions, get out of bed, wash, get dressed, face the world. It was like my sole purpose in life was to simulate anxiety and fear. It took me what felt like ages to get ready but I somehow managed to. I left the flat with plenty of time to spare. Who was I going to be working with tonight, I thought to myself? Will he be another Alex, another Laszlo? I wasn't eager to find out. I got to work and as I was walking towards the entrance a couple was approaching me who seemed to take a keen interest in me. I never look around when I'm out walking but I could always sense when people's eyes were on me. I would sometimes walk fast and take different routes whilst walking to avoid the more populous areas where there was a lot of traffic. I became used to doing that

CHAPTER 4: THE SUFFERING CONTINUES

to avoid human interaction. The couple was staring at me and I saw the man smile; my immediate thought was that he was making fun of me, mocking me. Maybe they could see my sorrow and pain and found it amusing. I don't know. I thought the worst of people. My mom once asked me if I insult people the way I thought they insulted me and I said "no". I wish that was enough, but it wasn't. I've always had trust issues throughout my life. As they got closer, I heard the man say something; I couldn't decipher what it was but then I saw her smile and assumed it was something negative about me. Everything was about me like I said. I believed I was the centre of everyone's world. I ignored this and didn't react but it started my shift off on the wrong foot. This was my last shift before I was going to be off for four days. I just wanted to get it over and done with. I walked in with my tail between my legs, head down and defeated. Laszlo greeted me in an orotund voice and I just smiled and said nothing. He quickly left and I was there on my own. After about five minutes the phone rang and it was the cover staff guy who explained that he was running late. I assured him that it was okay and that I would see him soon. He finally arrived. He seemed nice and quiet and I thought that the shift would go well based on how things looked. He took his seat and I introduced myself. He said his name was Cristof. He was a bit older than me, I'd say, by about ten years and he seemed like a nice enough guy. A few hours passed and we had an incident. A guy and three women appeared at the reception desk waiting for one of our residents to come down and meet them. It was Sarah. She stayed on the 20th floor and would often have people coming to visit her. At first, I didn't realise they were actually waiting for anyone. It just seemed as if they congregated inside the building as it was warm, and it was a very cold night outside. I waited a few minutes because I didn't want to attract any attention to myself. They were getting louder and louder and I was becoming more anxious about the situation unfolding before my eyes. After about five minutes of waiting, I decided to ask them who they were waiting for. One of the ladies replied, "Oh, we're waiting for our friend, Sarah". Then I felt a sense of relief as I knew exactly who they were talking about, but then just after she said that I heard the guy utter something. I couldn't interpret what it was that he said but my mind told me it was something derisive. He wanted to embarrass me in front of the women. His body language spoke volumes. I heard the word "p***y". In all the confusion I made out that word and I knew he was saying it to me. I did nothing. About two minutes later Sarah came running into the lobby all dressed up and ready to go out with her friends. She was wearing high heels, a red dress and a long furry coat. I didn't have a problem with her as she was always kind to me and my colleagues. They left. Even the way some of the tenants or landlords would look at me at reception, I felt like I was looked down upon, or was it that I felt like a failure, that I wasn't in a skilled job, making a lot of money and feeling good about myself. I was the result of problem after problem. They say when you think someone is negatively looking at you it's almost always because you think all they are looking at is exactly what you don't like about yourself. This is true but you can't come up with an excuse for someone hating the fact you were born. That's a problem with mankind.

    A few hours passed and there was a moment where it was quiet so Cristof and I were able to talk a little bit. He was rather laconic.

He told me he was married and had three children. He had done security work for fifteen years and had worked in many different places. We engaged in a ten-minute conversation and at some point, after connecting I heard him insult me. I couldn't catch a break, it was constant that I would hear people insult me, it was never-ending. I was simply tired of it. On this occasion, I did decide to ask if he had said something. I didn't ask him specifically if he used the word "idiot" which is what I heard. He smiled and said that he didn't. After that, I heard him insult me about three more times. Self-fulfilling prophecy. On my break, I just sat in the dark again contemplating suicide. I was just tired of being tired and I wanted out. I didn't know what else to do. I had previously had therapy – cognitive behavioural therapy (CBT) more specifically. It didn't help in practice and I couldn't keep the application going. I had that feeling again of feeling lost and alone, a pariah. A shadow in the dark. In the past, it had been worse. I remember there were times that I couldn't even leave my flat for three weeks on end. I would venture out at odd times like 3 am or 5 am to do my food shopping. I wouldn't get on public transport as I was not driving, and I was hypersensitive and alert to my surroundings at all times. I was never relaxed.

I went back to the desk. It just felt like Deja vu. I tried my best to feign happiness and shake off the visceral feeling I had. The shift quickly came to an end and I was so relieved to leave and go home.

A few months had passed and I had left the job I was previously doing. The anxiety and psychosis got to me and I couldn't cope with it anymore I needed a break from the work environment and being around people constantly. People who didn't like me for that matter. I was at home and alone for most of the time, hardly leaving my house. To say I had money problems was an understatement.

I was gambling and causing more anxiety due to this. I started gambling to try and make ends meet. I didn't want to work in an office environment so decided to make money by other means, to avoid human contact. This is when things began to get really bad. Anxiety is expensive. You'd sit in a cab rather than sit on a bus, you'd rather pay £5 home delivery for groceries than go to Tesco or Sainsbury's, you would rather order takeaway via uber eats than go downstairs and cook whilst your flatmates are around, you'd rather wash your vehicle yourself than go to a busy car wash. Anxiety is crippling and it shows no remorse. It doesn't let you off. It can take some of us years to realise that some things are bigger than our anxiety. Some never do. It's a blight, it can destroy your life. It's the worst thing I have ever experienced. Going on holiday isn't the same, meeting up with friends and family. It's a very dark place.

Part 2

Chapter 5: Understanding the Different Types of Mental Health Disorders

There are many different types of mental health disorders: for example, schizophrenia, schizoid, bipolar disorder, panic disorder, depression, anxiety, psychosis and others. Many of them are interchangeable with nuances but generally, they all relate to each other and in that way are easy to understand. When you have good mental health, it means you are generally able to think, feel and react in the ways that you need and want to live your life. But if you go through a bad period of poor mental health, you may find that the ways you are frequently thinking, feeling or reacting become difficult or even impossible to deal with. This can be as bad as having a physical illness, or even worse at times. Mental health problems affect maybe around one in every four people in any given year. That's 25% – that's how common it is. Chances are you know someone who suffers from it. They range from common problems such as depression and anxiety to rarer problems like schizophrenia and bipolar disorder. In this part, I will look into some of the different types of mental health disorders, their effects on you and how they can be treated. Remember this isn't an exhaustive list but it covers a wide range of the different types of mental health disorders that do exist today.

Bipolar Disorder

Is a mental health condition that affects your moods, which can swing from one extreme to another. It used to be known as manic depression.

People with bipolar disorder have episodes of:
- Depression – feeling very low and lethargic
- Mania – feeling very high and overactive

Symptoms of bipolar disorder depend on which mood you're experiencing. Unlike simple mood swings, each extreme episode of bipolar disorder can last for several weeks (or even longer), and some people may not experience a "normal" mood very often.

Depression

You may initially be diagnosed with clinical depression before you have a manic episode (sometimes years later), after which you may be diagnosed with bipolar disorder.

During an episode of depression, you may have overwhelming feelings of worthlessness, which can potentially lead to thoughts of suicide. If you're feeling suicidal, go to your nearest A&E department as soon as possible. If you're feeling very depressed, contact your

GP, care coordinator or local mental health crisis team as soon as possible. You could also call NHS 111 for an immediate assessment if you are based in the UK.

If you want to talk to someone confidentially, call the Samaritans, free of charge, on 116 123. You can talk to them 24 hours a day, 7 days a week. It's a little-known fact that getting help for mental health problems for young people in the UK isn't easy. But contacting your doctor and insisting on getting help is sometimes the only way to go about it. After all, no one cares about you as much as you do. Alternatively, if you are in the UK, visit the Samaritans website or email jo@samaritans.org.

Mania

During a manic phase of bipolar disorder, you may feel very happy and have lots of energy, ambitions, plans and ideas, spend large amounts of money on things you cannot afford and would not normally want. It's also common to not feel like eating or sleeping; you begin to talk quickly, and you also become annoyed easily. You may feel very creative and view the manic phase of bipolar as a positive experience. But you may also experience symptoms of psychosis, where you see or hear things that are not there or become convinced of things that are not true.

Living with bipolar disorder

The high and low phases of bipolar disorder are often so extreme that they interfere with everyday life. But there are several options for treating bipolar disorder that can make a difference. They aim to control the effects of an episode and help someone to live life as normally as possible.

The following treatment options are available:
- Medicine to prevent episodes of mania and depression – these are known as mood stabilisers, and you take them every day on a long-term basis
- Medicine to treat the main symptoms of depression and mania when they happen
- Learning to recognise the triggers and signs of an episode of depression or mania
- Psychological treatment – such as talking therapy, which can help you deal with depression, and provides advice about how to improve your relationships
- Lifestyle advice – such as doing regular exercise, planning activities you enjoy that give you a sense of achievement, as well as advice on improving your diet and getting more sleep

It's thought that using a combination of different treatment methods is the best way to control bipolar disorder. Help and advice for people with a long-term condition, or their carers, are also available from charities, support groups and associations. This includes self-help and learning to deal with the practical aspects of a long-term condition. Bipolar disorder, like all other mental health problems, can get worse during pregnancy. But specialist help is available if you need it.

What causes bipolar disorder?

The exact cause of bipolar disorder is unknown, although it's believed many things can trigger an episode.
These include:
- extreme stress
- overwhelming problems
- life-changing events
- genetic and chemical factors

Bipolar disorder is fairly common, and 1 in every 100 people will be diagnosed with it at some point in their life. You have Bipolar I which means you will have had at least 1 episode of mania that lasts longer than 1 week. You may also have periods of depression. Manic episodes will generally last three to six months if left untreated. Depressive episodes will generally last six to twelve months without treatment. You have Bipolar II which means it is common to have symptoms of depression. You will have had at least one period of major depression. And at least one period of hypomania instead of mania. Bipolar disorder can occur at any age, although it often develops between the ages of 15 and 19 and rarely develops after 40. Men and women from all backgrounds are equally likely to develop bipolar disorder. The pattern of mood swings in bipolar disorder varies widely. For example, some people only have a couple of bipolar episodes in their lifetime and are stable in between, while others have many episodes. If you have bipolar disorder, it may affect your driving. You must inform the Driver and Vehicle Licensing Agency of your country of residence if you are diagnosed with it.

Psychosis

Psychosis can be caused by stress, use of illicit drugs or alcohol usage and sometimes steroids, psychotic drugs, schizophrenia and mood disorders as well as other mental disorders.

Psychosis is divided into three categories: beliefs by way of delusions, hallucinations and formal thought disorders a.k.a disorganised speech and thinking. There are thought disorders, so some people believe people are out to kill them or have paranoid delusions. There are grandiose delusions like having supernatural powers. Delusions of reference is when people believe people are talking about them, are thinking about them and insulting them. This is the closest match to my symptoms. But I couldn't find any case specifically like mine. Most people hear other voices, not the voice of the actual person to who they are speaking. People hear voices coming from outside of themselves telling them nasty things or to do stuff which is called command hallucinations. The modality of the hallucinations consists of touch (tactile), smell (olfactory), sight, this is generally how hallucinations are categorised.

Disorders are defined by having confused thought processes which are incoherent and difficult to convey. Schizophrenia is one of the disorders associated with psychosis. You can have transitory short-term illnesses. Schizophrenia can occur at a young age which is risky.

Psychosis is generally treated with antipsychotic medications. There are many different medications on the market BUT the biggest risk is the side effects

Antipsychotics are sometimes used for over a year, sometimes two years, to take effect. Talking therapies like Cognitive Behavioural Therapy (CBT) also help people integrate back into Society and manage their mental health disorders. It's also very common with anxiety disorder.

Schizophrenia

Schizo means split in Latin, phrenia means mind.

It refers to the mind but it's not necessarily a split personality as a lot of people associate it with. It's actually a split from reality.

It results in a fragment of thinking.

Schizophrenia syndrome

Different patients will suffer from different symptoms. There are negative symptoms and cognitive symptoms. Most human symptoms are just an extreme version of a physiological process. There are as follows:

- ▸ The heartbeat process and tachycardia is a fast heartbeat which is a symptom.

- Body temperature fluctuates. It rises when you have an episode.

These are the psychotic symptoms.
- Delusions.
- Hallucinations.
- Disorganised speech disorganised behaviour.
- Or catatonic behaviour.

Delusions are false beliefs. Similar to schizophrenia, sometimes delusions make people think remarks are made against them. Hallucinations are another type of psychotic symptom – it's basically when a person thinks they are experiencing something that isn't actually happening, or there. Disorganised speech is when a person mixes words together and is not being coherent. There's disorganised behaviour which means you exhibit strange behaviour like you're doing cartwheels in the middle of a high street for no reason. Catatonic behaviour has to do with movements, posture and responsiveness. A person might be in an unresponsive stupor. You have negative symptoms too, so this is the removal or reduction of normal processes. So, for example, putting you in an emotional state and making you lose interest in things. There's something called 'the flat effect' which is an inappropriate response, so to speak, like if a person saw a lion approaching them in the middle of a busy supermarket, but they wouldn't find that weird as most people would. You also get short responses with no elaboration. For example, someone asks you your age and you answer but add nothing to that. There are cognitive symptoms that cause issues with memory, learning and understanding. As mentioned, there are three phases of schizophrenia; delusions, hallucinations and disorganised speech and behaviour.

Diagnosis for schizophrenia requires at least two of the following; delusions, hallucinations disorganised speech or behaviour symptoms. There must be signs of this for at least six months and at least one month of active symptoms. Substance abuse is also one of the causes of schizophrenia.

Antipsychotic medication can be prescribed for this condition. Autoimmune disorders, celiac disease and genetic diseases are also linked to schizophrenia.

As far as epidemiology goes, for men the onset tends to be around their mid-twenties and for women, it's their late twenties. Race doesn't affect this.

With schizophrenia and other mental diseases, one can attain help from many disciplines. There's talking therapy, meditation, hypnotherapy and acupuncture. All these have scientifically been proven to help alleviate symptoms of various mental health disorders. Medication and psychopharmacology is another method that can be used alongside therapy, for example. Antipsychotics, as mentioned previously, are a great way to alleviate symptoms. They improve one's tolerance level and help overcome mental health issues. There are risks of dependence and weight gains associated with antipsychotics, however. One can also suffer from withdrawal symptoms once they cease taking them. But this can be avoided as long as you are weaned off your medication correctly and gradually.

Schizoid Personality Disorder (SPD)

This is an uncommon condition in which people avoid social activities and shy away from interaction with others. They also have a limited range of emotional expression. It's a chronic and pervasive condition. People with schizoid disorder tend to be peculiar or odd. They are generally loners or prefer solitary activities. Many people with this condition can function fairly well although they tend to choose jobs that allow them to work alone like night security officers, library or lab workers. I know this is something I chose to do when my condition was at its worst. I always preferred lone working to avoid social interactions with others. Some of the common traits of schizoid behaviour include the following:

- ✓ They do not desire or enjoy close relationships with people
- ✓ They choose solitary jobs and activities
- ✓ They take pleasure in few activities, including sex
- ✓ Some have no close friends, except first-degree relatives
- ✓ They have difficulty relating to others
- ✓ They show little emotion

Schizoid, although similar to schizophrenia, has some differences. It's one of the less common types of mental health disorders but it tends to be long lasting if not treated early.

Schizoaffective disorder

Schizoaffective disorder is a condition where symptoms of both psychotic and mood disorders are present together during one episode or within two weeks of each other. There may be times that it can be hard to look after yourself. There may also be times between episodes when you feel okay. Some people have suggested that schizoaffective disorder sits in the middle of a continuum, with schizophrenia at one end and bipolar disorder at the other. Both mood disorders and psychotic symptoms are present in schizoaffective disorder.[6] Just as there is more than one type of mood disorder, there is more than one type of schizoaffective disorder. There's the manic type; in this type you have both psychotic and manic symptoms which occur within one episode. Depressive type means you have both psychotic and depressive symptoms occurring at the same time during an episode. Then you have the mixed type which means you have psychotic symptoms with both manic and depressive symptoms.[7] The psychotic symptoms are, however, independent of bipolar disorder. Some of the psychotic symptoms which are similar to schizophrenia include:

- Hallucinations – you may see things that others around you don't. For example, hearing voices, seeing visual hallucinations and other unexplained sensations.

---

[6] Mind, 'Symptoms', 2021 <https://www.mind.org.uk/information-support/types-of-mental-health-problems/schizoaffective-disorder/symptoms/> [accessed 15 August 2021].

[7] Mind, 'What Is Schizoaffective Disorder?', 2021 <https://www.mind.org.uk/information-support/types-of-mental-health-problems/schizoaffective-disorder/about-schizoaffective-disorder/> [accessed 15 August 2021].

- Delusions – you may hold strong beliefs that others don't share. An example is a fear that you are being watched, your thoughts are being read, you are powerful and able to control things that are, in fact, out of your control.

In general, you may feel your thoughts becoming very disorientated, very confused or feel frightened, angry, depressed, excited and/or elated.

Some of the mood symptoms which are also experienced in bipolar disorder include both manic and depressive symptoms:
- Manic symptoms – can include feeling uncontrollably excited or enthusiastic about something, making plans that are unrealistic and also being perilous and taking risks.
- Depressive symptoms – you may feel sad and lonely, always wanting to sleep, like you can't relate to other people, sometimes even feeling suicidal.

People diagnosed with mixed type schizoaffective disorder may switch between mania and depression in a short time. Schizoaffective disorder, schizophrenia and bipolar are similar but different. They can all involve feelings of elation for extended periods, rapid speech, racing thoughts, risk-taking behaviours, agitation, delusions and hallucinations. Despite its similarity to schizophrenia and bipolar disorder, schizoaffective disorder is commonly seen as a psychotic disorder with significant mood features rather than a mood disorder with psychosis. Schizoaffective disorder is also unique from the others in that it tends to have a longer first episode (at least a month) of simultaneous psychotic and mood symptoms. Difficulties with self-care and socialising aren't as noticeable as they are with schizophrenia. You can rule out other conditions by performing a physical exam. For example, an under or overactive thyroid can cause some of the symptoms (tiredness, anxiety, mood swings and depression) so in this case, the thyroid would need to be checked before someone is given a diagnosis. Recreational drugs can also cause some of the symptoms. Some people experience psychotic symptoms during a period of severe depression or a period of severe mania. But to receive a correct diagnosis you would have also experienced psychotic symptoms on their own without mood symptoms. If for example, you have schizophrenia and experience a short depression episode this wouldn't mean that your diagnosis should be changed to schizoaffective disorder. Some of the causes of schizoaffective disorder are stressful life events such as childhood neglect, experiencing a traumatic loss, being out of work or having money problems, childhood trauma such as sexual or physical abuse, neglect, traumatic events or losing someone very close to you. Brain chemistry is a theory is that suggests that people with schizoaffective disorder have more dopamine in their brains or that dopamine has different effects for them. Some research suggests that chemicals are also involved. Antipsychotics which are used to reduce symptoms of psychosis or schizophrenia can help to lower dopamine levels so as a result, this may reduce one's sensitivity when faced with a situation they perceive as baleful.

Body dysmorphic disorder (BDD)

It's an anxiety disorder related to body image. You may be diagnosed with BDD if you experience obsessive worries about certain flaws in your appearance that only you can see and that are usually barely noticeable.[8] You can also be diagnosed with it if you develop compulsive behaviours like frequent use of mirrors, for example.

If you have BDD these obsessions and behaviours cause emotional distress and disallow you from carrying out your day-to-day life normally. For this reason, BDD is closely connected to obsessive-compulsive disorder (OCD). As a result of BDD, it can be hard for a person to be around people and out in public. This invariably can affect your work life and relationships with people. BDD can also cause other concerns such as a feeling of shame, guilt or loneliness, depression or anxiety, or lead to misuse of alcohol and other drugs, suicidal thoughts, self-harm, feeling of needing unnecessary medical procedures such as cosmetic surgery, etc. Many people, as with other conditions, tend to not seek help because they worry that people will judge them or not be understanding. Some of the common obsessive worries about the body in people with BDD include negative thoughts about one specific area of the body, or several areas of the body that they think are out of proportion, disfigured, lacking symmetry or too big or too small.[9] These thoughts can cause you significant anxiety and you will spend a lot

---

8 Mind, 'About BDD', 2021 <https://www.mind.org.uk/information-support/types-of-mental-health-problems/body-dysmorphic-disorder-bdd/about-bdd/> [accessed 31 August 2021].

9 Mind, 'Symptoms'.

of time thinking about it. BDD can affect any area of the body but common areas are the chin, skin, hair, nose, lips or genitals. BDD has similarities to eating disorders in that in both cases you have a poor body image, worry excessively about your physical appearance and develop compulsive behaviours to try and deal with these worries. Some people who suffer from BDD also experience an eating disorder, but not all people with eating disorders have BDD. BDD and eating disorders aren't the same; for example, when a person is experiencing an eating problem such as anorexia or nervosa they are mainly concerned about their shape and their weight. Someone with BDD is likely to experience concerns about other areas of their body, too, like a specific facial feature.

Common compulsive behaviours include seeking constant reassurance about your appearance, exercising excessively, frequent body checking with your fingers, picking the skin to make it smooth, frequent weighing, comparing yourself with people in magazines or models, etc., using heavy make-up to try and hide an area you are concerned about.[10] Although it's not for certain what causes BDD, there is a correlation between certain things and BDD; these include abuse or bullying, low self-esteem, fear of being alone or isolated, perfectionism, genetics and depression.[11] BDD can be treated with cognitive behavioural therapy (CBT), medication or specialist services if all else fails. What CBT does is that it identifies a connection between your thoughts, feelings and behaviours. It

---

10 Mind, 'Symptoms'.
11 Mind, 'What Causes Body Dysmorphic Disorder (BDD)?', 2021 <https://www.mind.org.uk/information-support/types-of-mental-health-problems/body-dysmorphic-disorder-bdd/causes/> [accessed 24 August 2021].

also helps one to develop practical skills to manage them. For BDD, CBT aims to address the key features of BDD that gradually make you less anxious about your body. It focuses on improving your general attitude to body image and physical appearance, it addresses your concerns about the flaws you think you have and it reduces the desire to carry out unhelpful behaviour. With regards to medication, you may be prescribed antidepressants either on their own or in combination with your therapy if CBT alone doesn't correct your BDD, or if your BDD is causing you some impairment. The type of antidepressants typically prescribed are serotonin-specific reuptake inhibitors (SSRIs) which reduce obsessive thoughts and behaviours. SSRIs are known to cause unpleasant side effects. If the above methods are unsuccessful one can seek specialist services to deal with the specific areas of your BDD but CBT is generally very effective.

Anxiety disorder

There are many different types of anxiety disorders. General anxiety disorder (GAD)[12] is when someone has general worries about things in their everyday life. There's social anxiety disorder which is where one has extreme fears or anxiety when in social situations such as parties, workplaces or other environments where people are, this is something I suffered with. Panic disorder is the next type; it is when someone has regular panic attacks without a

---

12 Osmosis.

clear cause or trigger. This can leave you in perpetual fear of having another one.[13] There are phobias – extreme fear or anxiety caused by a particular situation such as leaving your house or fear of a particular object such as spiders or rodents. Post-traumatic stress disorder (PTSD) happens when you develop anxiety problems after going through something you found traumatic like fighting in a war. You may be diagnosed with obsessive-compulsive disorder (OCD) if you have repetitive thoughts, behaviours or urges. Health anxiety means you have obsessions and compulsions relating to your health and illness. BDD is another example of anxiety disorder. And finally, Perinatal anxiety or Perinatal OCD is when some people develop anxiety problems when they are pregnant, or within the first year of giving birth.

From time to time, we all experience anxiety disorder when anxious for longer periods than what is considered normal. It is basically when you are subjected to a frightening situation that is scary and uncomfortable. What happens is that your body releases hormones like adrenaline or cortisol (survival mode) and in that situation, it triggers the fight or flight response, and depending on what is happening determines whether you fight or run. An anxiety disorder is where that one experience tends to repeat itself, and because it's more frequent it's the body's way of trying to protect itself, keeping you safe.

Most people think anxiety is broken down into regular panic attacks and constant worrying. Anxiety is made up of many different

---

13 Mind, 'What Are Anxiety Disorders?', 2021 <https://www.mind.org.uk/information-support/types-of-mental-health-problems/anxiety-and-panic-attacks/anxiety-disorders/> [accessed 9 September 2021].

symptoms. Some include physical symptoms, never feeling good enough, trouble sleeping, terrifying intrusive thoughts including suicide, feeling like everyone hates you and feeling on edge. A common treatment for anxiety disorder is CBT which is a talking therapy. Antidepressants are also a common treatment for anxiety disorder. I suffered from this for about eight years – social anxiety specifically – but my anxiety was caused by my psychosis and what I have self-diagnosed "schizoid". it's very complex and each individual's experience of it is most likely going to be different. Anxiety is the most common type of mental health disorder along with depression. When you feel anxious you have this churning feeling in your stomach. When you have an episode, you may feel light-headed or dizzy, you could potentially get pins and needles, feel restless or unable to sit still, your breathing quickens, you get the sweats, feel nauseous and this can all also lead to you having panic attacks if this goes untreated. Our bodies naturally have this anxiety to protect us from danger. The problem is if you have a disorder, you are always having a feeling of dread even before you see a perceived threat and as a result, you go looking for threats to explain why you are feeling anxious. As I said, it's very common but can be treated.

Panic attacks

Panic attacks are a fear response. They are an exaggeration of your body's normal response to danger, stress or even excitement. When you have a panic disorder you may feel reluctant to go out alone or to public places because you are worried about having another panic attack. If this fear becomes very intense it may then be called agoraphobia which is a fear of being out and in open spaces. When you have a panic attack your heart pounds very quickly, you take quick shallow breaths, feel faint or dizzy, hot or cold, you sweat and tremble, feel nauseous, you may get pains in your chest and/or abdomen, find it hard to breathe, feel nervous or shaky and feel disconnected from your mind, body and surroundings. When having a panic attack, you may feel like you're losing control, going to faint, having a heart attack or are going to die. Imagine that people who have this disorder regularly have the feeling that they are going to die – that's horrible and so scary.

Panic attacks occur at different times for everyone. Some people have them once, then never again and others don't. Most panic attacks last between 5 to 20 minutes. They tend to happen very quickly and suddenly. They can be frightening, but there are things you can do to cope. You can focus on your breathing, for example, breathing slowly in and out whilst counting to 5, stamp on the spot which can help your breathing, focus on your senses for example taste the strawberry flavoured sweet you are eating and finally grounding techniques which help you feel in control. They are especially useful if you experience dissociation during panic attacks. After a panic attack think about self-care and the things you can do to make yourself better. It's important to pay attention to what your body needs after a panic attack. For example, you may need water as you will most likely feel dehydrated or maybe you may need to lay down and rest. It's also vital to talk to someone you trust about this. They can alert you about when you have another one and then you can discuss how they could potentially help you during an episode.

If you are experiencing a lot of panic attacks at unpredictable times and there doesn't seem to be a specific trigger then you may be diagnosed with panic disorder. It's common to experience panic disorder and other types of phobias together like agoraphobia. People who suffer from panic disorder may have some periods where they have few or no panic attacks but other times when they experience a lot of them.

Some studies indicate that people who have panic disorder might be sensitive to sensory experiences like sunlight, smells, sounds, changes in the weather, etc., but there isn't any concrete evidence as yet from researchers to confirm it. Panic attacks like anxiety can be caused by many things; for example, bad childhood experiences, your current life situation, physical and other mental health problems like depression, etc. Drugs and medication can also cause it if abused or not properly taken. Anxiety and, particularly, panic disorders can be treated with therapy; for example, cognitive behavioural therapy or applied relaxation therapy which involves learning how to relax your muscles in situations where you normally experience panic. SSRIs (selective serotonin reuptake inhibitor) is the best type of antidepressant used to treat panic and anxiety. For some people, this may cause side effects like sleep problems or make them feel even more anxious than usual. If they don't work consult your doctor or therapist and you will most likely be prescribed a different kind.

Beta-blockers are sometimes used to treat the physical symptoms of panic such as a rapid heartbeat, palpitations and tremors. They aren't however psychiatric drugs so they don't reduce any of the psychological symptoms.

Panic attacks are horrible and can honestly feel like you are going to die. It's important not to suffer in silence and seek help if any of your symptoms are similar to those I have covered. It's important that you contact your doctor and get the help that you need.

Borderline Personality disorder (BPD)

BPD is also known as emotionally unstable personality disorder (EUPD) it's a type of personality disorder. You may in some cases be diagnosed with BPD if you have problems with how you feel about yourself and other people. You have to have experienced at least five of the following things that have lasted for a while and have a big impact on your daily life to be diagnosed with it: you feel worried about people abandoning you, you find it hard to keep and maintain stable relationships, you feel empty a lot of the time, you often self-harm and have suicidal thoughts, you have feelings of serious anger which you can't control, you do things impetuously and which could harm you, you experience drastic emotional changes. For example, one minute you feel very happy and excited and the next you feel low and isolated. As you can see it can be a very broad diagnosis and that includes a lot of people with very different experiences.

BPD is caused by a combination of factors namely stressful or traumatic life events and genetic factors. Some of the traumatic life events can often include things like feeling afraid, upset or unsupported, family difficulties or instability such as living with a parent who has some sort of addiction to something, sexual physical or emotional abuse is another factor, or losing someone close to you like a parent for example.[4] If you had childhood experiences like these it could have led to you finding coping strategies and mechanisms to deal with it and this would have invariably changed your beliefs about yourself. These thoughts tend to cause you distress. You may also battle with feelings of anger, fear and sadness. Some people that get BPD may have not had any history of traumatic events and they develop it through other types of difficult experiences. With the genetic factors, evidence suggests that BPD is likely to be diagnosed if someone in your family has it too. There are debates however whether BPD is caused inherently by your parents or other environmental factors. A combination of factors may be involved. Genetics might make you more vulnerable to developing BPD, but it's often due to stressful or traumatic life events that these vulnerabilities are then triggered and become a problem. It is thought that BPD is more likely to affect women than men, however, both can develop it. Children can also be diagnosed with BPD but this is harder to diagnose as when you are young you are growing up you go through so many changes. Some symptoms of BPD can be very similar to other mental health problems such as bipolar disorder, PTSD, depression and psychosis. It's possible however to experience BPD and other mental health problems at the same time. There is a variety of things one can do to alleviate their symptoms of BPD, this includes; focusing on one feeling at a time. If you feel angry, frustrated or restless you could perhaps rip up a newspaper, hit a pillow, do some vigorous exercise, listen to

---

14 Charles H. Elliott, *Borderline Personality Disorder for Dummies, 2nd Edition: p15-50* (Indianapolis: John Wiley and Sons, 2020).

CHAPTER 5: UNDERSTANDING THE DIFFERENT TYPES OF MENTAL HEALTH DISORDERS

loud music, do practical activities to keep the mind preoccupied. If you are feeling depressed, sad or lonely you could wrap up nice and cosy and watch your favourite tv show, preferably comedy, write all of your negative thoughts and feelings on a piece of paper and tear it up, listen to music you find uplifting, write a comfort letter to the part of yourself that is sad or alone. If you feel anxious or tense you could make yourself a hot drink, noticing the taste, the smell of it the shape of the mug and the weight and how it feels in your hand. Take ten deep breaths, counting each one out loud. Write down everything you can think of about where you are right now, such as the colours of your surroundings, the date or the time. Take a warm bath or shower as this can help to change your mood and relax and calm you down. If you feel dissociative, drink a glass of ice-cold water or pour it over your head, clap your hands and notice the stinging sensation, chew a piece of ginger or chilli. If you feel like self-harming take a cold bath, rub ice over the area you want to hurt yourself or stick a plaster on your skin and peel it off. This will help distract you from what you want to do. It's also good to talk to someone, keep a mood diary, try peer support, look after your physical health e.g., through exercise, etc., find specialist support for abuse and bullying.

Several treatments can help, for example, talking therapies like dialectical behavioural therapy (DBT). This type of therapy uses individual and group therapy to learn the skills you need to cope with difficult emotions. It's a preferred treatment for women who often self-harm. There is also mentalisation-based therapy (MBT)[15] which aims to help you understand your and other peoples' mental states and to examine your thoughts about yourself and others. Then there are other therapies such as CBT, which I've covered already, but this type of therapy covers how your thoughts and beliefs affect your feelings and behaviour. Cognitive analytic therapy (CAT) combines CBT's practical methods with a focus on the relationship between you and your therapist. it examines how you relate to people, including yourself and what patterns have developed for you. Finally, there are other talking therapies such as schema-focused cognitive therapy, psychodynamic therapy, interpersonal therapy or arts therapies.

Psychiatric medication isn't recommended for treating BPD. This is because there aren't any drugs known to be effective. However, you might take medication for other mental health problems you are experiencing. In a crisis situation, your doctor may prescribe you a sleeping pill or a minor tranquiliser to help you feel calmer but this shouldn't be taken long term or it could have adverse effects on you.

Depression

Depression is a low mood that is chronic and lasts a long time and invariably affects your everyday life. At its mildest depression can mean just feeling low, at its most severe stage it can be life-

---

15 Mind, 'Treatment and Support', 2021 <https://www.mind.org.uk/information-support/types-of-mental-health-problems/schizoaffective-disorder/treatment-and-support/> [accessed 15 August 2021].

threatening as it can make you feel suicidal. If the low feelings interfere with your everyday life and persist for a couple of weeks it could be a sign that you are experiencing depression.[16] There are different types of depression: it's usually mild, moderate and severe depression. However, there are some specific types of depression. You have Seasonal Affective Disorder (SAD) which is depression that occurs at a particular time during the year or during a particular season. You have Dysthymia which is a continuous mild depression that lasts for two years or even longer; another name for it is persistent depressive disorder or chronic depression. Then you have prenatal depression which occurs during pregnancy; another associated name for it is antenatal depression. Then finally you have postnatal depression, which occurs in the first year after giving birth. Premenstrual dysphoric disorder (PMDD) is a severe form of premenstrual syndrome (PMS). Many women experience PMS but for some women, their symptoms are very severe which affects their everyday life and their ability to function optimally. When this happens, one might be diagnosed with PMDD. PMDD itself is not a type of depression but women who experience PMDD find that depression is a major symptom.

There are many symptoms or common traits of depression. These include psychotic symptoms, self-harm and suicide, the risk of isolation, and anxiety and depression as symptoms of other mental health problems. Some common signs of depression are feeling down, upset or tearful, being restless, agitated or irritable, feeling guilty or

---

16 Mind, 'About Depression', 2021 <https://www.mind.org.uk/information-support/types-of-mental-health-problems/depression/about-depression/> [accessed 24 August 2021].

worthless, feeling empty and numb, isolated and unable to relate to other people, no longer finding pleasure and enjoyment in things you used to enjoy, there's a sense of unreality, no self-confidence or self-esteem, you may feel hopeless and suicidal. Just remember that eventually, your competence will become your confidence. As a result of these symptoms, there are specific ways in which people with depression will then behave. They may avoid social events and activities that they usually enjoy; become suicidal or self-harm, find it difficult to speak and think clearly, their decision-making may become poor, loss of interest in sex and a decrease in libido, and they may find it difficult to remember or to concentrate on things. They tend to use more alcohol, tobacco and drugs than usual, find it hard to sleep or are sleeping too much, feel tired all the time; there can be drastic weight loss and loss of appetite, also weight gain or eating too much, and there can also be physical aches and pains with no known physical cause.[17]

If you experience an episode of severe depression, you may also experience some psychotic symptoms which include delusions such as paranoia, and hallucinations such as hearing voices which is also common in psychosis and schizophrenia. If you experience psychotic symptoms as a part of depression, they are likely to be linked to your depressed thoughts and feelings. An example is that you may become convinced that you have committed an egregious crime. These experiences can feel very real to you at the time, which in turn can make it hard to understand that these experiences are

---

17 Mind, 'Symptoms | Mind, the Mental Health Charity - Help for Mental Health Problems', 2021 <https://www.mind.org.uk/information-support/types-of-mental-health-problems/depression/symptoms/> [accessed 24 August 2021].

also symptoms of your depression. They can also be frightening and upsetting. Experiencing psychotic symptoms could mean you get a new diagnosis, but psychosis can be a symptom of depression.

If you are feeling low you may use self-harming behaviours to deal with the difficult feelings. When you are feeling low and hopeless you may contemplate suicide; whether you are only thinking of the idea or actually considering doing it, it can be frightening.

There's also a risk of isolation when it comes to depression. At times it can feel difficult to talk to someone about it so instead you may decide to cut everyone off as you suffer in silence. The more serious your symptoms are the more likely you are to feel lonely and isolated. Without the correct intervention and help depression can affect your relationships, work, finances and overall health. So, it's important to get help early.

It's very common to experience anxiety and depression together. They can sometimes have the same symptoms; for example, feeling restless, being agitated and struggling to sleep and eat. Depression can be a symptom of other mental health problems such as bipolar disorder, BPD and other personality disorders, schizoaffective disorder, too.

The causes of depression vary between each individual but some of the common causes are bad childhood experiences; for example, abuse from a parent or even a foster-parent – this is known as the Cinderella Effect – life events, other mental health problems, genetic inheritance, medication or recreational drugs and alcohol use, sleep or diet and exercise. Antidepressants work by changing the brain's chemistry and some argue that depression is caused by changes in the brain chemistry which are then rectified by the drugs. The evidence is weak, however. If changes to the brain chemistry occur, we don't know whether these are the result of actual depression, or in fact, its cause.[18] There are several ways in which you can help yourself if you suffer from depression. You can talk to someone you trust, try peer support, try mindfulness which involves giving your full attention to the present moment, which in turn helps to manage depression, you can look after your physical health through exercise and a healthy diet and good sleep, etc., stay active, keep a mood diary, spend a lot of time in nature. All these things can help you manage your depression and overcome it.

Many treatments can help with depression. These vary depending on the country you are in and how severe your depression is. Self-help is one of them. This can be delivered through a self-help programme that is recommended by your GP/doctor. A computer-based CBT programme for depression may also be recommended; this will help you to understand your depression and challenge negative thoughts about yourself. 'Beating the blues' is one example of computerised cognitive behavioural therapy (CCBT) that could be employed. Finally, a physical activity programme could be put in place. Again, this would be recommended by your doctor. You could join a group exercise class. These are run by qualified professionals and designed for people who suffer from depression. Many different talking therapies can be effective in treating depression. There's cognitive behavioural therapy (CBT), group-based CBT, interpersonal therapy

---

18 Mind, 'Causes', 2021 <https://www.mind.org.uk/information-support/types-of-mental-health-problems/schizophrenia/causes/> [accessed 15 August 2021].

(IPT), behavioural activation, psychodynamic psychotherapy and behavioural couples' therapy.

Several medications can be used to treat depression. These can be considered if CCBT or physical activity have not helped you. You may also try antidepressants, either on their own or in combination with talking therapy. There are different types of antidepressants. There are selective serotonin reuptake inhibitors (SSRIs), serotonin and norepinephrine reuptake inhibitors (SNRIs), tricyclics and tricyclic-related drugs, monoamine oxidase inhibitors (MAOIs) and other antidepressants that can be taken to manage your depression. Everyone is different, so different people may require different medications. Once you feel better and feel you want to come off your medication it's important to get support, preferably from a professional or from others who have come off the medication who understand its effects. Find out the possible risks of stopping the medication, and always remember to come off gradually and not just suddenly. There are alternative treatments too. These include art therapies, alternative and complementary therapies, mindfulness, ecotherapy which involves putting yourself in nature and taking in the elements, and finally, peer support.

If you have severe or complex depression you may need to be referred to a specialist. ECT which is electroconvulsive therapy should only be considered in extreme circumstances. According to NICE guidelines (National Institute for Health and Care Excellence), this can be if you are experiencing a long and severe period of depression in extreme circumstances and other treatments haven't worked or if the situation is life-threatening.

Repetitive transcranial magnetic stimulation[19] is another option for treatment if you haven't responded to the other treatments mentioned above. This treatment involves daily sessions lasting about 30 minutes which are spread over several weeks. Neurosurgery is also another option but this is rarely used and once again it's only chosen if all other treatments have failed. Whatever the case always consult your doctor if you are using a recommended treatment that isn't working for you and they can refer you to a specialist or advise you of other methods you can try to improve your depression. I have also included various ways that you can help yourself to overcome depression as well as other mental health afflictions later on in the book.

Anger

What is anger? Anger is normal and part of being human. It's a healthy emotion. We feel anger usually when we feel attacked, deceived, frustrated or unfairly treated. My definition of anger is the punishment we put on ourselves for other peoples' mistakes. Despite the belief that it's a bad emotion, it can be useful, for example, when we want to identify problems or things that are hurting us. It motivates us to create change and achieve our biggest goals. It helps us stay safe and defend ourselves in dangerous situations by triggering our fight or flight responses and aids our decision-making, to an extent. Most people will experience anger in ways

---

19 Mind, 'Treatments', 2021 <https://www.mind.org.uk/information-support/types-of-mental-health-problems/body-dysmorphic-disorder-bdd/treatments/> [accessed 24 August 2021].

that don't have a big impact on their lives. One needs to learn healthy constructive ways to deal with it so that it doesn't become overpowering. Anger can become a problem when it gets out of control or harms you or others around you. This is especially the case when you regularly express your anger through unhelpful or destructive behaviour; if it harms your mental and physical health, you haven't developed healthy ways to express it.

Anger has different effects on your body. It can give you a churning feeling in your stomach, tense muscles, you feel hot and your temperature increases, you sweat, have an urge to go to the toilet, you shake, you may feel dizzy and your legs go weak. Anger can also have effects on the mind. It can make you feel tense and unable to stay calm and relaxed, can make you feel guilty, it can also make you feel resentful towards others, you easily get irritated, feel humiliated and 'red mist' comes down on you. Recognising these signs is a great way in helping you choose the best way to deal with anger when you feel it. Of course, in that present moment, emotions are heightened, and adrenaline is pumping so it can cloud your judgement. Just remember to not judge your anger, let it go and try to think positive.

Everyone has their own triggers for what makes them angry. Different situations may invoke different reactions from different individuals. But some common situations which may trigger anger are when someone feels threatened or attacked, powerless, being treated unfairly, or being disrespected in any way. Thinking I was being disrespected, was the primary cause of most of my anger. How you interpret a situation can depend on many factors in life; for example, upbringing, past experiences and the current state of your life. You find that a lot of people who are classed as having an 'anger problem' have outbursts from events that occurred in their life in the past, and some a very long time ago.

There are many ways one can cope with anger, when they feel it in the moment and manage it in general. As mentioned before anger can produce adrenaline through the body so before you recognise the emotion you're feeling you may pay attention to your heart rate increasing, quickened breathing, your body becoming tense, your jaw or fists clenching.[20] Recognising these signs gives you a chance to think about how you will react to the situation. You can buy yourself time to think before reacting to any situation by: counting to 10, removing yourself from the situation by going for a saunter, or you could talk to a trusted person who isn't part of the situation who can calm you down and understand what you are going through. I always used to talk to my mom about such situations and she was a great help. There are some techniques you can employ to manage your feelings: you can breathe slowly, taking deep breaths each time, you breathe, relax your body, mindfulness techniques, exercise is a great way to distract yourself and not only is it beneficial for your health but it releases pent up tension you may feel. You can use up energy safely in other ways that invoke positive emotions like walking, reading, writing, listening to music, etc as these things can be cathartic, or you can try and do things to distract yourself mentally or physically like drawing, fixing something around the house or maybe watching your favourite television show.

---

20 Mind, 'Signs That You're Feeling Angry', 2021 <https://www.mind.org.uk/information-support/types-of-mental-health-problems/anger/anger-symptoms/> [accessed 24 August 2021].

It's important to learn what triggers your anger to find the best way to cope with it when it happens. You could perhaps keep a diary to highlight what it was that made you feel angry, how you behaved, how you felt, what the circumstances were and how you felt afterwards. After a while, you may see patterns emerge and thus it would be easier to identify the problem you have and how best to manage it. It's important to examine your thought patterns. When you feel angry or upset you may find yourself saying things like this is all their fault, they never listen, this always happens to me and other people should act differently and behave better. Replacing these words with 'sometimes' or 'could' when thinking about a situation can help you to break away from the negative thought patterns. Developing your communication skills is also a must here. Be more assertive and think through what it is you are saying and doing when you have an episode. It can make communication easier and hence resolve any conflicts you may have; it can stop tense situations from getting out of hand and it can benefit your self-esteem. I learned that being a good communicator has helped me immensely in understanding my anger better and talking my way out of tense situations. Everything can be resolved with words. It's important to remember to be impeccable with your word, say what you want. Repeat this as often as you can.

To become more assertive, you can try to think about the outcome you want to achieve; be specific, for example, you could try and say "I feel angry because…." Using the phrase 'I feel' avoids blaming anyone and thus feeling angry with them or feeling attacked by them. You can listen to others' responses and finally be prepared for anything; don't expect things to go right, or your way. My mom always said you can't control other people in this world, you can only control yourself. Yes, you can predict people's behaviour, but what if you get it wrong? It's vital that you take a deep look at your lifestyle as this can cause you to feel angry more easily. Avoid drugs and alcohol as they affect your emotions and actions and can be a factor in violence. Being more active helps, too; for example, going for long walks, travelling, taking up new hobbies or activities as it releases any tension you are holding on to, and benefits your self-esteem. Getting good sleep is another point; think about when you have a bad night's sleep, how cranky and irritable it makes you. If you have insomnia, then this is something you could consult your doctor about. Sleep deprivation can be a contributing factor to anger. Also, maybe consider changing your diet. Food is key I will cover how food can affect your mental health later on in the book. Learn to deal with pressure and how to stay calm under pressure, or when things change. One thing that's common in people with mental health problems is that we like routine and predictability; when things change, we often find ourselves panicking and doing things out of character as we feel we lose control. Finally, develop emotional resilience as this makes us feel like we can handle our difficult emotions a lot easier.

There are various treatments for anger problems, namely talking therapy or counselling, anger management programmes and help for abusive and violent behaviour. Talking therapies involve talking about your problems with a trained professional (such as a counsellor or psychotherapist) who will explore your anger and find ways to cope with it. Counselling is usually a short-term treatment and it involves you talking through a specific issue, for example, you have outbursts. Psychotherapy often lasts longer and tends to dive deep into past experiences to gain a comprehensive understanding of your anger, and the root cause of it. From this, you can learn why you exhibit anger the way you do and why certain situations make you angry. CBT is more of a short-term treatment and, as mentioned previously, it explores how your thoughts and feelings affect your behaviour.[21] If you need help it's important to speak to someone, perhaps your doctor, and they will best advise you on how to map a plan to manage the problem. I understand it can be hard to approach someone for the fear of being judged or misunderstood. I had that problem. I was suffering in silence for years before I sought help. It was advice from my parents that made me seek professional help. It's important to let people in and trust them. People are generally good and where they can help, they will. I remember feeling angry a lot when I thought someone was insulting me; it was just my immediate reaction but I learned to cope with this anger and manage it, evaluate it, record it and eventually, I became impervious to it, to an extent. So much so that things that I should have gotten angry about, I stopped getting angry about.

Anger management programmes are great as well. They can help you manage your anger and identify the patterns that cause it, and its effects. This can be done in a group setting or individually. Sometimes hearing other peoples' accounts of their anger can help make yours more lucid and understandable.

---

21 Jerry Wilde, *Treating Anger, Anxiety, and Depression in Children and Adolescents: A Cognitive-Behavioural Perspective* (Washington, DC: Accelerated Development, 1996).

If your anger means you are acting in an abusive or violent way it's important to get help. You may worry that seeking help may get you into trouble for what you have already done. But it's like in religion, you should come as you are; opening up and seeking help is the first step. No one will judge you because you have a problem and you are admitting to it. Depending on the country you are in there are different organisations you can contact to get help but it's important to start with your doctor. In the UK there's ADAPT which supports men over 18 to change abusive and violent behaviour, there's the Everyman Project in London which looks and helps perpetrators of domestic violence, the Domestic Violence Intervention Project which offers support to stop domestic abuse across London, the Phoenix Respect Programme is run by Gwent domestic abuse services for men who have been, or are at risk of, being abusive to their partners, the BRAVE Project is based in Bradford which is a confidential service comprising group-work, one-to-one counselling and telephone support for men to help change their abusive behaviour and many more.

Statistically, it tends to be men who are the perpetrators of domestic violence but sometimes men can also be the victims. We are all entitled to get help and no one should feel they can't be helped. It's important to open up and seek assistance as early as possible if you start noticing the signs mentioned above to prevent it from becoming a bigger problem. Talk to family and friends, ask for them to be mindful of your problem. After all, they are the closest people to you and if they are the victim, it's even more important that they can help you if you can't help yourself. It's not easy; anger takes over us and makes us do things we often regret but I'm hoping after reading this you will realise there's help out there for you and you are not alone.

Stress

We all experience stress in our lives. Life today is very demanding and fast-paced, and as a result, can lead to stress. There's no medical definition for stress but it can be managed by managing external influences and developing emotional resilience to it. Being under pressure is a normal part of life. It can help us take action, feel more energised and motivated and yield results. But if you start feeling overwhelmed by stress, these feelings can be unbearable for some. Stress can cause mental health problems; mental health problems can cause stress. Sometimes the symptoms of stress may be physical. You often feel tired, have headaches and an upset or turned stomach. Sleep and diet are often also affected by stress levels. When we feel stressed, our bodies also release hormones called cortisol and adrenaline. If you're often stressed then you are invariably producing high levels of these 'negative' hormones. We all experience stress differently depending on the situation we are in. Stress can affect us both physically and emotionally. Here is a list of ways you may feel when you are stressed: you often feel irritable, aggressive, impatient, over-burdened, you may feel anxious, nervous or worried, it may dampen your spirits and your ability to enjoy yourself, it can lead to depression, it can make you lose interest in life, you always have a sense of dread, you may worry about your health excessively, or feel lonely or neglected and misunderstood. In some cases, where people have severe stress, they can feel suicidal. Stress impedes your ability to make decisions; you may find it hard to stop worrying, you may start snapping at people, biting your nails, pick your skin, lose concentration easily, you may overindulge in food or eat a lot less, you may turn to drinking, smoking and alcohol usage, or feel restless like you can't sit still (akathisia), and you may also feel highly emotional and tearful. As I mentioned stress can also show clear physical symptoms. I know with my mental health problems I constantly exhibited certain symptoms which are noticeable when we are stressed. I became stressed about my mental health condition. My muscles would be tense, I perpetually felt tired, had chest pains regularly, started smoking, I often had indigestion and diarrhoea, I felt nauseous a lot, my blood pressure sky-rocketed, I would always clench my jaw and grind my teeth, my eyesight felt blurry and I would often feel anxious and panicky.

Stress is caused by events in your life that involve feeling under pressure, facing big changes, worrying about something like the example of myself that I gave. Stress can be caused by not having control over a situation, feeling overwhelmed, being uncertain and not working. The list isn't exhaustive but generally speaking, these are the things that tend to cause the average person stress. You may ask the question of why you feel stressed. This can depend on several things. Typically, it's because of your perception of the situation which may be connected to a past experience or your self-esteem, and your thought processes, for example. Your emotional resilience is another reason you may feel stressed. If you are not receiving enough support that can also stress you out and if you are not experienced at dealing with a particular type of pressure, this can also exacerbate your stress.

Several situations can cause stress for an individual. It can be personal reasons, friends and family, money, living situations or work. Some personal reasons could be, for instance, being ill or injured, being pregnant, suffering from the loss of a loved one or long-term health problems, organising a big and complicated event. Sometimes it's just everyday tasks such as travelling maybe to work, etc., or house chores that can lead to stress. Friends and family can be another factor. Marriage or getting married can cause stress – the thought of it and what it will entail; getting divorced or going through a break-up, the same. If you have a strained or difficult relationship with parents or friends or your children, this can also cause stress. Work is another stress-inducing facet; for example, if you lose your job, if you are unemployed for lengthy periods, if you retire, or exams and deadlines can also cause stress, troubled relationships with colleagues, starting a new job, the list goes on and on. There are many factors here that have an impact on your stress levels. Living conditions can also cause stress for example if you are indigent, or homeless, moving house and perhaps having issues with your neighbours, having a pest problem etc., We all know money, or the lack of it, is one of the biggest causes of stress in our world today. Debt and poverty are two major causes for concern and lead us to worry a lot and thus become stressed. Just remember to focus on abundance of wealth, not your debt, or getting out of debt, or not being able to afford because you attract more of what you think about. What we think about and thank about we bring about.

Sometimes even happy events can bring on stress; for example, expecting a new baby or getting married, starting a new job, etc. This is usually because it's a 'change' and this can make you worry or overthink which is stress-inducing. Plus, the pressure it may put on you can also be very stressful for most of us.

Like most afflictions in life, stress can be managed if the right steps are taken. Considering the contributing factors to your stress can be useful by reflecting on events and feelings you have on your own, or with someone you trust. This can help break down the barriers which are worsening your stress levels. Remember when we get stressed, we feel we are having the correct feeling and it's justified. One has to learn to not judge your own thoughts and just let them go. The more we judge them the more it becomes an issue. It may also be useful to consider issues that come up regularly and that you don't have to worry about them, they are normal and a part of life. It's not worth getting stressed over one-off situations, these moments will pass always remember that nothing lasts forever. Ongoing stressful events can of course lead to long-lasting stress and reoccurring stress but it's important to reflect on this and try and manage it. Finding a balance is key.

It's important to organise and manage your time, too. Prioritising the important to do things first. Making a list can help. Maybe while doing that you can also create timetables and post-it notes which can help you to deal with that. I found this very useful in my journey. It's important to also set smaller, more achievable goals. Work towards your big goal by creating smaller ones along the way. This way you won't feel overwhelmed. Varying your activities is also a good thing. Doing the same repetitive thing can lead to boredom and stress and as a result, depression. Try not to do too much at once. Take regular breaks and getaways. This refreshes the mind and recharges your battery. It's important to not be afraid to ask for help, whether it's a local support group, family, friends or your doctor. There's support out there and people generally are good and will want to help you. It's a good thing to also address some of the issues you are facing; for example, if it's at work you can consider discrimination at work policies, or if it's finances you can work on your financial education or health. There are plenty of courses you can sign up for these days and they are very useful. You must adapt to changes that can be unsettling and cause stress. Making lifestyle changes is also key i.e., through exercise, eating and being more active. Taking a break from your life is also crucial if you want to stay relatively stress-free.

There are a lot of treatments to help alleviate stress. There's medication, ecotherapy and other therapies that may help. I recommend CBT. Yoga and meditation are also treatments to consider. They reduce stress drastically and centre your thoughts, calm you down and in a sense, slow down your responses to things in a measured and positive way. Just because someone is talking to you at a thousand miles an hour doesn't mean you have to mirror them; you are in control and can slow things down and this will also reduce stress. Acupuncture is also great as it can pinpoint the points in your body that are causing stress. Aromatherapy and deep massages can also help to relax you and alleviate stress.

Eating problems

An eating problem is any relationship with food that you find difficult. Anyone can experience an eating disorder or problem. This is regardless of age, weight, gender or background. An eating disorder differs from an eating problem as an eating disorder is a medical diagnosis. This diagnosis is based on your eating patterns and includes medical tests on your weight, blood and body mass index (BMI). On the other hand, an eating problem is simply a relationship with food that you find difficult. Typically eating too much or too little, or just how you view food in general.

Eating problems go further than just food. They can cause difficult and painful feelings which can be hard to express, face and resolve. Eating problems can affect you in many ways; for example, you may feel depressed and anxious, tired most of the time, ashamed or guilty and also feel scared of other people finding out.[22] If you do have an eating problem you may find that it's hard to concentrate on your work, studies and your hobbies. You may suddenly lack spontaneity, you may develop short or long-term physical problems, you may find that you are bullied about food and eating, your appearance may suddenly change, you avoid social events and you may even drop out of college or school, quit your job or stop doing the things you enjoy. When it comes to friends and family you may become distant from them and disengaged, they may focus on the effects eating problems can have on your body, they may not

---

22 Mind, 'What Is an Eating Problem?', 2021 <https://www.mind.org.uk/information-support/types-of-mental-health-problems/eating-problems/about-eating-problems/> [accessed 24 August 2021].

understand how complicated the situation you have is, they only think you have a problem if your body looks different to how they think it should be. You will know when it's becoming a problem if it affects your everyday life and your ability to lead a normal life without it getting in the way. Look out for these signs and if it is an issue seek help immediately.

Many people with eating problems also have other mental health problems. Some common ones are depression, anxiety, OCD, phobias of certain foods, self-esteem issues and body image issues, self-harming and BDD. Suicidal thoughts are also common when you have a severe eating problem. You may feel death is the only way to escape. If that's the case and you have suicidal thoughts you must reach out and seek help.

Diagnosing an eating disorder can be difficult. Food is one of the many mediums through which our emotions and distress can be expressed. Getting a formal diagnosis can be complicated. If your problems with eating aren't easy for your doctor to categorise you may not get a diagnosis. You may have a difficult relationship with food which affects your mental health but doesn't fit into any current diagnoses. You may also be experiencing more than one disorder or symptoms from multiple disorders.

BMI is always one of the factors they take into account at your doctor's surgery when diagnosing you, but it shouldn't be the only one.

Bulimia is made up of bingeing and purging. Bingeing is eating large amounts of food in one go and purging is acting to get rid of food you have eaten after bingeing; you may feel guilty about what you have eaten. If you experience bulimia, you will most likely feel shame or guilt that you are overweight, depressed and anxious, very low and sad, be fickle, numb, stuck in a cycle of feeling out of control and trying to regain it; you can also feel very lonely. Bulimia can lead to you eating lots of food, bingeing on food that is bad for you, eating in secret, craving only specific types of foods, making yourself sick after eating food so as not to gain weight and becoming obsessive about your body image. Bulimia affects your body, too; you can either stay the same weight or experience frequent weight changes, be dehydrated which can cause bad skin, get irregular periods or none at all, it can harm your teeth and give you a sore throat from stomach acid, and by making yourself sick, it can also lead to you developing IBS, a stretched colon, constipation or even heart disease if you use laxatives.

Anorexia means you are not eating enough food. It's often related to low self-esteem, negative self-image and feelings of intense distress.[23] When you experience anorexia you might be unable to think about anything other than food, you may feel like you need to be perfect or are never good enough, have a need for control that you relinquish by eating, that you feel scared or are afraid of putting on any weight even if it's a little, losing weight isn't enough, like you want to disappear, get tired and not interested in the things you normally would be, anxious and panicky and finally, you may also feel depressed and suicidal. When you are anorexic you might reduce food intake, spend a lot of time on the scales and counting calories, hide food secretly or throw it away, avoid 'dangerous'

---

23 Mind, 'Types of Eating Disorders', 2021 <https://www.mind.org.uk/information-support/types-of-mental-health-problems/eating-problems/types-of-eating-disorders/> [accessed 24 August 2021].

foods like those with high amounts of calories or fat, use drugs that reduce your appetite or speed up digestion, spend most of your time thinking about losing weight, exercise a lot and you may also have very strict and structured eating times. Try to consider this, if you completely stopped eating, within the first six hours nothing would happen. Your body will turn to glycogen and convert it back to glucose and use it up for energy. After three days your body will use up fat for energy as it doesn't have enough carbohydrates to do just that, this is called ketosis. You don't have to be starving to be in a ketosis stage. It can also be for people on low carb diets or for example athletes who have just run a marathon as all the glucose has been used up. After three days, not only will you feel weak but your brain will begin to break down protein. Proteins release amino acids which can be converted into glucose. But this means that your body is cannibalising itself because most of muscle is made up of water, creatine and protein and therefore the muscles will start to shrink at this point. You will lose your libido too. For women, your menstrual cycle may stop to conserve energy. Bone density shrinks too. After one to two weeks, your immune system becomes very weak, as there are no vitamins and minerals so this is likely to lead to disease. Otherwise, your body will continue to use all sources of energy. Cardiac arrhythmia is a very common cause of those who die from anorexia. Starvation can cause death from up to three weeks to 70 days as documented in the Irish hunger strike in 1981. Survival all depends on how much water you have and how much fat your body has. Not to be morbid, but it's important you consider this if you choose to not eat or choose to not eat enough. You are putting yourself at risk.

Binge eating disorder means you are unable to stop eating even when you want to. It's like an addiction. You might rely on food to determine your mood. It's sometimes described as compulsive eating. When you experience a binge eating disorder you might feel out of control, as if you can't stop eating, ashamed of how much you actually eat, lonely and empty, very low, even worthless, unhappy about your body, stressed and anxious, too. When you experience a binge eating disorder you are likely to eat large amounts of food all at once, eat unhealthy foods, eat for comfort or when stressed, eat until you feel uncomfortably full or even nauseous and hide how much you eat. When you binge eat you put on weight a lot, feel sick often, have shortness of breath, develop health problems like IBS and acid reflux, develop issues linked to being overweight like type 2 diabetes, hypertension, joint and muscle pain.

If you get an 'Other Specified Feeding and Eating Disorders' (OSFED) it means you don't meet all the criteria for anorexia, bulimia and binge eating disorder. OFSED was previously known as an 'Eating Disorder Not Otherwise Specified (EDNOS).

Rumination Disorder is when you regularly regurgitate your food; you might re-chew, re-swallow or spit out the food you regurgitate.

PICA is when you eat things that aren't food that have no nutritional value; for example, chalk, metal and paint which is very damaging to your body.

Avoidant/Restrictive Food Intake Disorder (ARFID) is when you get a strong need to avoid all foods. This could be because of the smell, taste or texture. ARFID isn't linked to body image, more the process of eating itself.

Eating problems can be caused by many factors, namely having difficult life experiences, family issues maybe when you are young, or even when you are grown-up arguments and tension in your family can lead you to eat for comfort or as an escape; there's social pressure too, physical and mental health problems, medications you may be taking, genetic factors and triggers that make you eat more.

There are many ways in which you can recover from an eating problem and ways you can care for yourself. It's important to learn to not get affected by other peoples' comments about your weight or eating habits. Learn to cope with gaining weight. For example, during the 2020 covid-19 pandemic a lot of people were housebound which led to them eating a lot more than usual and burning fewer calories; being okay and understanding it was a difficult time can help you mentally accept and cope with an eating problem. It's important to talk to people you can confide in and that you trust, so they can support you adequately and understand your needs. It's also good to join peer support groups to share your experiences with people in similar situations and come together to find a way to manage it. Change unhealthy routines and exercise more. Be careful online; nowadays there are what we call 'keyboard warriors' who say heinous things online. This can affect you if you are already very conscious of your body. Maybe staying off social media is a good option here. Eat well, and look after yourself this is the best way you can help yourself through mindfulness, relaxation and working on your mental wellbeing.

Treating eating problems is crucial if you want to get better. It's important to talk to your doctor at the earliest opportunity. They can refer you to a specialist service and start you on your road to recovery. I know it can be scary and you may feel vulnerable but it's the only way to get the right help that you need. Online self-help programmes are another great way to get the ball rolling.[24] You can do this once you have officially been diagnosed with bulimia, binge eating disorder or if the symptoms of your eating problem are similar to those two. Similar to some other mental health problems you may be offered talking treatments for eating problems. There's CBT for anorexia, bulimia and binge eating disorder. There are no specific drugs for eating disorders but you may be prescribed medication such as antidepressants for underlying factors such as depression and anxiety. For best results, it's important that you take medication alongside your talking therapies. You could be hospitalised in more serious cases but this is something that your doctor would advise you on once you consult them. Once in the hospital, you can get help from doctors, dieticians, psychotherapists, social workers, occupational therapists, etc. Treatment can include talking therapies, medication refeeding which brings your food level back to a point that is healthy for you, and finally, you can work in groups with others experiencing eating problems, too. Your weight and general health will be monitored whilst you are there. They will also offer you guidance on buying, preparing and serving food, tips on how to cope with stress and anxiety, how to be more assertive and how to manage anger and frustration.

To summarise, eating is a big part of our daily lives – without food, we cannot survive. Food is our source of energy and it's a

---

24 Mind, 'Treatment and Support for Eating Problems', 2021 <https://www.mind.org.uk/information-support/types-of-mental-health-problems/eating-problems/treatment-support/> [accessed 24 August 2021].

very pertinent part of our existence. If you start to notice any of the mentioned symptoms whilst eating, or if your views on food gradually begin to change it's important to monitor this and if it gets out of hand it's important that you consult your doctor to seek medical advice before it becomes a more severe and potentially life-threatening problem.

Hoarding

Hoarding is acquiring and saving a lot of things irrespective of their value. When you are a hoarder, you are most likely to feel better when you get more items. You may feel very upset or anxious at the thought of losing your things and you also may find it hard to decide what to keep and what to get rid of. If you hoard you may feel you need things for the future, you may feel you cannot cope with your feelings if you lose your things, you have to dispose of things perfectly or not at all, your belongings make you happy and keep you safe, you find that your belongings are unique and special to you. Some relate hoarding to OCD but they are not the same. Hoarding can also be caused by other mental health problems such as dementia and a brain injury.

Hoarding may affect you in your everyday life in many ways; for example, you may buy the same things more than once because you can't find them, you may avoid letting people into your home which could mean if things need fixing, they don't get done and this, too, can cause you problems. You may find it hard to look after your physical health, for example, if you can't access your bathroom, or you may find it hard to eat healthy food or even gain entry to cook healthy food in the kitchen, certain parts of your home may become inaccessible, you may be unable to quickly vacate your home in the event of an emergency, you may distance yourself from people and you could feel ashamed and lonely which could affect your self-esteem.

There are many symptoms of hoarding. You may be diagnosed as a hoarder if you find it difficult to discard or part with possessions or if you are unable to use parts of your home because of the clutter everywhere. You may also be diagnosed if you are experiencing distress due to hoarding or it inhibits your ability to live a normal healthy life. Not all the symptoms are the same but this can give you an idea of what to look out for. Hoarding is different from collecting in that people who collect vinyl records, stamps, books or sports memorabilia, for example, choose them carefully and display them in an ordered way; hoarding is different. There's no order to it and it's more compulsive.[25]

People who hoard tend to acquire and keep items like clothing and shoes, drawings and photographs, toys, books, magazines and leaflets, post – both opened and unopened – boxes and food. Hoarding isn't limited to these items but these are some common ones. It's common to hoard these items in your home but some people also hoard them in their cars, garages and storage units. Things that aren't physical objects such as emails or Facebook messages, etc can also be hoarded online. Hoarding can also be extended to animals.

---

25 Mind, 'Symptoms of Hoarding', 2021 <https://www.mind.org.uk/information-support/types-of-mental-health-problems/hoarding/symptoms/> [accessed 24 August 2021].

CHAPTER 5: UNDERSTANDING THE DIFFERENT TYPES OF MENTAL HEALTH DISORDERS

For example, if you keep more animals than you can adequately look after i.e., providing food, shelter, toilet facilities and vet care this can also be identified as a form of hoarding behaviour.

No one knows exactly what causes hoarding. There are many different views and opinions on its causes. Difficult experiences and feelings can sometimes be linked to the cause of hoarding. Some people say hoarding helps them cope with other mental health problems, or distracts them from that anxious feeling. Being a perfectionist can also lead to hoarding. You see people who are perfectionists hoard because they are worried about making mistakes; they find it hard to be decisive, plan ahead or do tasks. This leaves them feeling vulnerable and it's a reason why they may turn to hoarding to fill that void. Childhood experiences of losing or not having possessions is another common cause of hoarding. This could include experiences like money worries and living in poverty, having belongings taken or thrown away and being deprived or neglected. Trauma and loss can also be linked to hoarding as can being a victim of abuse or attack, or if you have had a bad break-up, became ill, are feeling lonely or have come close to death. It's common for people who hoard to have a parent or sibling who also hoards. In the same sentence, genetics can make you susceptible to hoarding. Shared environments can also be a factor, you may have picked up the habits of a parent or sibling and taken on their hoarding ways later in life as a result. If you have a partner who hoards and you live in clutter this can also lead you to become a hoarder yourself. Other mental health problems such as depression, anxiety, OCD, bipolar disorder, psychosis, schizophrenia and personality disorder can also cause you to start hoarding.

If you are a hoarder or notice the signs of having that problem there are ways in which you can help yourself. You could talk to someone by seeking help from your doctor or online and find out ways in which you can stop hoarding and also understand why you do it. Peer support is a great way to get help; if you can share common stories with other sufferers this may put things into perspective for you. Keeping a diary and noting down all the times you feel down or stressed and end up hoarding can be a great way to improve your situation. You can spot patterns of behaviour and triggers and thus change them. Finding other activities to participate in is a great alternative. Finding new ways to relax, like taking walks, watching TV, writing, and exercising can be great to distract yourself from hoarding. Getting enough sleep and eating well can also help. Maybe consulting your local fire service for them to conduct a safety check could help as they are more than likely going to have to clear the clutter and make you feel safer and understand the risks of hoarding. This fear can help you change.

Using clutter image rating is a great way to assess whether or not your problem is severe or not and if it requires action. Talking therapies, especially CBT, is great for dealing with hoarding. It focuses on how your thoughts, beliefs and attitudes affect your feelings and behaviour;[26] so for example, if you have a childhood experience that makes you feel lonely and makes you hoard you can look into this. Your therapist might consider your beliefs on why you need to keep things, make you understand why it's so hard for you to

---

26 David F. Tolin and others, *CBT for Hoarding Disorder: A Group Therapy Program Therapist's Guide* (Chichester, UK; Hoboken, NJ: John Wiley & Sons, 2017).

get rid of things and help you learn the skills you need to help you cope with the difficult feelings you may have. Some therapists will even visit you in your home to gain a better understanding of your unique situation so that they can make an informed decision about the specific help you need, so this is something to also consider. There isn't specific medication for hoarding; however, certain medications like antidepressants which are used for anxiety, for example, can also be taken to help with your hoarding. Like any other mental health condition, hoarding is unique and can make you feel very isolated and trapped. It's important to seek help when you notice the signs and have a positive attitude about your situation. It's not your fault and you didn't always hoard so you can change that. It's simply a matter of understanding why you hoard to be able to stop. It may seem difficult at first to break the habit as you may not know where to start but talking to your doctor and seeking help online is key. I have never had an issue with hoarding but I can understand how some may be affected by it. It's simply something in the brain that has been distorted and can be fixed with the right actions.

Obsessive-compulsive disorder (OCD)

Obsessive-compulsive disorder has two main parts: obsessions and compulsions. Obsessions are unwelcome thoughts, images, urges, worries or doubts that constantly and repeatedly appear in your mind. They make you feel very anxious. Compulsions are repetitive activities that you do to reduce the anxiety caused by the obsession.[27] For example, repeatedly checking a window or door is locked, repeating a specific phrase in your head or checking how your body feels. You might find that sometimes both are manageable and at other times it can make your life very difficult. They are more likely to be severe if you are dealing with other difficulties in life such as finances, health, work or relationships. So, it's important to keep on top of these things.

Living with OCD is challenging. Many people live with obsessions like leaving the gas on or making sure the door is locked and compulsions like avoiding cracks on the pavement or never sitting at the front of a plane; these don't interfere with your daily life generally speaking. When you have OCD it's likely to affect your relationships. You will feel ashamed, lonely or feel anxious and it will disrupt your daily life. You are likely to avoid situations that trigger your OCD, so for example going to work, you may avoid doing that or using public transport, etc.[28]

There are several related disorders to OCD. They are similar to it in that they cause repetitive thoughts, behaviours and urges. There's perinatal OCD when you are pregnant, and Body Dysmorphic Disorder (BDD) which involves obsessive worrying about one or more flaws in your physical appearance and developing compulsive routines to deal with the things you worry about concerning the

---

[27] W. K Goodman, Matthew V Rudorfer, and Jack D Maser, *Obsessive-Compulsive Disorder: Contemporary Issues in Treatment*, 2016 p.10-27

[28] Polly Waite and Tim Williams, *Obsessive Compulsive Disorder: Cognitive Behaviour Therapy with Children and Young People* (London; New York: Routledge, 2009)

way you look. There's also compulsive skin picking (CSP) which is as it sounds – A person constantly picks at specific parts of the skin to relieve stress and anxiety. Trichotillomania is a compulsive urge to pull your hair. There's also hoarding which I covered before, and finally Obsessive-compulsive personality disorder.

Some of the symptoms of OCD are easy to spot. Obsessions are persistent thoughts, pictures, urges or doubts that emerge in your mind over and over again. They interrupt your thoughts against your control and can be frightening and disturbing. They will most likely make you feel anxious and uncomfortable. You may also feel unable to share such thoughts with others, you think there is something wrong with you but trust me that's not the case – you are perfectly normal and this can be rectified with the right treatment. Some examples of obsessions are fear of causing harm or failing to prevent it. So, for example, worrying about the harm you have already caused someone like hitting them with your car or worrying about the harm you are going to cause someone like pushing them in front of a moving train. Another example of an obsession is having intrusive thoughts, images and impulses. You may picture yourself doing something violent or abusive and as a result, these thoughts may make you start to believe that you are a dangerous person. Another example is having religious or blasphemous thoughts that go against your religious beliefs. There's also relationship intrusive thoughts that relate to doubting the strength of your partner's feelings for you, or whether the relationship is right for you, or you can have sexual intrusive thoughts like worrying that you are a paedophile or rapist, for example. Fear of contamination is another example of an obsession. You may worry that dirt or germs are everywhere and that you have been contaminated by them, or even worry that you might get a disease because of this – sort of like a hypochondriac constantly worries about their health or wellbeing. Then there's mental contamination where you experience feelings of dirtiness from someone who has harmed you in some way. There's also what they call symmetry: this is the order of things whether they are clean, organised, etc., and you may have a fear that something bad will happen if everything isn't right and perfect. The 'groinal response' is a known phenomenon whereby the individual is constantly checking their genitals due to intrusive sexual thoughts. The attention and anxiety may increase blood flow and physical arousal which can make you feel aroused by intrusive thoughts, when in fact the exact opposite is true. There are many different examples of obsessions people may be afflicted by. It's important to seek help if you notice any of these in yourself.

Compulsions, are repetitive activities you may feel you have to do. Simply put, a compulsion aims to try and deal with the distress caused by obsessive thoughts. You may have to continue with the compulsion until the anxiety dissipates. Compulsions are typically physical actions, mental rituals referred to as 'Pure O'[29] which stands for purely obsessional, or they involve a number (like completing a compulsion a specific number of times before you are satisfied). Some examples of compulsions are rituals, so, for example, washing your hands or things around you a lot, touching things in a particular order or at specific times and arranging objects in a

---

[29] Mind, 'Symptoms of OCD', 2021 <https://www.mind.org.uk/information-support/types-of-mental-health-problems/obsessive-compulsive-disorder-ocd/symptoms-of-ocd/> [accessed 24 August 2021].

CHAPTER 5: UNDERSTANDING THE DIFFERENT TYPES OF MENTAL HEALTH DISORDERS

particular way. Checking is another type of compulsion. Some may check doors and windows constantly to make sure they are locked, checking your clothes for contamination, checking your memory to make sure intrusive thoughts didn't occur, checking your route to work constantly to make sure you didn't cause a crash. There are correcting thoughts; for example, repeating a word, name or phrase in your head or as a soliloquy, counting to a certain number and replacing an intrusive thought with a different image. Some people also need reassurance so they consistently ask others to tell them that everything is okay.

There are also internal compulsions like checking how you feel, checking your bodily sensations, checking how you feel about a thought, repeating numbers in your head or checking if you still have a thought. A lot of people with OCD avoid doing things that trigger their compulsions or obsessions. So, for example, if you are worried that you will stab someone you will avoid going into a kitchen because you know there are knives in there.

There are three main causes of OCD that have been identified by researchers: personal experience, personality and biological factors.[30] Personal experience can be attributed to childhood experiences like bullying, neglect or trauma; if your parents had similar anxieties, this then could have been adopted by you and emulated. Ongoing anxiety and stress and pregnancy or giving birth can also trigger perinatal OCD. Some research suggests that people with certain personality types are more predisposed to OCD. An example is if

---

30 Mind, 'Causes of OCD', 2021 <https://www.mind.org.uk/information-support/types-of-mental-health-problems/obsessive-compulsive-disorder-ocd/causes-of-ocd/> [accessed 24 August 2021].

you are neat, meticulous and methodical with a high standard you may develop OCD. Some biological theories suggest that a lack of the brain chemical serotonin may play a role in OCD. Studies have also looked at genetic factors and how different parts of the brain might be involved in causing OCD but there is yet to be found any conclusive evidence of this.

Like any other type of mental health problem, there are ways you can manage it yourself. If you find that it's taking over your life and interfering with your daily activities you can try to improve your wellbeing. Different things work for different people and it's important to move at a pace that suits you and your situation. If something you try isn't working for you now you can stop it, and maybe try another option or come back to it later. You can try self-help resources that are available to you. Build your support network.[31] It's important to do this to share your condition with others as this might give you a better idea of what you can do to improve your condition and gain a better understanding of it. It's important to talk to someone you trust and to speak to your doctor. This may be hard but it's a good idea to confide in someone you trust or a professional to help you through your problem. It's important to let go and to manage your stress. Try a relaxation technique and try mindfulness as this reduces stress and anxiety greatly. Looking after your physical health is another very important aspect of self-care. It's vital that you get good sleep, consume a healthier diet and try incorporating physical activity into your routine, for example,

---

31 Mind, 'Treatment for OCD', 2021 <https://www.mind.org.uk/information-support/types-of-mental-health-problems/obsessive-compulsive-disorder-ocd/treatment-for-ocd/> [accessed 24 August 2021].

exercise and taking walks, etc. These improve your mood and can motivate you as well. CBT, as I mentioned earlier, focuses on how your thoughts, beliefs and attitudes affect your feelings and behaviour. Exposure and response prevention (ERP) is specifically designed for OCD. It encourages you to confront your obsessions and resist the urge to carry out compulsions that effectively exacerbate the problem, not solve it. During ERP your therapist will deliberately put you in a situation that would usually make you feel anxious. Instead of doing your usual compulsion to deal with it, you will be encouraged to try and tolerate the anxiety. I will go into this in greater detail later on in the book. ERP helps you to recognise that uncomfortable feelings will eventually go away even if you don't perform a compulsion. There's also cognitive therapy which focuses on identifying and altering negative thoughts about yourself. This helps you to change unhelpful responses and behaviours. As far as medication goes SSRIs are the best; they can be taken to alleviate symptoms of OCD. Clomipramine is a tricyclic antidepressant that you could be offered if the SSRI doesn't work. If your OCD gets progressively worse you may be referred to a specialist OCD service. But speak to your doctor – this is the first step. Stay positive and keep putting the tips and advice you receive into practice. It's gradual like a lot of things, but eventually, you will get better. I recommend looking at changing your lifestyle and physical health, also trying mindfulness and meditation as this can help you to stay calm and be more relaxed, especially about the way you react to situations which is ultimately what causes OCD in the first place.

Paranoia

Paranoia is feeling, or even thinking, that you are being threatened in some way, even if there is no evidence or hardly any evidence that you are. One can also describe paranoid thoughts as delusions.[32] There are many different types of threats that you might be scared and worried about. When you are paranoid, you may also get exaggerated suspicions.

Some common examples of paranoid thoughts are where you may think that you are being talked about and scrutinized by people, you may think that other people are trying to make you look bad or exclude you, you may also believe that you are at risk of being physically harmed or even killed, and you may feel that people are deliberately trying to upset you or are trying to take your personal belongings, you may believe that your thoughts and actions are being interfered with by others or that you are being controlled, or that the government is after you. These thoughts may be constant or they may be sporadic when you are in a stressful or upsetting situation. Most of the time people who suffer from paranoia have thoughts about threats or harm to themselves, but occasionally they have the same paranoid thoughts about doing that to other people. They say people are just an extension of our thoughts. Paranoid thoughts are simply your perception of what other people will think and do.

People perceive risks in different ways and believe different things in terms of there being good and evidence for suspicious

---

32 Mind, 'What Is Paranoia?', 2021 <https://www.mind.org.uk/information-support/types-of-mental-health-problems/paranoia/about-paranoia/> [accessed 24 August 2021].

thoughts. Suspicious thoughts are more likely to be paranoid if no one else shares this thought with you, there's no clear evidence for the suspicious thought, there is evidence to the contrary of the suspicious thought, your suspicious thought persists even after reassurance from other people, or your suspicious thoughts are based on feelings and ambiguous events. Not all suspicious thoughts are paranoid, however. Paranoia, like anxiety, is your body's way of protecting you and signalling to you that something is wrong. Justified suspicions are suspicions that you have evidence for. An example is if a lot of people's homes have been burgled on your street – it's not paranoid to think the same will happen to you. Justified suspicions keep you safe.

Paranoia is a symptom of some mental health problems but not a diagnosis in itself. It can be anything from mild to severe, and these experiences can be quite different for everybody else's. It all depends on how much you believe the thoughts, how much you think about the thoughts, how much the paranoid thoughts upset you and if the paranoid thoughts interfere with your everyday life. It's normal for many people to experience mild paranoia at some point in their lives. They say in fact, that one in three people will, at some point. This type of paranoia is called non-clinical paranoia. But this can change over time. At the far end of the spectrum is very severe paranoia which is also called clinical paranoia, or persecutory delusions. If this is the case you are more likely to need treatment. Paranoia can be a symptom of paranoid schizophrenia, delusional disorder and paranoid personality disorder. You may believe certain things as a result of your paranoid thoughts which can feel helpful when you have an episode but in the long run, they exacerbate it. These are typically safety behaviours: isolation, worry and sadness. paranoia and stigma. I know I used to isolate myself a lot to avoid situations where people could potentially insult me but this affected me adversely as I was imprisoning myself and hiding from the world. Remember that when you are alone the only company you have is your own thoughts. This can be a negative thing as you may start to isolate yourself even more from the outside world. Safety behaviours are the things you do to keep yourself safe; for example, avoiding certain people or places, which is something I did a lot. As a result, you stay indoors a lot and avoid people as much as you can. If you think someone is threatening you or wants to inflict harm upon you, you may behave suspiciously or aggressively towards them. You may push them away or decide you are better off without them. But the catch is that people may also start treating you differently and avoid you, too. It may become harder to keep friends and make new ones, which can erroneously make you feel that your beliefs were justified in the first place. If you have paranoia, you are likely to feel alone. You may feel as if no one understands you. I know I did, and still do at times. It can be difficult when other people don't believe what feels very real to you, as I did. Staying indoors and being anti-social ends up making you feel even more isolated. It's important to talk to someone you trust and to consult your doctor if you notice any of these types of thoughts and suspicions happening more regularly.

You might feel anxious and worried about your paranoid thoughts, or feel low and sad about what they mean and how they affect your life. Low mood and anxiety make you susceptible to paranoid thoughts.

CHAPTER 5: UNDERSTANDING THE DIFFERENT TYPES OF MENTAL HEALTH DISORDERS

There are a lot of misconceptions about what it means to be paranoid. It's vital to remember that you are not alone and that you don't have to put up with people treating you badly. It's important to talk to other people; share your experiences with others to gain a better understanding of the subject as a whole, take action with your mind and share this book with other people so they have a better understanding of what it means to have paranoia.

Exactly what causes paranoia is not known. There are many different theories on its causes. There are, however, general risk factors involved. Some of the things that can make paranoid thoughts more likely are having confusing experiences or feelings that you cannot explain. But it's also about the way you feel, because if you feel worried or anxious or have low self-esteem you will expect others to reject you. The way you think is also another thing that makes paranoia more likely in that you tend to come to conclusions quickly and it's hard to change your mind on your beliefs about certain matters.[33] Being isolated is another reason, and also if you have experienced trauma in the past. It's clear to see that many mental health problems are associated with some form of a bad life experience or trauma. It's because the mind is so traumatized by an event, or events, that it does everything it can to avoid it happening again. So, it creates a fear-based mechanism to cope, and this tends to be another mental health problem.

Childhood experiences can cause paranoia; for example, it can lead you to believe that the world is unsafe and that you can't

---

33 Mind, 'Causes of Paranoia', 2021 <https://www.mind.org.uk/information-support/types-of-mental-health-problems/paranoia/causes-of-paranoia/> [accessed 24 August 2021].

trust anyone, which would make you suspicious of everything and everyone. These things can negatively impact your self-esteem. An example is being bullied at school or abused at home. This then can affect you as you become an adult if the core beliefs about it aren't tackled. Being bullied at work or discriminated against can also cause paranoia in the long run. Your external environment is another contributing factor. Research suggests that paranoid thoughts are more common if you live in an urban environment or community where you feel isolated from the people that are around you rather than feeling connected to them. Media is a big factor here as well. In today's world, all we hear on the news is bad news and this can negatively distort your perception of the outside world. Mental health is another factor that can cause paranoia. If you are dealing with anxiety, depression or even low self-esteem you may be more likely to experience paranoid thoughts because you are more on edge, worry a lot and are looking for things to vindicate your negative feelings and thoughts. As with me and my psychosis, many people experience paranoid delusions as a result of it. Paranoia is sometimes a symptom of some physical illnesses such as Huntington's disease, Parkinson's disease, strokes, Alzheimer's disease and other forms of dementia. Hearing loss is another thing that can cause paranoia in some people. If you cannot hear any more you have to learn to lip read and this can cause misinterpretations quite easily, especially if you already have low self-esteem, etc. A lack of sleep can cause negative feelings and hallucinations. Fears and concerns are more likely to develop late at night so it's important to get good sleep and not to take it for granted. Genetics are also said to be one of the main causes of paranoia. Granted it's the brain chemicals and imbalances that can cause it and that may be attributed to environmental factors and life experiences but having a family member who suffers from it may also leave you predisposed to this problem. Recreational drugs are another cause of paranoia. This I know is a subject of huge debate. I know for a fact… well I strongly believe… that when I stopped smoking cannabis in my late teens it wasn't long after that that I started experiencing paranoid delusions and psychosis. My therapist suggested there may have been a possible link as to why I contracted my mental health illness. Cocaine, cannabis, alcohol, ecstasy, LSD and amphetamines may trigger paranoia. This is particularly more likely if you are already feeling low, anxious or are experiencing other mental health problems. Experts have found that some steroids, insecticides, fuel and paint are said to be associated with paranoia… Drinking alcohol, smoking or taking drugs may also stop the medication from effectively treating your symptoms. The relationship between paranoia and anxiety is complicated. Both are to do with reacting to some type of perceived threat. Anxiety can be a cause of paranoia but paranoid thoughts can also make you anxious.

You must take action straight away if you start to notice that you are feeling more and more paranoid. You could keep a diary and note any paranoid thoughts you might have, dissecting why you feel the way you feel, why you are thinking those thoughts and how you can change your thoughts to benefit you.[34] Look for support around you, learn to relax; maybe trying meditation or yoga could help centre

---

34 Mind, 'Self-Care for Paranoia', 2021 <https://www.mind.org.uk/information-support/types-of-mental-health-problems/paranoia/helping-yourself/> [accessed 24 August 2021].

your thoughts. Look after yourself, eat well, exercise and get good sleep. One very important thing is also to challenge your paranoid thoughts. Ask yourself if there is any evidence for your suspicions that can't be questioned. Are your worries based on your feelings rather than definite evidence? Is it likely that you would be singled out by everyone? Is there any evidence against your beliefs? Have you talked to other people about your worries? What would your best friend say? Do you still feel suspicious, even though people around you have reassured you that everything is okay? You don't have to necessarily stick to this list but it can be used as a guide to start asking the right questions and expedite the process by which you get better.

Talking therapies can help you to better understand your affliction and how to cope with it, CBT is also a great tool and one of the most successful and commonly used treatments for paranoia and many other mental health problems; psychodynamic therapy, counselling and family therapy can also help here. Arts and creative therapies are also popular as they are cathartic. It allows you to express yourself and how you are feeling, in a therapeutic environment. This type of therapy can be helpful if you are having difficulty talking about your experiences. If you have a diagnosis of paranoid schizophrenia or delusional disorder, you are likely to be offered an antipsychotic drug to reduce the symptoms you are experiencing. Antipsychotics may reduce paranoid thoughts or make you feel less threatened by them. With my psychosis and paranoia, I was prescribed aripiprazole and it works by correcting your negative perceptions about the world. The delusions and hallucinations are corrected too, and it generally gives you a more positive filter as to how you perceive the world and people. The severity of your paranoia or psychosis will determine the strength of the dosage you receive. I am on 10mg and have been for a few years now. It takes time for antipsychotics to take effect so if you are prescribed it, be patient. You may experience side effects but it worked out for me in the end. It suppressed my paranoid delusions immensely. If you have anxiety or depression your GP may offer you antidepressants or minor tranquillizers which will help you to feel less worried about the thoughts and stop them from getting any worse.

Tardive dyskinesia

Tardive dyskinesia (TD) is a side effect of antipsychotic medication. It can sometimes cause your body and face to make sudden jerky or slow twisting movements.[35] Anyone taking antipsychotics drugs could develop TD. Tardive means delayed or appearing late. Dyskinesia means abnormal or unusual movements. When you have TD you may feel self-conscious about the movements it causes, feel upset that you can't control exactly what your body is doing, find it hard to know or predict when the symptoms will come.

The main sign of TD is making movements that you don't normally make and are totally out of your control. TD can cause jerky movements, some examples are lip-smacking, moving your mouth or jaw, tapping or moving your hands or feet, movements in

---

35 Mind, 'Signs of Tardive Dyskinesia (TD)', 2021 <https://www.mind.org.uk/information-support/types-of-mental-health-problems/tardive-dyskinesia-td/td-signs-symptoms/> [accessed 25 August 2021].

your hips, upper body movements or blinking the eyes a lot. Slow movements include writhing or squirming for example wiggling fingers or twisting the fingers, arms, legs, neck or tongue. Then there are muscle spasms which are also called tardive dystonia. This is where you have movements that cause your muscles to suddenly tighten, which could last a short while or for a longer period. For example, making grunting noises, struggling to breathe and changes to your posture. If you have had schizophrenia, you may have experienced unusual movements before taking any medication, including involuntary moving legs and arms, or being restless, which can make it hard to identify symptoms of TD. TD is an unwanted side effect of medication, most commonly antipsychotic drugs. These drugs are likely to be part of your course of treatment if you have psychosis, schizophrenia, bipolar disorder, severe depression or anxiety. Some other drugs used for treating physical conditions can also cause TD as a side effect. When I started taking aripiprazole, I got akathisia which is a feeling of restlessness, and feeling like you can't sit still. It isn't quite the same as TD but similar. I quickly overcame it. Remember when you do take antipsychotics you may experience side effects but it's important then to consider changing your dosage to make it more bearable.

Anyone taking antipsychotics drugs is at risk of developing TD. Everyone gets affected differently. The risks depend on how long you have been taking them; the longer you have been taking the drugs the greater the risk. The dose you are on can also determine if you get it or not. Research also shows that the risk might also be greater if you are aged over 50 or are of African descent. Taking older first-generation antipsychotics are particularly associated with TD.

The newer second-generation ones are said to be safer and said to cause fewer side effects. Stopping and starting antipsychotics can also increase the risk of TD so it's very important that you speak to your doctor before you come off them or up the dosage, etc. Other side effects which affect your movement can also be caused by taking first-generation antipsychotic drugs; for example, symptoms that mimic Parkinson's disease such as shaking, stiffness, restless legs and akathisia. You may get TD when you start to come off antipsychotics and, in this case, you may decide to stay on your medication. Sometimes withdrawal can cause involuntary muscle movements or movement disorders that are similar to TD but it often gets better with time.

You may be prescribed Clonazepam which is a benzodiazepine tranquillizer used in epilepsy. Or Tetrabenazine which is a drug used to treat movement disorders usually Huntington's disease. The most common side effect of this drug however is depression. Melatonin is a drug licenced for sleep problems. This is another drug you may be prescribed to deal with TD. Sometimes herbal medicines that you can acquire over the counter without prescription may help with TD. These include Vitamin E, Vitamin B5 and Ginkgo Biloba.

If you notice any of these symptoms it's important to speak to your doctor. before taking any new medications; it's also important to speak to your doctor first even if it's over the counter stuff.

You can help yourself if you have TD by looking after your physical health, focusing on your well-being, finding specialist support and building your support network. First and foremost, it's important to identify whether, in fact, you have it or not. Using the above determinants is a great starting point.

Seasonal affective disorder (SAD)

SAD is a type of depression during particular seasons or times of the year. If you have SAD, you will be particularly affected by the weather. For example, you may find that your mood drops when it's cold or very hot and you may also notice changes in your sleeping and eating patterns. If your feelings interfere with your day-to-day life then it may be a sign that you have depression. If it keeps coming back at the same time of the year it may be diagnosed as SAD. Some of the symptoms of SAD are a distinct lack of energy, difficulty concentrating, avoiding people, difficulty sleeping, feeling sad and low, changes in your appetite, being more prone to physical health problems, losing your libido, other symptoms of depression and in severe cases having suicidal thoughts. If you have another mental health problem you may find that things get worse when you are affected by SAD.

The exact causes of SAD are unclear. Depression in general can lead to SAD. There are some known causes of SAD; for example, the effects of light. When light hits the back of your eye, messages go to the part of your brain that controls sex drive, temperature, sleep mood and activity. Therefore, if there isn't enough light these functions slow down and gradually stop. Some people may need more light than others. That means that they are more likely to get it during colder months, so as you can imagine it affects people who generally live in colder countries, too. At the same time, some people find that bright light is hard to cope with. Each individual is different. Disrupting the body clock is another cause of SAD.[36] Our bodies set our body clocks by the hours of daylight. One theory is that if you experience SAD, this part of your brain is no longer working correctly and as a result, your body clock slows down which can lead to tiredness and depression. Researchers believe this is because your sleep pattern – aka the 'sleep phase' -starts at a different time which is often described as having a delayed sleep phase. SAD is said to be more common in countries where there is a greater change in weather and daylight hours during different seasons. For example, England and Wales. People who live near the equator for a portion of their lives and then move further away are more vulnerable to getting SAD.

High melatonin levels is another cause of SAD. When it gets dark your body produces a hormone called melatonin which helps you get ready for sleep. Some people with SAD produce much higher levels of melatonin in the winter periods (the same as hibernation in animals).

Weather and temperatures can also cause SAD. All of us have different experiences of particular seasons and different weather. If, for example, it's hot you may feel more uncomfortable than when it's cold and this can contribute to causing SAD. It is more commonly associated with colder winter weather but some people also find difficulties with this in hot weather. Researchers have discovered a link between higher temperatures and poor mental health.

There are many things you can try out to improve SAD. During winter you can apply practical day-to-day tips by making the most of

---

36 Mind, 'Causes'.

natural light like going for strolls, sitting in parks, etc, you can plan ahead for winter, too. There are also summer practical day-to-day tips which you could apply. You could drink plenty of water, look for ways to get shade so you aren't exposed to too much light, visit indoor places and plan ahead for the summer. Talk to someone you trust. Understanding from others and empathy can improve your situation by making you feel less isolated and alone. Keep a diary and record your symptoms to help you understand why it happens. Plan for more difficult times, try peer support, learn ways to relax e.g., meditation, manage stress levels, spend a lot of time in nature, too. Finally, looking after your physical health by exercising more, eating better and sleeping well. Avoiding alcohol and drugs can also help.

To get treatment the first step is to consult your doctor. Your doctor may refer you for counselling or other talking therapies. Antidepressants can help too, either on their own or combined with talking therapy. This will most likely be SSRIs. Light therapy has also been said to be very useful in overcoming this condition. Some people use a lightbox which is a device that gives off strong white or blue light. There's also a lamp or an alarm that simulates dawn, which is called light therapy. Light therapy may not be suitable for you if you are also taking St. John's wort, as this can make your skin more sensitive to light. If you also have an existing eye problem you may want to consult your optician before you try a lightbox. Other therapies you could be given are arts and creative therapies which involve using arts-based activities in a therapeutic environment with the support of a trained professional. All this will help you to understand yourself better, help you resolve complicated feelings, help you to communicate and express yourself, too. Then there are complementary and alternative therapies that take a holistic approach to your physical and mental health; they consider all aspects of your physical and emotional wellbeing as a whole. There is also ecotherapy which involves doing outdoor activities in nature. Once all this is set in motion your doctor will likely schedule regular check-ups to see how you are progressing with the treatments. Remember we are all different and different things work for different people, and if a particular medication or talking therapy doesn't work for you, your doctor should be able to offer something else. If you have tried everything and it hasn't helped then your doctor may refer you to the community mental health team (CMHT); this is particularly true in the UK.

Suicidal feelings

A suicidal feeling is usually the result of the most severe form or effect of a mental health problem. Suicide is the act of intentionally taking your own life. Many people think about suicide at some point in their life, such is the stressful nature of the lives that we live nowadays. Different people have different experiences of suicidal feelings. You may feel unable to cope with the feelings you are dealing with. It's less of a feeling of wanting to die and rather feeling like you cannot go on living the life you have. These feelings may build over time and can change from moment to moment. When you feel suicidal you may feel hopeless like there is no point in living, overwhelmed by negative thoughts, you may feel unbearable pain that you can't see ending, useless and not wanted by others, desperate, you may feel like everyone would be better off without you, cut off from your body or physically numb and being fascinated by death.[37] When you are suicidal you may experience poor sleep, a big change in appetite, including weight gain or weight loss, have no desire to take care of yourself, wanting to avoid other people, you may make a will or give away your possessions, you may struggle to communicate and you may have urges to self-harm. I know when I felt suicidal, I often felt I couldn't go on living my life in the way that it was. The thought was incessant, and I struggled to abate this feeling. The length of time you remain suicidal varies between individuals, but it's common to feel as if you will never be happy again. With the right treatment and self-care, one can go on to make a full recovery and live a fulfilling life. The earlier you speak to someone and inform them of your situation, the quicker you'll be able to get the right support you need to overcome these feelings. It can be difficult, understandably, to open up and talk about it – this is something I definitely understand. Sometimes you can feel unsure of who exactly to tell, be in fear of being judged, worried they won't understand you or you are just unable to tell someone. My advice is first to talk to your loved ones and then speak to your doctor.

Suicidal feelings can affect anyone, of any age, gender or background. Some common causes of suicidal thoughts are mental health problems, bullying, all types of abuse, bereavement, the end of a relationship or the prospect of it ending, long-term physical pain or illness, big changes in your life like retirement or redundancy,

---

[37] Mind, 'Causes of Suicidal Feelings', 2021 <https://www.mind.org.uk/information-support/types-of-mental-health-problems/suicidal-feelings/causes-of-suicidal-feelings/> [accessed 25 August 2021].

money problems, housing problems including becoming homeless or being in huge debt, loneliness, being in prison, addiction or substance abuse, pregnancy or postnatal depression, doubts about sexual gender and identity, trauma and cultural pressure such as arranged marriages, etc.

Some medications such as antidepressants can cause suicidal feelings in a person. Research shows that young people under 25 years of age are more likely to experience suicidal thoughts when taking antidepressants (SSRIs). Some antipsychotic medications can also cause people to experience suicidal thoughts as they change the chemical balance in the brain. If you experience this it's important to speak to your doctor at once. Statistically speaking men are more prone to taking their own lives than women. This is said to be because they feel pressured to get on with things and are reticent about their feelings and thoughts; they choose suicidal methods which have a lower chance of survival like jumping in front of a train or off a tall building; men can sometimes be stubborn as there is pressure to always appear strong and thus believe they can cope without help. The Campaign Against Living Miserably (CALM) works to prevent male suicide in the UK. People from the LGBTIQ community are more likely to experience suicidal feelings and commit suicide. The main reasons for this are they could potentially deal with homophobia, biphobia and transphobia, stigma and discrimination, difficult experiences of coming out, rejection and a negative reception from other people. Your self-esteem may be affected by this and this can lead to suicidal feelings and thoughts.

It's important that you get help with these feelings. You can get support through your doctor/GP, helplines and listening services, peer support, talking therapies which help you to understand why you are experiencing suicidal thoughts and they can also help you implement coping strategies, medication such as antidepressants, antipsychotics and mood stabilisers and crisis services.

There are some ways in which you can help yourself now. You can make yourself safe by removing anything around you that could be used to harm yourself, follow a safety plan or crisis plan (actions you take to always stay safe), tell someone how you are feeling and open up. Use self-harm coping techniques like distracting yourself; for example, tearing something up into many pieces or taking a very cold shower or bath, and engage your senses. Steadying your breathing can also help as this can calm you down. Look after your needs by drinking a glass of water, eating something if hungry, sit somewhere comfortable or write down how you feel. Avoid alcohol or recreational drugs as these have been known to make matters worse in crisis situations. Going outside and getting fresh air can help. Contacting a listening service or helpline, too. This is vital – you also need to challenge your thoughts. You can tell yourself that you won't act today. Find reasons to live by writing down the things you look forward to, or will attain in future – having children can be a great motivating factor for many. Think about people you love and how they would feel if they lost you. Be kind to yourself and tell yourself that you can get through this. That's something I used to regularly say to myself when I felt suicidal and it really helped.

Going forward it's vital that you make a safety plan. By this, I mean detail the warning signs, coping strategies, the names of contact details of anyone who may be able to help, list down any helplines or listening services, etc. You need to learn to manage these difficult feelings. Take one day at a time, and don't suppress your feelings, as this can cause them to build up over time and by then it's too late. Make a happy box that can be filled with memories and items that provide comfort and help lift your mood when you feel morbid or down. You can put a favourite book, positive quotes, photos, letters, a cuddly toy or even notes to yourself in the box. You need to learn your triggers and identify patterns in your mood over time. You can track your feelings by using an online mood diary. Remember, don't blame yourself and be kind to yourself, as none of this is your fault. It's important also to value yourself. Write a letter to yourself and mention people you care about and what positive things mean a lot to you, make plans to look forward to, build your self-esteem, celebrate yourself and be around people that celebrate you and not just tolerate you, make time to do the things you enjoy doing for yourself, too. Try and connect with people by joining peer support groups and volunteering. This sense of belonging and purpose can also provide you with a reason to keep on living, and talking to other people who also have suicidal thoughts can help you feel better about your own feelings by letting you know you are not alone and that the support bubble is there to help you cope. Finally, getting good sleep, avoiding drugs and eating well and exercising are also key as they can improve your self-confidence and self-esteem and give you a positive outlook on life. The release of these endorphins alone can help improve your mood over time if you do them regularly. Keep doing these things and your outlook on life will change and you will begin to feel better and more positive. It's no quick fix but it's definitely worth it. You are amazing, you are relevant and you are important.

Post-traumatic stress disorder (PTSD)

PTSD is a mental health problem you may develop soon or just after experiencing traumatic events in your life. The condition was first recognised in war veterans. When you have it you sometimes experience difficulty sleeping and can also feel numb – this is called 'acute stress reaction'. A lot of people find that these symptoms disappear within a few weeks, but if your symptoms last longer than a month you may be given a PTSD diagnosis.

There are different types of PTSD. Namely Delayed-onset PTSD which is when your symptoms appear more than six months after experiencing trauma. Then there's Complex PTSD which is when you experience PTSD at an early age that lasts for a long time.[38] Finally, we have birth trauma which is a traumatic experience that happens during childbirth. If you experience symptoms while supporting someone close who's experienced trauma, this is called secondary trauma.

There are many known symptoms of PTSD. They include reliving what happened – having flashbacks of a traumatic event as if it's happening right now, intrusive thoughts and images, nightmares, intense distress and physical pain, sweating, nausea or trembling. Alertness and feeling on edge are another symptom; this includes panicking when remembering the trauma you experienced, being easily upset or angry, extreme alertness aka hypervigilance, interrupted sleep, irritability, difficulty concentrating, being easily

---

38 Shirley Porter, *Treating PTSD: A Compassion-Focused CBT Approach* (New York: Routledge, Taylor and Francis Group, 2018).

startled and some other symptoms of anxiety. When you have PTSD, you also exhibit behaviours that avoid feelings and memories – like feeling you have to keep busy, avoiding things that remind you of trauma, being unable to remember details of what happened, feeling emotionally numb, unable to express affection and just being cold, doing self-destructive things, too and one of the most common ones is using alcohol or drugs to avoid memories. Your beliefs and feelings may also be affected. You may feel like nowhere is safe and that you can't trust anyone and feel like nobody understands; you may blame yourself for what happened and feel overwhelmed by feelings of anger, sadness, guilt or shame.

The reason PTSD can have physical effects is that when we feel stressed emotionally our bodies release hormones called cortisol and adrenaline. This is the body's automatic way of responding to a threat aka flight, fight or freeze response. Studies have shown that the body continues to produce these hormones when the person is no longer in danger which also explains some symptoms like alertness. Some also experience headaches, dizziness, anxiety and stomach aches or even chest pains.

Some other effects of PTSD are difficulty looking after yourself, holding down a job, maintaining relationships and friendships, coping with change, decreased libido and also forgetting things easily. It's also common to experience other mental health problems alongside PTSD such as anxiety disorder, self-harm, depression, dissociative disorders and suicidal feelings.

PTSD can be caused by many things, usually due to a perceived life-threatening event. Some examples are being involved in a car crash, being raped or sexually assaulted, experiencing violence including military combat or a terrorist attack, doing a job where you repeatedly hear distressing things, being kidnapped, being abused or bullied, traumatic childbirth, losing someone close to you, being diagnosed with a life-threatening condition like AIDS or cancer and surviving a natural disaster like a flood or pandemics – like coronavirus, for example. Some factors may make you more vulnerable to developing PTSD such as experiencing repeated trauma, getting physically hurt, having no support bubble and being alone, previously experiencing anxiety and depression and dealing with extra stress at the same time such as bereavement, money worries, racism, being homeless, etc.

There are some tips available on how to cope with flashbacks which is one of the effects of PTSD. You can focus on your breathing; when you are frightened your breathing changes and this can increase fear and panic. Tell yourself that you are safe, comfort yourself, keep a diary and record when you do have flashbacks and carry objects that remind you of the present moment. You can carry these in a pocket or a bag with you at all times. It can bring you back when you have an episode. You must get to know the triggers that remind you of the traumatic experience such as sounds, smells, words and places. When you do this, you can avoid the feelings when this does happen. Confide in someone and let them in. Try peer support and talk to others who may also suffer from PTSD. Finding specialist support is also important to help you with your specific type of PTSD as we are all different. Look after your physical health too, this can help you going forward as it changes the brain's chemistry.

There are several treatments available that you can access through the NHS if you are based in the UK, such as talking therapies and medication. Some good talking therapies are trauma-focused cognitive behavioural therapy (TF-CBT) and Eye Movement Desensitisation and Reprocessing (EMDR) which involves rhythmic eye movements while recalling a traumatic event. Rapid eye movements are intended to create a similar effect to the way your brain processes memories and experiences while you sleep (REM). If you feel none of the above has helped contact your doctor and they may recommend something else. Remember we are all different and what works for you may not work for someone else. If you are offered medication for PTSD this will usually be antidepressants. While PTSD differs from depression, this type of medicine has been known to help. Some of the recommended antidepressants are paroxetine which can be prescribed by your GP, and mirtazapine, amitriptyline and phenelzine which can be prescribed by a specialist in the UK.

Trauma

When you go through very distressing, stressful and frightening events this is sometimes known as trauma. There's emotional and psychological trauma. These are events we find traumatic and it's also about how we're affected by our experiences. Traumatic events can happen to anyone at any age and have long-lasting effects. Going through further trauma can also cause you to start being affected by past experiences, or exacerbate existing problems. Some events that may be traumatic are likely to make you feel frightened, under threat, humiliated, invalidated, unsafe, vulnerable, trapped, rejected, ashamed and powerless. Trauma can happen in many ways; for example, on-off or ongoing events, being directly harmed, witnessing harm to someone else, living in a traumatic atmosphere and being affected by trauma in a family. Your experience of trauma might relate to your identity, including if you've been harassed, bullied or discriminated against.

Trauma can also cause mental health problems, or make you more vulnerable to developing them. PTSD and complex PTSD are some conditions that are known to develop as a direct result of trauma.[39] If you have trauma and didn't reach out to anyone, that feeling of being lonely could make the trauma execrable.

Our bodies respond to danger in different ways depending on who we are. But when we do face danger, as I said before, we release hormones called cortisol and adrenaline. This is the body's automatic way of preparing to respond to danger and it's not something we have control over. The generally known effects of this response are freeze, which is when you have a feeling of stupor and can't move or feel paralysed, flop which is doing what you're told without being able to protest, fight which is fighting, struggling or protest, flight which is as it sounds – leaving the situation or running away – and fawn, which is trying to please someone who actually inflicts harm upon you.[40] Research has shown that stress signals may continue long after the trauma is done. This might affect your mind and body

---

[39] Shoshana Ringel and Jerrold R Brandell, *Trauma: Contemporary Directions in Theory, Practice, and Research*, 2011.

[40] Mind, 'Effects of Trauma | Mind, the Mental Health Charity - Help for Mental Health Problems', 2021 <https://www.mind.org.uk/information-support/types-of-mental-health-problems/trauma/effects-of-trauma/> [accessed 25 August 2021].

and also the way you think, feel and behave which is a reason why CBT is a very useful treatment in dealing with trauma.

There are some common effects of trauma that can occur. Flashbacks involve reliving facets of a traumatic event or feeling as if it is still happening in the present, and panic attacks, dissociation which is when you become desensitized to the traumatic event by way of feeling aloof, spaced out and numb, almost detached in a way. Then there's hyperarousal which involves feeling anxious, on edge and unable to relax and which perpetually puts you in a state where you are looking for danger or threats. This is something I would do constantly due to my fear of being insulted by people. Some people may also experience sleep problems due to having a lot of nightmares, etc., and low self-esteem. Some experience grief too. Some self-harm as a result of trauma which is a coping mechanism or get suicidal feelings and many abuse alcohol and substances to cope with difficult emotions and memories.

Trauma can also affect you in that it makes you neglect to look after yourself properly, struggle to hold down a job, have difficulty trusting others or in maintaining and keeping relationships. You might also have difficulty remembering things, your libido may be affected and you may no longer be able to enjoy your leisure time. In some cases, trauma has a serious impact on your ability to work. The good news is that there are ways that you can help yourself going forward. If you are having flashbacks, you can tell yourself that you are safe, touch or hold objects that remind you of the present, describe your surroundings out loud and count objects of a particular colour or type. If you have panic attacks you can breathe slowly in and out while counting to five, stamp on the spot, eat a sweet and taste all of its flavours or touch something soft. If you feel spaced out you can chew a piece of ginger, clap your hands and notice the stinging sensation or you can drink a glass of ice-cold water. If you feel anxious or on edge you can make yourself a hot drink, and as you drink it notice the taste and smell, take ten deep breaths, counting each one out loud. You can write in detail everything about where you are right now. Taking a warm bath or shower helps, too, as it can change your mood and be a distracting physical sensation. If you feel sad, depressed or lonely you can wrap up in a blanket and watch your favourite TV show, write all of your negative feelings on a piece of paper and tear it up, cuddle a pet or a soft toy or listen to music you find uplifting. If you want to self-harm you could rub ice over where you want to hurt yourself to numb it, stick a plaster on your skin and peel it off or take a cold bath. You can also help yourself, in the long run, to deal with your trauma. You can confide in someone, learn ways to relax like mindfulness or meditation, try peer support, find specialist support and look after your physical health. This will make you feel better about yourself and give you something else to think about.

Just as with other mental health problems there are many treatments that can help; for instance talking therapies like body-focused therapy which addresses how trauma affects your body, EMDR[41] which involves rhythmic eye movements while recalling a traumatic event which is also used to treat PTSD as mentioned before, trauma-focused CBT, cognitive analytical therapy (CAT)

---

[41] Mind, 'Treatment for Trauma', 2021 <https://www.mind.org.uk/information-support/types-of-mental-health-problems/trauma/treatment-and-support/> [accessed 25 August 2021].

which looks at how past events and relationships can affect how you think, feel and act, and finally there's schema therapy which addresses unmet needs and difficult beliefs about yourself. Arts and creative therapies are also useful as they can help you to express yourself and they address painful feelings and experiences without using words. Medication, too, can be useful in treating trauma. Some people find medication helpful in managing mental health problems that are linked to trauma. The type you are given will depend on the specific mental health problem or symptoms you have.

Trauma can be difficult and it can make you feel alone and isolated. It's important that you speak to your doctor as there are treatments available that can help you overcome this. It may take some time but it's worth it as it can not only improve your quality of life but save your life too. We all deserve to live a healthy fulfilling life. Don't suffer in silence. Get help immediately. I can only imagine where I would be if I didn't seek help. Yes, I took many years to finally get the help I needed and I'm still battling with my mental health affliction but I'm much better informed about my condition and know how to manage it, and still do some of the day-to-day things I didn't foresee myself doing ever again.

Dissociation and Dissociative disorders

Many people experience dissociation during their life. When you feel dissociated you disconnect from yourself and the world around you. You may feel detached from your body or feel as though the world around you is unreal. It's one of the ways the mind copes with stress. Dissociation can be ephemeral, or it can be chronic. You may dissociate after you experience trauma. Some people dissociate to focus on completing a task or to calm down. You might experience dissociation as a mental health symptom of PTSD, depression, anxiety, schizophrenia, bipolar disorder or borderline personality disorder (BPD).[42] You can also experience dissociation as a side effect of alcohol or certain medications, sometimes even when coming off medication. Some people may have difficulty remembering personal information. You may have gaps in your life where you can't remember anything that has happened. Or you may not be able to remember information about yourself or about things that have happened in your life. Psychiatrists call this dissociative amnesia. Some people even travel to a different location or take on a new identity when they get there and do not remember their actual identity. Doctors call this dissociative fugue.[43] People with dissociative disorders may feel like the world around them isn't real They may see objects changing in shape, size or colour, see the world as lifeless or they may even feel as if other people are robots. Doctors and psychiatrists call this derealisation. Some people also feel like they are looking at themselves from outside like watching yourself in a film, feel as though they are just observing their emotions, feel disconnected from parts of their body, some also feel as though they are floating away. This is called depersonalisation by doctors.

---

[42] Paul F Dell and John A O'Neil, *Dissociation and the Dissociative Disorders: DSM-V and Beyond*, 2015 <page 2-35>.

[43] Mind, 'Dissociative Disorders', 2021 <https://www.mind.org.uk/information-support/types-of-mental-health-problems/dissociation-and-dissociative-disorders/dissociative-disorders/> [accessed 25 August 2021].

CHAPTER 5: UNDERSTANDING THE DIFFERENT TYPES OF MENTAL HEALTH DISORDERS

Identity alteration, as called by doctors, is when you feel a shift in your identity, speak in different voices, use a different name or names, switch between different parts of your personality, feel as if you are losing control to someone else, experience different parts of your identity at different times and act like different people too. When you dissociate you find it very difficult to explain or categorise the kind of person you are. You also feel as if there are different people inside of you. This is known as identity confusion by the experts.

Dissociative identity disorder (DID) is also called multiple personality disorder. This is when you experience severe changes in your identity. I watched a movie called 'Split' that depicted this type of disorder very accurately. The different states of your identity will most likely control your behaviour and thoughts at different times. This can happen in various ways. Each of your identity states may have different patterns of thinking and relating to the world. Your different identities may be portrayed as different ages and genders, you may feel that only one part of your identity feels like 'you', the different parts of your identity may have memories that conflict with each other, you may have no control over when the different parts of your identity take over, you may also experience amnesia when another part of your identity is in control which makes sense when you think about it. DID is sometimes still called multiple personality disorder (MPD) – that's because many people experience changes in parts of their identity as complete separate personalities. DID isn't a personality disorder – it's a way of coping and dealing with childhood trauma. DID may mean you look after yourself more. As different parts of your identity have different needs. You might also experience depersonalisation and derealisation. With regards to the fugue, you might experience a state of mind where you forget everything about who you are. You may or may not have dissociative symptoms that fit into any other diagnosis. This will be explained to you when you get examined. Many people who suffer from dissociative disorders also have other mental health problems such as BPD, depression, anxiety and panic attacks, OCD, suicidal feelings and hearing voices, too.

Dissociation is a normal defence mechanism that helps us deal with the trauma we experience. Some examples are war, kidnapping, rape or invasive medical procedures. This becomes dissociative when the environment you are in is no longer traumatic but you still act as if it is. During childhood, while the brain is developing, some examples of trauma that may lead to dissociative disorder are physical abuse, sexual abuse, severe neglect and emotional abuse. Trauma causes dissociation by activating the way we respond to threat. One theory is that when we experience what we perceive as a threat, our body reduces blood flow to areas in the front of the brain which is the analytical, thinking and rational part. This turns on areas in the back of the brain which are the automatic and instinctive parts. Using this part of the brain to freeze or flop helps protect us from the trauma we can't prevent or escape. But reducing the blood flow to the front of the brain means that it becomes more difficult to process what happens and may mean we experience dissociation as a result. The front of the brain includes areas that help us to understand where we are in the space-time continuum, use language and speech, store memories, feel connected to the body and interpret information coming through

CHAPTER 5: UNDERSTANDING THE DIFFERENT TYPES OF MENTAL HEALTH DISORDERS

our senses. Sometimes we split experiences into different parts so that we don't have to deal with them all together like memories, perceptions, thoughts and feelings. Some of the things that make dissociative disorders more likely are abuse or neglect that begins at an early age, abuse or neglect that lasts a long time, abuse and neglect that makes you scared, abuse or neglect that is done by someone you feel attached to when there is no adult who you have a good relationship with and can provide comfort and help you process and handle trauma.

If you have a dissociative disorder, you should ask your GP or psychiatrist to refer you for a full assessment. You may meet with a psychotherapist and a psychiatrist as part of the assessment. What's important is that the person assessing you establishes whether your dissociation is as a result of drugs or medication, a physical cause or any cultural or religious practices that may explain your experiences. Your diagnosis will depend on how you experience dissociation, whether you have symptoms and whether your symptoms are causing you distress or negatively affecting your life. Sometimes it can be difficult to diagnose dissociative disorders because sometimes mental health professionals don't get the correct training they need to deal with them. They don't understand enough of your mental health and life history to obtain the relevant information to get the right diagnosis. Some people coping with this disorder try to keep it hidden from others as it can be difficult to talk openly about their experiences. You may experience dissociative disorders alongside other mental health problems or on its own. As a result, it can be hard for professionals to know whether to give you a diagnosis of a dissociative disorder.

There are many ways in which you can help yourself going forward. You can keep a journal and document all the different times you have bad memories or when you have an experience of a different personality coming out. Try visualisation as this helps you feel safe. Like having a go-to place where you feel safe and away from harm. Look after your health, join peer groups and talk to other people who have similar experiences. Making a personal crisis plan can help too; you do this when you are well. It explains what you would like to happen if you are not well enough to make decisions about your treatment or other aspects of your life.

Talking therapy can help deal with dissociative disorders. For example, counselling and psychotherapy will help you explore traumatic events in your past, help you understand why you dissociate and develop alternative coping mechanisms. It also helps with the management of your emotions and relationships. It can be hard to get the right help and considering most talking treatments for dissociative disorders take several years this makes it extremely hard to get help. It's important to consult your doctor who will point you in the right direction. There are no specific medications used to treat dissociation. Antidepressants, antipsychotics and mood stabilisers are typically used to treat depression, anxiety, suicidal feelings, psychosis, etc., but your doctor may prescribe these to go alongside your dissociation in most cases as this could help. You will only get medication for DID if most of the different parts of your identity, or at least one dominant part of your identity, experiences the problem you are looking to treat.

Non-epileptic attack disorder (NEAD) is when you experience dissociation alongside seizures. These seizures don't seem to have a physical cause. These are called dissociative seizures or non-epileptic attacks. If you have dissociative seizures, you may have convulsions of the arms, head and legs which may affect one side or the whole body, lose control of your bladder, bite your tongue, go blank or stare in an unseeing way. It's said that dissociative seizures are caused by the brain dealing with overwhelming stress by shutting down.

Dissociation or dissociative behaviours can be hard to deal with. It can become your norm, a way of desensitizing yourself or switching off when you are faced with reliving the trauma. It's not a solution, rather it compounds the problem in the long run. If you are experiencing any of the mentioned symptoms and haven't yet sought help it's important you do so. There is help out there.

Postnatal depression and perinatal mental health

A perinatal mental health problem is one that you experience any time from becoming pregnant up to a year after giving birth. It's natural to experience a range of emotions when giving birth. If these emotions become problematic, however, you may be experiencing a perinatal health problem. Some of the common perinatal health problems are perinatal depression, anxiety, OCD, Postpartum Psychosis and Postpartum PTSD. Some women also experience eating problems after giving birth.[44] If you have a mental health

---

44 Mind, 'Perinatal and Postnatal Mental Health', 2021 <https://www.mind.org.uk/information-support/types-of-mental-health-problems/postnatal-depression-and-perinatal-mental-health/about-maternal-mental-health-problems/> [accessed 25 August 2021].

problem while you are pregnant it's important to talk to your doctor at once. Your doctor will help you make plans to manage your mental health during pregnancy. They may also make you aware of the extra support you will need. You may feel pressure to be happy or excited soon after having a baby even if you are suffering from a mental health problem, you may feel like you have to be on top of everything, worried that you're a bad parent, also worried that someone will take your baby away from you if you open up about how you are feeling. It's important that you know having these feelings isn't your fault and you can ask someone for support if you need it. Some women also get thoughts of hurting their own babies which can be frightening. You may be afraid to tell anyone about those feelings. But the more you can open up about those feelings, the sooner you can get the support that you need.

Perinatal mental health problems are caused by previous or other experiences of mental health problems, biological causes, lack of support, difficult childhood experiences, the experience of abuse, low self-esteem, stressful living conditions and major life events.[45] There is antenatal depression which occurs while you are pregnant, postnatal depression which happens during your first year after giving birth and perinatal depression happens anytime from becoming pregnant to around a year after giving birth. The difference between 'baby blues' and postnatal depression is that with baby blues you experience a brief period of low mood, feeling emotional and tearful for approximately 3 to 10 days after you give birth.

---

45 John L. Cox, Jeni Holden, and Carol Henshaw, Perinatal Mental Health: The Edinburgh Postnatal Depression Scale (EPDS); Manual, 2. ed (London: RCPsych Publ., Royal college of Psychiatrists, 2014).

During this period, you are likely to be coping with new demands and getting very little sleep, so it's natural to feel overwhelmed and emotional. Postnatal depression is a much deeper and longer-lasting depression. It usually develops within 6 weeks of giving birth and it can be gradual or very sudden. It also ranges from mild to severe depending on the person. There are some typical signs and symptoms of perinatal depression. You might feel down, or tearful, restless, guilty, empty and numb, isolated and unable to relate to people, feel a sense of unreality, low self-esteem, feel hopeless and despairing and you may even feel suicidal in more severe cases. When you have perinatal depression, you may find that you lose concentration very easily, find it hard to sleep, have reduced appetite and loss of interest in sex. Talking therapy namely CBT or Interpersonal therapy (IPT) are both very effective against perinatal depression. With regards to medication, antidepressants are the most commonly given type of medication. Electroconvulsive therapy (ECT) involves sending an electric current through your brain, causing a brief surge of electrical activity within your brain (a seizure); this treatment aims to relieve symptoms of mental health issues. It's usually given under a general anaesthetic. It allows you to care for and bond with your baby as soon as possible.

You must take care of yourself if you experience perinatal depression. You can do this by being kind to yourself, i.e. not beating yourself up about being a parent. Remind yourself that you are human and you are learning as you go to a degree. Be kind to yourself. Keep a mood diary and track any changes in your mood; this can help you notice if any activities, places or people make you feel better or worse. Look after your hygiene and stay healthy. This small thing makes a huge difference in how you feel in the long run. Speaking to people with similar experiences can also help. It makes you realise you are not the only one suffering from this condition. In the UK you can contact Infoline or visit a local Mind to find peer support options in your area. Contact specialist organisations. PANDAS is a great option – they help to treat antenatal and postnatal depression.

Perinatal anxiety or antenatal anxiety happens while you are pregnant, postnatal anxiety happens during the first year after giving birth and perinatal anxiety happens any time from becoming pregnant to around a year after giving birth. There are some well-known signs and symptoms of perinatal anxiety. The effects on your body are that you may feel a churning feeling in your stomach, pins and needles, feel light-headed or dizzy, feel restless or unable to sleep, an increase in your breathing rate, sweating or hot flushes, nausea, needing the toilet more or less often, having panic attacks and grinding your teeth, especially at night. Perinatal anxiety also has many effects on your mind. It can make you feel tense, nervous or unable to relax, feeling a sense of dread, or fearing the worst. It can make you feel like other people can see that you are feeling anxious or are looking at you. You are unable to stop worrying. You may worry that you are losing touch with reality. You most likely ruminate, which is thinking a lot about bad experiences or thinking over a situation again and again. You may experience depersonalisation which is when you feel disconnected from your mind or body and/or you may experience derealisation which involves feeling disconnected from the world around you like it isn't real at all. Talking therapy is very useful in treating perinatal anxiety. Particularly CBT. Your doctor may give you access to online CBT programmes to try yourself, or even prescribe self-help books to help you to learn to manage your anxiety. To help deal with perinatal anxiety in the long run you can try shifting your focus onto something small, like the details of a picture or the texture of something you are wearing. If you engross yourself in this act, it can help distract you and calm you down. You can learn some breathing techniques or try some physical activity and if none of this helps you can contact Anxiety UK and No Panic who will offer you support and advice on your existing problem with anxiety.

You may develop postnatal PTSD which is also known as birth trauma. Some causes of postnatal PTSD include difficult labour with long and painful delivery, an unplanned C-section, emergency treatment and other unexpected and traumatic experiences during birth. Some common signs and symptoms of postnatal PTSD include re-living aspects of trauma i.e., flashbacks and intrusive thoughts and nightmares, being over-alert or on edge making you easily angry or upset, finding it hard to sleep, becoming very irritable, finding it hard to concentrate, being easily startled, or self-destructive and reckless. You might also find yourself avoiding feelings and memories (which includes feeling like you have to keep busy), avoiding situations that remind you of trauma, being unable to remember details of what happened, feeling emotionally numb or cut off from your feelings, being unable to express affection, and using alcohol and recreational drugs to avoid memories, etc. Another sign of postnatal PTSD is having difficulties with your beliefs and feelings which may include feeling like you can't trust anyone, that nowhere is safe, and nobody understands, blaming yourself for what happened and feeling overwhelming anger, sadness and guilt.

Some useful therapies in treating postnatal PTSD are trauma-focused CBT and EMDR. It is common to experience anxiety alongside PTSD so therefore, your doctor may offer you medication to treat those symptoms.

Postpartum psychosis, sometimes called puerperal psychosis, can be overwhelming and frightening. It means after birth psychosis. If you have postpartum psychosis, you are most likely to experience a mix of psychosis, depression and mania. If you have it you may feel excited or elated, severely depressed, have rapid mood changes and feel confused or disorientated. You may behave in strange ways, mainly being restless, unable to sleep, unable to concentrate and you may even experience psychotic symptoms like delusions and hallucinations.

If you have a family history of mental health problems, particularly postpartum psychosis, you are at risk of developing it yourself. You may also be more vulnerable to developing it if you have bipolar disorder or schizophrenia, or if you have had a traumatic birth or pregnancy or have previously experienced postpartum psychosis. You can also develop postpartum psychosis even if you have no history of mental health problems. When it comes to medication you are most likely going to be offered an antipsychotic drug to manage your mood and psychotic symptoms. You may also be offered antidepressants. If your symptoms are severe and other treatments don't work the doctor may offer you ECT. In some cases, you may need to be admitted to the hospital but this all depends on what the doctor finds when he/she investigates.

It's important that you build your support network, manage daily tasks and look after your physical and emotional health going forward.

To summarise, mental health is a big issue in the world today. It affects our moods, emotions and how we see ourselves. Many people suffer in silence without getting the help they actually need. It's got a stigma about it which makes some people reluctant to step forward and take action. It's normal to experience some of the mental health conditions outlined and there's nothing wrong with seeking the help you need. Many people's mental health condition gets worse as they don't seek the help they need. I understand at first it can be difficult to speak out or to fully realise that help is needed but I can only tell you from my personal experiences with mental health that it's vital that you don't take it for granted. I know I did. I still regret it to this day. If I had sought help earlier who knows how different things may have been, but instead, I'm still here trapped in the abyss. I have got the tools I need to help me manage it but I'm still not out of the woods yet. Every day I try to practice what I have learned to help improve my situation and lead to a better quality of life that I had missed out on for about a decade. You don't have to be afraid anymore or live in a cocoon; you are great, you are powerful and you deserve to lead a happy and healthy life. Making small changes is the key – day to day minute changes lead to a big change overall. This is no easy fix; it can take some people years to finally get better but taking the first step is a start to a happier life. Don't let your affliction dictate how your life should be. You are in control; you set your own destiny. Remember all the tools that you can use to manage your problem. Eventually, you will get better.

Chapter 6: The truth about some mental health afflictions

What a lot of people who don't have anxiety disorder and other mental health afflictions don't realise is that there are certain things that people with anxiety usually say, think and do.

1. We tend to make excuses and not to go to parties and other social outings we get invited to. I constantly did this. From meetings with friends, dates with women, to no end. You just say you can't attend functions when you're asked because of your anxiety.
2. We eat foods and drink drinks that exacerbate our disorder. For example, artificial sweeteners, aspartame sugar, table salt, the list goes on. All these things raise the chances of contracting cardiovascular disease. Not only that but it makes the anxiety worse. Eating a carbon and plant-based diet is best to inhibit diseases, too. These foods have live enzymes and magnesium which produce serotonin, a natural calming agent, in the body. Kale, watercress, avocados to name but a few are good foods to eat. Alcohol also inhibits the production of serotonin.

3. We tend to judge by appearances, thinking that someone who outwardly looks okay is fine, when in fact they may be suffering from anxiety inside and are definitely not okay. People who suffer from anxiety tend to be very good at hiding their discomfort and struggles, usually, due to their vulnerability and maybe the embarrassment, they feel for having it.
4. We tend to be people-pleasers as a means to disarm others so they do not offend or attack us (depending on your mental health affliction). It's a defence mechanism, a way to keep us safe. Remember our brain is designed for survival and self-preservation, not happiness.
5. We tend to be afraid of change, unfamiliar things or people, the unknown. "Tomorrow" is our worst nightmare.
6. We tend to focus on creating the worst possible outcomes for ourselves. We focus on the things that go wrong so we miss out on the things that go right. Letting go and surrendering to everything is true freedom from bondage and affliction.
7. We are always outside of our bodies, as I mentioned before, and in our minds. Overthinking, stressing, worrying.
8. We hardly ever ask for help, afraid of even more judgement.
9. We put others' needs before our own. We like to please others we become servile.
10. We hate to be told to calm down in a situation where we are having a panic or anxiety attack.
11. We are very attuned to all our senses. We constantly live in them due to our brain's overactivity and use.
12. We always run away from ourselves. Psychologist Fritz Pearl said "We need to be in the here and now"; all your power lies in

the present moment. We tend to live in a past adverse moment and thus worry about another bad or worse future moment. The shock it has on the body scares the brain so much that it becomes hyper-vigilant. Like the burnt toast effect, it draws for its weapon at any sound or movement to prevent being caught off guard, so to speak.

13. We become perfectionists. Analysing every little decision we make, how fast we are driving, if we are taking too long to pay at the shop, if we should join the queue or not. We are super critical of our own behaviour and not only that, we also judge our thoughts. We put ourselves down and blame ourselves if we experience an episode, "it's because I did this or that" this self-censorious deprecation eventually debilitates us. Nothing we do is good enough because it has to be perfect but it can't be. So, in the end, we do nothing instead. Just wait and wait.

This list isn't exhaustive but very common with people who suffer from some form of anxiety disorder. It's constant. It's the engine that powers the vehicle. Imagine living that way. I have, I do.

There are three statements that people who suffer from an anxiety disorder of some sort will always make. First is that something bad is going to happen, secondly that there's not enough time, and lastly that there's no way out. Recognise and realise that all three of these thoughts and beliefs are connected to the external world and disconnected from yourself but because of societal norms, years and years of conditioning, we accept these things as part of who we are. Let me ask you a question. What was the day that you accepted an hour was indeed an hour? By the systems, we put in place and are taught to never question. But we all live by that system and definition. Why don't we question that? Challenge it or even ignore it and define it in our own way. Change it. Have you ever tried? Imagine we discover that there is and can be another definition.

Something I wasn't aware of when my disorder was at its worst was that I needed to not necessarily change my thoughts and beliefs, but rather not judge them. Neither accept them as good nor bad. That way you don't take any action to counter them, nor do you internalise them and let them grow. There are different types of anxiety and worry. There's personal, like how you see yourself. I'm too fat, I'm not good enough, etc., or external worries. – what people think of you – they think I'm ugly, unattractive, unintelligent – or worrying about the government. I believe that anxiety somehow comes from childhood, school years through living up to society's expectations of us. Moreover, anxiety comes from the desire to control the external world which we can't. The idea is to not feel like you are a victim. The minute you accept that you are, you subconsciously expect to be attacked or for bad things to come after you. It's a state of mind. It isn't real. Just a perception and essentially perception shapes reality. I didn't know this. I still suffer from anxiety and psychosis; however, armed with this new knowledge I'm at least able to discern it rather than just viscerally surmising facts.

As I mentioned, one of the things people with anxiety disorder and some other mental health afflictions say is they must become perfect to function in society and just on a day-to-day basis. This is fallacious. You don't have to be perfect; just say to yourself that you already are perfect. Letting go of perfection is where perfection actually begins. You can't just always remain in the waiting room, waiting to get out of the darkness only to end up not being saved. You have to force your way out. After all, you were once in the light. There's a saying "you can't bring something out of you if it isn't already there." Dig deep and find yourself again. It's a work in progress but you will actualise it. Make it an obsession.

We also have to let go of who we think we are. You are not tall, short, white, black, a man, a woman, rich, poor. Let go of the identity society has given to you, you are an infinite being. You have to drum this into your mind. Reprogramme your brain. Debug the current version. Block out other peoples' energy. Do you, be you, be limitless, be inscrutable. Represent infinite possibilities. Be the change you want to see in others.

See it as it's happening *for* me', not '*to* me'. See it as a reminder of what you need to work on about yourself. When you stop fear from holding you back you can use it to push you forward and achieve greatness. Like Tony Robbins once said. 'wants' don't get met consistently, 'standards' do. Be the standard you know you'd like to be, don't just think it. Remember anxiety isn't just in the mind, it's in the whole body. Whatever you think you embody. When you feel anxious, stressed, depressed. Ask yourself at that moment what you are doing. Start doing things that don't trigger the anxiety. Think of yourself as unlimited, free to express yourself and be whoever you want to be. If you look at animals, they don't seem to get shy or become bashful and sheepish around other animals. They just are themselves. They urinate where they want, sit where they want. My point is just let go of what society has told you that you should use as a barometer to who you are.

The truth is we generally experience certain types of mental health problems because we are trying to fit in over a long period. Fit in. Be something we are not. You need to question and lose your identity. Think of this example. You spend your whole life working and being laborious and diligent but always underpaid and undervalued. While adding value will invariably increase your salary, if you are doing a job that you don't love, or the job doesn't fit you, you do it just to pay a bill. You are neglecting your true core essence. You are devoid of true identity by default. It's not just what you think you are supposed to be, more that you don't know what to be. You get lost. This over time will spark some form of anxiety disorder or other mental health disorder. You are not doing you. You are going against it. As I stated, don't try to escape your thoughts, rather learn how to stop judging them as that causes overthinking which is the biggest cause of unhappiness. Just accept your thoughts as once you begin judging them you judge who you are and always try and do what others deem as acceptable or as desirable. Don't use the Cinderella effect. We often judge others which essentially makes us judge ourselves. Comparisons, separation. The Facebook depression. Oh, he's doing so well or looks great, etc. You are unique, incomparable to anything and anyone. Surround yourself with people that celebrate you, not just tolerate you. You become who you hang around with, after all.

You are not the job that you do, although schools teach us that we are in a way. That we are quantifiable. It's all BS, belief systems and b"l s"t... You are enough; nothing is ever as serious as we think. We have nothing to lose because one day we will die, as Steve Jobs, the American business magnate, once said. Stop overthinking.

Overthinking causes unhappiness, but not only that – it also turns us into perfectionists.

Immerse yourself in nature; it calms us, humbles us, gives us time to become attuned to the world around us – the beauty, the marvel of it all. We are in the world, but we also are the world.

One thing I think about more nowadays after teaching myself more about my condition is that when I feel so anxious, in certain moments I don't realise that perhaps others are just as anxious as I am. Have you noticed that when you feel anxious and panicky that everything else around you is, too? The truth is when you are calm everything around you becomes calm too. This is why I meditate, listen to Solfeggio frequencies, eat well and exercise. It's not easy, I have my moments. I'm far from where I need to be but I'm working on myself every day and so should you.

It's important to love yourself and spend time with yourself. Appreciate yourself when you are alone, be the debonair and urbane man or woman. You will see that if you are comfortable in your own presence, then when in social settings, people will be comfortable with you. Don't let them question why you are being you. Or challenge that you aren't being you. People often do this when they aren't convinced you are happy with how you are behaving. Address any inferiority complexes you might have. You are enough. You are important.

Just be you and worry less about them. Do things that make you smile and then that joy will spread. Change your eating habits, be more aware of what your body is doing, stand as if you are hanging by your teeth, get rid of the low pose, don't take anything for granted, change your behavioural patterns, challenge yourself regularly to start doing without what you've become accustomed to. Change your routines and habits, even if it's something small. Become aware of what triggers your anxiety, not only that, but how to use that to build a system that keeps you away from the triggers. It won't be easy; it's a process, but if you practice this day in day out you will eventually become it. As I say I've been to hell and back, I'm more informed about ways to help myself and then help others. You are me and I am you.

Chapter 7: Money, Money, Money

As I said at the end of Part 1, times got hard. I was desperate for money and didn't see any coming in anytime soon. I was even more depressed because of this. As if my mental health problems weren't enough! Money in itself isn't evil, it's just energy, but what people are willing to do for money can be evil. But it's all by design. It's systemic and designed to oppress, reward and separate people. I wasn't working as I had left my previous job in Islington as a concierge. I couldn't take the audible hallucinations anymore; I was tired of getting beaten up, so to speak. I'm not proud of it but I had to go on benefits to make ends meet and to get by. I guess there's no shame in that. It is there for a reason. I was one of the priority groups due to my mental health problems. What I received in my monthly payments was hardly enough to get by. It was just enough to pay my rent, eat, fill up my car, visit friends occasionally. I hated that existence. Just getting by. Hand to mouth. I had several opportunities throughout my life to put some money away but I always failed to do so. They say to get rich when it comes to money you have to earn it, keep it and grow it. I earned it alright but was unable to keep it and grow it. I was between a rock and a hard place because on one hand, I wanted all the finer things in life, nice clothes, gadgets, to travel as I have a wanderlust, especially anywhere with water as I am a thalassophile. On the other hand, I was unable to work with people in the work environment because of my terrible affliction. I didn't know what to do. I had to figure out a way to earn money, keep it and grow it. I turned to gambling and stock trading. This was the beginning of a terrible period in my life. I can't believe that as of the year 2018 there were approximately 37 million gambling accounts in the UK of which 33.5 million were active. Gambling is certainly a billion-dollar industry. They say gambling is a mug's game; I disagree, or maybe I'm just in denial. Gambling is meant to give us a fair chance of winning money but how can it truly be fair if you are wagering against getting hooked on it. Either way, I set up a gambling account with a company called Betway. Initially, I would gamble on live football matches like a lot of people do, but later I got into virtual football matches and casino slots. One thing gambling revealed to me is that I have an addictive personality. Granted there is a psychology behind how they get you hooked just like with nicotine, alcohol, drugs, money and so on. I remember my first bet was for £10 – it was for both teams to score in a Manchester United versus Everton match. Both were explosive teams, good on the counter-attack so I figured there would be a lot of goals. I won. I made £20 profit because the odds were 2/1. Meaning for every pound you stake you win £2 profit. I found this number-crunching interesting and believed it was a legitimate way in which I could earn some extra money. At least that was the idea. Bit by bit I would stake a few bets and win. Yes, I lost some too but I was up overall. I was actually starting to be happy. Not only was this a distraction from my mental health problems and a solution, but it was fun.

CHAPTER 7: MONEY, MONEY, MONEY

The problem is as people we tend to create a new problem to solve an existing one. At first, it was every few days and then it became a daily thing. From morning to night, I would sit on my laptop or phone and place bets. This was when I got into virtual betting mainly on football and dog racing. As live football wasn't perpetually on, I needed this to stimulate me. Looking back on it now it's one of my biggest regrets in life. All the money I've thrown away because I was trying to escape the reality of life and create a new one.

At one point, I started staking £100 per bet with the hope of returning about £150-£200 profit each time. This is when I should have realised that it was getting out of hand, but I didn't. I just kept on doing it. A few months passed, no job came and I was just stuck at home thinking I was going to get rich by clicking buttons. Naïve? Brave? Stupid? Who knows? No one can judge me except me. I once heard that the hardest thing to do as an individual is to look at yourself in the mirror and critique yourself. It's so true.

At some point, I had earned nearly £10,000 in profit which I made with the woman I was dating at the time. Little old me convinced her to give gambling a try, I lured her in. Most of that money was made on virtual football. We both started with about £1,500 each and ended up with about £12,000 each. I truly believed I had found a solution to my problem. The funny thing was when I had all that money, which to me was a lot at the time, I still didn't feel satisfied nor fulfilled. I actually felt rather numb. Money isn't everything and I'm not only saying that because I don't have any. It truly doesn't buy you happiness. I have always said that money isn't the answer, it's the question. It just leaves you with more uncertainty and more questions. My girlfriend, Ayesha at the time, and I would stay up all night studying patterns and paradigms to the virtual football games. We were convinced we had it figured out. Then we basically lost it all. There was only what we started with left. Easy come easy go. Just as quickly as we had won all that money, we squandered it. It was like a bad dream. I just remembered feeling so depressed the day this all happened. All the plans I had for that money had been destroyed in minutes. I got greedy, or I got cocky. I had made a handsome amount and I thought I could make more and more. The idea was to make enough to relieve my girlfriend of having to endure the pain of working in a job she hated and staying in the rat race. This was how much I cared for her. That night I had an empty feeling inside of my soul; I just couldn't see the point in living anymore. I felt cursed like I had no luck and nothing was going my way on top of being stuck in my mental prison. It was all too much to handle. Somehow Ayesha was able to fall asleep. I didn't sleep a wink I just lay there on the bed staring through the computer screen feeling guilty that I had sold her a dream and destroyed it at the same time. I cared more about how she felt than I did myself. I was willing to do anything to get that money back. Don't get me wrong, because of my psychosis, I would hear insults from her every day just like I did with everyone else. But she stuck by me and even when I asked her constantly if she had insulted me, or when we were out if she had heard someone else insult me, she stuck by me and supported me. I've never felt such love from someone before, or maybe it was just tolerance. She's nowhere to be found today.

That night I told myself I would win twice as much as we lost. I had a figure in my head of £40,000. £20,000 each. I wasn't going to see the next day if I didn't. Then it happened! I saw the bet that I

CHAPTER 7: MONEY, MONEY, MONEY

was waiting for all night. It was a virtual game. The score I was after was 0 – 0. It was 10/1 odds meaning if I staked £100 I would win £1000 profit. I took our last bit of money that she had entrusted to me and just a minute before bets were closed for that game I froze. I was overcome with fear. Fear of making it worse, losing everything, fear of having a better life, fear of failure, fear of Ayesha leaving me. I just froze. I had about £3000 in the account and if I staked it all it would have returned about £30,000. It happened! I sat there and wanted to cry – I couldn't believe it. Then I figured it all out. Gambling companies base their business model on customers' fear, the quintessential and most predictable human emotion. They know in such situations you will be too scared to take the risk, that you would rather go for a safer bet, for example with 1/2 odds which isn't guaranteed anyway. You would ignore your deep visceral intuition and play it safe and lose. Then when you lose you would risk more money to win back what you lost. It's a vicious cycle. I never forgave myself that night. I could have fixed everything, made it perfect. She would have cherished me, extolled me, but I failed because I was a scared little man. Pathetic. So, what did I do? Out of pure frustration, I just staked £3000 on the very next bet on both teams to score and I lost everything. I just wanted to drive my car off a cliff. Quietly without her realising, just ridding her of the burden in her life. Me. I had all sorts of thoughts running through my mind. I truly was lost. I didn't even know how I would tell her that I had lost everything and made matters worse. I stayed up all night, desperately trying to escape my reality. I just felt like everything was rigged and designed to make me fail, that nothing would go my way. It never did. I was at one of the lowest points that I had ever been in in my adult life. I was so sure about gambling. I was so passionate about it. I was convinced it would work. It didn't. The morning quickly came and I had to take the responsibility of telling her I'd lost the rest of our money. As soon as she woke up she asked me what happened. The look I gave her said it all. She sighed and let out a huge gasp. I just laid my head flat on my chest and said nothing, the room was silent. A few minutes went by as she laid back down and I could hear her weeping. I felt terrible. It was the worst feeling that I think another human being has ever made me feel. I just lay next to her and held her tight, and with that embrace, I knew she forgave me. It broke her, it broke me. We carried on dating for a few years after that before she finally left the country for her own personal reasons. What I wish I knew back then about money is the best way to make money is by learning more. Warren Buffett said, "the more you learn the more you earn." I also found out later that financial intelligence is everything. We need to understand accounting, tax, investments and the law to be more productive when it comes to money. Isaac Newton said, "You have to stand on the shoulder of giants." Basically, learn from people that have already been successful and emulate them. I wish I knew this back then.

I stopped gambling for some time after this. I finally got a new job working in Watford in a call centre. The money was terrible. Nothing to write home about. After all my expenses, I was left with almost nothing. I couldn't save any money. Pointless. You know those jobs that are menial and hand to mouth. I deserved better than this. So, I signed up for a tourism and hospitality management postgraduate course that I never managed to complete. Not sure if it was laziness or a lack of motivation but I couldn't complete it. I enrolled in this course because I had over a decade of experience in hospitality. I was tired of being in a dead-end job, being undervalued and overworked and being around bad people at that. I know I wasn't that type of person to just be average I always wanted more from my life.

My anxiety and psychosis were still extremely bad. I would hear things daily from all sorts of people that I encountered. When I started working in this call centre which dealt with the management of car parks throughout the UK, it started off as quite fun. For the first two weeks, I was required to train on day shifts. This allowed me to become familiar with the team and chat and make new friends. I think most of the people I befriended were female. Don't get me wrong, I heard things from females, too, but I perceived them as being less of a threat. I will admit my natural virile nature took precedence. I was very flirtatious and debonair around the women that worked there. It was just a lot of sexual tension in the office as you would expect in an open office environment. I was there to do my job; this wasn't all fun and games for me. I just liked the fun nature of the office I was in. It was a big distraction for me and strangely I felt like I fitted in. Things changed, however, when I was assigned to a night shift which was actually the shift I was hired to do. I always preferred the night shift. Less pressure, no management breathing down your neck, more freedom. Of course, my anxiety and anti-social nature fitted in with that perfectly. After getting used to everyone on the day shift the moment finally came for me to start my first official night shift. A lot of the girls I had bonded with, namely Henna, who was a new supervisor and started on the same day that I did, Sarah who was a customer support advisor and so, too, was

Amal. They all worked on day shifts and evening shifts so the latest they would finish was around 10 pm and I started at 8 pm so didn't get to see them for long anymore. Everything felt like it had changed. There were two-night shift teams. Each had three staff members. On my team was Tricia and Henry. I heard a lot about Tricia, that she was very truculent and had had several run-ins with other staff members in the past. Henry was gregarious, very sociable and loquacious, my worst nightmare. The first shift started off very tense. Henry was also fairly new to the team. I'm sure you can understand how high labour turnover is in that type of industry. I sat opposite Henry and next to Tricia. Henry was Dutch and Tricia was from Barbados. No one was talking during the first shift. Everyone was wary of Tricia who was the night supervisor. We all trod on eggshells around her as gossip spread like a wildfire about her temperament. She was indeed very stern and hard-nosed. She didn't mince her words and had this air of seriousness about her. I never once heard any insults from her and I'm not sure why that is. It just never happened. Henry, on the other hand, I would hear insults from all the time. From the second shift onwards, I heard him say all sorts of things to me in front of the other staff members and I remember thinking to myself that I would just ignore him and keep my distance. For whatever reason, I felt angrier when this would happen when women were present, or when anyone was for that matter. It was easier to ignore insults when alone with one person than in a group. No one likes to feel ridiculed in front of others.

It got so bad that I came to the realisation that I couldn't work in that environment anymore. I tried my best to keep ignoring him and taking the punches but enough was enough. One day I confronted him about it. He denied ever saying anything to me but it was like I had armed him with the special bullets it took to get to me and he exploited that. He never once thought that maybe I had a problem and was troubled. The same night I confronted him about everything I also spoke to my supervisor, Tricia, about the tension between Henry and me. She seemed completely tactless towards me and had no empathy. She was cold but had to afford me the professional courtesy of offering me words of encouragement and support. I spoke to Henna a lot even outside of work, as did I with Amal. Henna was middle-eastern, a bit younger than me but was a supervisor on day shifts, and Amal was Ethiopian.

One day I went to work and again I believed Henry had insulted me and this time I just gave up. Just the feeling of being ridiculed in front of an audience was horrible. I thought he had put his middle finger up to me as well as calling me an idiot. This was in the middle of a normal innocuous exchange. The minute it happened my heart started racing, I was clouded by doubt and anger. I didn't know what to do or why I deserved that. I had tried and tried. So, I decided to apprise Henna of it. There was a lot of underlying issues with the way the office was being managed, a lot of personality clashes and egos; I could see this. She told me I was lucky not to be on day shifts as those were far worse. She was lovely; during my lunch breaks, she would bring me food from home as she lived locally and she would just offer me some company and a way to vent out my frustrations. I was lucky to have met her; she was amazing. She also suffered from social anxiety and struggled to fit into the new group at first. Also, being younger a lot of people didn't give her the respect she deserved. Our mental afflictions were different but it's what made us get close. We had each other's backs. She became a good friend of mine. One day I came in to work for my night shift. The feeling I had was like I was sure I couldn't go on doing that job. I have had that feeling previously. I know myself. I had had enough. I had been toying with the idea of just walking out for weeks. Just the feeling I would have before I even arrive at work, the dread, the anxiety the fear of being insulted – my heart would race, my brain would hurt. I did everything I could but the insults just wouldn't stop from Henry and co. It was like everyone was out to get me and disrespect me. On this particular day, I just felt like a ghost. I felt invisible and irrelevant – an outsider. To make matters worse Tricia and Henry were bonding and would deliberately leave me out of their little bubble. I didn't mind that but I just hated the feeling of being omitted. It wasn't FOMO, it was a form of bullying, I felt. Just wrong and unacceptable. Midway through the shift I just stood up and walked outside for a cigarette. I tried my very best to clear my head and shake off the feeling I had. I needed the money and like my mom would always say, nothing lasts forever. This feeling would pass. But I couldn't keep going on. I was going to explode in a bad way. I walked back in and just sat down for half a minute and then I just started packing my stuff up. Of course, Tricia was surprised by this. Henry looked like he had a smile of satisfaction on his face. He had won and got me to quit. What a wicked character, I thought to myself. I just picked up my stuff without saying a word and headed for the door. As I strode off, Tricia quickly asked me where I was going. I just explained to her that I would email the manager and she would be filled in at a later date. She did seem marginally concerned but I didn't care. I didn't need her sympathy; it was too late for all that anyway. The drive home was long but therapeutic. I listened to music and just concentrated on what my next move was going to be to make money. Gambling. I thought to myself that I would become rich from it, that I would be one of the few people who consistently beat the house and would never need to work again or be around people again. I read the book "Rich Dad Poor Dad" by Robert Kiyosaki and I just wanted out of the rat race. Going nowhere quickly. I don't know if I truly believed gambling was the answer but I know I was desperate for something else. They say to have something you never had you have to do something you never did. I was willing to try this out again. Besides the idea of it seemed fun and I had had some success with it in the past. I just didn't overcome and face my fears at the right moments.

I got home at around two in the morning and immediately deposited £100 into my betting account. I hadn't touched it for a while. I was back and ready to try again. I was going to get what would be my final paycheque within seven days so I was okay, somewhat. I also expected to receive untaken holiday pay. I was going to make it. I would survive and live off this gambling money that I was sure I was going to make.

About two months had passed. I was still in the same place. I had won money, lost it, won it and lost it. I then decided to up the ante. Up my stake. I didn't have the money so I decided to apply for a loan of £2500. It was from a payday loan company that rip people off for a living but it didn't matter because I was going to double it in one bet and pay it straight back. I was approved for the loan because I lied about still working and my credit score was still good. It just took a few minutes. This was the beginning of a vicious cycle, that I now wish I had never started. I deposited the entire amount of £2500. I lost the bet and I remember feeling like I was having a panic attack. Apart from my overdraft and student loan, I had never really been in debt. No car finance, mortgages, big loans, etc. I didn't know what I had done. All I know was that my immediate reaction was to fix the problem. So, I applied for another loan. This time it was for £2000 from another payday loan company called Satsuma. They approved my application. The money was deposited into my NatWest account two minutes later. I felt better. I sighed and just told myself I needed to win two 1/1 bets or thereabouts to get all the money back, pay off the loans and still have a profit. In theory, it wasn't that difficult. Especially on virtual football. I waited a day and then deposited the £2000 into my betting account. I spent about two days just making small bets of about £10, I was in fear of losing all the money. Eventually, I mustered up the courage to make my bet it was for £1960 and the profit would have been £2450. I was confident but afraid at the same time, an oxymoron. I lost the bet again and my heart sank. I've never had that feeling before. This time I started thinking about suicide and just feeling cursed and indignant. I couldn't understand what was going on. It didn't make any sense to me. I did it again. I found another company that was willing to lend me £900. I lost it again. Before I knew it I had accumulated about £8,000 worth of debt with about seven loan companies. I had never been as unsure about anything in my life as I was about the situation, I found myself in. I started chastising myself, blaming myself and being hard on myself for my poor financial intelligence and decisions, blaming my mental health problems for the situation I was in. If I had kept all that money, I would have had a comfortable

£8000 in my account plus money from my last job. A much better alternative. I started receiving benefits and I was looking for new employment. I had set up a debt management plan soon after and was paying about £50 per month to all my creditors monthly as that was all I could afford. They said with that payment schedule I would be debt-free in about 17 years and 3 months. This meant nothing to me, I was just happy to have some breathing space. I couldn't deal with all the phone calls and emails coming in from my creditors. This was the best solution. For a while, I felt depressed and my anxiety was exacerbated. I became even more reclusive than usual. I would ignore calls from friends and family, wouldn't venture out for more than one reason. I was just in a cocoon. Estranged from the world.

About a month later I found a job in Earls Court working in another hotel. It was rundown and housed what some would consider being lower social class people. It was full of unsavoury characters. Charging on average £30 per night what else was there to expect. I did, however, like the job as I worked alone on shift and didn't have to see anyone except customers, and staff for about 10 minutes to hand over. It was the year 2020. The hotel group consisted of about five hotels all in the southwest area of London. I saw a lot of things in that hotel that I hadn't seen before. I had to call the police about three times in my short time working there. I still would hear insults from customers regularly but I was able to ignore it as with most of them I wouldn't see them more than once. Then there was coronavirus which greatly affected the hospitality industry in general. At some point, the hotel even had to temporarily close as business was so bad and numbers weren't adding up. My money situation wasn't any better. I even had difficulty paying rent for some months. My first paycheque wasn't due for about three and a half weeks and I still had the urge to gamble. I was an addict. I had been deceived by the system as I imagine many others are, too. I thought of ways in which I could raise money to pay off my debts. I started asking friends and family if I could borrow money from them. I managed to get about £1500 from people I knew. I tried to win all my money back again, this time making smaller bets of £100 and making £100 every day, so after three months I would be more than okay. The money did stretch and last but I was still not taking steps forward. I eventually lost all that money and had accumulated even more debt. My parents did send me £3000 of their hard-earned money to pay off some of my debt as I had explained to them what I had done and the mess I had created. I felt terrible. I paid off some of my debt but was still £5000 in a hole, not including student loans and overdrafts. I felt like I couldn't breathe. It's strange but debt made me feel claustrophobic in a way. I can only describe it like that. I wasn't saving money from my job. I was earning significantly more than my previous job, but then I would just gamble my savings away and make my situation worse. This went on and on until one day I eventually decided to stop gambling. I just went cold turkey. It wasn't easy and even today I still get the urge to put money into my account. I closed my account and I haven't looked at it since. Paul Merson wrote the book 'Hooked' and he said addiction wants you on your own. It imprisons you and isolates you.[46] What keeps you coming back is the chance that you could win and win big, but if

---

46 PAUL MERSON, HOOKED: *Addiction and the Long Road to Recovery.* (S.L: HEADLINE BOOK PUBLISHING, 2022).

that's not enough winning your money back is. My gambling got so bad that at times I even considered suicide. I had no one to help me. I was ashamed to talk about it. I remember once I was just sitting in my car thinking of the best way to end it all. If you consider my mental health problems and the gambling, too, it was all too much for me to handle. I wanted to just end the pain and suffering. So I drove to a deserted area near the countryside. I wasn't familiar with the area I just drove and drove until I reached a place where no one would find me. I found a place to park off-road and just sat in my car contemplating suicide. My head was in my hands; I was scared, scared of the unknown. These are the moments life demands that you must submit to. I sat there trying to summon up the courage to accelerate ferociously and just find a tree to crash into. Then my phone rang – it was my mum. She saved my life. I never spoke a word of it to her but I know somehow, she was my angel sent to protect me. After the phone call, I drove home and slept for hours and hours. The thing with gambling is that it's a rollercoaster, the ups and the downs. It was taxing on my heart. My girlfriend told me a story of a friend of a friend of hers whose partner committed suicide due to having a gambling debt. I could relate to that. It's crippling and it can ruin your life. A lot of these gambling companies prey on innocent, good people's desire to make a little bit of change at the cost of becoming addicted to it. It's deep psychological manipulation, the biggest crime if you ask me. I know that I said fear is what limits your wins, but gambling is never an honest way for any company to make legitimate money. Gambling is terrible. It's something people do out of desperation. This just reminds me of what I mentioned earlier about what the great Thoreau said, "The masses of men live in quiet desperation. What we know as resignation is actually confirmed desperation." For most of us, gambling is something we do on the off chance that we could win so big that it can change our lives. A bit like the lottery. I learned my lesson the hard way. What's worse, I started smoking even more. Even after witnessing my uncle passing away from cancer caused by smoking. I was addicted.

If you suffer from a gambling addiction visit www.gamstop.co.uk for the opportunity to self-exclude yourself from all betting sites in the UK.[47] This can help you to cease gambling. It worked for me. You can also visit www.gamcare.co.uk they offer a range of services to help with gambling cessation,[48] from a self-assessment tool, to changing your behaviour, to money management and even a course. Give it a try – it's worth it. Gambling is a serious problem and it can ruin lives. At the start it is insidious but if left unchecked it can get out of hand and you don't want that. My advice is to stop while you are ahead.

---

47 GAMSTOP, 'Gambling Self-Exclusion Scheme', 2021 <https://www.gamstop.co.uk/> [accessed 7 September 2021].

48 GamCare, 'Home - GamCare - The Leading Provider of Support for Anyone Affected by Problem Gambling in Great Britain', *GamCare*, 2021 <https://www.gamcare.org.uk/> [accessed 18 September 2021].

Chapter 8: The other side of pain

You are what you think. You are what you feel. You are what you believe you are. I learned about the law of attraction much later on in my life. One of the seven hermetic principles – the law of correspondence. This is very powerful and relevant. I didn't understand the pertinence of this principle. It applies to your very core being and frequency. Every day we live our lives this principle is in effect. Just think when you tell yourself you don't want to get stuck in traffic because you are late for work. What happens? You get stuck in traffic. When you tell yourself that you may not get a promotion at work that you so badly want. What happens? You don't get it. When you tell yourself that your partner may be disloyal to you what happens? They cheat on you. Equally, when you tell yourself you will have a great blissful day. What happens? You tend to have a great day. When you tell yourself that you will get that brand new car you always wanted. What happens you eventually get it. It's powerful, but it's also divine timing. Things don't necessarily happen exactly when you want them to but they do eventually manifest as long as you believe they will wholeheartedly. One way or another. It's not only what you think but also what you believe, feel and know.[49] If you wholeheartedly believe these things will happen, they most often do. We are more powerful beings than we know. We can manifest things just by feeling and believing them. It's all energy. Where focus goes, energy flows. This I found to be so true with my mental health affliction, I can also relate it to this principle. Every day I was certain that I would attract negativity and insults and that people wouldn't like me, and what happened every day? People insulted me. Whether it was real or not I still believed it was. The thing is its energy. Our bodies are made up of energy through atoms, molecules and cells. Everything is energy and energy can be manipulated to do what you command it to do. It's like a river, it just flows with the current. What people don't often realise is that the current can be changed to one's benefit or determent. I was fixated and obsessed with this idea that people wanted to insult me. I would wake up every day and believe that it was my fate and that it couldn't be changed. I never thought to myself that in the past this never used to happen and that in general everyday life these things don't happen. It was no longer relevant because I had to change my belief system, I was limited in what I was able to believe and think. I heard this saying that you shouldn't be the bi**h of your own brain. Basically, you shouldn't let your brain control you, tell you what to do or think or limit you. Just like any other muscle in the body the brain can be trained and developed too. They say it takes about 66 days to make a particular behaviour become automatic and between 18 and 254

---

49 Rhonda Byrne, *The Secret*, 1st Atria Books/Beyond Words hardcover ed (New York: Hillsboro, Or: Atria Books; Beyond Words Pub, 2006).

days for that new habit to be formed. According to Philippa Lally, a psychologist from University College London, it takes a little over two months and up to 254 days to form a new habit. There are myths about this. Dr Maxwell Maltz coined the idea that a habit can be formed through 21 days of doing the same thing over and over; this was far from being true. It was popular amongst people but later got debunked. I didn't know this before. I also love the saying, 'good habits are hard to form but easy to live with and bad habits are easy to form but hard to live with.'

I found this article on the formation of a new habit and how some of the most successful people managed to do it.

The habits of highly successful people allow them to consistently perform behaviours that breed success. Everything from eating well to responsible spending to task completion and beyond requires habits that make such behaviours part of our daily life. Michael Jordan spent his off seasons taking hundreds of jump shots a day. Award-winning Phillies pitcher Roy Halladay routinely does a 90-minute workout before practices. The young Venus and Serena Williams would wake up at 6:00 am to hit tennis balls before school. Highly successful people have learned to develop good habits, and it takes discipline, courage and hard work on a daily basis to keep those habits in place. It makes perfect sense to adopt habits that will facilitate success, yet, why are some so difficult to adopt?

Most people believe that habits are formed by completing a task for 21 days in a row. 21 days of task completion, then voila, a habit is formed. Unfortunately, this could not be further from the truth. The 21-day myth began as a misinterpretation of Dr Maxwell Maltz's work on self-image. Maltz did not find that 21 days of task completion forms a habit. People wanted it to be true so much so, however, that the idea began to grow in popularity.

Tom Bartow, who successfully started advanced training for Edward Jones and has since become a highly sought after business coach, developed the following model of what habit formation looks like:

The three phases of habit formation:

Phase 1: THE HONEYMOON[50]

This phase of habit formation is characterized by the feeling of "this is easy." As all married people will tell you, at some point, even the greatest honeymoon must end. The honeymoon phase is usually the result of something inspiring. For example, a person attends a highly motivational conference, and for the first few days after the conference, the individual is making positive changes in his or her life.

Phase 2: THE FIGHT THRU

Inspiration fades and reality sets in. A person finds himself struggling with positive habit completion and old habits seem to be right around the corner. The key to moving to the third phase of habit formation is to win two or three "fight thru's." This is critical. To win the fight thru, use the following techniques:

---

50 LiveWell Team, 'The Three Phases of Habit Formation', LiveWell, 2019 <https://www.strengthandrehabilitation.com/post/2019/01/08/the-three-phases-of-habit-formation> [accessed 5 September 2021].

RECOGNIZE: Recognition is essential for winning the fight thru. When you have entered the fight thru, simply say to yourself, "I have entered the fight thru, and I need to win a few to move past this." Winning each fight thru will make it easier to win the next. Conversely, when you choose to lose a fight thru, you make it easier to lose the next one.

ASK 2 QUESTIONS: "How will I feel if I do this?" and "How will I feel if I don't do this?" Bring EMOTION into the equation. Let yourself feel the positive in winning the fight thru and the negative in losing.

LIFE PROJECTION: If the above 2 techniques haven't moved you to action, then imagine in great detail how your life will be in five years if you do not begin making changes. Be honest with yourself, and allow yourself to feel what life will be like if the changes are not made.

Phase 3: SECOND NATURE

Entering second nature is often described by feelings of "getting in the groove." Once in second nature, the following are three common interruptions that will send a person back to the fight thru:

THE DISCOURAGEMENT MONSTER: An individual allows negative results to discourage him or her into thinking, "This isn't working, and there is nothing I can do."

DISRUPTIONS: An individual experiences significant change to his or her current pattern (e.g., vacations, holidays, illness, weekends).

SEDUCTION OF SUCCESS: An individual begins to focus on positive results and begins to think, "I'm the special one. I have finally figured out how to have great results with the not-so-great process."

If a person experiences an interruption that sends him or her back to the fight thru, winning two or three fight thru's will bring him or her back to second nature.

Most people want positive habits to be as easy as brushing their teeth. HELLO…LET'S BE ADULTS HERE…being great isn't easy. Greatness requires sacrifice. It requires doing things that others won't or can't do. GREAT HABITS ARE FORMED DAILY. Truth be told, good habits require consistent commitment. Highly successful people have learned to develop good habits. Make the commitment to make it past the fight thru, no matter how many times you go back to it, to reach new levels of success.

Published by Forbes 2013

The thing is you may discover that you have the talent to succeed but do you have the guts to fail. The law of attraction and the formation of new habits are commingled. It's all about the mind's ability to yield a result based on a repetitive thought, action or belief. It became so easy for me to wake up and believe my new reality was permanent. It's like I didn't see myself losing myself. It was insidious and gradual. I just believed this was my fate and that it would never end and so I attracted it more and more. It's a simple paradigm shift. It takes a bit of change and programming to reconfigure your brain but if you don't believe it will happen, it won't happen. As the saying goes, 'those who think they can and those who think they can't are both usually correct.' I gave up too easily and didn't have enough fight thru's. Now don't get me wrong, we are creatures of habit. We do things automatically. sometimes without even applying thought to it and changing habits is hard, especially when you consider how fast the world moves in this current age. 96% of our cognitive decisions are done without us actually consciously making those decisions even though we think we are. This is something we do daily. There's real power in the principle of the law of attraction. We don't realise how often we apply this to our everyday lives. I only realised how relevant this was to my particular case when I started applying it consciously to my life. I would wake up every day and attract the very thing I didn't want. The mind cannot negate the negative aspect of this law. You attract exactly what you think of. The universe doesn't give us what we want, it gives us what we are. This law is always in action and never stops. If I knew the energy it took me to think and attract positive was the same as the negative, I would have applied this to my life before and completely turned things around. Today, I still suffer from anxiety and psychosis but it's a lot milder and more manageable. But mentally I'm still stuck in that dark place and find it hard to escape. There was an experiment I once saw on the internet – I believe it was YouTube – where they tested the negative bias, we human beings have. It's a lot easier to think negatively than positively although it takes the same amount of energy. A man was asked to stand with his eyes closed and extend his arms out as far as possible. Then someone stood in front of him and told him to imagine all the things he felt negative about in his life. Whilst doing this the person tried to use force to push his arms back down to his sides. It was effortless, the man relented and gave in, there was no fire in his belly nor did he put up a fight. He then did the same experiment, but this time told the man to stand with his arms extended and asked him to think of all the positive things in his life and again tried to push his arms down back to his sides but this time it was met with strong resistance, no matter how hard the person tried to push his arms down he couldn't. The man believed in the positive things, they made him strong and he couldn't be halted. This experiment showed me that we are at our most powerful in the present moment and that when it comes to positive things, we believe in them so much that nothing can penetrate that bubble. Conversely, when we feel defeated and dejected, we easily fold and relinquish our power. It's just in the human psyche it's the negative bias we all have. Most of us wake up worrying about our day rather than celebrating the day, it's just a lot easier. It's from all the years of conditioning through media, family friends, history. It's all designed to make us have a negative bias and always dwell on negativity and expect it. We do this subconsciously without even realising it at the best of times. Think about it. We always worry about our finances, our relationships, our spirituality and the relevance of it to the afterlife, our children, our bodies. The list goes on. Media makes us believe that we are not enough and that we are supposed to feel inept or feel inadequate, that whatever you have isn't enough and that you need more. It's by design. It's a system. It affects all of us. Just always remember that it's not a question of who will let you, it's a question of who will stop you. You are formidable and you deserve great things in your life.

Here's another example of how effective the law of attraction is. During the presidential election in 2016 when Donald Trump was voted into the White House, so many people didn't like him, nor what he stood for. People were against him, yet all the energy they had emitted on how much they didn't want him to be the new president-elect led to him being voted into the White House. Another example is how people focus on anti-war protests and movements. Essentially, they are looking for equality and world peace but because they are focusing on war and stopping it they are still giving energy to the "war" and thus the wars and separation in the world continue year after year. I once worked with a man who used to always worry about contracting cancer because he smoked too much. He would constantly say he DIDN'T want cancer. He didn't help himself by continuing to smoke, but what eventually happened? I found out that he had contracted cancer and was in a really bad way at that time. The message is simple: there is power in the tongue, mind and soul. We have divine power and are infinite beings, everything is energy and is connected, and we have dominion over this earth as children of God. When we say and do things, even little things, they affect us and everything around us. One thing I also learned when I was doing cognitive behavioural therapy (CBT) is that our feelings are caused by our thoughts and that we attract what we think about. Emotions and feelings are the highest form of energy we can emit. For example, love, fear, anxiety. Love is the most powerful. Love lends a unique quality to efforts. If you do things out of love, your efforts are more likely to be fruitful. We are emotional beings and are constantly being led by how we feel. We believe in our feelings more than we understand our thoughts. We are constantly thinking, I believe we have on average over 100,000 thoughts a day. This figure has been disputed over the years and is said to vary greatly. But just think about how often our brains are working. We are never not thinking if you think about it.

Chapter 9: How to overcome and cope with mental health afflictions

There are many methods I've discovered that can help eradicate/alleviate anxiety and psychosis amongst other mental health conditions. Some are my own methods and some I have learned through therapy and through things I've read throughout the years. The list isn't exhaustive but I am currently using it to my advantage.

- Exercise regularly
- Consider having a vegan diet
- Talking therapies especially CBT
- Exercise the mind i.e., through reading a lot, meditation and so on
- Taking prescribed medication
- Apply the Gray's Line method
- Using colours to overcome mental health problems
- Present moment focus
- Consider a best-case scenario (positive assumptions)
- Adjust your mental grinder accordingly
- If you have auditory hallucinations audio record your interactions with people
- Go on vacations regularly or take time outs

- Get good sleep and rest
- Abstain from drinking alcohol, beverages with high caffeine content and smoking
- Deep breathing exercises – counting to 10
- The Theory A and Theory B approach
- Laughing a lot
- Learn what triggers your anxiety and learn how to cope with it
- Be okay with not having control over everything
- Anxiety Blueprint
- Challenge your negative thoughts
- Situation, Reaction and Learning point record
- Acupuncture
- Embrace moments of stillness and quietness
- Develop new habits that help to improve you
- Have a positive attitude and set goals, shift your paradigm
- Keep reminding yourself that these moments (anxiety and panic attacks) will pass
- Remind yourself that you are normal
- Consider playing different frequencies and tapping into your chakras
- Join self-help groups or local early intervention centres – realise you are not alone
- Family and friend intervention

Regular exercise

Regular exercise is a must when it comes to mental health problems. It helps free the mind and balance the body, spirit and mind. Regular exercise reduces the feeling of anxiety, depression and general negative moods by improving your self-esteem and belief and your general cognitive function. It also releases endorphins which is exhilarating. They call it 'runner's high.' You make better decisions and have better and more positive thoughts. Research has found that exercise has also been found to reduce social withdrawal and low self-esteem.[51] One obvious factor, too, is that you look great. More often than not when you look great you feel great, too. Tony Robbins once said something like our body is a representation of our standards. He said, "wants don't get met consistently, standards do." If you make it your standard to look good and be healthy this affirms your mental state of believing you are worthy and being your best version. It's not about vanity, it's just about knowing and feeling good about yourself without any compromises. A lack of exercise, according to the experts of the British Nutrition Foundation, can lead to dementia and depression.[52] In an article, I once read by Ashish Sharma M.D., Vishal Madaan M.D., and Frederick D.Petty M.D. PhD it states that people who lead sedentary lifestyles are more likely to be affected by chronic diseases which are also

---

[51] *Exercise, Health and Mental Health: Emerging Relationships*, ed. by Guy E. J. Faulkner and Adrian H. Taylor (London; New York: Routledge, 2005).

[52] British Nutrition Foundation, 'Home – British Nutrition Foundation', 2021 <https://www.nutrition.org.uk/> [accessed 7 September 2021].

associated with medication side effects.[53] These diseases include diabetes, hyperlipidaemia and cardiovascular disease. Aerobic exercises e.g., jogging, swimming, cycling, walking, gardening and dancing have been proved to reduce anxiety and depression. These mood improvements can be attributed to an exercise-induced increase in blood circulation to the brain by an influence on the hypothalamic-pituitary-adrenal (HPA) axis, and thus on the physiologic reactivity to stress. This physiological influence is probably mediated by the communication of the HPA axis with several regions of the brain which also includes the limbic system which is known for controlling motivation and mood; the amygdala, which generates fear in response to stress; and the hippocampus which relates to memory formation as well as mood and motivation. Other benefits of physical activity include self-efficacy, social interaction and distraction. Exercise has been reported to be especially useful and helpful for people with schizophrenia since they are already vulnerable to weight gain due to antipsychotics. There was a 3-month physical conditioning programme that showed improvements in weight control and reported increases in fitness levels, exercise tolerance and reduced blood pressure levels. There is also said to have been an increase in energy levels and upper body strength levels. 30 minutes a day of exercise 3 days a week is enough to attain such results. Some other health benefits of exercise include:

---

[53] Ashish Sharma, Vishal Madaan, and Frederick D. Petty, 'Exercise for Mental Health', *Primary Care Companion to the Journal of Clinical Psychiatry*, 8.2 (2006), 106 <https://doi.org/10.4088/pcc.v08n0208a>.

CHAPTER 9: HOW TO OVERCOME AND COPE WITH MENTAL HEALTH AFFLICTIONS

1. Improved sleep
2. Increase in libido
3. Better endurance
4. Stress relief (reduction in cortisol levels and increase in serotonin)
5. Improvement in mood
6. Increased energy and stamina
7. Reduced tiredness
8. Weight loss
9. Reduced cholesterol and improved cardiovascular fitness

Exercise is crucial for managing mental health problems. It balances the body and mind and helps to regulate hormone levels. You need to get out of the mind and back into the body. Exercise and regular physical activity are good in general and are something everyone should look to incorporate into their everyday lives. After all, it's one of the four pillars of life: health, wealth, love and happiness. It has helped me with my social anxiety and psychosis. I try to exercise regularly and keep improving myself mentally and physically. I noticed a reduction in stress levels, better moods and decision making also an ability to stay calm during an anxiety episode. We have to realise the body is the subconscious mind. If your body is unhealthy, that has a knock-on effect on the mind as the two are connected. We may not be fully aware of the effects our unhealthy bodies have on our conscious mind but there is definitely a correlation between the two.

Veganism

Veganism has become very popular in recent times. So many people are becoming vegans and implementing a meat-free diet. Research has shown the positive effects this can have on mental health afflictions as well as your general health.[54] I exercised a 7-day vegan challenge and I immediately saw the difference in my anxiety and stress levels. Most vegan foods contain calcium, magnesium like kale and watercress, potassium like bananas and pumpkin seeds and vitamin B, all these generally lower stress and anxiety levels in the body. Researchers from Benedictine University discovered that there were little to no differences in the depression levels in people who had a vegan diet, conversely, people with a meat-full diet however had higher anxiety and stress levels. Foods to stay away from when you suffer from mental health problems are fried food, cereals, candy, pastries, high-fat dairy products like milk or full-fat milk. These are more likely to cause anxiety and depression. Rather look to eat more fibre-rich grains, fruits, vegetables and if pescatarian, fish as well, as this will more than likely balance your moods and stress and hormone levels. We are made of carbon amongst other things so eating a rich carbon-based diet is key; this results in chemical affinity where your body reacts positively to the food you give it as it recognises it as it's made up of the same thing. Milk or cheese is one of the worst things you can consume as the body doesn't recognise the foreign nature of the cells in this food. Over time this can lead to an overactive liver and kidneys and eventually disallows the body

---

54 Elanor Clarke, *Little Book of Veganism*, 2015.

from producing sufficient insulin levels which can lead to diabetes and other medical conditions like heart disease and even cancer. As far as beverages go tea is very good for severe anxiety but coffee is one beverage to avoid due to its excessive potassium levels. Kava tea relaxes the mood, calms and eases fears. This is because it contains kavalactones which have been found to affect the brain in the same way as anxiety medications. Vitamins are also good for reducing anxiety, namely Vitamin D, magnesium, Ashwagandha which is a herb, valerian root which is also a herb are good for you. Vitamin C is also good for mood and cognitive function and reduces anxiety and depression. Believe it or not, even drinking water and staying hydrated can calm you down. It's the little things we take for granted that make all the difference. According to the nutritionist, Geeta Sidhu-Robb, a vegan diet can affect your mood immensely. There are four ways in which this can be done. It makes you feel less depressed just like with exercise. This is because of the elimination of fatty acids e.g. arachidonic acid, which is found in meat and is associated with depression. Vegan diets also have better carbohydrates present which increases the hormone serotonin, it's calming for the body and makes you feel good.

Vegan diets help improve your mood. They contain higher levels of vitamins and nutrients than meat diets, and these help to fight off illnesses and diseases. Vitamin C for example boosts the immune system as it produces antibodies and stimulates the production of white blood cells which combat illnesses. Vitamin E is another good and necessary vitamin as it has antioxidants that help fight off infection. When you are ill or unwell you feel tired, moody and lethargic so eating a vegan-based diet can help curb this.

Vegan diets can also help improve sleep. Eating more foods with calcium and magnesium in them can help to improve one's sleep. A lack of good sleep can put anyone in a bad mood. The highest source of magnesium comes from kale, watercress, spinach, avocados and pumpkin seeds.

Vegan diets can reduce stress levels and eradicate the production of the hormone, cortisol.[55] A vegan diet lowers your blood pressure, cholesterol intake and weight. This will positively reduce your stress and anxiety levels. Potassium, calcium, magnesium and vitamin B all lower stress levels. Antioxidants in vitamins A, C and E help reduce free-radical damage which increases when we are stressed. Life as we know it is very stressful it comes in many forms and from many different directions. Having a well-balanced meat-free diet can help to reverse this and lead to a more improved mood. Vegan diets can affect men and women differently, but generally, they all improve our mood and thus we feel better and are happier. There are concerns that vegan diets are more expensive but if you think about it your body is all you have to take you through this journey, we call life and it's a worthy investment. Invest in yourself first. Another thing is we are creatures of habit so changing to a new meat and dairy-free diet may be challenging at first but as I've always remembered it's question first, answer second. The why of it all is crucial. We all know smoking a cigarette can give a great feeling in the moment but if you asked yourself why you are smoking and the negative effect it can have on your health long term you would most likely stop. The

---

[55] Winston J Craig, 'Health Effects of Vegan Diets', *The American Journal of Clinical Nutrition*, 89.5 (2009), 1627S-1633S <https://doi.org/10.3945/ajcn.2009.26736N>.

same applies to implementing a vegan diet. There are several recipes that you can find online now and videos you can watch on YouTube which will help you find a healthy, tasty diet.

There is a study that states that 45% of Australians aged between 16-85 years of age will suffer from mental illness at some point in their lives. Some of these mental health disorders include depression, OCD, schizophrenia, generalised anxiety and eating disorders and then some. If left untreated this can lead to suicidal thoughts. According to the Australian Bureau of Statistics in 2007 mental illness cost $20bn. This figure also consists of loss of labour productivity and labour force participation. The number of mental health services subsidised by Medicare doubled to nearly 4 million cases, mental health service expenditure increased to $3bn and also the number of GP visits concerning mental health in 2007 was estimated to be around 12 million. The population of Australia at that time was around 21 million. The total cost of mental health grew to $30bn the same year.

A link between a vegan diet and mental health was looked into. It was based on 620 patients who were subdivided into three categories: 283 vegans, 109 vegetarians and 228 omnivores. They assessed the patients using the depression anxiety stress scale-21 (DASS-21) The results concluded that vegan females had much lower stress scores than non-vegans, whilst male vegans reported lower average anxiety scores.

In 2015 a study in America that tried to establish whether having a plant-based diet improved depression, anxiety and productivity was published by the American Journal of Health Promotion. The study incorporated 10 worksites of a major UDS insurance company and 292 subjects with a body mass index (BMI) greater than 25 and/ or a previous diagnosis of type 2 diabetes. Some followed a vegan diet for 18 weeks and some were told to eat as they normally would. Their mood was measured using a short form-36 questionnaire whilst work productivity was measured using the work productivity and impairment questionnaire. The group of people who became vegan showed significantly improved depression, anxiety and productivity compared to the other group. There was even another study in Queensland Australia consisting of about 12,000 households or individuals. The study looked into the fruits and vegetables that the subjects ate and then rated their level of satisfaction, stress, vitality and other mental health markers. The more fruits and vegetables people ate, the better they felt. The average Australian has a high meat-based diet and thus have, and are likely to suffer from depression, stress and anxiety.

You are what you eat. Food is an essential part of our everyday lives; it ensures we are well centred and have a balanced hormonal level and also dictates our moods and stress levels. As I said, I tried this 7-day vegan challenge out and I could immediately see the difference. I advise that you do try this out and see if it works for you. People underestimate the importance of food and the effects it has on our minds and body's chemistry. I do admit I'm not a total vegan (I like meat too much) but it's worth trying it out. I do have times when I only eat vegan food for a week or so. I also believe that moderation is key. I do consume many fruits, vegetables, fibre, etc. The 7-day vegan challenge will amaze you. Again, it's all about forming new habits and breaking the mould. A lot of us eat foods based on our cultures. But this doesn't necessarily have to be you. Do what works for you. Don't be afraid to try new things and improve your quality of life.

Cognitive behavioural therapy (CBT)

Cognitive behavioural therapy (CBT) is one of the most popular forms of talking therapy that is recommended for people with mental health afflictions. It was originally used to treat depression. It combines cognitive therapy (what you think) with behavioural therapy (what you do). Aaron Beck, a psychoanalyst from the University of Pennsylvania Medical School, described the basic concept of CBT as being when individuals who suffer from depression have a set of beliefs about themselves. These thoughts then cause them to have negative thoughts while responding to adversity, and these thoughts cause them to retreat within themselves and as a result, they become more depressed. He felt that this contradicted contemporary thinking about depression as back then treatments for depression focused too much on the past and previous experiences rather than day-to-day beliefs and experiences.[56] By realising this Beck revolutionised this treatment of depression. Later on, it became so effective that it was eventually used to treat other non-depression disorders. It is said that CBT can be effective in up to 75% of all cases. Essentially, CBT is changing your automatic negative thoughts that contribute to and exacerbate emotions, depression and anxiety. In a

---

56 Joaquin Selva, 'What Is Cognitive Behavioral Therapy (CBT)? A Psychologist Explains', *PositivePsychology.Com*, 2021 <https://positivepsychology.com/what-is-cbt-definition-meaning/> [accessed 9 September 2021].

sentence, your thoughts cause your feelings. This is a very veracious concept.[57] CBT helps you to overcome problems more positively by breaking them down into smaller parts. CBT is based on the idea that the way we think about situations can affect the way we feel and behave. For example, if you interpret a situation negatively then you might experience negative emotions as a result. Those bad feelings might lead you to behave in a bad way. This also relates to the ladder inference that I mentioned before. Negative thinking starts from childhood onwards. An example is if you didn't receive enough attention from your parents or praise you may grow up not feeling worthy or good enough. If your negative interpretation of this goes unchecked then these patterns in your thoughts feelings and behaviour can become part of a continuous cycle, as illustrated on the next page:

---

57 NHS, 'How It Works - Cognitive Behavioural Therapy (CBT)', Nhs.Uk, 2019 <https://www.nhs.uk/mental-health/talking-therapies-medicine-treatments/talking-therapies-and-counselling/cognitive-behavioural-therapy-cbt/how-it-works/> [accessed 30 August 2021].

Figure 1: Cognitive Behaviour

```
                          ┌─────────────────────┐
                          │      Feeling        │
                          │ I feel low/depressed │
                          └─────────────────────┘
                              ↗           ↖
          ┌──────────────────┐             ┌──────────────────────┐
          │    Behaviour     │             │      Thoughts        │
          │Withdraw from others│ ←―――――――→ │I've let everyone down│
          │  Avoid friends   │             │They'll be angry with me│
          │                  │             │ I'm not a good friend │
          └──────────────────┘             └──────────────────────┘

                          ┌─────────────────────┐
                          │      Feeling        │
                          │   I feel anxious    │
                          └─────────────────────┘
                              ↗           ↖
          ┌──────────────────┐             ┌──────────────────────┐
          │    Behaviour     │             │      Thoughts        │
          │Get away from the │ ←―――――――→  │   I can't do this    │
          │    situation     │             │  What is wrong with me│
          │ Avoid it in future│            │Everyone is looking at me│
          └──────────────────┘             └──────────────────────┘
```

CBT is different from other talking therapies in the sense that it focuses on your current problems rather than focusing on issues from your past. All our behaviours are broken down into patterns and paradigms; CBT aims to amend these for your benefit. You can apply it daily to every aspect of your life. CBT has also been found to be useful in several other mental health conditions, namely;

- Bipolar disorder
- Borderline personality disorder
- Panic disorder

- Phobias
- Eating disorders such as bulimia and anorexia
- Obsessive-compulsive disorder (OCD)
- Post-traumatic stress disorder (PTSD)
- Psychosis
- Schizophrenia
- Schizoid
- Insomnia
- Alcohol misuse

CBT is also said to be useful in treating people with other long term health conditions such as;
- Irritable bowel syndrome (IBS)
- Chronic fatigue syndrome (CFS)
- Fibromyalgia

CBT cannot cure the physical symptoms. However, it can help individuals cope better with their symptoms.

If CBT is recommended you usually have one or two sessions weekly or fortnightly. The course of treatment usually lasts for 10 to 20 sessions with each session running for about 60 minutes. In each of these sessions, you will work on breaking down your problems into their separate parts such as your thoughts, physical feelings and actions. These will be analysed and your therapist will then be able to help you work out how to change unhelpful thoughts and behaviours. After doing so, you will put these changes into practice in your daily life and during each session assess the effectiveness of the changes made. The essence of the sessions is to teach you to apply the skills you have learned during treatment to your daily life. This helps stop the negative impact on your life even after the course has been completed. This is what happened in my case, although I would sometimes forget to apply what I'd learned. I was just so used to seeing the world through a certain filter that I didn't think I could change the way I saw things.

As with any treatment or medication, there are pros and cons. CBT, although very effective, also has these. Some of the advantages of CBT are that it can be used where, for example, medicine alone hasn't worked. It can be completed in a short time relative to other talking therapies. It can be used in everyday life even after treatment is complete, and is good for you in general.

One of the disadvantages of CBT is that it can be time-consuming to carry out the extra leg work needed in your own time to permanently apply the changes. It takes commitment; the therapist can advise you but you need to do most of the work yourself, too. It may not be useful for people with complex mental health needs or learning difficulties. It involves confronting your emotions and anxieties and thus can lead to a heightened anxious or fearful state initially. It focuses on the individual's capacity to change themselves (thoughts and feelings). If there is a wider problem this may not be dealt with. e.g., family problems, or money or relationship problems which all have a significant impact on one's health and well-being. Another disadvantage is that CBT doesn't address an unhappy childhood or a previous abusive relationship so it is argued that it may not be as effective as some other forms of therapy as it doesn't always reconcile these different things.

The mind

The mind is like a muscle and just like any muscle it also needs to be trained and developed regularly to be stronger and better. This improves its efficiency and allows for better decision making, it increases one's intelligence and ability to deal with mental health issues. There are many ways in which this can be done; for example, through reading a lot of articles, books, columns and so on. Meditation is also very good, not just for the mind, but also for the body and spirit. The brain is like the control room for your body. It's the most important organ in you and thus must be carefully looked after.

Reading

Reading can be a good way to open up the mind to new ideas and ways of thinking. We live in a world now where information is ubiquitous through the world wide web. It's easy to purchase an e-book if you'd rather not have a physical copy. The truth is 'the more you learn, the more you earn,' as Warren Buffet always says. Not only does reading make you smarter and more perspicacious but it gives you new ideas and also improves your lexicon and language skills. It can also have a positive effect on your earning potential, as it allows you to come up with new improved ways to make money and just generally approach situations in a more astute way. Reading has been said to also reduce stress, if you can lose yourself in a good book this can drastically reduce stress and anxiety levels. I remember in 2016 in one of my plethora of jobs I would always make a conscious effort to read during my lunch breaks and it really put my mind at ease and just put me in a different more positive place. I felt much calmer and happier. It's said that reading just 6 minutes a day can reduce stress levels by 60%,[58] by slowing down your heart rate, easing muscle tension and altering one's state of mind. A surprising statistic. Reading is also said to put us in a meditation-like state and brings the same health benefits of deep relaxation and inner calm. Avid readers have better sleep, lower stress levels, lower rates of depression and higher self-esteem than non-readers. Reading helps with concentration levels and thus you don't easily get distracted by other people which was one of the main causes of my own anxiety. Reading can also improve memory and thinking skills. The positive effects of reading (that good feeling) carry on even after you have finished reading and have a long-term lasting effect. Reading is also said to reduce the chances of getting dementia. One thing about reading is that it allows you to embrace ambiguity – the unknown, which is one of the things I struggled with, with my own psychosis. I was always unsure if people were saying things to me. Reading allows you to be okay with not knowing and embracing not knowing. It also gives you a more positive outlook on life so you are more likely to not assume the worst, but assume the best. I can attest to this. Reading makes us more empathetic. Literary fiction stimulates our everyday

---

58 PowerofPositivity, 'Science Explains: Reading 6 Minutes A Day Helps Reduce Stress And Increase Happiness»', *Power of Positivity: Positive Thinking & Attitude*, 2020 <https://www.powerofpositivity.com/reading-6-helps-reduce-increase-happiness/> [accessed 7 September 2021].

lives and increases our ability to feel empathy for others. In a test to compare a group of people who read literary fiction compared to those who read literary non-fiction, those who read fiction proved to have the most empathetic response. This is because the neurons that ignite in our brains when we perform an action ourselves, but especially when seeing someone else perform that action, sparks our ability to empathise According to Keith Oakley, professor emeritus of cognitive psychology at the University of Toronto, the most important part of being human is the social aspect; fiction can help us to do this even more effectively. He says a piece of fiction is a piece of consciousness being passed from mind to mind. When you read you are taking a piece of consciousness that you make your own.

Reading makes us more mentally flexible. Reading poetry and other texts that require the reader to question the meaning has been shown to cause changes in the pattern of the brain's activity. A test was done where people were asked to rate texts based on their "poeticness". It was found that where texts were more complex it required the reader to rethink their meaning. More activity happened in key areas of the brain as well as heightened literary awareness. Researchers found that the sustained experience of reading poems might increase mental flexibility through the process of reappraisal of meaning and the acceptance of new meaning. One of the study's authors, Professor Philip Davis, director of the Centre for Research into Reading, Literature and Society at the University of Liverpool, states that greater mental flexibility allows people to adapt better to changing situations. People who have greater mental flexibility are more likely to find new solutions to situations rather than just being led by habit.

Reading improves rationality and creativity. A study was undertaken to compare the need for cognitive closure between readers of essays and short stories. These findings led to the conclusion that reading fictional literature could lead to better procedures for processing information generally, including those of creativity. Due to the ambiguous nature of fiction, readers are forced to be more accepting of ambiguity which is believed to be a key factor in creativity, according to professor Maja Djikic. When you can entertain multiple perspectives, it becomes easier to see new possibilities.

I have included a few quotes by famous people about reading;

Stephen King said: "Speaking personally, you can have my gun, but you'll take my book when you pry my cold, dead fingers off of the binding." He also said: "If you don't have time to read, you don't have the time (or the tools) to write. Simple as that."

> Charles William Elliot said: "If you only read the books that everyone else is reading, you can only think what everyone else is thinking."

> Ralph Waldo Emerson said: "I like nonsense, it wakes up the brain cells. Fantasy is a necessary ingredient in living."

> Mark Twain said: "The person, be it a gentleman or lady, who has not pleasure in a good novel, must be intolerably stupid."

Oscar Wilde said: "Books are the quietest and most constant of friends; they are the most accessible and wisest of counsellors, and the most patient of teachers."

Reading helps to expand the mind and change your view. It also helps change how you approach situations and become okay with adapting rather than just reacting, which is one of the biggest setbacks of mental health. This is why reading is essential in helping to overcome mental health conditions.

Meditation

Meditation is great for dealing with mental health problems. It allows for better concentration and focus. It also improves self-awareness and self-esteem, and lowers anxiety levels and stress. Meditation also helps to foster kindness and tactfulness, can help increase your tolerance for pain and help fight addiction especially substance addiction.[59] Sara Lazar, Associate Researcher in Psychiatry, Massachusetts General Hospital and Assistant Professor in Psychology, Harvard Medical School found that meditation can change the structure of the brain, thickening key areas of the cortex that help a person control their attention, emotions and self-control. Meditation over time can also help to regulate negative thoughts, improve memory and the ability to learn new things.

---

59 Holly J Bertone, 'Which Type of Meditation Is Right for You?', *Healthline*, 2020 <https://www.healthline.com/health/mental-health/types-of-meditation> [accessed 30 August 2021].

There are 9 main types of meditation;

- Mindfulness meditation which is used in Buddhism – You pay attention to your thoughts as they pass through your mind. You don't judge the thoughts or become involved with them. You just observe and make note of any patterns.
- Spiritual meditation – Mainly used in eastern religions such as Hinduism, Daoism and Christianity. It's similar to prayer in that you reflect on the silence around you and seek a deeper connection with your God and the universe. Essential oils are used to heighten the spiritual experience; for example, frankincense, myrrh, sage, cedar, sandalwood, palo santo
- Focused meditation – Involves concentration using any of the five senses. It's good for people who need extra focus in their life. An example is focusing on something internal like your breathing, or you can bring in external influences to help focus your attention.
- Movement meditation – For example walking through the woods, gardening. Most people associate movement meditation with yoga. These gentle movements are good as you can let the movement guide you and you connect to the motions. Movement meditation is good for people who like to let their minds wander.
- Mantra meditation – Is prominent in many teachings mainly Hinduism and Buddhism. This type of teaching uses a repetitive sound to clear the mind. It can be a word, phrase or sound. It can be loud or quiet. After you chant this

mantra for some time you will be more in tune with your environment. This allows you to experience deeper levels of consciousness and awareness.
- Visualisation meditation – Enhances feelings of relaxation, peace and calmness by visualising positive scenes or images. With this technique, it's vital to imagine a scene vividly and apply all five senses to add as much detail as possible. Another form of visualisation meditation involves imagining yourself achieving your goals which increase focus and motivation. It's a bit like the law of attraction. Visualisation meditation boosts your mood, reduces stress and promotes inner peace which is good for people who have mental health problems.
- Transcendental meditation[60] – Is very popular. A bit like mantra meditation but it's a bit more changeable. It's good for people who like structure and are serious about maintaining a meditation practice.
- Progressive relaxation – Also known as body scan meditation it reduces tension in the body and promotes relaxation. Often this involves tightening and relaxing one muscle group at a time throughout the body. In some instances, it may also encourage you to imagine a gentle wave flowing through your body to help release any tension. It's great for relieving stress in the mind and body, and releasing built-up tension. It's most effective before bedtime and in the morning just when you wake up before you start your day.

---

60 Bob Roth and Inc OverDrive, *Strength in Stillness* (S.I.: Simon & Schuster, 2018) <https://api.overdrive.com/v1/collections/v1L1BqQAAAA2G/products/fecd246a-e8f0-4190-b8be-9f57f975332a> [accessed 7 September 2021].

- Loving-kindness meditation – This form of meditation is used to strengthen your ability to show compassion, kindness and acceptance towards others and oneself. It involves opening the mind to receive love from others and then sending a series of well wishes to loved ones, friends and acquaintances and all living sentient beings. It's very good for those people who are holding onto feelings of anger and resentment as it helps disperse that negative energy.

All have their own benefits but are all generally similar in their effects on the brain and mood. It has been proven that mediation brings stability to the mind and strengthens the connection between the mind, body and spirit, it's holistic. It's something I have looked into and continue to apply to my life every day. It helped suppress my anxious and negative thoughts by reinforcing them with more positive calm thoughts.

Medication

Medication has been proven to be extremely helpful in treating mental health afflictions. For anxiety, some popular drugs known as benzodiazepines include alprazolam (Xanax), clonazepam, chlordiazepoxide, diazepam and lorazepam.[61] Some medications that are recognised for treating depression as well as OCD, general

---

61 National Institute of Mental Health, 'Mental Health Medications', 2021 <https://www.nimh.nih.gov/health/topics/mental-health-medications#part_2362> [accessed 5 September 2021]

anxiety disorder and PTSD include selective serotonin reuptake inhibitors (SSRIs) for example fluoxetine, citalopram, sertraline. Then there are serotonin noradrenaline reuptake inhibitors (SNRIs) very similar to SSRI's but more effective some include duloxetine (Cymbalta and Yentreve) and venlafaxine (effexor). Then you have noradrenaline and specific serotonergic antidepressants (NASSAs) these are useful for people who are unable to take SSRIs but they do cause drowsiness when first taken. One of the main ones in the UK is mirtazapine (zispin). You also get tricyclic antidepressants (TCAs) but this medication is no longer usually recommended as they have worse side effects than SSRIs and SNRIs also if an overdose is taken, they are far more dangerous than the others. In addition, TCAs are useful for other mental health conditions as well as bipolar disorder. Some examples of TCAs are amitriptyline (tryptizol), clomipramine (anafranil), imipramine (Tofranil), lofepramine (gamanil) and nortriptyline (allegron). Finally, we have Monoamine oxidase inhibitors (MAOIs); these are an older type of antidepressant hardly used these days as they cause serious side effects. Some examples of MAOIs include tranylcypromine, phenelzine and isocarboxazid. These are the main types of anti-depressants.

CBT is a more popular treatment for people who suffer from depression and anxiety as it has a longer-lasting effect than medication alone and there's no risk of side effects. Antidepressants are said to increase the levels of chemicals in the brain called neurotransmitters. Certain neurotransmitters such as serotonin and noradrenaline are linked to mood and emotion. These neurotransmitters are also useful in treating long term pain. The Royal College of Psychiatrists estimates that 50 to 65% of people treated with an anti-depressant will see an improvement compared to 25 to 30% of those taking placebos. Anti-depressants are usually taken in tablet form. You will usually start on a low dosage. It's important to continue taking the medication even if side effects occur. Never come off antidepressants without consulting your doctor first as this could harm you. Once you are ready to come off the doctor will wean you off the medication by gradually reducing your dosage.

Determining whether someone has schizophrenia may involve taking a physical exam, tests and screenings, a psychiatric evaluation and diagnostic criteria for schizophrenia. Schizophrenia requires lifelong treatment for it to be effective. In some cases, hospitalisation may be required. Antipsychotics are the most commonly prescribed drugs to help treat schizophrenia and other mental health conditions such as schizoid and psychosis. They control symptoms by affecting the brain's neurotransmitter dopamine. Some of these medications take months to take an actual effect so don't be deterred if you don't see results immediately; it's gradual, over time. Some of these drugs have serious side effects. When I started taking aripiprazole I suffered from akathisia, tardive dyskinesia and fatigue. After a while, this subsided. Antipsychotics are split into second-generation and first-generation medications.[62] The second generation is the newer. These have lower risks of side effects. Some examples of them are;

- Aripiprazole (Abilify)
- Asenapine (Saphris)
- Brexpiprazole (Rexulti)

---

62 National Institute of Mental Health.

- Cariprazine (Vraylar)
- Clozapine (Clozaril)
- Iloperidone (Fanapt)
- Lurasidone (Latuda)
- Olanzapine (Zyprexa)
- Paliperidone (Invega)
- Quetiapine (Seroquel)
- Risperidone (Risperdal)
- Ziprasidone (Geodon)

Some first-generation antipsychotics include;
- Chlorpromazine
- Fluphenazine
- Haloperidol
- Perphenazine

These are often cheaper than second-gen medications so for long term treatment this may be preferable. Some antipsychotics may be given as intramuscular or subcutaneous injections, administered every two to four weeks depending on the medication.

All in all, all medications used to treat mental health problems are good because they regulate your thinking patterns. They change the mood and give you happier more positive thoughts. If, for example, like me, you suffer from auditory hallucinations (psychosis) these medications help to regulate this and reduce the severity of the belief that you are hearing things by changing your beliefs and promoting more positive thoughts. The medication rebalances dopamine and serotonin which in turn improves mood behaviours, decision making and thinking. Where dopamine levels are too high medications like aripiprazole help with symptoms like hallucinations. They also increase dopamine activity in areas of the brain where it is low, helping with symptoms like poor motivation. It's worth noting that people who take antipsychotics may suffer from weight gain as one of the common side effects. Just consult your doctor to get more information before taking these drugs. Make sure it's right for you before you take it. As with anything important it will take a while to work and to yield results.

The Gray's Line method

Something I learned in my years of suffering from psychosis is the Gray's Line method. It's simple. It measures your anxiety levels over time against the actions you take to eradicate it. The illustration on the next page describes this concept:

Figure 2: Gray's Line

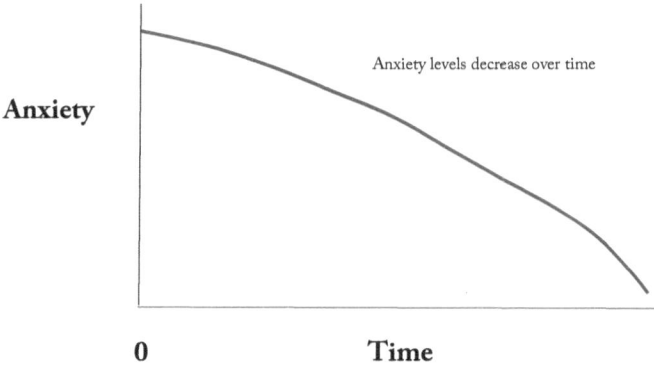

Essentially your anxiety levels will decrease over time the less you respond to the stimulus that sparks a reaction to your anxiety levels. The key is to learn to do nothing when you have these episodes. Acknowledge that you are having an episode e.g., manic episode or panic attack, etc., and over time you will condition your mind to be okay with doing nothing to counter it. This in effect will calm the mind and increase your ability to subdue this seemingly indomitable feeling. This also regulates the dopamine levels in the brain and reduces stress over time. It applies to most mental health afflictions. I used this method to eradicate my psychosis and anxiety and I can't emphasise enough how effective it was. I'm not out of the woods yet, but I certainly am coping much better with my affliction. One thing to also note is that a lot of the time people who suffer from mental health problems may not completely overcome their affliction –

rather they find ways to manage it and cope with it. Which makes it more tolerable. Combining this method with meditation is a great way to deal with mental health problems. The Gray's Line method is also a great way to find inner calm and peace internally and realise that you can be impervious to the outside world to a certain degree. We don't always have to be reactive to things. Once you are at one with yourself you can ward off external negative influences that affect you internally. We are subjected to millions of different scenarios throughout our lives that require us to take action, or so we think. The truth is that sometimes not reacting is reacting. The amount of energy it takes to decide whether or not to take an action plus the action taken itself is taxing on the mind. Imagine constantly having to feel fear, uncertainty, stress, anxiety during an episode you may have. This over time affects you adversely and can take its toll on the brain. Now don't get me wrong, it's difficult to not react and to subdue your natural primal reactions when you are in a state of panic. It's hard to find that moment of inner calm and peace in light of a perceived dangerous situation. It's instinctual for human beings to always do something about it. It's difficult at first because in some situations you don't want to look inept or weak, a walkover, so you feel you must react to defend your integrity. I found that when there was an audience to me being insulted, I had to react to it and do something about it. This method trains you on how to be less stimulated in harmful situations. We live in a world full of stimulants and it's very easy to get lost in that, so much so that it can become habitual. Unlearning this is one of the most effective ways you can overcome mental health afflictions. Over time your mind will become accustomed to stressful situations and realise they will pass. They will pass even quicker the less you react to them. Fear is a state of mind, danger is real. This is true but, in most situations, we go through in life, although we perceive them as dangerous, nine out of ten times they are innocuous. This method gives you the resources you need in adverse situations to be astute and calm under pressure. It can also help avert aggression and things like violence if that is something you suffer with due to your mental health affliction. You take a second, and calmly assess situations to your benefit so you can come out of them unhurt. It gives you better judgement and more patience and understanding of yourself and others.

I found this to be very interesting during my research into ways in which one can overcome mental health problems.

Colour

Different colours have different psychological and emotional effects on us, from things like pictures to advertisements to nature to people. Introducing colours that implore you to be more positive is a great way to help with your mental state. One of the colours that I found to be interesting is red which denotes excitement, happiness and joy. Red captures attention, hence why successful companies like Coca-Cola use it to brand their items. YouTube is another one that uses the red colour to build excitement before you stream and watch their videos.

Orange represents creativity, adventure, enthusiasm, success and balance and brings fun to any picture. Logos like Nickelodeon and the Home Depot are orange. Nickelodeon is a children's channel –

the logo represents the creativity and enthusiasm that a children's channel needs.

Yellow represents optimism and being motivated and positive. It revolves around sunshine. It also represents deceit and warnings. A lot of companies use this colour to denote something positive and bright. Companies like IKEA and Ferrari use this colour. Many people dream of driving a Ferrari. This luxury brand is associated with happiness, summer and a carefree lifestyle. Ikea also uses this colour to advertise its brand to be attractive to people buying new homes or decorating them. This is a milestone for many people, ergo it's filled with happiness and optimism for the new change.

Pink is associated with femininity, playfulness and immaturity and unconditional love and is usually targeted to a female audience. Some examples are Victoria's secret and Barbie. Victoria's secrets websites highlight some key product information in pink and black.

Green represents nature and money, growth, fertility, health and generosity. There are also some negative associations with the colour green such as envy and jealousy.

Although many fallaciously believe blue represents sadness and loneliness it also means to be dependable and reliable.

Purple represents being creative and being a vanguard in whatever it is that you do.

Grey represents the calmness of the mind and soul and is the most effective for altering mental state when suffering from mental health problems. Personally, I feel the most powerful colours to deal with mental health problems are red, green, grey and yellow. Maybe you could try changing the colours of the walls in your home or being in nature more often. Appreciate the beauty of the colours you surround yourself with and connect to them as this can have very positive psychological effects on you. Perhaps purchasing things which have those colours in them can also help. The mind is always active and it's the little things that have the biggest effect on our minds, the things we take for granted every day.

Present moment focus

Present moment focus is another great tool in helping one cope with mental health problems. All your power lies in the now, not in the future or the past. Given the fast and hectic pace of our lives today most of us are perpetually anxious, stressed and unhappy, which is the new norm. Sometimes we don't even realise it but the tendency to get sucked into the past or future can leave us worn out and feeling out of touch with ourselves. Being present in the moment is a solution to this.

Being in the present moment means that we are aware and mindful of what is happening at this very moment. We are not distracted by ruminations on the past or concerns about the future but centred in the here and now. All of our attention is focused on the present moment. This helped me, especially serving as a distraction from my hallucinations and anxiety. So, I focus on, for example, the features of a person I'm talking to, their very being, how their face moves when they speak, how they have dressed, things like that. This takes my attention away from hearing negative things.

Author, Myrko Thum is quoted as saying: "*The present moment is the only thing where there is no time. It is the point between past and future. It is always there and it is the only point we can access in time. Everything that happens, happens in the present moment. Everything that ever happened and will ever happen can only happen in the present moment. It is impossible for anything to exist outside of it."*[63]

This is very powerful and salient. Being present-minded is the key to staying healthy and happy. It helps you fight anxiety, cut down on your worrying and ruminating. It also keeps you grounded and connected to yourself and everything around you. It can help to reduce stress and decrease the impact on our health and calms us and helps us cope with negative emotions like fear and anger. Some factors that contribute to us not being able to live in the now include: our minds wander a lot, facing a lot of uncertainty in the present moment which can cause anxiety. We often edit out bad parts of our experiences, making our past seem more enjoyable than it really was. Sometimes it is good to think about the past, present and future. Where would we be if we didn't look over our past successes and mistakes and learn from them? Where would we be if we didn't prepare for the future or for what's to come? It requires a healthy balance. The problem is we tend to overindulge our thoughts in either the past or the future and thus we lose power in the present moment. It's important to think about both past and future in small doses so as to not overindulge and get lost in it. Learn from your mistakes and take your lessons from the past and focus on a healthy future in a low anxiety way i.e., by not worrying too much about

---

[63] Courtney E Ackerman, 'How to Live in the Present Moment: 35 Exercises and Tools (+ Quotes)', *PositivePsychology.Com*, 2021 <https://positivepsychology.com/present-moment/> [accessed 5 September 2021].

what you have no control over. Think about the future just long enough and then prepare for it. Align everything you desire with your core frequency. Make sure you stay in the present moment for the majority of your time. Like everything, it just takes practice to perfect this. Being present in the moment is a great way to stop worrying so much. Below are six steps to become more present in the moment and reduce the amount of anxiety you suffer from.

- Focus on your breathing
- Find your flow. Make the most of your time by losing track of it. Put down your phone. Just switch off.
- Improve your ability to accept what you cannot change and what you can change
- Enhance your engagement
- Avoid worrying about the future by fully experiencing the present
- Cultivate unselfconsciousness. Let go and stop judging yourself, because the moment you judge others you judge yourself.

These are great ways to be more in the now and let go and just live and be happy. Yoga is also good for being present in the moment, mainly due to the focus on the breath. Breath is always here and now and it's constant. Our present is rooted in its flow, as Kelle Yokeley, founder of Yoga Mindset says. When we focus our attention on the breath, we have no choice but to be present in the moment. Another great reason why yoga is closely associated with the present moment is because of the postures you do with your body. You may find that as soon as you get into a good pose your mind can become distracted; this is called 'monkey mind'. Yoga's gentle transition from one position to the next is a good opportunity to cultivate the ability to stay present. The transitions mimic the changes we experience as we go from working to resting to cooking to cleaning to sleeping and everything else in between. If you do enjoy yoga and want to work on present moment awareness, try this affirmation: "I am present and aware of this moment; it is full and it is great."

There are five ways in which one can strengthen present moment focus: do a mindful body scan, write in a journal, visualise your daily goals, take many walks in nature, conduct a mindful review of your day. All these helps you become more present in the moment.

It's important to note that present moment focus can be applied in many different forms. Find the one which works best for you, depending on your desires. Personally, I found that focusing on little things helped attune my mind to my surroundings and served as a distraction from the one thing I kept focusing on. So, for example, when driving I paid attention to the steering wheel in as much detail as possible. The way it felt, the material, the slick surface of it, the circular shape of it; I felt the connection between it and the tyres turning. Or, for example, I'd just park my car in the park and just focus on the green and the trees and the way the leaves swayed as the wind blew. I'd pay attention to the birds singing – the sound in detail. It's a way to train your mind and to also stop worrying and focusing on things that are negative when they happen. It's natural to dwell on things as they happen based on the past or the future. As I mentioned before the ladder inference is another good example of why we focus on the past and the future. One of the reasons I was so focused on the future was because each time I would encounter someone who insulted me I'd want to avoid it happening again at all costs. Yoga and meditation are also great for aiding present moment focus as they centre the mind and body and strengthen your ability to control what you think and when.

In any situation, you have the power to decide whether it's positive or negative.

The best case scenario rule

The best case scenario rule is key to overcoming mental health problems. As I have previously said, I suffer from psychosis and social anxiety. I would often have auditory hallucinations and be paralysed as a result of not knowing for sure what insult was dished out to me and why. Where this rule applies is that I have the power to surmise that whatever was said to me could have been positive and not negative, especially when I didn't hear it clearly. In situations where I think I've clearly heard the word, I can apply this principle to come up with a different but similar-sounding word that's positive, perhaps. It's all about positive reinforcement in the mind. Doing this over time conditions the mind to always make positive conclusions. So even if someone is insulting you or gesticulating at you negatively, you automatically assume it was something positive. It takes the same amount of energy to make these positive conclusions as it does with negative conclusions. I would always think people were saying something negative. I remember once I was at the airport sitting in the departure lounge. There was a crowd of people and a man walked past that had his eye on me. He clearly worked at the airport and I thought he said something to me as in my mind he was fixated on me. I didn't see him notice anyone else but me. What I could have done is applied this principle and assumed he said something positive, or that he wasn't talking to me at all. A part of this principle also involves thinking of the most likely outcome. So, for example, if you think someone called you 'stupid' you then ask yourself how likely that is in reality, especially if you haven't done anything to offend them. The more you realise that these things don't just happen, the more you will be able to cope with this affliction over time. In this day and age, let's be honest, it's much easier to accept the negative over the positive. We live in a vain world where everyone is comparing themselves with everyone else. Social media, on television, at work. It's very easy to have a negative bias. This simple process of thinking positive goes a long way. Affirmations are also a great way to prepare your mind for the harsh world out there. Affirmations aren't wishful thoughts, rather they use neuroplasticity to change the feelings of fear to those of confidence. Neuroplasticity lets the human brain form synaptic connections and takes the necessary action. Some examples of affirmations could be telling yourself 'I am more than adequate', 'I am safe', 'I am great', 'I am intelligent', 'I am attractive', 'I am kind', 'I can slow my breathing when I feel like', 'I will overcome the situation if I remain courageous', 'I will be successful', 'I am strong and independent'. There are many more you can come up with. These are some great affirmations to have and apply. Saying 'I am' is powerful. You are programming your mind to always be conscious of these facts about yourself, in situations of uncertainty, these will guide you and, in a way, ground you and calm you down. They can be written down, said verbally or even tattooed on your body. You will learn not to take everything so personally. You will realise the world isn't out to get you. I always say the universe is pantagruelian and we are infinitesimal in comparison. All our problems, worries, doubts, concerns pale in significance to the sheer scale of the cosmos. Remind yourself of this every day and you will begin to worry less about your shortcomings and problems. I did and this has helped me a great deal. I even say this randomly to myself throughout the day to etch it in my mind.

Anxiety is the most common form of mental health problem in the world today. Our ever-changing society leads us to live anxiety-filled lives. This can cause an onset of stress, depression and even bring on suicide. It's important to find ways to distract yourself during an anxiety attack or episode.

The mental grinder

The mental grinder is another key principle that can help you understand your mental health disorder and at the same time cope with it. It's a simple concept. The following is a diagram better illustrating the way it works:

Figure 3: The Mental Grinder

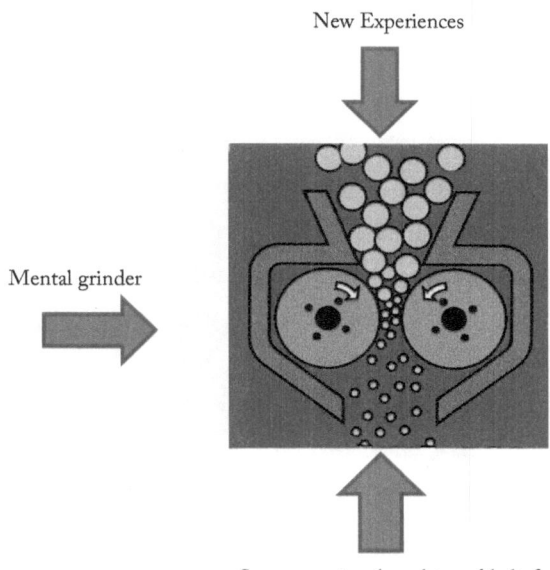

The way it works is when you have a mental health problem, for example, psychosis, your mind begins to filter things out and replace them with the same usual patterns of thought. So, for example in my case, I was used to hearing insults from people that I had an interaction with. One day someone compliments me. This is the new experience, but in my brain, the grinder will crush it into what I'm used to which is an insult, so I dismiss the compliment or new experience. Your mind is a system that is designed to adapt and respond according to patterns. As things change around you your mind contorts, warps and moulds them into, let us say, shapes of things it's familiar with. The world is full of contrast and is ever-changing. Learning about the mental grinder is a good way to be more aware of these responses and change them to your benefit. This isn't only a principle that applies to mental health but rather to everyday life in general. We shape our lives every day through our experiences and interactions – biological, psychological and social. The key is learning to be more conscious of this and altering it when it doesn't benefit you. Being open to new suggestions and ideas is a great way to rid yourself of mental bondage. Being adaptive and welcoming new experiences is a great way to keep the mind flexible and alert, while also ensuring you don't omit new positive experiences by filtering them out. In life, it's important to take things as they come. This can be difficult as we are a net result of all of our experiences. Who you are today is simply a result of all of your thoughts in your life up to that point. We walk around feigning happiness and positivity but most of us are stuck in our old habits and old negative thoughts. That when positive things come our way, we are either quick to dismiss them or we are unable to discern their meaning. It's easier said than done. Most of the time we are taking out our anger on the next person because of the previous person. It's important to make a conscious effort to keep an eye on your mental filters making sure to not let them get saturated with negativity from the past. Living in the past can block new great opportunities. For example, if you are unemployed and for a long time have been receiving job application rejections, it can lead you to feel dejected, to a point where you start assuming all responses will be a 'no'. This is because of your mental grinder. New doors are everywhere – you just have to be prepared to walk through them. The definition of success is where preparation meets opportunity.

Stay prepared as opportunities will always come. You don't want to miss them because you chose to not stay ready. Remember, if you stay ready you don't have to get ready.

This concept may seem strange to some but, as I have mentioned, I mainly suffered from auditory hallucinations. Some olfactory and some tactile, but my main affliction was auditory hallucinations – at least that's what I realised once I become more aware of what my affliction actually was. I discovered a simple way to check whether or not this was, indeed, happening. This approach doesn't work with all types of auditory hallucinations.

Audio record

Audio record your interactions with people. I started doing this some years back. I would have a plethora of audio recordings to sift through. It was a very accurate way of determining if people were actually insulting me. There were even times when I would remember a specific point in a conversation where I'd heard something, but I found that in all the recordings I went through there wasn't one that confirmed my suspicions that people were insulting me. It can be tedious but it works. The problem however with this approach is that it didn't change my belief that people were insulting me, even though there was proof that they weren't. It didn't change my beliefs that people still would or wanted to. That part takes time and for other interventions to take effect. Over time the more I realised that nothing was being said, the more I started to change my beliefs about it. I admit it can be awkward to secretly record your interactions with people and even more awkward listening back to it, but I must say it helped me a lot. I was amazed at how wrong I was. If you do this for a long enough period and you suffer from auditory hallucinations it may just work for you. It does have its limitations, however. I would hear things being said in the actual person's voice that I was interacting with. Some people have hallucinations in a constant generic voice not representing the people they are talking to so it's impossible to record that. I would use my phone and position it in such a way that there would be clear recordings and no interference. I applied this method for about six months and didn't once hear an insult when listening back to the recordings. Combining this method with other methods can be very useful to help alleviate your mental health disorder, whatever it may be. On the other hand, if you do indeed hear insults, then you can seek professional medical advice accordingly and find the next steps to take to overcome your affliction. In my case I was lucky and I proved myself wrong.

Taking regular time outs and going on vacation

Taking regular time outs and going on vacation is another great tool that you can use to overcome mental bondage. It doesn't have to be fancy expensive holidays to the Caribbean or Seychelles. Just little getaways can go a long way. I found being around water and open spaces helped me. Being a thalassophile this was particularly helpful. Holidays can make us mentally sharper and more creative. This can give you a newfound motivation for when you come back.

Today's life can be very fast-paced and demanding. A study found that three days after a vacation travellers felt well-rested, less anxious and in a better mood. It is also said that just 30 minutes of being in nature every week can significantly reduce the symptoms of depression and anxiety by up to 7%. Travelling and taking little breaks also has a positive effect on health, relationships, business performance and the well-being of communities. When you are taking a break, you can leave your worries behind and focus on spending quality time with loved ones. This can take your mind off your mental health problems. This may not solve your problems overnight but taking regular breaks can help alleviate some of your symptoms, whether it's in a hot remote place, dipping your toes into a pool, soaking up the sun, doing unusual fun activities or experiencing new cultures, all this can give you a mental boost.

Scientists say that the psychological benefits of taking holidays can last for 30 days after returning home. Now, holidays can be expensive but it's worth the money based on the psychological relief you can get from it. Putting money away every month that goes towards little breaks, I feel, is very pertinent to improving your mental health.

Some of the main benefits of taking regular breaks include a massive reduction in your stress and cortisol levels. There was a study conducted which compared people who went on holidays to those who didn't. The ones who didn't had much higher blood pressure and stress levels and didn't sleep well. As mentioned before, holidays also make us mentally sharper and more creative. If you are exhausted you won't be functioning at your best. Just like when you are at work, if you don't take regular breaks your productivity levels will drop. Travelling helps you stay active and thus improves your mental health. Travel broadens your mind literally. It also increases creativity and cultural awareness. When you travel to new places your mind goes into overdrive through new sounds, smells, sights and so on. Your brain takes in new surroundings and this can make you more culturally aware. This is great for the mind and can help you to overcome mental health problems. Having something to look forward to can help boost the mind, especially something like a holiday or short break. It starts happening from the moment you click to book it. Your mind goes into overdrive and the excitement alone can have a positive effect. I personally always loved to travel and always have. Whenever I travelled to Dubai, I had this feeling that's incomparable and for the time I was there and a while after I got back, I felt so refreshed and so positive and motivated. Travel can help with depression. Studies show that just six days away triggers genetic changes which reduce stress, boost the immune system and lower levels of proteins which are linked to dementia and depression.

Some writers such as Ernest Hemingway, Aldous Huxley and Mark Twain drew inspiration from travelling abroad, too. Creativity is related to neuroplasticity, or how the brain is wired. Neural pathways are influenced by environment and habit which means they are also sensitive to change. New sounds, tastes, smells and sensations can spark different synapses in the brain and can revitalise the mind.

Adam Galinsky, a professor at Columbia Business School found that cognitive flexibility is the mind's ability to switch between different ideas, which is a key component of creativity. He said the key is multicultural engagement, immersion and adaption. Someone who lives abroad and doesn't engage with the local culture will get less of a creative boost than someone who travels abroad and engages in the local environment. For example, going to Cancun for a week on a spring break probably won't make you more creative. But going to Cancun and living with the local fishermen might.

In one of his studies published in 2015 in the Academy of Management Journal, Galinsky and three other researchers examined 270 high-end fashion houses, totalling 11 fashion lines.[64] The research looked at creative directors' experience working abroad and the fashion houses, innovations, or the degree to which final, implemented products and services are novel, and useful from the standpoint of external audiences. The level of creativity of a given product was rated by a pool of trade journalists and independent buyers. It was discovered that there was greater creative output for those who spent time abroad than those who did not. It was also found that the more countries the executives had lived in, the more creative the lines were. However, it was found that those who had worked and lived in three countries or more showed higher levels of creativity than those who hadn't worked abroad at all, but were less creative than those who had worked in a smaller number of countries. Galinsky concluded that this was because the executives who had spent time in more countries didn't have enough time to fully immerse themselves in the culture for it to take effect on them. Galinsky and his colleagues also found that living in a culture that differed greatly from their own proved to reduce creativity levels

---

64 Brent Crane, 'For a More Creative Brain, Travel', *The Atlantic*, 2015 <https://www.theatlantic.com/health/archive/2015/03/for-a-more-creative-brain-travel/388135/> [accessed 30 August 2021].

compared to living in the sort of cultures that were more similar to their own. The reason for that, they hypothesised, was that a significantly different culture might come with an intimidation factor that may discourage people from fully immersing themselves in it. No immersion would therefore mean no changes associated with living in a foreign country.

Mary Helen Immordino-Yang, an associate professor of education and psychology at the University of Southern California, says that cross-cultural experiences have the potential to strengthen a person's sense of self. Engaging with people from different backgrounds than your own, and the ability to get out of your own comfort zone or expand it, helps one build a strong and acculturated sense of self. Ones' ability to differentiate our own beliefs and values is tied up in the richness of the cultural experiences that we have had. Travelling abroad and embracing other cultures also resulted in peoples' restoration of faith in humanity. Galinsky says that experience, when people treat you in similar ways abroad, leads to an increase in trust in mankind. This trust plays an important role in enhancing creativity. A lack of cultural diversity hampers creativity as it results in closed-mindedness. It disallows people from thinking outside of the box.

For some travelling abroad may be expensive, so as an alternative maybe look at a short break or getaway, fully immerse yourself in where you go and the culture and the people; this will have a profound effect, not only on your creativity, but your general mental health. In the long run, it reduces stress and the risk of depression. Regular holidays or getaways are essential for ensuring you lead a healthy life and have a good mental health balance.

Sleeping and resting well

Sleeping and resting well are crucial for your mental health. In fact, a lack of good sleep can exacerbate your mental health affliction. You are probably aware that poor sleep affects mood. After a sleepless night, you may be more irritable, short-tempered and vulnerable to stress. Studies have shown that even partial sleep deprivation has a significant effect on mood. It can also lead to feelings of worry and stress, poor decision making and low self-esteem. Poor sleep leads to worrying. Worrying leads to poor sleep it's a vicious cycle. A lot of us find it hard to sleep, stay awake or we wake up earlier than we intend to. Some of us have problems that disturb our sleep due to things like panic attacks, flashbacks, nightmares and psychosis. Due to some mental health problems such as psychosis, schizophrenia and depression some people find it hard to even get out of bed every day. Some even sleep too much due to mental health problems such as depression or psychosis.

If you have problems sleeping it could lead to you feeling anxious, depressed or even suicidal. It's more likely that you will have psychotic episodes. Poor sleep can trigger mania, psychosis or paranoia. Sleeping problems can also make you feel lonely and isolated. It affects decision making and your ability to focus and plan things. This can lead to impulsive or unfocussed decisions. You can also have problems in your day-to-day life with things like work, family and friends. In addition, sleep can cause you to suffer from other mental health problems in the long run. As mentioned, a lack of good sleep can be caused by anxiety which causes repetitive thoughts and worries that constantly keep you awake. Panic attacks can also become more prominent if you suffer from a panic disorder. Depression can also affect sleep and a lack of sleep can exacerbate your depression by way of making you sleep more (seasonal affective disorder – SAD), being less productive and anti-social and this can also cause insomnia. Trauma is another thing that can cause one to have a sleep deprivation issue, which in turn worsens the effects of the trauma itself. Night terrors, flashbacks and nightmares can plague you in your sleep and thus reduce the quality of sleep you have. Paranoia and psychosis can make it hard to sleep, too. You may hear voices or see things you find frightening or disturbing. Mania can also be a factor that can affect sleep and sleep quality. It generates feelings of energy and elation so you may not feel tired or that you want to sleep and this can cause insomnia in the long term. Medication is another thing that can affect sleep. A lot of medications have side effects like insomnia, nightmares, fatigue. The thing is if you cease taking certain drugs this can lead to sleep problems. Americans are notoriously sleep-deprived. Sleep problems typically affect 50% to 80% of patients in a typical psychiatric practice, compared with 10% to 18% of adults in the general U.S. population. Sleep problems are particularly common in patients with anxiety, depression, bipolar disorder and attention deficit hyperactivity disorder (ADHD).

Every 90 minutes a normal sleep cycles between two major categories of sleep. During quiet sleep, a person progresses through four stages of increasingly deep sleep. Body temperature drops, muscles relax, and heart rate and breathing slow down. The deepest stage of quiet sleep produces physiological changes that boost the immune system. The other sleep category, REM (rapid eye movement) sleep, is the period when people dream. Body temperature, blood pressure, heart rate and breathing increase to levels measured when people are awake. It's said REM enhances learning and memory. Scientists have discovered that sleep disruption which affects levels of neurotransmitters and stress hormones adversely affects the brain by impairing thinking and emotional regulation. This can trigger insomnia. There are over 70 different types of sleeping disorders, most commonly sleep apnoea and insomnia, various movement syndromes and narcolepsy. It is estimated that 65% to 90% of adults and 90% of children with major depression suffer from sleep deprivation. Most patients with depression have insomnia but one in five suffer from obstructive sleep apnoea. Insomnia and other sleep problems affect outcomes for patients with depression. Studies show that depressed patients who suffer from insomnia are more likely to think about suicide.

69% to 99% of bipolar disorder sufferers reported less need for sleep during a manic episode. Bipolar depression studies report that 23% to 78% of patients sleep excessively (hypersomnia) studies and also report that a lack of sleep can trigger mania. Sleep problems also adversely affect mood and contribute to relapse.

Sleep problems affect more than 50% of adults with generalised anxiety disorder. It's also common with people who have PTSD and may occur in panic disorder, OCD and phobias. A study has shown that it took young people who had anxiety disorder longer to fall asleep than a normal person. Insomnia is also a risk factor for developing an anxiety disorder. Insomnia can worsen the symptoms of anxiety disorders or prevent recovery.

Various sleep problems affect 25% to 50% of children with ADHD. Problems include difficulty falling asleep, shorter sleep duration and restless slumber. Sleep-disordered breathing affects up to 25% of children with ADHD, and restless legs syndrome or periodic limb movement disorder which also disrupts sleep affect up to 36%. Children with sleeping disorders may become hyperactive, inattentive and emotionally unstable.

Overcoming sleep problems can be broken down into lifestyle changes and behavioural pattern changes. Abstaining from drinking alcohol, caffeine and nicotine can help improve sleep. Alcohol depresses the nervous system which actually helps some people fall asleep. Nicotine is a stimulant that speeds up the heart rate and thinking. Regular aerobic activity helps you fall asleep faster, spend more time in a deep sleep and awaken less often during the night. This is because the body needs this time to repair itself and heal. Often aerobic activity also makes your body very tired hence why you sleep better. Staying awake longer can help one sleep better at night, also keeping distractions away, like televisions, etc., can improve sleep quality. Relaxation techniques can also help, namely meditation, yoga, guided imagery and breathing exercises. They reduce anxiety and the too many thoughts that you may otherwise have. CBT reverses one's thoughts from negative to positive and builds confidence and in turn, this improves sleep.

In conclusion, sleep is vital to ensuring one has a healthy mind and body. Long term sleep deprivation can affect mental health and if you already have existing mental health problems sleep deprivation can worsen this. It's a cycle. A lack of sleep can worsen your condition and your condition can worsen your sleep. If you do notice you are having difficulty sleeping tackle it now and don't let it linger for too long as this can have a very adverse effect on you in the long term.

Alcohol, caffeine and nicotine

Alcohol, caffeine and nicotine are the most consumed psychotropic drugs worldwide. Their use is frequent in patients with schizophrenia. There is a relationship between depression and alcohol consumption. These drugs can all create dependence. Alcohol is harmful to the brain; it can cause intoxication with impairment of cognition, delirium tremens, and dementia. Nicotine causes cancer cardiovascular disease. Frequent drinking that's associated with malnutrition is said to cause damage to the central nervous system (CNS).[65] Patients with bipolar depression are more likely to abuse alcohol during periods of their illness. Patients with schizophrenia are more likely to consume all three substances at a high rate to alleviate their dysphoria.

Consumption of alcohol by way of beer and wine goes way back. Some physicians prescribed beer and this has been found on Sumerian clay tablets (c 2100 bc). Egyptian doctors in their medical papyri (c 1500 bc) included beer and wine in about 15% of their prescriptions. Alcohol, which is an inebriating substance, is consumed because it relieves the mind from anxiety and inhibitions.

---

65 'PubMed Central Full Text PDF' <https://www.ncbi.nlm.nih.gov/pmc/articles/PMC3181622/pdf/DialoguesClinNeurosci-5-175.pdf> [accessed 30 August 2021].

The Diagnostic and Statistical Manual of Mental Disorders, Fourth Edition (DSM-IV)3 divides alcohol use disorders into two categories: alcohol abuse and alcohol dependence. Abuse means one doesn't adjust appropriately to the environment or situation which results in adverse consequences; for example, neglect of children or work or marital problems, driving whilst drunk. Dependence is indicated by a loss of control and continued drinking despite alcohol-related problems, and by evidence of tolerance or symptoms of withdrawal. A typical example is that a subject wants to stop drinking but cannot; drinking in the morning is characteristic. Alcohol and depression are interrelated. In a booklet written by Bode, a German physician, they found that regular drinking could be a consequence of the depression caused by adverse climate; for instance, alcohol being consumed by Italians moving to the inclement London weather, or in German colonial officers posted in tropical countries. Bode also added that alcoholism could be one of the first symptoms of melancholia which is the usual term for today's depression. He added that the melancholic patient turned to alcohol to alleviate symptoms of anxiety, guilt, sorrow and sadness. In the case of alcohol-induced mood disturbances, alcohol is clearly primary and depression secondary. Mood disturbances are characteristic of heavy drinkers, particularly during the withdrawal phase. When not drinking alcoholics tend to report depression, irritability, suspiciousness, lethargy, apprehension, anxiety and a lack of focus. About a quarter of recently detoxified alcoholics have a depressive syndrome. This usually remits in less than one month without specific treatment. The clinical course of depression when it coexists with alcoholism is generally benign and self-limited, most patients become euthymic (having bipolar disorder but being in neither a manic or depressed state) within 2 to 3 weeks of abstention without antidepressant treatment.[66] With some depressed alcoholics, a more chronic depression persists. In that case, antidepressants should definitely be used since they will invariably lower relapse rates.

The opposite of alcohol-induced depression, depression-induced alcoholism can also be observed. Drinking may be secondary to depression when alcohol is used to self-medicate. The patient may drink to relieve his/her mind from sorrow, fear and despondency or to combat loneliness. Since consumption of alcohol has a mood-lifting effect, but this approach has only short terms benefits. Chronic use of alcohol is more likely to make the subject more withdrawn, more depressed and more anxious. Although depression can lead to alcoholism, most cases of alcoholism are not explained by primary depression. Mood disorders are particularly suspected in certain circumstances, notably in females and in the cases of early-onset drinking. The chance of bipolar disorder should also be kept in mind. Women may be more at risk of developing this secondary alcoholism than men. Early-onset drinking may often be secondary, not a primary psychiatric disorder. A study by *Roy A DeJong J Lamparski D et al 'mental disorders amongst alcoholics arch gen psychiatry' 1991;48:423-427* found that 81% of 339 alcoholics had associated mental disorders. Alcoholics with the onset of heavy drinking before 20 years of age had more antisocial personality traits, drug abuse, bipolar disorder, panic disorder,

---

66 Marc-Antoine Crocq, 'Alcohol, Nicotine, Caffeine, and Mental Disorders', *Dialogues in Clinical Neuroscience*, 5.2 (2003), 175–85.

suicide attempts and paternal alcoholism than alcoholics with onset after 20 years old.[67]

The association between alcohol and depression can be inferred from the findings of numerous familial, epidemiological and molecular genetic studies.

It's been found that the early onset of bipolar disorder tends to precede that of alcoholism. It has also been found by the independent familial aggregation (clustering of disease within families) that an early onset of alcoholism than nonbipolar depression suggests that unipolar mood disorders are frequently secondary to alcoholism. The most commonly abused drug in both bipolar I (episodes of severe mania often with depression) and bipolar II (a less severe form of mania) is alcohol. Bipolar I subjects appear to have higher rates of substance abuse and dependence than bipolar II subjects.

There are empirical studies that show a link between genetics and alcoholism. The depressive spectrum hypothesis by Winokur states that persons under the age of 40 who have developed unipolar depression tend to have more alcoholism and antisocial personalities than their male relatives. However, researchers were unable to consolidate the relationship between mood disorders and drinking. There is a consensus that genetic factors are salient where the vulnerability of mood disorders is concerned and it's likely that hereditary factors influence the appearance of alcoholism, too. Both are probably influenced by genetic factors. Men metabolise a large

---

67 Roy A DeJong and J Lamparski, *Mental Disorders amongst Alcoholics Arch Gen Psychiatry*, 1991.

fraction of alcohol in the stomach before it is absorbed, whereas women don't as they have less active stomach enzymes. 20% of alcohol is absorbed into the bloodstream through the stomach and 80% through the intestine. In women, it's higher during ovulation. Up to 90% of alcohol consumed is metabolised in the liver.[68]

Alcohol interferes with the central metabolism of the neurotransmitters, especially indolamines, which are involved in the pathophysiology and drug treatment of mood disorders. It's been found that men and women who are diagnosed with severe depression at the time they are admitted for inpatient treatment of alcohol dependence have much shorter times to alcohol relapse. This suggests that it's very important to diagnose and treat depression in alcoholic patients who have been admitted for treatment. Antidepressants have shown efficacy in the treatment of alcoholism that's combined with depression and sometimes even in its absence. Antidepressants are particularly helpful in the reduction of craving and relapse figures during a period of detoxification. Antidepressants should be started if depression continues after 2 to 4 weeks of alcohol withdrawal, although some authors recommend using them much earlier to curb craving and the risk of relapse. The choice of medication is usually determined by the availability of many classes of drugs which is different in each country. Your doctor might prescribe drugs to treat your condition, for example, Citalopram which has been shown to reduce alcohol consumption in nondepressed people who have alcohol dependence. Fluoxetine

---

68 'PubMed Central Link' <https://www.ncbi.nlm.nih.gov/pmc/articles/PMC3181622/> [accessed 30 August 2021].

was able to prevent relapses in weaned alcoholics. Trazodone, which decreases cravings for alcohol in detoxified alcohol-dependent subjects at low doses. Viloxazine, which is was shown to be superior to placebo on the reduction of alcohol consumption.

Nicotine

Tobacco is native to America where it's said to have been cultivated by man around 5000 to 3000bc. On his very first trip to America, Columbus went to Cuba, he came into contact with Indians smoking it. Like caffeine, nicotine is a stimulant. Nicotine is not directly associated with psychiatric disorders; however, it's been observed that psychiatric patients smoke more than the general population. A study in rats showed that nicotine produces selective degeneration in the medial habenula, which is a dense region of nicotinic cholinergic receptors. These receptors respond to drugs such as nicotine. They are found in the central and peripheral nervous system, muscle and many other tissues of many or organisms. Pregnant women are at risk as prenatal exposure to tobacco inflicts damage to the developing brain of the child. Nicotine has a neuroprotective action in neurodegenerative disorders such as Parkinson's and Alzheimer's disease. The onset of smoking typically occurs in the teenage years. In America, in a study, it was said that the median age was 16 to 17 years old. According to French epidemiological data, the mean age of smoking onset is 14 years old, so it's clear to see smokers are getting younger and younger throughout the world. Smokers claim that smoking relieves stress, and it helps them concentrate and perform. This is consistent with studies suggesting that smoking helps improve attention, learning, reaction time and problem-solving. Studies suggest that nicotine increases the speed of sensory information processing in smokers, eases tension, improves mood and reduces depression and anger. The peer pressure and societal factors that make a person decide to start smoking also play a role in making them delve into other substances and generally, different patterns of behaviour. There's an association between the use of various psychoactive substances in adolescents. The National Household Survey which was conducted by the National Institute of Drug Abuse 1985 found that, among 12 to 17-year-olds, the proportion using alcohol and marijuana was 74.2% and 47.3% respectively, among current smokers, as compared with just 23.5% and 5.8%, respectively, among non-smokers'. A Canadian study of 13,549 students showed that adolescents who consumed alcohol or cannabis or who smoked cigarettes were also more likely to use stimulants like amphetamines and diet pills for recreational purposes. Smoking is also more common in people whose parents or partners smoke. While many young people are exposed to the pleasurable effects of nicotine, only a few go on to become regular smokers. Some people also turn to food, substances, and acts to alleviate feelings of boredom, anxiety, emptiness, etc. Smoking is said to be one of the coping mechanisms, too, because of its rapidity of action, as nicotine reaches the brain in seconds and acquiring cigarettes requires hardly any effort and isn't that expensive and inaccessible. I even remember times when teenagers hanging outside shops would ask me, as an adult, if I could purchase cigarettes for them and I always refused. There are similarities in the psychological factors that lead smokers to try out other substances. As a result, cigarette smoking is associated with the use of other substances, and the quantity of alcohol and nicotine consumed tends to follow parallel curves (moderate drinkers tending to moderate smokers and heavy drinkers tending to heavy smokers). Statistically, cigarette smoking and nicotine dependence are more prevalent in people who have a history of child abuse and neglect, also in children whose parents have problems with drugs, alcohol and in single teenage mothers, in children who are fostered, in school dropouts, unemployed youths and adolescents who are incarcerated and those in vocational schools. By high school graduation, 28% of adolescents smoke cigarettes, but their peers who are dropouts rake in a 70% rate of smoking. In adults, smoking is more prevalent in divorcees and single parents. Smoking is also associated with alcohol and caffeine consumption.

Studies show that smoking cessation can only be successful when an individual has made up their mind, is motivated and has devised a personal strategy for how and when to stop. This is greatly influenced by the person's psychological motivation. During the cessation process, the smoker will have to overcome the discomfort due to dependence and will also have to reverse established habits reinforced by sociocultural factors. The practice of smoking is by and large part a habit, a learned behaviour with some elements of conditioning, which is elicited by multiple stimuli including colours, tastes, smells, aromas, locations, times of the day like in the morning or after dinner or after a task, people, familiar surroundings. It only takes two days for nicotine to be completely out of your system if you stop smoking. The prevalence of signs and symptoms at two days post cessation in individuals who quit smoking without any assistance is as follows: anxiety 49%, craving 37%, decreased heart rate 61% depression 31%, difficulty concentrating 43%, hunger 53%, irritability 38%, nocturnal awakening 39%, restlessness 46%.[69] Most symptoms begin six to twelve hours following smoking cessation, peak in one to three days and last an average of three to four weeks. Craving and hunger are generally the only remaining symptoms four weeks after cessation.

During the late 1950s, almost 80% of men in western European countries were tobacco smokers. A lot of them started during the war. Soldiers were used as test dummies to see the effects of smoking following traumatic experiences that they might be subjected to in war. A prevalence of 42% was reported in the USA in 1965. In western countries, however, it has decreased to 20-25% due to educational efforts. This has also been due to the socioeconomic gradient over the past few decades. In Britain, in 1990 only 16% of professional men and women were cigarette smokers, while 48% of men and 36% of women in unskilled manual occupations continued to smoke. A similar trend emerged in the USA. One has to remember that in the pre-war days it was seen as unacceptable for women to smoke but since then they have campaigned and advertised on many platforms images of women smoking to encourage it.

Nicotine replacement therapy (NRT) is a type of pharmacotherapy and it can be used to help smokers quit that find it difficult to do it on their own. It's available in the form of nicotine gum and

---

69 Marc-Antoine Croq, 'Alcohol, Nicotine, Caffeine, and Mental Disorders', *Dialogues in Clinical Neuroscience*, 5.2 (2003), 175–85 <https://doi.org/10.31887/DCNS.2003.5.2/macrocq>.

transdermal patches. NRT facilitates the early period of cessation by reducing the severity of the withdrawal symptoms such as craving and affective discomfort. Behavioural treatment itself is more efficacious than NRT and when combined, success rates are far higher. However, the will to quit plays a huge part in cessation rates as well, it's been found. Bupropion which was originally introduced as an antidepressant double the abstinence rate. In a double-blind, placebo-controlled study the abstinence rates at 12 months were 15.6% in the placebo group as compared to 16.4% in the nicotine patch group, 30.3% in the sustained-release bupropion group and 35.5% in the group given bupropion and the nicotine patch. It's been theorised that bupropion, which is a weak inhibitor of synaptic reuptake of dopamine, may maintain stimulation of the pleasure response areas of the brain in the absence of nicotine by enhancing dopamine activity in the nucleus accumbens which is the part of the brain where addiction and pleasure are triggered. Numerous tests have been conducted on rats to determine this fact.

Caffeine

Tea and coffee are major sources of caffeine. Caffeine is also found in maté, in small concentrations in cocoa, and in caffeinated soft drinks like red bull. Coffee originates from Ethiopia. Europeans then started cultivating it when they colonised. Tea has been around a lot longer. It dates back to China around the 3rd century AD. An average cup of coffee contains 100mg caffeine, whereas a cup of tea or 0.3L glass of cola drink contains about 40% of that amount.

Around 80% of inhabitants of affluent countries drink tea or coffee daily, it's a stimulant: it lifts mood, elevates alertness, etc. Caffeine stimulates feelings of well-being, motivation for work and desire to socialise. Patients with schizophrenia have a high intake of caffeine.

Like nicotine, caffeine use is reinforced by the taste and smell of coffee, the hedonic psychoactive effect of mental stimulation and the strong desire to avoid the feelings you have if you withdraw from it. Withdrawal symptoms are relieved by caffeine intake, that goes without saying. Some of the signs and symptoms of withdrawal include headache, impaired concentration, depression, anxiety – although drinking coffee itself can also cause anxiety, irritability, nausea or vomiting and muscle aches and stiffness. The withdrawal syndrome shows an onset 18 to 24 hours after cessation and it peaks 20 to 48 hours after abstinence and its duration lasts between two days to a week.

No psychoactive drug has been studied in so many individuals as have alcohol, nicotine and caffeine. Betel and khat are amongst some other drugs that are widely consumed in Asia and Africa. They are popular for their mild stimulant properties. In recent times there has been an inclination towards decriminalising the use of cannabis and it seems to be growing in acceptance and popularity; after all, it's been around for thousands of years, used for healing and much more. The study, 'Overlapping addictions and self-esteem among college men and women' *Addict behaviour 1999;24:565-571* states that there is a large correlation between people who are addicted to alcohol, drugs, nicotine and caffeine to gambling, internet use, television and video games. Men scored higher than women in alcohol, cigarettes, gambling and television addictions but women scored higher on chocolate and caffeine. As mentioned, before tests on animals have shown that things such as food, sex and playing stimulate a midbrain reward circuit involving dopamine and the nucleus accumbens. In humans, however, this is more complex as we have a conscious capacity to evaluate, in the prefrontal cortex of the brain, whether pleasurable activities are appropriate and acted upon, or should be deferred or resisted. This duality of the human, oscillating biological urges and conscious choice has always been a fundamental question in our history, this has been highlighted by our love of intoxicants and games which are discussed in religious texts.

Deep breathing

Deep breathing can really help a patient with a mental health affliction during an episode they have. It regulates the heart rate and calms you down. When you breathe in air, blood cells receive oxygen and release carbon dioxide. Carbon dioxide is a waste product that's carried through the body when you exhale. Not breathing properly can upset the oxygen and carbon dioxide exchange and contribute to anxiety, panic attacks, fatigue and other physical and emotional disturbances.

Breathing can add to the level of anxiety one experiences. A lot of people aren't aware of the way they're breathing. There are two types of breathing patterns:
- Diaphragmatic (abdominal) breathing
- Thoracic (chest) breathing

When people are anxious, they tend to take rapid and shallow breaths that come directly from the chest. This type of breathing is called thoracic breathing. Shallow breathing causes an upset in the oxygen and carbon dioxide levels in the body which results in a rapid heart rate, dizziness as you are taking in too much oxygen, muscle tension and other physical sensations. As your blood is not properly being oxygenated this signals a stress response that invariably contributes to anxiety and stress. Diaphragmatic breathing more likely occurs in babies or when you are asleep or very calm. There is a way you can determine which way you are breathing at any time. Put one hand on the upper abdomen near the waist and the other on the middle of your chest. As you breathe notice which hand raises the most. If you are breathing correctly the hand on your stomach should expand and contract with each breath the most. During an anxiety or panic attack, you are most likely to breathe from your chest.

Some good breathing exercises are:

- ❖ Inhale slowly and breathe through your nose. Relax your shoulders. Your abdomen should expand and your chest should rise very little.
- ❖ Exhale slowly through your mouth. As you blow air out, purse your lips slightly, but keep your jaw relaxed. You could potentially hear a soft whooshing sound as you do this.
- ❖ Repeat this exercise several times until you start to feel better

This is especially good during an anxiety or panic attack, or just generally when you are having a mental health episode.

Several other breathing exercises have been popularised to help deal with anxiety attacks. Lengthen your exhale. Deep breaths in are linked to the sympathetic nervous system which controls the flight or fight response. Exhaling is linked to the parasympathetic nervous system which influences the body's ability to relax and calm down. Taking too many breaths too quickly can cause you to hyperventilate. This reduces the amount of oxygen-rich blood that flows to the brain. Here are ways you can apply the long exhale method to improve your overall mental health during an anxiety attack.

1. Before you take a big deep breath try to exhale instead
2. Try spending a bit longer exhaling than you do inhaling. E.g., inhale for five seconds then exhale for eight seconds.
3. Try this for two to five minutes.

This can be done either by standing, sitting or lying down on your back whichever you feel most comfortable with. The website healthline.com illustrates how breathing can help to alleviate stress as shown below:

Figure 4: Breathing

B	BOX BREATHING	Breathe in- Hold- Breathe
R	ROLL YOUR SHOULDERS	Releases Tension
E	EXTEND YOUR ARMS	Hands Clasped, Reach Up with Palms Up
A	ADJUST YOUR POSTURE	It Affects M-O-O-D
T	TALK ABOUT IT	Text A Friend
H	HYDRATE	Drink Some Water

Practice belly breathing.[70]

---

70 Sarah Dalton, 'Breathe Deeper to Improve Health and Posture', *Healthline*, 2020 <https://www.healthline.com/health/breathe-deeper-improve-health-and-posture> [accessed 5 September 2021].

1. Sit down relax your head chest and body
2. Place one hand on your chest and one on your stomach above your belly button.
3. Breathe in through your nose, notice your stomach rise. Your chest should remain relatively still.
4. Purse your lips and exhale through your mouth. Engage your stomach muscles as you do this too.

For this type of breathing to become automatic, you will need to practice it daily. Try this exercise three or four times a day for up to ten minutes each time.

Breath focus is the next one. When breathing is focused and slow it can reduce anxiety. Do this in a quiet location and position.

1. Take a slow deep breath through your nose
2. Notice how your belly and upper body expand.
3. Exhale
4. Do this for several minutes paying attention to this rise and fall of your belly
5. Choose a desired word to focus on and vocalise during your exhale. For example, "safe" or "calm" or "peace"
6. Imagine your exhale washing over you like a gentle wave
7. Imagine your exhale taking negative thoughts and energy away from you
8. When and if you get distracted bring your attention back to your breath and words

Equal breathing is the next one. This technique comes from pranayama yoga and means you are inhaling for the same time as you are exhaling. Here is a step-by-step process to apply this method of breathing.

1. Shut your eyes and pay attention to the ways you normally breathe for several breaths.
2. Slowly count 1-2-3-4 as you inhale through your nose.
3. Exhale for the same four-second count
4. As you inhale and exhale, be mindful of feelings of fullness and emptiness in your lungs.

Resonant breathing is also called coherent breathing. It calms anxiety and gets you into a relaxed state. Try this method:

1. Lie down and close your eyes
2. Gently breathe in through your nose, mouth shut, for a count of six seconds.
3. Don't fill your lungs too full of air
4. Exhale for six seconds, don't force the air out
5. Continue for up to 10 minutes

Yoga breathing pranayama is a wellness practice with ancient roots. Breathing is at the heart of each variation of yoga. It's centred and focused on breathing.

Lion's breath. Which, as it sounds, involves exhaling forcefully. Here is the way it's done:

1. Get into the kneeling position, crossing your ankles and resting the bottom of your feet.
2. Bring your hands to your knees, stretching out your arms and fingers
3. Take a breath in through your nose
4. Breathe out through your mouth and vocalise the word "ha"
5. During the exhale open your mouth as wide as possible and stick your tongue out directing it down towards your chin.
6. Focus on the middle of your forehead (third eye-pineal gland) or the end of your nose while exhaling
7. Relax your face as you inhale again
8. Repeat this up to six times

Alternate nostril breathing is another method. Rest your left hand on your lap and put your right hand in the air. Then rest the pointer and middle fingers of your right hand on your forehead in between the eyebrows. Close your eyes exhaling and inhaling through the nose.

1. Take your right thumb and use it to close the right-hand nostril and inhale slowly through the left.
2. Pinch your nose gently closed between your right thumb and middle finger holding it for a moment.
3. Use right ring finger to close your left nostril and exhale through the right waiting for a brief moment before inhaling again
4. Inhale slowly through the right nostril
5. Pinch your nose gently closed again pausing for a second or two

6. Open the left side and exhale waiting for a moment before inhaling again
7. Repeat this cycle up to 10 times each cycle should take approximately 40 seconds.

Guided meditation is another useful tool that can help your breathing and reduce anxiety and stress levels. It interrupts the patterns of thinking that perpetuate stress. You can practice this method by sitting in a cool, dark, comfortable place, then listening to calming recordings like solfeggio frequencies while relaxing your body and steadying your breathing. This method helps you visualise a calmer, less stressed reality. It can also help you gain control over intrusive thoughts which will and do trigger anxiety.

To summarise, breathing techniques are a vital part of overcoming mental health afflictions. They calm you down and give you a more placid feeling. It's easier to deal with further anxiety or panic attacks when your breathing is stronger, deeper more in tune with the rest of your body. It's vital to practice these techniques regularly to train your body to breathe this way by default. This will help reduce the chances of having episodes of anxiety, etc going forward.

Figure 5: The Theory A and Theory B approach

Theory A	Theory B
The problem is people just don't like me and will insult me or antagonise me	I *worry* that people don't like me and *misinterpret* people's actions as insults
There have been some occasions when I've not let people in and they have insulted me	The more I think I've heard something the more likely it is to happen again
Sometimes I leave conversations and I feel I may do this in a rude way	The more anxious I am the more likely I am to hear things
There have been four or five occasions where I have been in a confrontation and been insulted	My filter is usually very negative and I always think the worst of people. I can't imagine someone murmuring a compliment instead
	These things have been instigated by me and no one has ever clearly confronted me out of the blue

This approach is very useful. It distinguishes between what you know and what you think. I used the example of my struggles with hearing insults from people. I realised that the more anxious I felt the more likely I was to hear things. I also realised that my negative filter made me think the worst of people and thus made me believe they were insulting me when I was unsure about what was being said. So, it's clear to see that we must not always go based on what we think, but there is a clear link between our beliefs and what actually happens. Yes, sometimes things are happening but the problem is your filter is so traumatised that you ALWAYS think it will happen over and over again. So, you are living in fear of the same thing happening again. This principle applies to many matters of mental health. When it's at its worst it can then become hallucinations, and that's the worst stage to be in. it's important to not allow yourself to be a passenger, take control and try and stop thinking about what will happen. Wait for bad things to happen because more often than not they don't.

Laughter

Laughter is so important to change your state of mind. Laughter decreases stress hormones and increases immune cells and infection-fighting antibodies which in turn improve your disease resistance. Laughter triggers the release of endorphins which is the body's natural feel-good chemicals. Endorphins promote an overall sense of well-being and can also temporarily relieve pain in some cases. Laughter activates multiple regions of the brain: the motor cortex, which controls muscles; the frontal lobe, which helps you understand context; and the limbic system which modulates positive emotions. Laughing is similar to antidepressants in that it activates the release of the neurotransmitter serotonin which is the same brain chemical affected by the most common type of antidepressants, SSRIs. Laughter therapy is a cheap alternative to other methods to alleviate mental health problems. It doesn't require specialised preparations, such as suitable facilities and equipment, and it's easily accessible and acceptable. Laughter has now been incorporated into therapy generally. It decreases serum levels of cortisol, epinephrine, growth hormone and 3,4-dihydrophenylacetic acid[71] (a major dopamine catabolite), indicating a reversal of the stress response. Depression is a disease where neurotransmitters in the brain, such as norepinephrine, dopamine, and serotonin, are reduced, and there is something wrong in the mood control circuit of the brain. Laughter can change dopamine and serotonin activity. Endorphins secreted by laughter can help when people are uncomfortable or in a somewhat depressed mood. Laughter is effective and scientifically supported as a single or adjuvant therapy to help with mental illness. Laughter has existed in all societies throughout the ages. There is a well-known proverb, "A merry heart doeth good like a medicine" (proverbs 17:22). has been used through the ages and records show physicians have been advocating the potentially curative aspects of humour for hundreds of years. Humour improves positive emotions, gives pain relief, strengthens the immune system and moderates stress levels. Severe mental health illnesses such as major depression, schizophrenia, bipolar disease, OCD, panic disorder, PTSD, borderline personality disorder are said to disrupt a person's motivation, thought processes, emotions, mood, interpersonal relationships and behaviours. These come with difficulties such as self-esteem issues, coping with anxiety, depressive and suicidal thoughts, coping with traumatic experiences, coping with strong

---

71 JongEun Yim, 'Therapeutic Benefits of Laughter in Mental Health: A Theoretical Review', The Tohoku Journal of Experimental Medicine, 239.3 (2016), 243–49 <https://doi.org/10.1620/tjem.239.243>.

hostility and sexual drives interpersonal and intrapersonal conflicts; including shame and guilt, loss of the ability to enjoy life, social alienation and internalised stigma, as well as institutionalization. These conditions necessitate significant intervention. Treatment can be hard and interventions include many medications and therapies. A book written by Darwin called *The Expression of the Emotions in Man and Animals* speculated that the evolutionary basis of laughter had its function as a social expression of happiness and that this rendered a cohesive survival advantage to the group. In support of his theory, laughter has been found to occur in social contexts over 95% of the time. In addition to regulating conversation, it enhances social relations by producing pleasure in others through simple contagious processes, and by rewarding others' actions, thus encouraging social activities. Laughter itself is enough to promote short term well-being.

In conclusion, laughter can relieve stress as it makes us feel good. Laughter causes positive physical effects. It increases our intake of oxygen-rich air which helps our heart and our muscles. It also activates our stress response which increases our heart rate and blood pressure and then cools it down, leaving us feeling relaxed and satisfied in a sense. Laughing also stimulates circulation which alleviates some of the symptoms of stress and it cancan lower blood pressure, which can help people who may have weight issues. This has to do with the way our arteries respond when we are amused. Research shows that after watching a funny movie, our arterial compliance (the elasticity of some large blood vessels) improves for the next 24 hours. Laughter can also burn calories. Obviously, it's not like exercising but research shows 10-15 minutes of laughing can burn 50 calories. Laughter can also make us smarter by making connections between disparate pieces of information, one of the key ways to measure intelligence. Try to laugh more even if you don't know the science behind it. It can truly help to improve your mental health.

Learn what triggers your mental health problems

Learn what triggers your mental health problems and learn how to cope with them. It's important to realise what triggers your mental health affliction. Once you know this you can put things in place to prevent it, or manage it when you have an episode. I realised that what triggered mine was people and crowds, but mainly interpersonal situations where I would have to interact with people. Just the idea of it made me anxious because I was always afraid of something negative being said to me in the conversation. In a way, I lost my basic ability to interact with people. It's a basic social skill one learns when young. So, I would avoid people as much as I could. Once you are aware of what causes your problem you can avoid situations where it might happen. For example, although it's not advisable, my problem was caused by being around people. So, what did I do? I tried to avoid people as often as I could. I'm not saying that this can always be a method you can use but it's also good to be aware of the triggers and avoid them where possible. Another example is if you feel anxious in open spaces you could avoid going to places that are too open and vast. Deep breathing when you feel the onset of an episode coming on is another great way to cope with it, as mentioned previously. There are many deep breathing techniques you could use to alleviate the symptoms of anxiety, etc. It's also important to be fully aware of what triggers your mental illness because in doing so you are on top of it and can manage it as long as you have the right tools in place. There are some drawbacks to being aware of it and that is because it can make you more aware and conscious of your mental health problem, and thus perpetuate it. You can start to think obsessively about it and even bring on an episode in this way. This can be managed by ensuring you just keep on top of it rather than obsess about it and let it cripple you.

Be okay with not having control over everything

In life, it can almost become instinctive to want to take control over adverse situations. Reacting is the one way we as humans feel like we can potentially take control over a situation. Doing nothing is very difficult as explained with Gray's Line. The more one tries to take control over a situation the more emphasised it becomes. The more control you yearn for, the more difficult it can be to deal with when you realise you are losing control. Learn to let go and just be in the now. You have more power when you are in a position of submission than you think. I understand when you have a problem with mental illness it's normal to want to react or control a situation, but a lot of the time this can make the situation a whole lot worse. You are creating the potential for anxiety and stress when you do this. It's not a requirement to react to everything that happens in your life. It's wise to pick what you will react to and what you won't react to. As long as you can think to yourself "is this worth reacting to?" That in itself means you are aware and have the power to not. There's a saying: "don't spend five minutes worrying about something now that won't be relevant in five 'years' time." Just let go and try to be free in the mind and the body. Submit to everything, be at one with everything. Don't interrupt the flow. Eventually, your mental illness will improve the more you can do this. By being in control sometimes you can attract negative outcomes. My advice is to just let things be and subtly pass through life, not being passive but being pedestrian, sometimes.

Anxiety Blueprint

Some questions you can ask yourself when it comes to your anxiety are:

> What if this happens again? I couldn't cope if I felt like that again. What do I do if I start to feel worse? I've still got so many things to change and how can I cope on my own?

These questions can be subdivided into things like my triggers, my most unhelpful thoughts and my most unhelpful behaviours. So, for example, in my case, my triggers are social situations. My most unhelpful thoughts are that people will insult me no matter what, and my most unhelpful behaviours are being quiet or avoiding interacting with people. It becomes a cycle and you then worry about it happening every time you are in a social situation. You also feel alone. It's good to note this information down to see the patterns in your behaviour and thoughts, and this way you can make the necessary changes to avoid it holding you back all the time.

Challenge your negative thoughts

Depression, poor self-esteem and anxiety are often the result of irrational negative thoughts. Someone who regularly receives positive feedback at work might feel that they are horrible at their job because of one negative criticism. Their irrational thought about job performance will dictate how they feel about themselves. Challenging irrational thoughts can help us change them. Here are some questions you can ask yourself which can help to assess your thought.

> Is there substantial evidence for my thought?
> Is there evidence contrary to my thought?
> Am I attempting to interpret this situation without all the evidence?
> What would a friend think about this situation?
> If I look at the situation positively, how is it different?
> Will this matter a year from now? How about five years from now?

Asking these questions regularly in these situations will change your brain's way of thinking. It's important to do this to rid yourself of always thinking negatively. Like they say, why spend five minutes worrying about something now that won't matter in five years. Changing the way you see situations will invariably decrease your negative thoughts over time and thus improve your mental health. You deserve to be happy. To an extent, you can control how you interpret things. It's better to do so in a way that serves you well.

Figure 6: Situation, Reaction and Learning point record

Situation	Anxiety at the start (thought and rating out of 10)	Reaction	End Anxiety (out of 10)	Learning Point
Approaching the end of the road, about to turn onto the main road. Very narrow – another car approaching me.	8/10	Over compromised and gave way to the oncoming vehicle but was nervous and feared my action may have provoked the other driver.	6/10	I tried to disarm the driver by being over-friendly. I was nervous about getting onto the main road which had more people on it. Need to stay calm
In queue in the post office, queue kept getting longer behind me.	9/10	Biting nails, tapping my leg, humming to myself, looking straight ahead, got nervous and anxious.	3/10 (I was relieved when I left)	People trigger my anxiety, the more people the worse it gets. I need to be calm and not focus on them and realise that the situation is innocuous and normal.

You can apply this method to any situation that triggers your mental health problem. It's a good way to document your behaviours and reactions and what you can do the next time to avoid it. Sometimes we don't see what we are doing because we are in the situation. When you read back on this it will show you where you may be making the wrong choices and applying the wrong thoughts. You can see that your reactions can either increase or decrease your anxiety at the end of the event. Most of the time, as people, we do things to make ourselves feel less anxious, but we don't realise that reacting can perpetuate the cycle.

Acupuncture

Acupuncture is one of the treatments for mental health that I haven't looked into. I find this approach very interesting. Approximately 25% of people in the UK will suffer from a mental health problem each year. The majority of these cases are for anxiety and depression. It is predicted by the World Health Organisation (W.H.O.) that by the year 2030 depression will be the leading cause of disability in the entire world. Some of the symptoms of anxiety and depression include poor concentration, diarrhoea, palpitations, shortness of breath, lassitude, low self-esteem, irritable bowel syndrome, migraines, suicidal thoughts and much more. Stressful events often trigger anxiety and depression, such as bereavement, illness and financial difficulties. The most common types of treatment for these afflictions is usually drugs or therapy. The former has mixed results in both the short-term and long-term and can result in a plethora of side effects such as drowsiness, slurred speech, akathisia, and so on. Long-term use can lead to addiction and neurotoxicity.

Acupuncture has no long-term risks associated with it and has been shown in many studies to be relatively safe. It has also been noted that acupuncture is as safe as drugs. In the York study, it was found that acupuncture was clinically effective, safe and cost-effective as a treatment for depression. What acupuncture does is it reduces sensitivity to pain and stress. It also promotes relaxation and deactivating the analytical brain which is of course responsible for anxiety and worry. Acupuncture also regulates the levels of neurotransmitters and hormones such as serotonin, noradrenaline, dopamine, GABA, neuropeptide which alters the brain's mood chemistry to eradicate negative affective states of the mind (Lee 2009; Yuan 2007; Zhou 2008). In addition, acupuncture also stimulates the production of endogenous opioids that affect the automatic nervous system. It's known that stress activates the sympathetic nervous system while acupuncture activates the opposing parasympathetic nervous system which in turn triggers a relaxation response in the mind and body. Acupuncture also reverses pathological changes in levels of inflammatory cytokines which are associated with anxiety and depression and results in a reduction in stress-induced changes in behaviour and biochemistry. One can combine acupuncture with other conventional treatments without this affecting the course of the treatment. Acupuncture is a form of traditional Chinese medicine (TCM) it has been more widely used as a treatment for pains and aches. In TCM your "Qi" is the flow of energy through your body. Qi flows through your body on energy channels known as meridians. It's believed that your energy becomes blocked in some way which results in illness. This is present with physical symptoms such as an aching back or emotional symptoms such as stress and anxiety. Acupuncture is said to remove these blockages and restore energy flow, balancing your organs, mind and your body. The needles from the acupuncture inserted into the body are said to release endorphins in the body and thus changing the neurotransmitters in the brain. Endorphins are the body's natural painkillers. Ergo an increase in these hormones provides a boost to your body and mind. There have been arguments put forward that acupuncture is a placebo effect but this hasn't been confirmed or proven. The hands-on connection can make some people, typically people dealing with depression, feel much better, regardless of the actual needlework that goes into it. Some side effects associated with acupuncture can be itching at the area of treatment, soreness, bleeding from the needlepoint, muscle twitching, drowsiness, tiredness, bruising around the needlepoint and so on. There have been cases where the improper practice of acupuncture has led to spinal injury, infection and respiratory and cardiac problems.

Each practitioner may target different acupoints when they insert the needles. Each point corresponds to a part of the meridian or qi that's being targeted for relief. These acupoints are located all over the body from your head to your neck and even legs and feet. These acupoints are commonly targeted to alleviate depression.

A study in 2013 showed that electroacupuncture, which is a type of acupuncture that uses a mild electric current transmitted through the needles was just as effective as Prozac in easing depression. Acupuncture is said to also increase libido.

Acupuncture treatment can be used over a range of time. This ranges from once a week to six days a week. If you are considering doing this type of treatment it's good to indulge in your own research about it first. Study the potential benefits and risks involved. Remember it can be pricey so it's good to also consider that when making your decision. I personally have never tried this treatment but doing my research I think if nothing else has worked for you it may be worth a try and it's also good to combine it with other treatments as it can be even more effective, according to research.

Embrace moments of stillness and quietness

Find your inner peace and stick with it. Meditation is a great way to connect with your inner soul and calm yourself. When you have inner quiet and peace you aren't easily perturbed by outside influences. You are most likely to be able to ignore negative things that try to penetrate your mind. You will find that if you arm yourself with this calmness when you have an episode you will be able to ward it off. Not only are calmness and stillness good for anxiety but also generally helpful in improving your ability to connect with people on deeper spiritual levels. It allows us to empathise and relate to people through positive energy. Being at one with nature is a great way to gain stillness and quietness. Just sitting in the park in a quiet place watching the trees sway as the wind brushes the branches from side to side can be very therapeutic and calming. I'd suggest implementing this into your weekly or even daily activity. Make

CHAPTER 9: HOW TO OVERCOME AND COPE WITH MENTAL HEALTH AFFLICTIONS

time for it as it will greatly improve your quality of life. When you are calm you make better decisions, too. You are less stressed, less impulsive, you are more discerning and more astute when it comes to deciding on what to do. As with everything, it does take practice and repetition to make it a part of your essence. At first, it can seem a bit strange to just sit somewhere peaceful and do nothing. We live in a world that is overstimulated and demands instant gratification which makes it hard for us at the best of times to just be still and quiet. The mind like every other muscle in the body needs rest, it needs time off, time to recharge and refresh itself. Overuse can cause stress and many other mental and physiological complications. Learn to be at one with everything. Do nothing sometimes. Surrender to everything and you are powerful. Let the current take you, feel it – don't fight it or oppose it. I sometimes would just sit at the beach by myself, find a quiet place and meditate. It doesn't have to be the beach if you enjoy nature or greenery you could go to a park or the woods or a hilltop; there are many options. For some, it could even be going for a long drive regularly as driving can be therapeutic too. I found driving to be helpful. I would just put on some solfeggio frequencies and just get lost in the moment, clear my mind and just drive. I tended to head out during the evenings when there were fewer people and cars. I only realised just how beautiful London is on these drives that I took. It's very built up but beautiful at the same time. I really marvelled at its beauty and felt more connected to it. It's not just about the people, it's about the place, too. I think being calm and still in a world like ours is very difficult with the many challenges we face every day, stress-inducing situations, problems at work, with partners, friends and family, money issues. It can lead you to a dark place. This is why staying on top of it by being still is very necessary. It really makes a huge difference in centring your focus and thoughts. Many of us have anxiety attacks or panic attacks because we get distracted by outside influences but if you are centred and calm this is less likely to be the case. It's often the things we take for granted in life that mean the most to our well-being and livelihood. Mind therapy is one of them. I once heard the saying that 'what costs doesn't count and what counts doesn't cost'. It's often the things that are free and accessible that hold the most value in making us happy; little things like a pleasant interaction with another human being, or being complimented by someone, or helping someone who is destitute or helpless. These are the things to value – not just how big your house or car is, or what job you do. It's about making a difference in the world and helping others and if your mind is calm and still you are of better service to others.

New habits that help to improve yourself

It's important to develop new habits that help to improve yourself if you struggle with mental health problems and in general. The state of mind is determined by habits and paradigms. We all get stuck in routines and habits. It's what defines us as humans. Day to day activities and thoughts makes us who we are in a sense. There's a saying. "Heaven on earth is when your habits align with your goals and dreams, hell on earth is when they don't". In other words, if you are a sportsman and it's your passion and dream to become a professional one, but you never play sport as a habit or go to the gym, then that's hell on earth. It's clear in that case you need to evaluate what your habits are and maybe change them. Mark Cuban, the owner of the basketball franchise, Dallas Mavericks, once said that in life it's important to focus on what you tend to do the most – the thing or things that are effortless and you do religiously. Perfect those things and you will become successful at them and in turn be able to help others once you are in an established position. He was saying your habits are what determine your future. But he wasn't advising you to change them, just perfect them and use them as tools to support or create a goal and dream. Gary Vaynerchuk, the Belarusian-American entrepreneur, once said, "it's important when you are on your way to success and you are following your dream, to not worry about telling people what to do and how to become successful, rather just by being the example yourself". This can also be linked to a person's habits as this, by definition, is what you tend to do every day and if you are not doing it you are thinking of it. My point is you should form habits that support your dreams and passions. We only have one life to get things right, you don't get another chance; so if you need to fail whilst trying a thousand times it's better than not trying at all, as trying today is worth a lot more than tomorrow. It only takes two months to form a new habit after all. Think about that for a minute. With regards to mental health, some habits you can form to improve it are getting better sleep that is regimented, being mindful, intermittent fasting, exercising and eating well, taking regular breaks, opening up and just being more open-minded to things and ideas and thinking positive thoughts. These can all improve your mental health tenfold. One new habit you can form is the 4:55 drill.[72] It's an end of day routine. At 4:55 or about five minutes before the end of a shift at work. You pull out a 3x5 index card or sticky note and jot down the three most important things you need to get done the following day. Leave it face up on your desk so as soon as you walk in it's staring you in the face. There are two benefits to forming this new habit

1. It decreases anxiety and stress about work during the evenings. Writing down to-do's puts your mind at ease and relaxes it because you know exactly what you need to do the next day.
2. It also reduces friction in the morning. One of the common causes of procrastination is uncertainty about how or what tasks you need to do. This then leads to anxiety which then leads to us impulsively checking Facebook or YouTube in an attempt to distract ourselves from that discomfort. By being clear about what we need to do, it maximises our chance of staying focused and efficient.

There are many benefits to forming new habits. It's important to stay on top of things and to be aware of when your habits lead to negative things like procrastination, or exacerbating your mental health problems. Routines are part of human life but there are good routines that help put your life in order and help with the efficacy when it comes to what you desire and want to get done. I strongly advise that you consider this approach.

---

[72] Nick Wignall, 'The 4:55 Drill', *Nick Wignall*, 2018 <https://nickwignall.com/the-455-drill/> [accessed 7 September 2021].

Having a positive attitude and setting goals

Having a positive attitude and setting goals is important, too. You must shift your paradigm and change your mindset. Success is a mindset. I understand it can be hard to see things positively when you have a mental health problem. Every day you are plagued by the problem you have, and this can be like a dark cloud hanging over you. But there's a silver lining to every cloud. It's vital that you reinforce positive thoughts. Remind yourself that once upon a time you were okay and that you did live a healthy happy life before the onset of your mental health issue. I always heard my therapist say that to me. He always urged me to remember the fact that I wasn't always burdened by this affliction, and that I did have an anxiety and psychosis free existence before this. So, if that was possible, it's possible to get it back. Positivity can go a long way. Just thinking positive thoughts to yourself can change the framework that determines your mood on a day-to-day basis, and in the long run, this can reverse any mental health problem you might have. Remember, reasons to live give reasons to die. Set goals for yourself and do everything you can to actualise them. There is no conviction without inconvenience. Enjoy the journey. The world is beautiful and so are you. Remember without commitment one will never start and without consistency, one will never finish. A question opens the mind, a statement closes it. Ask the right questions. Positivity motivates you; it lifts your mood and enables you to treat others in a good way. Even in the event of an episode, you may interpret it differently and more positively if you just change your mindset. When you feel positive you believe you can achieve so much more than when you are negative. Give it a try it does make a lot of difference. There will be difficult days and days where things don't go your way but don't let your success go to your head and your failure go to your heart. Keep moving forward and trying and you will get to where you want to get to. Success comes from within not from without as said by Ralph Waldo Emerson.

Keep reminding yourself that these moments (anxiety and panic attacks) will pass

My mom always taught me that no situation is permanent. Nothing in life lasts forever. It will by all means pass. Sometimes you just need to sit there and take it knowing that it will eventually be over. Mental health afflictions can make one think that the world is coming to an end and that when you feel panic, stress, anxiety, etc., that the feeling will last forever. Many people also live in fear of an anxiety attack happening again, such is the scary nature of each episode you may have. Anxiety by definition is the desire to escape the present moment. The fear and shock of the event is so severe it then triggers the flight, fight, freeze, fawn or flop response. Something happens and it's so traumatic or unsettling that you live in perpetual fear of it happening again. You avoid doing certain things that may trigger it or going to certain places that may trigger it. You end up just doing nothing and can potentially become depressed or even suicidal – this is anxiety disorder. It can leave you feeling overcome by lassitude and just a general lack of desire to do anything to avoid it happening again. That's debilitating, it's frightening; trust me, I've been there.

Telling yourself and reminding yourself that it will pass is crucial if you want to overcome the battle in the long run. It isn't easy. It takes time. It can be done, however, if you constantly remind yourself that it's not a permanent situation. If you think about it, all of us go through stuff we would rather not do on a daily basis. For example, being stuck in traffic and late for work, working with someone you don't particularly get on with, having to study hard for an exam, having a cold or the flu, having arguments with loved ones, etc., but we don't let those things cripple us and stop us from doing them again. If you look at anxiety in the same way you then realise it's a choice. Fight or flight in a sense. If you treat it like something annoying that you have to put up with daily, it may be easier to live with it and eventually become impervious to it. Anxiety for example is a normal thing. We all have it. It's our mind or body's way of protecting us in dangerous situations. For example, you are in the wild and you see a large male lion in the distance walking in your direction. Anxiety will then kick in and then the fight, flight or freeze response, and so on. The problem when you have the disorder is that you perceive innocuous situations as dangerous or menacing when they are not, so your anxiety response is overstimulated and overactive. It's the burnt toast effect. The toaster expels the bread when it starts to overheat but that's not a life-threatening or necessarily dangerous situation. It's important to not overthink it or dwell on your issues when you have an episode; just remember it will pass as with everything else. Imagine things could be worse – you may have a life-threatening ailment that you can't escape because the suffering and pain is a constant reminder of it. See it more positively and realise it's just in your mind, it's just a mental disorder that can be undone. It's not your fault that it's gotten to this point. But you can get yourself out of it with the right actions. The mind can become comfortable in any situation and once that happens it will refuse to see things differently; it's your job to change that. One thing that always keeps me going is the knowledge that these anxious moments will pass; it can be uncomfortable, but it won't last forever. I always remind myself of this when I'm having an episode. It really does help me and I'm sure it will help you, too.

Remind yourself that you are normal

There's nothing wrong with you. Having a mental health affliction doesn't make you abnormal. It's very common in the world, especially with anxiety. Don't believe you are strange or different; you are perfectly normal. I used to think there was something wrong with me because of my anxiety and psychosis. I would ruminate on it all the time and wonder why I was cursed. I simply didn't understand that it's just a simple chemical imbalance in the brain and that it's something that could be treated with the right intervention. In life, things do happen. Things that we cannot explain or understand. Don't blame yourself or beat yourself up because of this. It's not your fault. You didn't choose to start feeling this way or believe in this; it just happened. Life today is tough: it's very stressful, competitive, ruthless. One can easily get lost. It's important to stay on top of your mental health and protect yourself by implementing the tools that have been mentioned. We all walk different paths and go through different things in life but the truth is that one man's story is every man's story. You are not alone.

Consider playing different frequencies

Consider playing different frequencies and tapping into your chakras to overcome your mental health problems and rebalance your mind and body. Solfeggio frequencies refer to specific tones of sound that promote various aspects of the body and mind. These frequencies date way back in history. They are said to be the fundamental sounds in both western Christianity and eastern Indian religions, chanted by the Gregorian monks and also in ancient Indian Sanskrit chants. Our chakras are situated along the length of the spine, from the pelvic floor to the crown of the head. The system of chakras originated in yogic philosophy and the word chakra (pronounced chuhk-ruh) translates as "circle" or "wheel" due to the centralised locations in the body where energy channels, known as nadis, converge.[73] It's often referred to as the body's energy ecosystem. When the ecosystem is out of alignment our emotional and physical being is negatively affected. We can then put in place a wide range of healing techniques, from meditation to music, and massage to Reiki, which helps in unblocking and realigning the system. It's very important to note this. Some say

---

[73] Relax Melodies, 'The Science Behind Solfeggio Frequencies | Relax Melodies', 2021 <https://www.relaxmelodies.com/blog/science-behind-solfeggio-frequencies/> [accessed 30 August 2021].

there are 114 chakras but in today's studies, they are narrowed down to 7.

1. The root chakra (Muladhara) is located at the base of the spine in the tailbone area and radiates the colour red. It forms our foundation and is associated with aligning instincts and feelings. It also directs energy around the body
2. The sacral chakra (Swadhisthana) is located at the lower abdomen about 2 inches below the navel and it's portrayed as orange. It's related to emotions, desires and feelings as well as sensations and reproductive functions.
3. The solar plexus chakra (Manipura) is located in the stomach area and it's associated with the colour yellow. It's related to ego, self-discipline and identity. It offers confidence and allows one the ability to achieve goals
4. The heart chakra (Anahata) is located at the centre of the chest just above the heart and it's associated with the colour green. I think this one is a bit more obvious – it's related to love, both self-love and love towards others. It determines our beliefs, ethics and values.
5. The throat chakra (Vishudda) is located in the throat and is associated with a light blue/turquoise colour. This relates to our ability to communicate verbally. It puts you at a higher spiritual place if you are in tune with it, and grants us artistic abilities to be expressed.
6. The third eye chakra (Ajna) which is located in the forehead between the eyes, also called the brow chakra, is associated with a dark blue/purple colour. It's considered to be the gateway

to enlightenment and is related to seeing both intuitively and physically. It's central to inner perception, dreams, goals and ambitions and allows us to see the big picture.
7. The crown chakra (Sahasrara) is located at the very top of the head and it's associated with a violet/white colour. It's about our connection to the mother earth and the universe. It represents a state of higher consciousness similar to the nirvana stage of Buddhism, for example. When developed this chakra brings wisdom, knowledge and understanding of the world, people and of course, oneself.

Dr Joseph Puleo, a physician and researcher found that there are six measurable tones that bring the body back into balance and aid in healing. In total there are nine different frequencies that are now known. There's 174Hz which is one of the three additional frequencies above the sol-fa syllables responsible for pain relief, 285Hz which is also one of the new frequencies said to bring balance and deep healing to your life as it aligns you with the rhythms and tones that form the basis of the universe, 396Hz which liberates fear and guilt from the mind and is connected to the root chakra, 417Hz which is responsible for undoing situations and facilitating change and is connected to the sacral chakra, 528Hz which is for transformation and miracles (DNA Repair) and is connected to the solar plexus chakra, 639Hz which relates to connections with people and relationships and is connected to the heart chakra, 741Hz which awakens your intuition and visceral knowledge and is connected to the throat chakra, 852Hz which returns order to your spirit and is connected to the third eye chakra, and 963Hz (the God frequency) is associated with awakening intuition and activating the pineal gland. It's also called the pure miracle tone. It awakens your crown chakra (Sahasrara) and also raises the positive energy and vibrations and helps us connect to our source or God. We are all made of atoms, cells and molecules, and thus we are all energy and we all vibrate on many different frequencies. It's a bit like the string theory. It's worth noting that some may overlap.

It's important to note that most of the music we consume is played on the 440Hz frequency which actually doesn't align with our minds and souls. There was a test done with water to study the responsiveness of water to different frequencies played, and it was found that 440Hz created a pattern in the water that was abrasive and the sounds were dissonant when compared to the Solfeggio frequencies where the patterns were beautiful and magical. Since our bodies are made up of more than 70% water or liquid this gives testament to the importance of the tones we play and hear in our daily lives.

The Schumann resonance explains why Solfeggio frequencies produce more positive effects on the body than any other sounds or tones. In 1952, German Winfried Otto Schumann mathematically documented the electromagnetic resonances between the earth's surface and the ionosphere which is the electrically charged part of the earth's atmosphere. He discovered that these electromagnetic waves, which originate from lightning discharge, resonated at a low frequency between 7.86Hz to 8Hz. He determined that this frequency was, in essence, the earth's heartbeat. It's since been coined 'the Schumann resonance' after him, its founder. Doctoral candidate, Herbert Konig, took this further. He studied the connection between the Schumann resonances and found them to match various levels of human brain activity when comparing EEG recordings with the earth's electromagnetic fields. Konig discovered that the resonances matched five different brainwave states: delta, theta, alpha, beta and gamma. These are the daily brainwave states that occur during activities, from sleeping to creating to learning. So, the question is how do Schumann's resonances relate to Solfeggio frequencies? These frequencies have such positive effects because they resonate in harmony with the Schumann resonance of 8Hz. Musically, the frequencies are derived by beginning at 8Hz and working up the musical scale octave by octave until the C note is vibrating at the 256Hz frequency and the A note is vibrating at 432Hz. When music is tuned to match with this frequency this is known as scientific tuning. Many ancient musical instruments were constructed for 432Hz tuning, and before the mid-20th century 432Hz was the standard of instrument tuning until 440Hz became the norm. 432Hz is known for having deep calming and soothing effects. An Italian study shows that music tuned to 432Hz slows down the heart rate compared to 440Hz. This frequency fills the mind with feelings of peace and well-being, making it perfect for use with yoga, gentle exercise, meditation and sleep. 528Hz can heal and repair the body. A 2018 study in Japan showed that music tuned to 528Hz frequency significantly reduces stress in the endocrine systems and autonomic nervous systems even after just five minutes of listening. There was another study published in the journal of addiction research and therapy that the frequency 528Hz reduced the toxic effects of ethanol, the principal ingredient for alcoholic drinks, on cells. Even more amazing was that the frequency also increased cell life by about 20%.

396Hz helps improve subconscious fears, worries and anxiety. It also eradicates the feelings of guilt and subconscious negative beliefs blocking one's path to achieving goals. Listening to music on this frequency helps to uplift mood, it makes you feel more secure and it gives power to your goals and dreams. I listen to this frequency all the time and I can see the difference. I listen to all the Solfeggio frequencies as I feel they all work together holistically. 639Hz helps balance emotions and lift the mood; it promotes communication, love, understanding, empathy, and harmony in interpersonal relationships. Music set to this frequency is perfect when you are in need of a boost of love and positivity.

741Hz helps with problem-solving, cleansing the body and self-expression. It also helps awaken intuition and promote simple and pure living. It can also be useful in overcoming your mental health problems as can all the frequencies mentioned above.

852Hz replaces negative thoughts with positive ones, making it ideal when nervousness or anxiety is bringing you down.

Each Solfeggio frequency is powerful and useful as overall it will uplift you and edify you. You can turn your life around just by listening to these frequencies (let them do the work). I use and listen to them all the time and I can see the difference where my mental health and general health is concerned.

Join self-help groups

Join self-help groups and contact your early intervention centre and just realise you are not alone in this. I understand it can be hard to admit you need help but speaking to others who fully understand what you are going through can really help to improve your situation. It took me years to finally admit I needed help and I regretted it as my condition got worse as I suffered in silence. Early intervention centres and groups can help you identify exactly what your condition is and how to eradicate it effectively. They will have experts on hand who can help you get better by providing regular counselling sessions and other methods to apply to help you.

Family and friend intervention

Family and friend intervention is also important. Relationships are vital when you suffer from mental health problems. It's important to have good company around you whether it be a girlfriend, a brother, a sister, a parent or a good friend, as they are most likely the people who will empathise with you the most and care about you while you go through what you are going through. I am currently in a great relationship with a woman who empathises with me and is very patient and understanding. I am able to fully open up to her about my condition and she always gives me good advice and even does things that help me with my anxiety. It's also important to have close people around you as you can open up to them and tell them how you feel without feeling exposed or vulnerable. After all, this is what family and friends are for so give it a try.

In conclusion, mental health is a very prominent subject. It's somewhat taboo, especially in the UK. A lot of people suffer in silence and don't get the help they need. I know, it took me years before I took action, mainly because I was worried about exposing myself in a sense, about how people would perceive me, and I was worried that people would humiliate me because of it. It can be especially hard to admit your weaknesses and ask for help when you are a man. It's ego; it's self-preservation. I hope after reading this book you have a better sense of what having a mental health problem means and that you are not alone. You are normal, you are enough. One man's story is every man's story. If you feel any of the mental health conditions, I have covered relate to you in any way and have not yet sought advice and help, I urge you to do just that. Don't be like me and let the problem get worse and worse before taking action. You are in control and this is something that no one can take away from you. The world is a wonderful place and you belong in it. It's okay to feel lost sometimes. Just remember at some point you didn't have this affliction and you can get back to that place if the right steps are taken. Always aim to be your best version. It's the little things that we do every day that yield the big results during a lifetime.

Before I end the book, I will leave you with this little quote I came up with. There's a saying 'don't bite off more than you can chew' that we are all familiar with. I always say 'Bite big, chew small'. What I mean by this is have an objective, a goal that you want to achieve. Whether it be to eradicate your mental health condition, or to become successful, or to buy that dream home you have always wanted. Set a big goal and take little nibbles at it every day until you manifest it. You are an infinite being and no one can stand in your way but you. Step into the light and once you do help others, too. As the saying goes – each one teach one.

Thanks for reading.

The End

Epilogue

To summarise mental health is a serious issue but it can be treated with the right intervention and actions. Being a sufferer myself I've applied many of the methods mentioned and they have greatly improved my mental health. I'm not out of the woods yet but I have a much better understanding of my condition and how to manage it. Being at one with yourself and at peace with the world is very important and this is why meditation and listening to frequencies can really ground you and level the cortisol levels and healthily increase the dopamine levels in the brain. It's important not to take mental health for granted. If you are someone fortunate enough to not suffer from it, this is a great read as it raises awareness of what's out there and how to help people you may know who suffer from mental health issues. It's rife and very common. Anyone can get it and anyone can help if the right tools are used as mentioned. The aforementioned list isn't exhaustive but it's what's helped me according to my own experience and research. I just wish everyone a speedy recovery and remember you are normal; you are not alone and you will get through it. Just persevere and keep working on it every day and you will eventually get there.

List of useful contacts in the UK for mental health conditions

https://www.mind.org.uk/information-support/local-minds/ to find help in your local area in the UK

Infoline: 0300 123 3393
Email: info@mind.org.uk
Post: Mind Infoline, PO Box 75225, London, E15 9FS

Our Infoline provides an information and signposting service. We're open 9am to 6pm, Monday to Friday (except for bank holidays).

Ask us about:

mental health problems
where to get help near you
treatment options
advocacy services.

Anger Problems

Alcoholics Anonymous (AA)
0800 9177 650
help@aamail.org (email helpline)
alcoholics-anonymous.org.uk
Help and support for anyone with alcohol problems.

Beat
0808 801 0677 (adult helpline)
0808 801 0711 (youthline)
0808 801 0811 (studentline)
beateatingdisorders.org.uk
Offers information and advice on eating disorders, and runs a supportive online community. Also provides a directory of support services at Help Finder.

British Association for Counselling and Psychotherapy (BACP)
bacp.co.uk
Professional body for talking therapy and counselling. Provides information and a list of accredited therapists.

Cruse Bereavement Care
0808 808 1677
cruse.org.uk
Information and support after a bereavement.

Galop
0207 704 2040 (LGBT+ hate crime helpline)
0800 999 5428 (National LGBT+ domestic abuse helpline)
help@galop.org.uk
galop.org.uk
Provides helplines and other support for LGBTIQ+ adults and young people who have experienced hate crime, sexual violence or domestic abuse.

Men's Advice Line
0808 801 0327
mensadviceline.org.uk
Confidential advice and support for men who have experienced domestic violence and abuse by a current or ex-partner or family member.

Mind Tools
mindtools.com
Tips and articles on personal effectiveness, management and leadership.

Moodjuice
moodjuice.scot.nhs.uk
Online self-help guides on topics including depression, anxiety and stress.

National Domestic Abuse Helpline
0808 2000 247
nationaldahelpline.org.uk
Free 24-hour helpline for women who have experienced domestic abuse and violence, with all female advisors. Also offers a live chat and can help to find refuge accommodation. Run by the domestic violence charity Refuge.

National Self Harm Network (NSHN)
nshn.co.uk
Survivor-led online support forum for people who self-harm, their friends and families.

Refuge
0808 2000 247
refuge.org.uk
Support, information and advocacy for women and children who have experienced domestic violence and abuse.

Respect
respect.uk.net
Information and support for people who are worried about their violent or aggressive behaviour towards loved ones, and for male victims of domestic abuse.

Samaritans
116 123 (freephone)
jo@samaritans.org
Chris, Freepost RSRB-KKBY-CYJK
PO Box 90 90
Stirling FK8 2SA
samaritans.org
Samaritans are open 24/7 for anyone who needs to talk. You can visit some Samaritans branches in person. Samaritans also have a Welsh Language Line on 0808 164 0123 (7pm–11pm every day).

Turning Point
turning-point.co.uk
Health and social care services in England for people with a learning disability. Also supports people with mental health problems, drug and alcohol abuse or unemployment.

Welsh Women's Aid
0808 80 10 800 (Live Fear Free Helpline)
welshwomensaid.org.uk
Information and support for women and children who have experienced domestic abuse, including a directory of local services.

Women's Aid (England)
Women's Aid Live Chat support
womensaid.org.uk
Information and support for women and children who have experienced domestic abuse, including support by live chat, a directory of local services and a forum.

Body Dysmorphic Disorder (BDD)

Body Dysmorphic Disorder Foundation
bddfoundation.org
Support and information for people affected by body dysmorphic disorder.

British Association for Behavioural and Cognitive Psychotherapies (BABCP)
babcp.com
Information about cognitive behavioural therapy and related treatments, including details of accredited therapists.

Improving Access to Psychological Therapies (IAPT)
nhs.uk/service-search/find-a-psychological-therapies-service
Information about local NHS therapy and counselling services, which you can often self-refer to (England only).

National Institute for Health and Care Excellence (NICE)
nice.org.uk
Produces guidelines on best practice in healthcare.

NHS Service Finder
nhs.uk/service-search
Searchable database of NHS services in England.

OCD Action
0300 636 5478
ocdaction.org.uk
Information and support for people affected by OCD and hoarding, including online forums and local support groups.

OCD UK
03332 127890
ocduk.org
Charity run by and for people with OCD.

Borderline personality disorder (BPD)

Borderline Arts
borderlinearts.org
Uses the arts to raise awareness of borderline personality disorder and reduce stigma.

The Consortium for Therapeutic Communities
therapeuticcommunities.org
Online directory of therapeutic communities across the UK.

FRANK
0300 123 6600
talktofrank.com
Confidential advice and information about drugs, their effects and the law.

Harmless
harmless.org.uk
User-led organisation that supports people who self-harm, and their friends and family.

The National Association for People Abused in Childhood
(NAPAC)
0808 801 0331
support@napac.org.uk
napac.org.uk
Supports adult survivors of any form of childhood abuse. Offers a helpline, email support and local services.

National Institute for Health and Care Excellence (NICE)
nice.org.uk
Produces guidelines on best practice in healthcare.

NHS UK
nhs.uk
Information about health problems and treatments, including details of local NHS services in England.

Personality Disorder
personalitydisorder.org.uk
Website commissioned by the UK department of health. Includes information and details of local services in England.

Samaritans
116 123 (freephone)
jo@samaritans.org
Chris, Freepost RSRB-KKBY-CYJK
PO Box 90 90
Stirling FK8 2SA

samaritans.org
Samaritans are open 24/7 for anyone who needs to talk. You can visit some Samaritans branches in person. Samaritans also have a Welsh Language Line on 0808 164 0123 (7pm–11pm every day).

Depression

Anxiety UK
03444 775 774 (helpline)
07537 416 905 (text)
anxietyuk.org.uk
Advice and support for people living with anxiety.

British Association for Counselling and Psychotherapy (BACP)
bacp.co.uk
Professional body for talking therapy and counselling. Provides information and a list of accredited therapists.

Campaign Against Living Miserably (CALM)
0800 58 58 58
thecalmzone.net
Provides listening services, information and support for anyone who needs to talk, including a web chat.

Cruse Bereavement Care
0808 808 1677
cruse.org.uk
Information and support after a bereavement.

Depression UK
depressionuk.org
Depression self-help organisation made up of individuals and local groups.

Do-it
do-it.org
Lists UK volunteering opportunities.

The National Association for People Abused in Childhood (NAPAC)
0808 801 0331
support@napac.org.uk
napac.org.uk
Supports adult survivors of any form of childhood abuse. Offers a helpline, email support and local services.

National Institute for Health and Care Excellence (NICE)
nice.org.uk
Produces guidelines on best practice in healthcare.

NCT
0300 330 0700
nct.org.uk
Provides information, support and classes for parents.

NHS UK
nhs.uk

EPILOGUE

Information about health problems and treatments, including details of local NHS services in England.

Papyrus HOPELINEUK
0800 068 41 41
07860 039967 (text)
pat@papyrus-uk.org
papyrus-uk.org

Confidential support for under-35s at risk of suicide and others who are concerned about them. Open daily from 9am–midnight.

Samaritans
116 123 (freephone)
jo@samaritans.org
Chris, Freepost RSRB-KKBY-CYJK
PO Box 90 90
Stirling FK8 2SA
samaritans.org

Samaritans are open 24/7 for anyone who needs to talk. You can visit some Samaritans branches in person. Samaritans also have a Welsh Language Line on 0808 164 0123 (7pm–11pm every day).

Sane
sane.org.uk

Offers emotional support and information for anyone affected by mental health problems.

Togetherall
togetherall.com
Online mental health community (formerly called Big White Wall). Free in some areas through your GP, employer or university.

UK Council for Psychotherapy (UKCP)
psychotherapy.org.uk
Professional body for the education, training and accreditation of psychotherapists and psychotherapeutic counsellors. Provides online register of psychotherapists offering different talking treatments privately.

Dissociation and dissociative disorders

Childline
0800 1111
childline.org.uk
Support for children and young people in the UK, including a free helpline and 1-2-1 online chats with counsellors.

Clinic for Dissociative Studies
020 7794 1655
clinicds.co.uk
Information and treatment for people with dissociative disorders. Accepts NHS referrals.

Epilepsy Action
epilepsy.org.uk
Information about coping with epilepsy, seizures and non-epileptic attack disorder (NEAD).

European Society for Trauma and Dissociation
estd.org
Society for professionals working with trauma and dissociation.

First Person Plural
firstpersonplural.org.uk
Support and information for people with complex dissociative disorders and their family and friends.

The International Society for the Study of Trauma and Dissociation (ISSTD)
isst-d.org
Academic society providing information for professionals and the general public about trauma and dissociation research.

The National Association for People Abused in Childhood (NAPAC)
0808 801 0331
support@napac.org.uk
napac.org.uk
Supports adult survivors of any form of childhood abuse. Offers a helpline, email support and local services.

National Society for the Prevention of Cruelty to Children (NSPCC)
0800 800 5000 (for adults concerned about a child)
0800 1111 (18 or under – Childline helpline)
nspcc.org.uk
Support and information for children and anyone worried about a child.

Non-Epileptic Attack Disorder (NEAD)
nonepilepticattackdisorder.org.uk
Provides information and support for people who experience non-epileptic attacks.

Positive Outcomes for Dissociative Survivors (PODS)
0800 181 4420
pods-online.org.uk
Information, support and resources for people with dissociative disorders.

Survivors UK
020 3322 1860 (SMS)
074 9181 6064 (WhatsApp)
survivorsuk.org
Support for men who have experienced rape or sexual abuse, including text lines and an online chat service.

The Survivors Trust
0808 8010 818
thesurvivorstrust.org
Lists local specialist services for survivors of sexual violence, including advocates and Independent Sexual Violence Advisors (ISVAs).

Eating problems

Anorexia and Bulimia Care (ABC)
03000 11 12 13
anorexiabulimiacare.org.uk
Advice and support for anyone affected by eating problems.

Association for Family Therapy and Systemic Practice (AFT)
aft.org.uk
Information about family therapy, including a directory of therapists.

Beat
0808 801 0677 (adult helpline)
0808 801 0711 (youthline)
0808 801 0811 (studentline)
beateatingdisorders.org.uk
Offers information and advice on eating disorders, and runs a supportive online community. Also provides a directory of support services at HelpFinder.

British Association for Behavioural and Cognitive Psychotherapies (BABCP)
babcp.com
Information about cognitive behavioural therapy and related treatments, including details of accredited therapists.

British Association for Counselling and Psychotherapy (BACP)
bacp.co.uk
Professional body for talking therapy and counselling. Provides information and a list of accredited therapists.

National Institute for Health and Care Excellence (NICE)
nice.org.uk
Produces guidelines on best practice in healthcare.

Overeaters Anonymous Great Britain
oagb.org.uk
Local support groups for people with eating problems.

Papyrus HOPELINEUK
0800 068 41 41
07860 039967 (text)
pat@papyrus-uk.org
papyrus-uk.org
Confidential support for under-35s at risk of suicide and others who are concerned about them. Open daily from 9am–midnight.

EPILOGUE

Samaritans
116 123 (freephone)
jo@samaritans.org
Chris, Freepost RSRB-KKBY-CYJK
PO Box 90 90
Stirling FK8 2SA
samaritans.org
Samaritans are open 24/7 for anyone who needs to talk. You can visit some Samaritans branches in person. Samaritans also have a Welsh Language Line on 0808 164 0123 (7pm–11pm every day).

Student Minds
studentminds.org.uk
Mental health charity that supports students.

Tommy's
tommys.org
Information and support for people affected by stillbirth, miscarriage and premature birth.

YoungMinds
0808 802 5544 (Parents Helpline)
85258 (Crisis Messenger for young people – text the letters YM)
youngminds.org.uk
Committed to improving the mental health of babies, children and young people, including support for parents and carers.

Hoarding

Age Cymru (Wales)
08000 223 444
ageuk.org.uk/cymru
Information and support for older people.

Age UK (England)
0800 678 1602
ageuk.org.uk
Information and support for older people.

British Psychological Society (BPS)
bps.org.uk
Information about psychology, including a list of chartered psychologists.

Help for Hoarders
helpforhoarders.co.uk
Help for people experiencing hoarding and their families, including support groups and an online forum.

Hoarding Disorders UK
07950 364 798
hoardingdisordersuk.org
Support for people affected by hoarding, including support groups.

Hoarding UK
020 3239 1600
hoardinguk.org
Support for people affected by hoarding, including support groups.

National Institute for Health and Care Excellence (NICE)
nice.org.uk
Produces guidelines on best practice in healthcare.

NHS UK
nhs.uk
Information about health problems and treatments, including details of local NHS services in England.

OCD Action
0300 636 5478
ocdaction.org.uk
Information and support for people affected by OCD and hoarding, including online forums and local support groups.

Rainbow Red
07931 303310
rainbowred.co.uk
Provides an ice breaker form for people wanting to seek help with hoarding.

Samaritans

116 123 (freephone)
jo@samaritans.org
Chris, Freepost RSRB-KKBY-CYJK
PO Box 90 90
Stirling FK8 2SA
samaritans.org
Samaritans are open 24/7 for anyone who needs to talk. You can visit some Samaritans branches in person. Samaritans also have a Welsh Language Line on 0808 164 0123 (7pm–11pm every day).

The Silver Line
0800 4 70 80 90
thesilverline.org.uk
Provides support, information, friendship and advice for older people (over 55) who may feel lonely or isolated.

Obsessive-compulsive disorder (OCD)

Carers UK
0808 808 7777
029 2081 1370 (Carers Wales)
advice@carersuk.org
carersuk.org
Advice and support for anyone who provides care.

Improving Access to Psychological Therapies (IAPT)
nhs.uk/service-search/find-a-psychological-therapies-service

Information about local NHS therapy and counselling services, which you can often self-refer to (England only).

National Institute for Health and Care Excellence (NICE)
nice.org.uk
Produces guidelines on best practice in healthcare.

NHS Service Finder
nhs.uk/service-search
Searchable database of NHS services in England.

OCD Action
0300 636 5478
ocdaction.org.uk
Information and support for people affected by OCD and hoarding, including online forums and local support groups.

OCD UK
03332 127890
ocduk.org
Charity run by and for people with OCD.

Royal College of Psychiatrists
rcpsych.ac.uk
Professional body for psychiatrists. Includes information about mental health problems and treatments.

Triumph Over Phobia (TOP UK)
topuk.org
Provides self-help therapy groups and support for those with OCD, phobias and related anxiety disorders.

Anxiety and panic attacks

Anxiety Care UK
anxietycare.org.uk
Helps people with anxiety disorders.

Anxiety UK
03444 775 774 (helpline)
07537 416 905 (text)
anxietyuk.org.uk
Advice and support for people living with anxiety.

British Association for Counselling and Psychotherapy (BACP)
bacp.co.uk
Professional body for talking therapy and counselling. Provides information and a list of accredited therapists.

Improving Access to Psychological Therapies (IAPT)
nhs.uk/service-search/find-a-psychological-therapies-service
Information about local NHS therapy and counselling services, which you can often self-refer to (England only).

National Institute for Health and Care Excellence (NICE)
nice.org.uk
Produces guidelines on best practice in healthcare.

NHS Service Finder
nhs.uk/service-search
Searchable database of NHS services in England.

No More Panic
nomorepanic.co.uk
Provides information, support and advice for those with panic disorder, anxiety, phobias or OCD, including a forum and chat room.

No Panic
0300 7729844
nopanic.org.uk
Provides a helpline, step-by-step programmes, and support for people with anxiety disorders.

Samaritans
116 123 (freephone)
jo@samaritans.org
Chris, Freepost RSRB-KKBY-CYJK
PO Box 90 90
Stirling FK8 2SA
samaritans.org

Samaritans are open 24/7 for anyone who needs to talk. You can visit some Samaritans branches in person. Samaritans also have a Welsh Language Line on 0808 164 0123 (7pm–11pm every day).

Triumph Over Phobia (TOP UK)
topuk.org
Provides self-help therapy groups and support for those with OCD, phobias and related anxiety disorders.

Paranoia

British Association for Behavioural and Cognitive Psychotherapies (BABCP)
babcp.com
Information about cognitive behavioural therapy and related treatments, including details of accredited therapists.

British Association for Counselling and Psychotherapy (BACP)
bacp.co.uk
Professional body for talking therapy and counselling. Provides information and a list of accredited therapists.

Carers UK
0808 808 7777
029 2081 1370 (Carers Wales)
advice@carersuk.org
carersuk.org
Advice and support for anyone who provides care.

Mood Diaries
medhelp.org/land/mood-tracker
moodscope.com
moodchart.org
moodpanda.com
Some examples of mood diaries – many more are available. Mind doesn't endorse any particular one.

The National Association for People Abused in Childhood (NAPAC)
0808 801 0331
support@napac.org.uk
napac.org.uk
Supports adult survivors of any form of childhood abuse. Offers a helpline, email support and local services.

National Paranoia Network
nationalparanoianetwork.org
Information and support for people who experience paranoid thoughts.

Rethink Mental Illness
0300 5000 927
rethink.org
Provides support and information for anyone affected by mental health problems, including local support groups.

Samaritans
116 123 (freephone)
jo@samaritans.org
Chris, Freepost RSRB-KKBY-CYJK
PO Box 90 90
Stirling FK8 2SA
samaritans.org

Samaritans are open 24/7 for anyone who needs to talk. You can visit some Samaritans branches in person. Samaritans also have a Welsh Language Line on 0808 164 0123 (7pm–11pm every day).

Post-traumatic stress disorder (PTSD)

Anxiety UK
03444 775 774 (helpline)
07537 416 905 (text)
anxietyuk.org.uk
Advice and support for people living with anxiety.

ASSIST Trauma Care
assisttraumacare.org.uk
Information and specialist help for people who've experienced trauma or are supporting someone who has.

Birth Trauma Association
birthtraumaassociation.org.uk
Support for anyone affected by birth trauma, including partners.

EPILOGUE

Body Psychotherapy Network
bodypsychotherapynetwork.co.uk

An organisation aiming to provide a community, a platform and a voice for Body Psychotherapy and body psychotherapists.

Combat Stress
0800 1381 619
combatstress.org.uk
Treatment and support for armed forces veterans who have mental health problems.

Disaster Action
disasteraction.org.uk
Information and support for people affected by major disasters in the UK and overseas.

EMDR UK & Ireland
emdrassociation.org.uk
Professional association of EMDR clinicians and researchers in the UK and Ireland. Provides extensive information about EMDR.

Freedom from Torture
freedomfromtorture.org
Supports survivors of torture.

Help for Adult Victims of Child Abuse (HAVOCA)
havoca.org
Information and support for adults who have experienced any type of childhood abuse, run by survivors.

Lifecentre
0808 802 0808 (freephone)
07717 989 022 (textline)
lifecentre.uk.com
Support for survivors of rape and sexual abuse, and anyone supporting them. Includes a helpline, text support and email counselling.

Moodjuice
moodjuice.scot.nhs.uk
Online self-help guides on topics including depression, anxiety and stress.

The National Association for People Abused in Childhood (NAPAC)
0808 801 0331
support@napac.org.uk
napac.org.uk
Supports adult survivors of any form of childhood abuse. Offers a helpline, email support and local services.

National Institute for Health and Care Excellence (NICE)
nice.org.uk
Produces guidelines on best practice in healthcare.

NHS UK
nhs.uk
Information about health problems and treatments, including details of local NHS services in England.

PTSD Resolution
0300 302 0551
ptsdresolution.org
Helps veterans, reservists and their families with trauma and distress.

RoadPeace
08454 500 355
roadpeace.org
Information and support for people bereaved or seriously injured due to road crashes.

The Survivors Trust
0808 8010 818
thesurvivorstrust.org
Lists local specialist services for survivors of sexual violence, including advocates and Independent Sexual Violence Advisors (ISVAs).

Victim Support
0808 168 9111
victimsupport.org.uk
Provides emotional and practical support for people affected by crime and traumatic events.

Postnatal depression and perinatal mental health

Action on Postpartum Psychosis (APP)
app-network.org
Information and support for anyone affected by postpartum psychosis.

Anxiety UK
03444 775 774 (helpline)
07537 416 905 (text)
anxietyuk.org.uk
Advice and support for people living with anxiety.

The Association for Post Natal Illness
020 7386 0868
apni.org
Provides support for women experiencing postnatal depression.

Birth Trauma Association
birthtraumaassociation.org.uk
Support for anyone affected by birth trauma, including partners.

The Breastfeeding Network
0300 100 0212
breastfeedingnetwork.org.uk
Support and information about breastfeeding and perinatal mental health.

Child Bereavement UK
0800 028 8840
childbereavementuk.org
Support when a baby or child of any age is dying, or a child is facing bereavement.

Family Action
0808 802 6666
family-action.org.uk
Supports families of any kind, including with mental health problems.

Family Lives
0808 800 2222
familylives.org.uk
Information and support for parents and families.

Fatherhood Institute
fatherhoodinstitute.org
Information, research and training to support fathers and their families.

Gingerbread
0808 802 0925
gingerbread.org.uk
Advice and practical support for single parent families.

Home-Start
home-start.org.uk
Support for families with young children, including details of local services.

The Lullaby Trust
0808 802 6868 (Bereavement support)
0808 802 6869 (Information & advice)
lullabytrust.org.uk
Information and support for people affected by Sudden Infant Death Syndrome (SIDS).

Maternal OCD
maternalocd.org
Information and support for people experiencing perinatal OCD, and their families.

The Miscarriage Association
01924 200799
miscarriageassociation.org.uk
Information and support for anyone affected by miscarriage, molar pregnancy or ectopic pregnancy.

Mood Diaries
medhelp.org/land/mood-tracker
moodscope.com
moodchart.org
moodpanda.com
Some examples of mood diaries – many more are available. Mind doesn't endorse any particular one.

The National Association for People Abused in Childhood (NAPAC)
0808 801 0331
support@napac.org.uk
napac.org.uk
Supports adult survivors of any form of childhood abuse. Offers a helpline, email support and local services.

NCT
0300 330 0700
nct.org.uk
Provides information, support and classes for parents.

Netmums
netmums.com
Online community for parents, which also facilitates local meet-ups.

NHS UK
nhs.uk
Information about health problems and treatments, including details of local NHS services in England.

No Panic
0300 7729844
nopanic.org.uk
Provides a helpline, step-by-step programmes, and support for people with anxiety disorders.

OCD Action
0300 636 5478
ocdaction.org.uk
Information and support for people affected by OCD and hoarding, including online forums and local support groups.

OCD UK
03332 127890
ocduk.org
Charity run by and for people with OCD.

PANDAS Foundation
0843 28 98 401
pandasfoundation.org.uk
Information and support for anyone experiencing a mental health problem during or after pregnancy.

EPILOGUE

Pink Parents
pinkparents.org.uk
Information for gay and lesbian parents.

Postpartum Men
postpartummen.com
Information and support for new fathers experiencing depression, anxiety and other mental health problems, including an online peer support forum.

Sands
0808 164 3332
sands.org.uk
Information and support for anyone affected by the death of a baby.

Start4Life
nhs.uk/start4life
Information on pregnancy, breastfeeding and parenting from the NHS.

Tommy's
tommys.org
Information and support for people affected by stillbirth, miscarriage and premature birth.

Psychosis

Bipolar UK
0333 323 3880
bipolaruk.org
Information and support for people affected by bipolar disorder, hypomania and mania.

Hearing Voices Network
hearing-voices.org
Information and support for people who hear voices or have other unshared perceptions, including local support groups.

Mood Diaries
medhelp.org/land/mood-tracker
moodscope.com
moodchart.org
moodpanda.com
Some examples of mood diaries – many more are available. Mind doesn't endorse any particular one.

National Institute for Health and Care Excellence (NICE)
nice.org.uk
Produces guidelines on best practice in healthcare.

National Paranoia Network
nationalparanoianetwork.org
Information and support for people who experience paranoid thoughts.

Rethink Mental Illness
0300 5000 927
rethink.org
Provides support and information for anyone affected by mental health problems, including local support groups.

Samaritans
116 123 (freephone)
jo@samaritans.org
Chris, Freepost RSRB-KKBY-CYJK
PO Box 90 90
Stirling FK8 2SA
samaritans.org
Samaritans are open 24/7 for anyone who needs to talk. You can visit some Samaritans branches in person. Samaritans also have a Welsh Language Line on 0808 164 0123 (7pm–11pm every day).

Schizophrenia

Carers UK
0808 808 7777
029 2081 1370 (Carers Wales)
advice@carersuk.org
carersuk.org
Advice and support for anyone who provides care.

Hearing Voices Network
hearing-voices.org
Information and support for people who hear voices or have other unshared perceptions, including local support groups.

National Paranoia Network
nationalparanoianetwork.org
Information and support for people who experience paranoid thoughts.

Rethink Mental Illness
0300 5000 927
rethink.org
Provides support and information for anyone affected by mental health problems, including local support groups.

Royal College of Psychiatrists
rcpsych.ac.uk
Professional body for psychiatrists. Includes information about mental health problems and treatments.

Samaritans
116 123 (freephone)
jo@samaritans.org
Chris, Freepost RSRB-KKBY-CYJK
PO Box 90 90
Stirling FK8 2SA
samaritans.org

Samaritans are open 24/7 for anyone who needs to talk. You can visit some Samaritans branches in person. Samaritans also have a Welsh Language Line on 0808 164 0123 (7pm–11pm every day).

Time to Change
time-to-change.org.uk (England)
timetochangewales.org.uk (Wales)
National campaign to end stigma and discrimination against people with mental health problems in England and Wales. The campaign for England ended in 2021, but its resources are still available online.

Schizoaffective disorder

Bipolar UK
0333 323 3880
bipolaruk.org
Information and support for people affected by bipolar disorder, hypomania and mania.

British Association for Behavioural and Cognitive Psychotherapies (BABCP)
babcp.com
Information about cognitive behavioural therapy and related treatments, including details of accredited therapists.

British Association for Counselling and Psychotherapy (BACP)
bacp.co.uk
Professional body for talking therapy and counselling. Provides information and a list of accredited therapists.

Carers UK
0808 808 7777
029 2081 1370 (Carers Wales)
advice@carersuk.org
carersuk.org
Advice and support for anyone who provides care.

Hearing Voices Network
hearing-voices.org
Information and support for people who hear voices or have other unshared perceptions, including local support groups.

Intervoice
intervoiceonline.org
International network for people who hear voices.

Mood Diaries
medhelp.org/land/mood-tracker
moodscope.com
moodchart.org
moodpanda.com
Some examples of mood diaries – many more are available. Mind doesn't endorse any particular one.

National Institute for Health and Care Excellence (NICE)
nice.org.uk
Produces guidelines on best practice in healthcare.

Samaritans
116 123 (freephone)
jo@samaritans.org
Chris, Freepost RSRB-KKBY-CYJK
PO Box 90 90
Stirling FK8 2SA
samaritans.org
Samaritans are open 24/7 for anyone who needs to talk. You can visit some Samaritans branches in person. Samaritans also have a Welsh Language Line on 0808 164 0123 (7pm–11pm every day).

Sane
sane.org.uk
Offers emotional support and information for anyone affected by mental health problems.

Seasonal affective disorder (SAD)

Campaign Against Living Miserably (CALM)
0800 58 58 58
thecalmzone.net
Provides listening services, information and support for anyone who needs to talk, including a web chat.

Depression UK
depressionuk.org
Depression self-help organisation made up of individuals and local groups.

National Institute for Health and Care Excellence (NICE)
nice.org.uk
Produces guidelines on best practice in healthcare.

NHS UK
nhs.uk
Information about health problems and treatments, including details of local NHS services in England.

Rethink Mental Illness
0300 5000 927
rethink.org
Provides support and information for anyone affected by mental health problems, including local support groups.

Samaritans
116 123 (freephone)
jo@samaritans.org
Chris, Freepost RSRB-KKBY-CYJK
PO Box 90 90
Stirling FK8 2SA
samaritans.org

Samaritans are open 24/7 for anyone who needs to talk. You can visit some Samaritans branches in person. Samaritans also have a Welsh Language Line on 0808 164 0123 (7pm–11pm every day).

Sane
sane.org.uk
Offers emotional support and information for anyone affected by mental health problems.

Stress

Anxiety UK
03444 775 774 (helpline)
07537 416 905 (text)
anxietyuk.org.uk
Advice and support for people living with anxiety.

Togetherall
togetherall.com
Online mental health community (formerly called Big White Wall). Free in some areas through your GP, employer or university.

Health and Safety Executive (HSE)
hse.gov.uk
Information and guidance on health and safety law in the workplace.

International Stress Management Association
isma.org.uk
Information about stress, including details of practitioners who may be able to help you.

Mind Tools
mindtools.com
Tips and articles on personal effectiveness, management and leadership.

NHS UK
nhs.uk
Information about health problems and treatments, including details of local NHS services in England.

Samaritans
116 123 (freephone)
jo@samaritans.org
Chris, Freepost RSRB-KKBY-CYJK
PO Box 90 90
Stirling FK8 2SA
samaritans.org
Samaritans are open 24/7 for anyone who needs to talk. You can visit some Samaritans branches in person. Samaritans also have a Welsh Language Line on 0808 164 0123 (7pm–11pm every day).

Stressbusting
stressbusting.co.uk
Information about stress, including causes, treatments and coping techniques.

Stress Management Society
stress.org.uk
Information about stress and tips on how to cope.

Time to Change
time-to-change.org.uk (England)
timetochangewales.org.uk (Wales)
National campaign to end stigma and discrimination against people with mental health problems in England and Wales. The campaign for England ended in 2021, but its resources are still available online.

Suicidal feelings

Campaign Against Living Miserably (CALM)
0800 58 58 58
thecalmzone.net
Provides listening services, information and support for anyone who needs to talk, including a web chat.

Gender Identity Research & Education Society (GIRES)
gires.org.uk

Works to improve the lives of trans and gender non-conforming people of all ages, including those who are non-binary and non-gender.

Maytree Suicide Respite Centre
020 7263 7070
maytree.org.uk
Offers free respite stays for people in suicidal crisis.

The Mix
0808 808 4994
85258 (crisis messenger service, text THEMIX)
themix.org.uk
Support and advice for under 25s, including a helpline, crisis messenger service and webchat.

Mood Diaries
medhelp.org/land/mood-tracker
moodscope.com
moodchart.org
moodpanda.com
Some examples of mood diaries – many more are available. Mind doesn't endorse any particular one.

NHS 111 (England)
111
111.nhs.uk
Non-emergency medical help and advice for people in England.

NHS 111 (Wales)
111 (Hywel Dda, Powys, Aneurin Bevan and Swansea Bay (including Bridgend) Health Boards
0845 46 47 (all other areas of Wales)
111.wales.nhs.uk
Non-emergency medical help and advice for people living in Wales. The contact number for this service differs depending on which area of Wales you are in.

Papyrus HOPELINEUK
0800 068 41 41
07860 039967 (text)
pat@papyrus-uk.org
papyrus-uk.org
Confidential support for under-35s at risk of suicide and others who are concerned about them. Open daily from 9am–midnight.

Sane
sane.org.uk
Offers emotional support and information for anyone affected by mental health problems.

Samaritans
116 123 (freephone)
jo@samaritans.org
Chris, Freepost RSRB-KKBY-CYJK
PO Box 90 90
Stirling FK8 2SA

samaritans.org
Samaritans are open 24/7 for anyone who needs to talk. You can visit some Samaritans branches in person. Samaritans also have a Welsh Language Line on 0808 164 0123 (7pm–11pm every day).

Shout
85258 (text SHOUT)
giveusashout.org
Confidential 24/7 text service offering support if you are in crisis and need immediate help.

Stay Alive
prevent-suicide.org.uk
App with help and resources for people who feel suicidal or are supporting someone else.

Students Against Depression
studentsagainstdepression.org
Information and support for students experiencing suicidal feelings, including a helpful safety plan template.

Survivors of Bereavement by Suicide (SOBS)
0300 111 5065
uk-sobs.org.uk
Emotional and practical support and local groups for anyone bereaved or affected by suicide.

Switchboard
0300 330 0630
switchboard.lgbt
Listening services, information and support for lesbian, gay, bisexual and transgender communities.

Togetherall
togetherall.com
Online mental health community (formerly called Big White Wall). Free in some areas through your GP, employer or university.

Tardive dyskinesia (TD)

Bipolar UK
0333 323 3880
bipolaruk.org

Information and support for people affected by bipolar disorder, hypomania and mania.

The Dystonia Society
dystonia.org.uk
Information and support for anyone experiencing dystonia (a type of tardive dyskinesia). Includes a helpline, online forum and support groups.

Hearing Voices Network
hearing-voices.org

Information and support for people who hear voices or have other unshared perceptions, including local support groups.

Medicines and Healthcare Products Regulatory Agency (MHRA)
mhra.gov.uk
Regulates medicines in the UK and runs the Yellow Card scheme for reporting side effects.

The National Tremor Foundation
tremor.org.uk
Help, support and advice for anyone living with any form of tremor.

NHS 111 (England)
111
111.nhs.uk
Non-emergency medical help and advice for people in England.

NHS 111 (Wales)
111 (Hywel Dda, Powys, Aneurin Bevan and Swansea Bay (including Bridgend) Health Boards)
0845 46 47 (all other areas of Wales)
111.wales.nhs.uk
Non-emergency medical help and advice for people living in Wales. The contact number for this service differs depending on which area of Wales you are in.

Parkinson's UK
0808 800 0303
parkinsons.org.uk
Information and support for anyone affected by Parkinson's disease and Parkinson's symptoms, including support groups and an online community.

Trauma

ASSIST Trauma Care
assisttraumacare.org.uk
Information and specialist help for people who've experienced trauma or are supporting someone who has.

Association for Cognitive Analytic Therapists (ACAT)
acat.me.uk
Information about cognitive analytic therapy, including a list of accredited therapists.

British Association for Counselling and Psychotherapy (BACP)
bacp.co.uk
Professional body for talking therapy and counselling. Provides information and a list of accredited therapists.

Chiron Association for Body Psychotherapists
body-psychotherapy.org.uk
Information about body-focused approaches to therapy.

EMDR UK & Ireland
emdrassociation.org.uk
Professional association of EMDR clinicians and researchers in the UK and Ireland. Provides extensive information about EMDR.

First Person Plural
firstpersonplural.org.uk
Support and information for people with complex dissociative disorders and their family and friends.

FRANK
0300 123 6600
talktofrank.com
Confidential advice and information about drugs, their effects and the law.

Freedom Programme
01942 262 270
freedomprogramme.co.uk
Free support programme for people affected by domestic violence.

Mind Recovery Net
mindrecoverynet.org.uk
Publishes information on recovery colleges, including a searchable list of providers.

The National Association for People Abused in Childhood
(NAPAC)
0808 801 0331
support@napac.org.uk
napac.org.uk
Supports adult survivors of any form of childhood abuse. Offers a helpline, email support and local services.

National Institute for Health and Care Excellence (NICE)
nice.org.uk
Produces guidelines on best practice in healthcare.

NHS Service Finder
nhs.uk/service-search
Searchable database of NHS services in England.

National Survivor User Network (NSUN)
nsun.org.uk
Independent, service-user-led charity for people with experience of mental health issues. Provides information, networking opportunities and peer support.

One in Four
0800 121 7114
oneinfour.org.uk
Offers advocacy services, counselling, and resources for adults who have experienced trauma, domestic or sexual abuse in childhood.

Positive Outcomes for Dissociative Survivors (PODS)
0800 181 4420
pods-online.org.uk
Information, support and resources for people with dissociative disorders.

Rethink Mental Illness
0300 5000 927
rethink.org
Provides support and information for anyone affected by mental health problems, including local support groups.

Samaritans
116 123 (freephone)
jo@samaritans.org
Chris, Freepost RSRB-KKBY-CYJK
PO Box 90 90
Stirling FK8 2SA
samaritans.org
Samaritans are open 24/7 for anyone who needs to talk. You can visit some Samaritans branches in person. Samaritans also have a Welsh Language Line on 0808 164 0123 (7pm–11pm every day).

Schema Therapy Institute
schemainstitute.co.uk
Information about schema therapy.

Sensorimotor Psychotherapy Institute
sensorimotorpsychotherapy.org
Information about sensorimotor psychotherapy, including a directory of therapists.

Somatic Experiencing Association UK
seauk.org.uk
Information about somatic experiencing, including a directory of therapists.

The Survivors Trust
0808 8010 818
thesurvivorstrust.org
Lists local specialist services for survivors of sexual violence, including advocates and Independent Sexual Violence Advisors (ISVAs).

Together UK
together-uk.org
Supports people with mental health problems, including through peer support.

UK Psychological Trauma Society
ukpts.co.uk
Forum for professionals to share ideas and knowledge about trauma, including a list of dedicated NHS and private trauma services in the UK.

Victim Support
0808 168 9111
victimsupport.org.uk
Provides emotional and practical support for people affected by crime and traumatic events.

Please visit www.mind.org.uk if the specific mental health problem you suffer from isn't on this list as they cover many more conditions which may be relevant to you.

Bibliography

Ackerman, Courtney E, 'How to Live in the Present Moment: 35 Exercises and Tools (+ Quotes)', *PositivePsychology.Com*, 2021 <https://positivepsychology.com/present-moment/> [accessed 5 September 2021]

Bertone, Holly J, 'Which Type of Meditation Is Right for You?', *Healthline*, 2020 <https://www.healthline.com/health/mental-health/types-of-meditation> [accessed 30 August 2021]

British Nutrition Foundation, 'Home – British Nutrition Foundation', 2021 <https://www.nutrition.org.uk/> [accessed 7 September 2021]

British Psychological Society, Division of Clinical Psychology, and Anne Cooke, *Understanding Psychosis and Schizophrenia*, 2017

Byrne, Rhonda, *The Secret*, 1st Atria Books/Beyond Words hardcover ed (New York: Hillsboro, Or: Atria Books; Beyond Words Pub, 2006)

Clarke, Elanor, *Little Book of Veganism.*, 2015

Cox, John L., Jeni Holden, and Carol Henshaw, *Perinatal Mental Health: The Edinburgh Postnatal Depression Scale (EPDS); Manual*, 2. ed (London: RCPsych Publ., Royal college of Psychiatrists, 2014)

Craig, Winston J, 'Health Effects of Vegan Diets', *The American Journal of Clinical Nutrition*, 89.5 (2009), 1627S-1633S <https://doi.org/10.3945/ajcn.2009.26736N>

Crane, Brent, 'For a More Creative Brain, Travel', *The Atlantic*, 2015 <https://www.theatlantic.com/health/archive/2015/03/for-a-more-creative-brain-travel/388135/> [accessed 30 August 2021]

Crocq, Marc-Antoine, 'Alcohol, Nicotine, Caffeine, and Mental Disorders', *Dialogues in Clinical Neuroscience*, 5.2 (2003), 175–85

Croq, Marc-Antoine, 'Alcohol, Nicotine, Caffeine, and Mental Disorders', *Dialogues in Clinical Neuroscience*, 5.2 (2003), 175–85 <https://doi.org/10.31887/DCNS.2003.5.2/macrocq>

Dalton, Sarah, 'Breathe Deeper to Improve Health and Posture', *Healthline*, 2020 <https://www.healthline.com/health/breathe-deeper-improve-health-and-posture> [accessed 5 September 2021]

DeJong, Roy A, and J Lamparski, *Mental Disorders amongst Alcoholics Arch Gen Psychiatry*, 1991

Dell, Paul F, and John A O'Neil, *Dissociation and the Dissociative Disorders: DSM-V and Beyond*, 2015 <page 2-35>

Elliott, Charles H., *Borderline Personality Disorder for Dummies, 2nd Edition:* 2nd edn (Indianapolis: John Wiley and Sons, 2020)

Faulkner, Guy E. J., and Adrian H. Taylor, eds., *Exercise, Health and Mental Health: Emerging Relationships* (London; New York: Routledge, 2005)

GamCare, 'Home – GamCare – The Leading Provider of Support for Anyone Affected by Problem Gambling in Great Britain', *GamCare*, 2021 <https://www.gamcare.org.uk/> [accessed 18 September 2021]

GAMSTOP, 'Gambling Self-Exclusion Scheme', 2021 <https://www.gamstop.co.uk/> [accessed 7 September 2021]

Goodman, W. K, Matthew V Rudorfer, and Jack D Maser, *Obsessive-Compulsive Disorder: Contemporary Issues in Treatment*, 2016 <http://www.vlebooks.com/vleweb/product/openreader?id=none&isbn=9781317200239> [accessed 8 September 2021]

MERSON, PAUL, *HOOKED: Addiction and the Long Road to Recovery.* (S.l.: HEADLINE BOOK PUBLISHING, 2022)

Mind, 'About BDD', 2021 <https://www.mind.org.uk/information-support/types-of-mental-health-problems/body-dysmorphic-disorder-bdd/about-bdd/> [accessed 31 August 2021]

———, 'About Depression', 2021 <https://www.mind.org.uk/information-support/types-of-mental-health-problems/depression/about-depression/> [accessed 24 August 2021]

———, 'Causes', 2021 <https://www.mind.org.uk/information-support/types-of-mental-health-problems/schizophrenia/causes/> [accessed 15 August 2021]

———, 'Causes of OCD', 2021 <https://www.mind.org.uk/information-support/types-of-mental-health-problems/obsessive-compulsive-disorder-ocd/causes-of-ocd/> [accessed 24 August 2021]

———, 'Causes of Paranoia', 2021 <https://www.mind.org.uk/information-support/types-of-mental-health-problems/paranoia/causes-of-paranoia/> [accessed 24 August 2021]

———, 'Causes of Suicidal Feelings', 2021 <https://www.mind.org.uk/information-support/types-of-mental-health-problems/

suicidal-feelings/causes-of-suicidal-feelings/> [accessed 25 August 2021]

———, 'Dissociative Disorders', 2021 <https://www.mind.org.uk/information-support/types-of-mental-health-problems/dissociation-and-dissociative-disorders/dissociative-disorders/> [accessed 25 August 2021]

———, 'Effects of Trauma | Mind, the Mental Health Charity - Help for Mental Health Problems', 2021 <https://www.mind.org.uk/information-support/types-of-mental-health-problems/trauma/effects-of-trauma/> [accessed 25 August 2021]

———, 'Perinatal and Postnatal Mental Health', 2021 <https://www.mind.org.uk/information-support/types-of-mental-health-problems/postnatal-depression-and-perinatal-mental-health/about-maternal-mental-health-problems/> [accessed 25 August 2021]

———, 'Self-Care for Paranoia', 2021 <https://www.mind.org.uk/information-support/types-of-mental-health-problems/paranoia/helping-yourself/> [accessed 24 August 2021]

———, 'Signs of Tardive Dyskinesia (TD)', 2021 <https://www.mind.org.uk/information-support/types-of-mental-health-problems/tardive-dyskinesia-td/td-signs-symptoms/> [accessed 25 August 2021]

———, 'Signs That You're Feeling Angry', 2021 <https://www.mind.org.uk/information-support/types-of-mental-health-problems/anger/anger-symptoms/> [accessed 24 August 2021]

———, 'Symptoms', 2021 <https://www.mind.org.uk/information-support/types-of-mental-health-problems/schizoaffective-disorder/symptoms/> [accessed 15 August 2021]

———, 'Symptoms | Mind, the Mental Health Charity – Help for Mental Health Problems', 2021 <https://www.mind.org.uk/information-support/types-of-mental-health-problems/depression/symptoms/> [accessed 24 August 2021]

———, 'Symptoms of Hoarding', 2021 <https://www.mind.org.uk/information-support/types-of-mental-health-problems/hoarding/symptoms/> [accessed 24 August 2021]

———, 'Symptoms of OCD', 2021 <https://www.mind.org.uk/information-support/types-of-mental-health-problems/obsessive-compulsive-disorder-ocd/symptoms-of-ocd/> [accessed 24 August 2021]

———, 'Treatment and Support', 2021 <https://www.mind.org.uk/information-support/types-of-mental-health-problems/schizoaffective-disorder/treatment-and-support/> [accessed 15 August 2021]

———, 'Treatment and Support for Eating Problems', 2021 <https://www.mind.org.uk/information-support/types-of-mental-health-problems/eating-problems/treatment-support/> [accessed 24 August 2021]

———, 'Treatment for OCD', 2021 <https://www.mind.org.uk/information-support/types-of-mental-health-problems/obsessive-compulsive-disorder-ocd/treatment-for-ocd/> [accessed 24 August 2021]

———, 'Treatment for Trauma', 2021 <https://www.mind.org.uk/information-support/types-of-mental-health-problems/trauma/treatment-and-support/> [accessed 25 August 2021]

———, 'Treatments', 2021 <https://www.mind.org.uk/information-support/types-of-mental-health-problems/body-dysmorphic-disorder-bdd/treatments/> [accessed 24 August 2021]

———, 'Types of Eating Disorders', 2021 <https://www.mind.org.uk/information-support/types-of-mental-health-problems/eating-problems/types-of-eating-disorders/> [accessed 24 August 2021]

———, 'What Are Anxiety Disorders?', 2021 <https://www.mind.org.uk/information-support/types-of-mental-health-problems/anxiety-and-panic-attacks/anxiety-disorders/> [accessed 9 September 2021]

———, 'What Causes Body Dysmorphic Disorder (BDD)?', 2021 <https://www.mind.org.uk/information-support/types-of-mental-health-problems/body-dysmorphic-disorder-bdd/causes/> [accessed 24 August 2021]

———, 'What Is an Eating Problem?', 2021 <https://www.mind.org.uk/information-support/types-of-mental-health-problems/eating-problems/about-eating-problems/> [accessed 24 August 2021]

———, 'What Is Paranoia?', 2021 <https://www.mind.org.uk/information-support/types-of-mental-health-problems/paranoia/about-paranoia/> [accessed 24 August 2021]

———, 'What Is Schizoaffective Disorder?', 2021 <https://www.mind.org.uk/information-support/types-of-mental-health-problems/schizoaffective-disorder/about-schizoaffective-disorder/> [accessed 15 August 2021]

National Institute of Mental Health, 'Mental Health Medications', 2021 <https://www.nimh.nih.gov/health/topics/mental-health-medications#part_2362> [accessed 5 September 2021]

NHS, 'How It Works - Cognitive Behavioural Therapy (CBT)', *Nhs. Uk*, 2019 <https://www.nhs.uk/mental-health/talking-therapies-medicine-treatments/talking-therapies-and-counselling/cognitive-behavioural-therapy-cbt/how-it-works/> [accessed 30 August 2021]

Osmosis, *Generalized Anxiety Disorder (GAD) – Causes, Symptoms & Treatment*, 2016 <https://www.youtube.com/watch?v=9mPwQTiMSj8> [accessed 31 August 2021]

Porter, Shirley, *Treating PTSD: A Compassion-Focused CBT Approach* (New York: Routledge, Taylor and Francis Group, 2018)

PowerofPositivity, 'Science Explains: Reading 6 Minutes A Day Helps Reduce Stress And Increase Happiness', *Power of Positivity: Positive Thinking & Attitude*, 2020 <https://www.powerofpositivity.com/reading-6-helps-reduce-increase-happiness/> [accessed 7 September 2021]

'PubMed Central Full Text PDF' <https://www.ncbi.nlm.nih.gov/pmc/articles/PMC3181622/pdf/DialoguesClinNeurosci-5-175.pdf> [accessed 30 August 2021]

'PubMed Central Link' <https://www.ncbi.nlm.nih.gov/pmc/articles/PMC3181622/> [accessed 30 August 2021]

Relax Melodies, 'The Science Behind Solfeggio Frequencies | Relax Melodies', 2021 <https://www.relaxmelodies.com/blog/science-behind-solfeggio-frequencies/> [accessed 30 August 2021]

Ringel, Shoshana, and Jerrold R Brandell, *Trauma: Contemporary Directions in Theory, Practice, and Research*, 2011

Roth, Bob, and Inc OverDrive, *Strength in Stillness* (S.I.: Simon & Schuster, 2018) <https://api.overdrive.com/v1/collections/

v1L1BqQAAAA2G/products/fecd246a-e3f0-4190-b8be-9f57f975332a> [accessed 7 September 2021]

SAS, 'Are You Stuck in a Crazy Eight?', *Sunshine and Showers Positive Mental Health*, 2013 <http://www.sunshineandshowers.co.uk/1/post/2013/04/are-you-stuck-in-a-crazy-eight.html> [accessed 30 August 2021]

Selva, Joaquin, 'What Is Cognitive Behavioral Therapy (CBT)? A Psychologist Explains', *PositivePsychology.Com*, 2021 <https://positivepsychology.com/what-is-cbt-definition-meaning/> [accessed 9 September 2021]

Sharma, Ashish, Vishal Madaan, and Frederick D. Petty, 'Exercise for Mental Health', *Primary Care Companion to the Journal of Clinical Psychiatry*, 8.2 (2006), 106 <https://doi.org/10.4088/pcc.v08n0208a>

Team, LiveWell, 'The Three Phases of Habit Formation', *LiveWell*, 2019 <https://www.strengthandrehabilitation.com/post/2019/01/08/the-three-phases-of-habit-formation> [accessed 5 September 2021]

Tolin, David F., Blaise L. Worden, Bethany M. Wootton, and Christina M. Gilliam, *CBT for Hoarding Disorder: A Group Therapy Program Therapist's Guide* (Chichester, UK; Hoboken, NJ: John Wiley & Sons, 2017)

Waite, Polly, and Tim Williams, *Obsessive Compulsive Disorder: Cognitive Behaviour Therapy with Children and Young People* (London; New York: Routledge, 2009) <http://www.ECU.eblib.com.au/patron/FullRecord.aspx?p=380846> [accessed 8 September 2021]

Wignall, Nick, 'The 4:55 Drill', *Nick Wignall*, 2018 <https://nickwignall.com/the-455-drill/> [accessed 7 September 2021]

Wilde, Jerry, *Treating Anger, Anxiety, and Depression in Children and Adolescents: A Cognitive-Behavioral Perspective* (Washington, DC: Accelerated Development, 1996) <http://www.123library.org/book_details/?id=107763> [accessed 9 September 2021]

Yim, JongEun, 'Therapeutic Benefits of Laughter in Mental Health: A Theoretical Review', *The Tohoku Journal of Experimental Medicine*, 239.3 (2016), 243–49 <https://doi.org/10.1620/tjem.239.243>

www.ingramcontent.com/pod-product-compliance
Lightning Source LLC
Chambersburg PA
CBHW020132130526
44590CB00040B/366